Beyond the Living Dead

Contributions to Zombie Studies

White Zombie: Anatomy of a Horror Film. Gary D. Rhodes. 2001

The Zombie Movie Encyclopedia. Peter Dendle. 2001

American Zombie Gothic: The Rise and Fall (and Rise) of the Walking Dead in Popular Culture. Kyle William Bishop. 2010

Back from the Dead: Remakes of the Romero Zombie Films as Markers of Their Times. Kevin J. Wetmore, Jr. 2011

Generation Zombie: Essays on the Living Dead in Modern Culture. Edited by Stephanie Boluk and Wylie Lenz. 2011

Race, Oppression and the Zombie: Essays on Cross-Cultural Appropriations of the Caribbean Tradition. Edited by Christopher M. Moreman and Cory James Rushton. 2011

Zombies Are Us: Essays on the Humanity of the Walking Dead. Edited by Christopher M. Moreman and Cory James Rushton. 2011

The Zombie Movie Encyclopedia, Volume 2: 2000–2010. Peter Dendle. 2012

Great Zombies in History. Edited by Joe Sergi. 2013 (graphic novel)

Unraveling Resident Evil: *Essays on the Complex Universe of the Games and Films.* Edited by Nadine Farghaly. 2014

"We're All Infected": Essays on AMC's The Walking Dead *and the Fate of the Human.* Edited by Dawn Keetley. 2014

Zombies and Sexuality: Essays on Desire and the Living Dead. Edited by Shaka McGlotten and Steve Jones. 2014

...But If a Zombie Apocalypse Did Occur: Essays on Medical, Military, Governmental, Ethical, Economic and Other Implications. Edited by Amy L. Thompson and Antonio S. Thompson. 2015

How Zombies Conquered Popular Culture: The Multifarious Walking Dead in the 21st Century. Kyle William Bishop. 2015

Zombifying a Nation: Race, Gender and the Haitian Loas on Screen. Toni Pressley-Sanon. 2016

Living with Zombies: Society in Apocalypse in Film, Literature and Other Media. Chase Pielak and Alexander H. Cohen. 2017

Romancing the Zombie: Essays on the Undead as Significant "Other." Edited by Ashley Szanter and Jessica K. Richards. 2017

The Written Dead: Essays on the Literary Zombie. Edited by Kyle William Bishop and Angela Tenga. 2017

The Collected Sonnets of William Shakespeare, Zombie. William Shakespeare and Chase Pielak. 2018

Dharma of the Dead: Zombies, Mortality and Buddhist Philosophy. Christopher M. Moreman. 2018

The Politics of Race, Gender and Sexuality in The Walking Dead: *Essays on the Television Series and Comics.* Edited by Elizabeth Erwin and Dawn Keetley. 2018

The Subversive Zombie: Social Protest and Gender in Undead Cinema and Television. Elizabeth Aiossa. 2018

Parenting in the Zombie Apocalypse: The Psychology of Raising Children in a Time of Horror. Steven J. Kirsh. 2019

Beyond the Living Dead: Essays on the Romero Legacy. Edited by Bruce Peabody and Gloria Pastorino. 2021

Beyond the Living Dead

Essays on the Romero Legacy

Edited by BRUCE PEABODY and GLORIA PASTORINO

CONTRIBUTIONS TO ZOMBIE STUDIES
Series Editor *Kyle William Bishop*

McFarland & Company, Inc., Publishers
Jefferson, North Carolina

This book has undergone peer review.

LIBRARY OF CONGRESS CATALOGUING-IN-PUBLICATION DATA

Names: Peabody, Bruce Garen, 1969– editor. | Pastorino, Gloria, 1968– editor.
Title: Beyond the living dead : essays on the Romero legacy / edited by Bruce Peabody and Gloria Pastorino.
Description: Jefferson, North Carolina : McFarland & Company, Inc., Publishers, 2021 | Series: Contributions to zombie studies | Includes bibliographical references and index.
Identifiers: LCCN 2021033626 | ISBN 9781476678375 (paperback : acid free paper) ♾
ISBN 9781476642628 (ebook)
Subjects: LCSH: Romero, George A.—Criticism and interpretation. | Zombie films—History and criticism. | BISAC: PERFORMING ARTS / Film / Genres / Horror | LCGFT: Zombie films.
Classification: LCC PN1998.3.R644 B49 2021 | DDC 791.4302/33092—dc23
LC record available at https://lccn.loc.gov/2021033626

BRITISH LIBRARY CATALOGUING DATA ARE AVAILABLE

ISBN (print) 978-1-4766-7837-5
ISBN (ebook) 978-1-4766-4262-8

© 2021 Bruce Peabody and Gloria Pastorino. All rights reserved

No part of this book may be reproduced or transmitted in any form or by any means, electronic or mechanical, including photocopying or recording, or by any information storage and retrieval system, without permission in writing from the publisher.

On the cover: A zombified version of Pellizza da Volpedo's *Fourth Estate*

Printed in the United States of America

McFarland & Company, Inc., Publishers
Box 611, Jefferson, North Carolina 28640
www.mcfarlandpub.com

For Big Daddy

Acknowledgments

Bruce Peabody thanks his colleagues in the Department of Social Sciences and History for creating a professional home conducive to research, debate, and joyful learning. He is also grateful to his coauthor and coeditor Gloria Pastorino, whose erudition, humor, and humanism (and hatred of alliteration) are without peer. As always, Bruce appreciates the forbearance, love, and patience of his family, especially Stephanie, Violet, and Isaac, who never questioned the value or sanity of writing a non-fiction book about armies of the dead. Thanks also to Jill and the Fit Fam Virtual for keeping us moving when the world went still. Finally, Bruce thanks his older brother Roy for being a mentor and guide through the world of the fantastic and macabre. Roy was and remains a gifted teacher and critic. From an early age, he exposed Bruce to horror essentials like James Whale, *Famous Monsters of Filmland*, *Invasion of the Body Snatchers*, and *Them*. Roy made sure Bruce grew up with monsters because he knew they make for rewarding company over a lifetime.

Gloria Pastorino thanks Martin Donoff, friend, colleague, patient soundboard and first reader, whose suggestions and intelligence are invaluable. She is grateful for Bruce Peabody's sense of humor, quick intellect, wit, grace under fire, and for having the idea to collaborate on this project. Working with him is like riffing. She would like to thank Normand Beaulieu for his love and unwavering support, her brother Ugo for being an outstanding and resilient fighter of what feeds off human bodies and for being a constant loving presence in her life, and her brother Diego, who was always encouraging and would have been behind this book 100 percent. Thanks to Romero, for the nightmares.

We both thank Dean Geoffrey Weinman for research released time and grant-in-aid support that made this book possible.

Table of Contents

Acknowledgments	vi
Introduction: Are They Coming to Get Us? Gloria Pastorino	1
Splat Panel Shocks: Romero, EC Horror and Innovation Emma Austin	15

No Grave Can Hold Them: *Night of the Living Dead* and the Rise
   and Rebirth of Zombies in Comics
   Chera Kee
	32

Blowing It All to Hell: Zombie Films as Allegorical Westerns Gloria Pastorino	54
Dead Men Telling Tales: From *Night of the Living Dead* to *Zone One* Angela Tenga	80

The Night of Spaghetti Horror: The Flesh-Eating Frenzy of Italian
   Zombies and Cannibals
   Fulvio Orsitto *and* Gloria Pastorino
	98

From Fiddler's Green to Juiced Up Islands: The State of the State
   in Romero's Zombie Narratives
   Bruce Peabody
	117

"They're [Still] Coming to Get You": White Liberals as the Zombie Horde
   in Jordan Peele's *Get Out*
   Cammie M. Sublette
	143

Rousseau, Romero, and the "Sentiment of Existence": The Search
   for Perfectibility in *Dawn of the Dead*
   Benjamin Isaak Gross
	155

*Conclusion: Do Not Go Gentle into That Bad Night: Humanism,
  Violence, and Plumbing the Romero Legacy*
    BRUCE PEABODY   170

Filmography   189
Bibliography   193
About the Contributors   205
Index   207

Introduction

Are They Coming to Get Us?

Gloria Pastorino

It is a well-known fact that in 1968 George A. Romero reinvented zombies in cinema, becoming the new master of horror, whose example has been followed and adapted to fit different cultural and socio-historical circumstances for over fifty years. Considering the sheer number of films and TV series directly or indirectly inspired by Romero, spin-offs, spoofs, reinterpretations, and sequels, his influence is hard to dispute. Even though the zombie-craze of the 1970s and '80s began to relent in the last decade of the twentieth century, when comparatively few zombie films were made, the beginning of the new millennium, with the attacks on New York's World Trade Center in 2001 and the spread of hard-to-defeat viruses, saw a resurgence of the genre, which has continued to evolve not just in film but in TV series, graphic novels, videogames, novels, performance art, and collective "happenings" such as the zombie walks that routinely take place in North American cities.[1] As Peter Dendle remarks, "the resurrection of the zombie on screen in the 2000s came as a surprise to everyone…. The genre has reinvented itself."[2]

While the impetus behind this volume was the death of Romero in 2017, whose life and career deserve celebration, and the 50th anniversary of *Night*'s release in 2018, it was also born of a series of reflections on the proliferation of dystopian, apocalyptic, and end-of-the-world narratives following the 2001 terrorist attacks. The political response to that catastrophic event has been the development of strategies, rhetoric, and policies based on fear and amplified by the media: fear of more attacks, of the annihilation of Western values, of the end of capitalism, of hidden forces undermining our society and the way of life as we know it.[3] In the past two decades, American TV series especially and, to a certain extent, films have offered consolatory formulas and storylines in which people faced with disastrous situations on the brink of total destruction inevitably affirm that "It's going to be ok." These include the plethora of TV series that have flourished to state unequivocally that there is no enemy smart enough, no case hard enough, and no threat scary or deviant enough to defeat superior American intelligence, scientific methods of investigation, resilience, and ingenuity (*CSIs*, *NCISs*, *Cold Case*, *Criminal Minds*, *24*, *Designated Survivor*, etc.). As ultimately reassuring as such shows are, they do not reflect the reality that less than 50 percent of reported crimes are solved. However, people's perception of criminality rates, which have declined substantially since the early '90s, is that crime has increased.[4] The color-coded alarmist threat advisory of the Bush administration and the crime fighting campaign focus of the Trump administration have contributed to maintain a heightened sense of awareness of an unspecified imminent danger.

Pre-millennium catastrophic science-fiction or dystopian films usually offered a similar kind of reassurance, although salvation for humankind often rested on the shoulders of few (or just one) brave, self-sacrificing individuals. The highest grossing film of 1998, *Armageddon* (Michael Bay), and the similarly themed *Deep Impact* (Mimi Leder) from the same year both offer the possibility of total destruction from wayward comets or asteroids, with a last-minute save that prompts discourses on the valor of heroes. Viral threats, natural but maliciously manipulated or man-made in the form of bioterrorism, make their way into end-of-the-world-as-we-know-it scenarios with *Outbreak* (Wolfgang Petersen, 1995) and Terry Gilliam's much more complex *12 Monkeys* from the same year. Beginning with the HIV/AIDS scare and spread in the mid–1980s, Ebola, Hand-Foot-Mouth disease at the turn of the century, and then West Nile fever, SARS, MERS, avian flu, swine flu and Zika, the possibility of viral outbreaks that could turn into pandemics has been a world-wide concern, played out in more or less catastrophic films. Oddly prophetic in these COVID-19 times, when a flu virus pandemic has forced the world to modify its habits, Steven Soderbergh's *Contagion* (2011) showed how easy it would be to spread a virus globally and how difficult to contain or cure it. Audiences of such films need to face their fears by seeing them on the big screen, identifying, of course, with survivors of total destruction or devastation, sometimes in a world so drab as to be unrecognizable. Scenarios that offer reassurance, especially from authority figures, in the midst of hopeless circumstances break the tension and turn dystopias into something that structurally is more akin to comedy, a genre that, notwithstanding an inevitable problem or impediment for its protagonists, assures a happy ending.

The driving force of zombie narratives, on the contrary, has always been a building and stubborn fear that today's "worst" may give way to even greater calamities tomorrow and that human salvation is dependent on too many variables to be permanent or even possible. However, post–9/11, the new need to comfort a scared viewing public has seeped into some recent American zombie films as well, like *World War Z* (Marc Forster, 2013) which documents a zombie pandemic,[5] making it clear that even they have become ways to exorcise fears. On the opposite end of the spectrum are new millennium parodies such as *Shaun of the Dead* (Edgar Wright, 2004)[6] and *Fido* (Andrew Currie, 2007), which ultimately find a way to integrate domesticated zombies into our already automaton-like existence, or rom-zom-coms—the ultimate reassuring narratives—such as the *Romeo and Juliet*–inspired *Warm Bodies* (Jonathan Levine, 2013, based on Isaac Marion's 2011 novel of the same title) and the CW series *iZombie* (2015–19, based on Chris Roberson and Michael Allred's comic book series), which both feature zombies who become or stay human by eating just the brains of the living. While they all use Romero as the ultimate reference, the idea of sustenance through brains alone is probably indebted to Dan O'Bannon's campy 1985 *Return of the Living Dead*, where indestructible reanimated corpses, quite limber, fast, and able to speak, seek brains not to "feel the pain of being dead" and rotting. All these new zombie narratives offer ways to coexist with a zombie threat and integrate the "different" in society, eliminating or limiting its capacity to harm.

As Susan Sontag wrote in 1965, the allure of science-fiction films that deal with collective fears is that they "distract us from terrors—real or anticipated—by an escape into exotic dangerous situations which have last-minute happy endings" or "normalize what is psychologically unbearable, thereby inuring us to it."[7] Her analysis of post–World

War II and Cold War sci-fi narratives is relevant in understanding post–9/11 films and TV series in which catastrophe and near-total annihilation is averted. What all these narratives have in common is the idea that human error accompanied by unchecked technological innovation brings destruction on the rest of humanity. Acquiescence, acceptance, or even enthusiasm for a kind of progress that marginalizes humans and destroys or subverts nature is what makes humans partly responsible for the debacle. Sontag concludes that sci-fi films provide an "inadequate response"[8] to assuage our fears: their inherent moral simplification makes them insufficient to deal with anxiety-inducing threats at a global level and offers a sort of "daddy knows best" attitude that finds no confirmation in reality. This sentiment was echoed in 2012 by Jon Towlson, who analyzes the tendency of reassuring post–9/11 narratives to emphasize that "patriarchal authority is infallible and governments are necessary to protect us,"[9] while facts make it clear that they are, on the contrary, often at the root of our problems.

George A. Romero's films embrace Sontag's idea of our co-responsibility in bringing about the destruction of an American society that is itself incapable of defeating urgent threats effectively. However, his twentieth-century zombie films offer no reassurance from either governmental agencies, which divulge contradictory or downright irresponsible information, or any sort of patriarchal figure. His zombies are humans gone bad, past their expiration date, who still retain two fundamental human traits post-mortem: hunger and the need to survive. His first three zombie films are not consolatory: they provide extremely narrow escapes for very few people, making the hypothesis of a satisfactory survival of the species doubtful. The America that in 1986 Jean Baudrillard sees as a "paradoxical" self-declared "achieved utopia"[10] is sternly criticized by Romero in all of his films, as he exposes and plays with such oxymoron, demonstrating that one person's utopia is always someone else's dystopia. From his critique of the US involvement in the Vietnam War and of domestic politics that marginalize blacks and consider them expendable (*Night of the Living Dead*, 1968), to his skewering of a consumerism that literally consumes humans (*Dawn of the Dead*, 1978), to the obscenity of scientific experiments on human beings and the obtuseness of police states that offer no humane solutions (*Day of the Dead*, 1985), Romero's pre-millennium zombie films offer a sometime humorous, always grotesque, and rather hopeless portrayal of the socio-political realities of his country of birth.[11]

In these three films zombies are an inexorable, undiscriminating payback for all, punishing the weak, the overbearing, and the arrogant, as well as the righteous. Moreover, Romero's twentieth-century zombie films are unrelentingly bleak: they offer no heroes who discover a cure, plan, or trick to save humanity at the last minute, thanks to individual ingenuity and resilience after all official authorities have failed. There are also no heroines to be rescued or love stories developing under extreme circumstances. "Innocent" children, women, girlfriends are all killed in *Night*, as is Ben, the only person resembling a hero in the film.[12] In *Dawn*, Stephen, Fran's love interest, dies—a fate shared by Sarah's boyfriend in *Day*. Those who survive the night in his first film are a haphazard redneck militia accompanied by a Sheriff who incites people to use everything in sight as target practice.[13] In *Dawn*, only two of the original four survive after having each lost a significant other,[14] flying away from the mall overtaken by zombies in a helicopter with little fuel left.[15] In *Day*, three of the thirteen survivors barricaded in an underground bunker manage to escape aboard a helicopter to what looks like an exotic island when the dead have their day.[16] The fate of the scattered humans who survive in these films is uncertain and their status and presence lacks any conscience-clearing catharsis.

Romero's three new millennium zombie films are equally grim, but in a different way: they leave a wider opportunity for survival but also less hope that this prospect is worthwhile. The critique of current politics is still present, although focused even more specifically on the impossibility of creating communities that will not be self-destructive or enter into unyielding conflict. Thus, the underlying question of these last three films is more clearly whether it is worth saving a humanity ready to torture, annihilate, and sacrifice the living even when in the face of a destructive omnipresent threat. Be it an oligarchy concentrating all resources to the detriment and shameless exploitation of the multitude (*Land of the Dead*, 2005), or a navel-gazing new generation believing that only what is filmed and photographed is real (*Diary of the Dead*, 2007),[17] or remarkably similar communities that are unable to coexist peacefully because of philosophical or ideological differences (*Survival of the Dead*, 2009), the general feeling of these films is that humanity has problems of its own, bigger than even the threat posed by the destructive reanimated dead. In these last three films, those who escape imminent death still carry with them the seeds of defeat, an outlook that is notably distinct from *Dawn* and *Day*'s endings, which leave us with admirable or at least appealing characters, who can snatch moments of cooperation and imagine a better future, even if its prospects are uncertain and its outlines hazy. In contrast, the model of Romero's later films is the one that has influenced most other zombie narratives of the past two decades, which are characterized by both the dubious morality of their protagonists and the constant feeling of being under attack. Through the ubiquity of this threat, zombies become a polysemic signifier of anything that can go wrong in the new millennium and of anyone who disturbs what some may perceive as "the American" way of living (terrorists, Muslims, migrants, tsunamis, viruses, our own fears of losing status/riches/things, etc.).

Cultural and social anxiety dominate and cause zombie narratives. Kyle William Bishop and Philip Simpson (quoting psychoanalyst Charles B. Strozier) compare the new millennium paranoia to "the worst days of the Cold War, when nuclear annihilation seemed imminent."[18] The possibility of disaster calls for a culprit, and zombies are perfect stand-ins for any sort of monster to be blamed: "infectious disease, biological warfare, euthanasia, terrorism, and even rampant immigration,"[19] in Bishop's words. Of course, the threat may come from the outside or the inside, be natural or man-made, and no amount of vigilance may ever prepare anyone for it. As Peter Dendle writes in the introduction to his second zombie encyclopedia, the most devastating realization that comes from all zombie films since *Night of the Living Dead* is that "in a time of crisis, people will not be able to depend on authorities for help."[20] Recent COVID-19 events surely confirm this statement, as does the anecdote Dendle recounts about the public advisory issued by the Department of Homeland Security in 2003, to keep "a 'disaster supply kit' on hand containing duct tape, scissors, battery-powered radio, plastic sheets for covering doors and windows ('pre-measured and cut'), and first aid supplies."[21] Duct tape sales spiked, even though none of the items listed could do much against terrorists, viruses, zombies, or hurricanes, as events tragically demonstrated two years later with Hurricane Katrina. Max Brooks, author of *The Zombie Survival Guide* and *World War Z*, claims he wrote his first book partly as a response to the lack of governmental response to HIV.[22] The Centers for Disease Control on May 16, 2011, posted on its website "Preparedness 101: Zombie Apocalypse," as a tongue-in-cheek attempt to advise on what tools and plans people should have at their disposal in case of an emergency. Even though the page contains some useful information, its cuteness hardly masks the sense of unpreparedness it actually communicates.[23]

The viral angle is particularly interesting in the sub-genre's resurgence post–9/11, if seen as a development of the virus outbreak films of the 1990s and of an already existing paranoia about the spread of uncontainable diseases. As Dahlia Schweitzer argues in *Going Viral*, fear of being wiped out by an infectious disease was cultivated, marketed, politically manipulated, and spread by media looking for sensational news to get audiences from the 1990s on: "Since drama sells copy—and movies, and books, and even public policy—this kind of dramatic language would continue to be embraced and the idea of a global threat perpetuated and carefully groomed."[24] The Ebola threat, in particular, was grossly exaggerated by the media and contributed to making people feel more insecure and some more racist, since it came from a mysterious and demonized Africa. Ironically and sadly, all the catastrophic scenarios painted in the past quarter of a century have not prepared anyone for the lethal and global effects of the recent COVID-19 pandemic, which has shown how actually vulnerable humans are to a known virus, let alone an unknown one. Zombies make the metaphor real: fighting them has the flavor of taking action, as opposed to the abstract idea of fighting "terror" or vague, invisible, microscopic enemies. Schweitzer quotes two scientists, a molecular biologist and a Nobel-Prize-winning virologist, who describe viruses as able to grow even in dead cells, bringing them back to life, "'neither living nor dead,' placing them in 'the twilight zone between the living and the nonliving.'"[25] The viral justification for turning into a zombie also explains the rapidity of movements of millennial zombies: they spread fast and turn dead people often in a matter of seconds.[26] A film that was in the final stages of production before 9/11, Danny Boyle's *28 Days Later* (2002), marks the beginning of this new type of virally infected zombie that thrives on the speed of dissemination (of information, of global travel, of contagion) typical of the new era.

One of the main differences between the new zombies and Romero-inspired ones is their mutation, in terms of mass behavior, from herd to swarm, as Lars Schmeink argues, drawing from Colin Tait, Hardt and Negri,

> in that "they possess the ability to look for openings, utilize crude skills, and eventually overwhelm via their inherently cooperative nature" (Tait 67). Utilizing a collective intelligence, the swarm becomes a single entity and, not caring for its individual components, urges onwards towards its goal. Visually, most films enact this variant of zombie morphology in terms of fluidity, in which the metaphor of the "wall" becomes the metaphor of the "wave." singular drops are lost, arrested in their motion, but the wave itself is unstoppable, moving by replacing the front particles with new ones from the back.[27]

The swarm, to continue the biological reference, acts according to "a 'taxis'—an innate behavioral response causing an organism to move towards or away from some particular stimulus,"[28] as argued by Derksen and Hick. The stimulus is eating human flesh, undeterred—which seems to be the perception of all third-millennium threats: the inherent aim for total destruction. The herd/swarm distinction partially explains the heightened feeling that people must band against a definite threat; Adam Lowenstein identifies this as "wound culture,"[29] seeing historical trauma (such as the attacks on the World Trade Center and the Pentagon) as the extension of "personal identity ... to the realm of national identity."[30] Several articles and books have been written on the appropriateness of the zombie as metaphor for terrorism; Kevin J. Wetmore sees this especially in their need "to replicate themselves, to contaminate,"[31] responding to the symbolic impact of an attack to the perceived epicenter of capitalism. However, it is the very fluidity of the zombie metaphor that makes it applicable to both motivated and unmotivated attacks, exposing, more than anything, vulnerability. "The viral contagion, just like viral terror, is undetectable, turns the familiar into the monstrous within seconds, and is destructive to any social order," argues Schmeink, making preemptive policies practically impossible and turning any ideological identification between zombies and terrorists or migrants (both nameless and faceless categories) an easy target of political manipulation, as we have seen in both the Bush and Trump administrations. Thus, the easy rhetorical polarization of "us" and "them" provides the ethical justification of eliminating remorselessly whoever threatens our way of life, conveniently disregarding the enemy's humanness.

The demonization of the "other" is part of what fuels the politics of fear, to the point that in 2001 Americans willingly agreed to what Italian philosopher Giorgio Agamben, after Carl Schmitt, calls a "state of exception," i.e., the "voluntary creation of a permanent state of emergency"[32] that effectively relaxes if not repeals the traditional rule of law and sacrifices democracy by making into laws measures that are the product of a political emergency. As Agamben explains, "the state of exception appears as the legal form of what cannot have legal form."[33] The USA Patriot Act, acronym for "Uniting and Strengthening America by Providing Appropriate Tools Required to Intercept and Obstruct Terrorism Act," signed into law by President George W. Bush a little over a month after the attacks on the Twin Towers and renewed in 2015 as the Freedom Act, "gives sweeping search and surveillance to domestic law enforcement and foreign intelligence agencies and eliminates checks and balances that previously gave courts the opportunity to ensure that those powers were not abused … threaten[ing] the basic rights of millions of Americans."[34] At the core of this law there is the elimination of the legal status of individuals, under the claim of *necessitas legem non habet*, or necessity knows no laws. Thus, third-millennium zombie films offer extreme versions of the suspension of legality and sacrifice of civil liberties, where need assumes the legal form of measures that are inherently lawless, and "security," sought at all costs, proves unattainable. The state of exception is triggered by the threat of zombie attacks, but the constancy of this hazard inures spectators and audience members to violence, danger, and state of exception itself. In fact, while a real and definitive threat, zombies become almost background noise in these post-zombie apocalyptic scenarios that emphasize the impossibility of creating or maintaining stable communities of survivors.

Similarly, in real life, the feeling of being under constant threat has characterized the past two decades and tainted every normal social action (being under constant internet and video surveillance even when walking down a street, getting through security at airports with no shoes and only micro-containers of liquids, having endless security checks that enhance the feeling of living in an insecure world, etc.). Meanwhile, the real threat is somewhere in the background, more in the back of everyone's mind than around the corner. We can see some of these dynamics in the most successful and longstanding zombie TV series, *The Walking Dead* (2010–present, now in its tenth season), which in many ways is the truest heir of Romero's ideas. The series has gone from a first season in which zombies are a real, hard-to-defeat, inexorably lethal presence to being a marginal nuisance now that all characters have developed superhero fighting skills and paramilitary combat abilities.[35] Unless a character is distracted, zombies are seen, heard, perceived, and dealt with before they become lethal for the group. The series ideally picks up where Romero left off, showing survivors coming together and organizing themselves into communities of unlikely allies, who find strength in numbers and in the will to survive. Unlike in other new zombie depictions where, in the words of Romero, "it seems like they all joined health clubs,"[36] these undead walk slowly rather than running, respecting the convention of moving with determination but with understandably slowed-down motor capacities post-mortem, and they are "secondary … sort of like, annoyances."[37]

In the teeth of this menace, the human instinct is to band together and, from the very beginning, the protagonist, Sheriff Rick Grimes, looks for meaning and other people like him to survive in the new world configuration. From the first season on, the focal group of the story revolves around other communities of survivors, each with distinct philosophies and personalities. Rick's itinerant survivors interact (and fight) with, join, and absorb characters from these alternative and usually rival groups, which include a self-sufficient family in a farmhouse, a town led by a seemingly fair but actually deranged tyrant (Woodbury), a community of cannibals (Terminus), a hospital in a tall building with selfish, corrupt doctor/kidnappers (Grady Memorial Hospital), an idyllic walled town inhabited by people who never had a real war with a horde of walkers (Alexandria), Wolf people, an agrarian community (Hilltop) extorted by a mafia-like group (The Saviors) that also gets food from another community (The Kingdom), a maritime community of only women (Oceanside), whose men have been killed by the Savior Mafiosi, and finally a community that walks with the dead wearing the skins of dead people as masks in order to camouflage (the Whisperers). All these communities are responses to the search of security in a world made unreliable by the presence of the undead. The characters' ability to stay together or build alliances determines their ability to keep zombies at bay. As Dawn Keetley observes, "*The Walking Dead* [is] a ground-breaking narrative, most importantly because it is the first such narrative in which the survivors are already infected."[38] In fact, a zombie bite only accelerates the inevitable: once dead, all humans in this post-apocalyptic reality turn into zombies. The ambiguity of the title is resolved by Rick in both the fourth volume of the comics (*The Heart's Desire*: "We are the walking dead!," 130) and at the end of Season 2 of the TV series ("Beside the Dying Fire": "We're all infected"). Keetley concludes that "the absolute opposition between human and zombie, along with the series of binaries that structure that opposition—human/non-human, normal/monster, living/dead, mind/body, rational/irrational, conscious/unconscious—are impossible to maintain. Humans and zombies are not opposed but are now evolving together."[39]

As Zygmunt Bauman argues in his seminal *Liquid Times*, progress is "a chase after utopias" or, rather, "an effort to run away from failed utopias."[40] All the communities in *The Walking Dead* are imagined or promised utopias in a dystopian world: they reflect co-habitation problems that we find in every existing country, in varying degrees, and which are a part of the composition of every "imagined political community," as Benedict Anderson defines nations. In the TV series, each community tries to weed out whatever (and whomever) does not fit in their world to create a more perfect assembly of people, whose common goal is to live a secure, simple life. The fact that people are banded together only because of need, rather than out of choice, highlights the limitations of such a society. However, in Season 9 the four main communities (Alexandria, Hilltop, the Kingdom, and Oceanside), faced with the new common threat posed by the Nazi-like Whisperers and remembering the full-blown war with the Saviors, sign a mutual protection pact, inspired by a poster of the preamble of the Constitution of the United States of America one of the lead warriors from Alexandria had seen while looting the Smithsonian museum (season 9, "A New Beginning").[41] This almost reiterates that pre-zombie-apocalypse America was, in fact, as close to a realized utopia as anyone can come, but it also confirms that nationalism stems from the invention of a nation to protect like-minded people from foreign threats (zombies but also threatening communities of living humans). If nationalism has negative connotations, rooted "in fear and hatred of the Other ... [with] affinities with racism,"[42] Anderson also reminds us that "nations inspire love, and often profoundly self-sacrificing love."[43] However, in these scenarios, the most important preoccupation is finding a way to coexist with the living: the dead are just a problem that nobody has any qualms exterminating so that "healthy" communities can continue to exist. That is how zombies, once again, are a polysemic generic threat that just needs to be eliminated remorselessly. Those living humans who try to hold on to dearly departed undead are clearly unhealthy individuals who put the community of survivors at risk, as seen in Romero's *Survival of the Dead* and in two separate instances in *The Walking Dead* (at the farmhouse in Season 2 and in the Governor's house in Woodbury in Season 3).

What makes the undead interesting in both Romero's three new millennium films and in the zombie "renaissance" more generally is the versatility and polymorphous nature of the threat they pose. In fact, while total destruction of the human race, one human meal at a time, is a present threat from the very beginning of *Night of the Living Dead*, in the last two decades this threat has come to symbolize the self-destructiveness of humans at all levels, from the personal to the political. From the standpoint of biopolitics, zombie films, TV series, graphic novels, etc., draw attention on one very important distinction: the actual biological life, easy to destroy (which Roberto Esposito calls "zoe") and the "political forms of life" ("bíos") that constitutes what existence we would like to preserve. Such a distinction helps us to understand that the dispatching of the undead invariably impacts our human capacities. In contrast with so many other zombie works, Romero shows that our compassion dies when zombies are seen as non-human instead of no-longer human; the battle over the dead is a battle for ourselves. Over the course of his films, Romero highlights the inhumanity of taking pleasure in destroying and torturing them. Other zombie films revel in the acts of mass destruction. This has the effect of both blurring the line between humans and zombies (since the audience enjoys what Jerrold Hogle calls the "sick fun"[44] of both of their "predations"), and subtly linking the dead enemies with the faceless masses of living people killed in modern warfare from a distance by "intelligent bombs," without considering their humanity. Thus, this turn to biopolitics helps explain how mass destruction of lives can be seen as a self-destructive, "autoimmune" reaction, whereby the sustained effort to immunize our societies against a constant threat makes us attack and destroy other humans, thus damaging the body politic (humanity) and dragging it into an endless cycle of violence. Lars Schmeink concludes that

> Biopolitics is thus the practice of excising unhealthy, bad, or wrong specimens from the governed social body, by deciding which life is worth living and which is expendable. It is this excised body that Giorgio Agamben describes with his concept of *homo sacer*, "who *may be killed and yet not sacrificed*"—the "bare life" of man that is outside of law and the social body, defined within only by exclusion from it. In (liquid) modern times, groups of expendable lives are declared *homo sacer* by a biopolitical sovereign in order to assure their lawful exclusion, and even extermination, from the social body.[45]

In zombie films, to avoid contagion, the undesirables have to be killed; however, as we have seen, zombies are not just monstrous versions of humans but rather allegories of perceived threats to life as we know it.

These monstrous doubles are Romero's legacy: the reinterpretation of the Haitian model of living dead (who are living humans paralyzed by powerful medicine that turns them into subjects of someone else's will)[46] into a perversion of resurrection, of the Eucharist, and of Armageddon that only a disillusioned Catholic could devise in these terms. Romero could have developed Richard Matheson's vampire idea, since his *Night of the Living Dead* is in part inspired by *I Am Legend* (1954), but he opts for creatures less potentially sensual and "romantic" to go beyond 19th-century vampirism and dependence (à la Baudelaire, Stoker, Strindberg, etc.).[47] His zombies survive in their "reborn" state through the consumption of a body—just as Catholics literally eat the body of Christ to keep on living in god's grace. The only thing that can stop them is the destruction of the brain (the site of human intelligence, not of divine essence), not a crucifix, or garlic, or a stake through the heart: god is dead, so protection and salvation cannot come from him. It cannot come from his agents on earth either: priests are generally absent from Romero's zombie films, with the exception of *Dawn of the Dead*, where a priest shows up in a basement filled with living people who could not leave their dead alone and, as a consequence, are turned into zombies as well. There too, religion brings no solace. As Gregory Waller notes, "Instead of admonishing the men to have faith and to follow the ways of tradition, the priest cryptically warned Peter and Roger that 'we must stop the killing or we lose the war.'"[48] Since interrupting the cycle of death seems to be an unlikely proposition for humans, salvation, if at all possible, is more readily available for the undead through the flesh of the living; as Jean-Baptiste Thoret states: "zombification is a process of transformation that evokes a monstrous rebirth—every bitten human is then reborn in an altered form."[49] However, in Romero's films the feeling that the undead are a reflection of Americans' worst defects lingers in each film, when it is not explicitly stated (as in *Dawn*). David Pagano observes that "returning from death with no revelation and no insight beyond whatever rapacious desire had been immanent within humans all along, Romero's zombies are both autopoetic and insignificant ... their infernal danger is precisely the transubstantiation of 'us' into 'them.'"[50] A recent TV series, *iZombie*, makes the transubstantiation even more explicit and elegant: highly functioning undead may continue to live a mostly normal life by eating human brains; however, by eating a dead person's brain they also internalize images and experiences from that person's life, inheriting their personality as well, for a limited time, until the next brain is eaten.[51] The Eucharist makes humans participate in the nature of the divinity by intaking Christ's body through the wafer: spiritual enlightenment, salvation, cleansing of sins, and rebirth should come to those who partake in the communion with the Host, until the next communion. *iZombie* marks a new trend of normalization of the interaction between zombies and humans (as Andrew Currie's *Fido*, or the series *Santa Clarita Diet*, 2017–19, do as well), that departs from Romero's vision, while still paying constant homage to him (for instance, zombies who do not sustain/save themselves through eating brains become the zombies we are used to seeing, going "full Romero"). While not focusing on the full-fledged monsters, the show uses zombies as powerful allegories of societal discrimination. The most obvious one could be seeing infected but otherwise healthy zombies as HIV positive humans, different from the ones sick with AIDS.[52]

Clearly, the scope of Romero's six zombie films has given rise to a very rich and varied body of work that goes well beyond the confines of the horror genre, also bleeding into comedy and drama. Because of the complexity and the versatility of the material Romero inspired, the guiding principle of this book is assembling academicians from different disciplines and intellectual perspectives to interpret the director's inspiration and legacy through different theoretical lenses. The scholars who adhered enthusiastically to this project are specialists in film and media studies, cultural studies, literary criticism, and political science. They were all asked to focus on Romero and reflect on what is his legacy. In doing so, inevitably they ended up also reflecting on the socio-political and cultural elements that shaped Romero's films. The result is a series of investigations into pop culture, films, and politics at the core of the director's oeuvre, as well as into how he shaped other directors, creating new trends both domestically and abroad, originating a series of sub-genres. The essays in this volume are not meant to offer a comprehensive interpretation of Romero's films or cover the breadth of zombie mediatic products post-Romero, but rather to contribute original interpretations of a cultural phenomenon that has permeated popular culture for over 50 years. While discussing the cultural relevance of Romero's legacy, authors also examine the political ramifications of his films.

The two essays that open the volume are a complementary view of how comic books of the 1950s and '60s helped shape Romero's aesthetic. We felt that no single analysis of the comics' impact on Romero's imagination could be exhaustive, since, as Tom Engelhardt writes,

> by 1953, more than 150 horror comics were produced monthly, featuring acts of torture often of an implicit sexual nature, murders and decapitations of various bloody sorts, visions of rotting flesh, and so on. Miniature catalogs of atrocities, their feel was distinctly assaultive. In their particular version of the spectacle of slaughter, they targeted the American family, the good life, and reverend institutions. Framed by sardonic detective narrators or mocking Grand Guignol gatekeepers, their impact was deconstructive.[53]

The publisher of EC, William Gaines, defended his horror and science-fiction comics as products of the environment in which Cold War children lived. Romero's take from his first film on expands on that idea and adds his rendition of "embarrassingly un-American-looking atrocities"[54] witnessed in the news from the South-East-Asian front and the domestic one, proving that, in 1968, the violence he portrayed on screen was sadly American. Romero and his friend Stephen King were both interested in the "irreverence and uninhibited presentation"[55] of EC, even though the director was more attracted to expressing the anger of his times[56] through the allegory of zombies. Emma Austin focuses on the relationship between Romero's zombies and contemporaneous horror films in the 1970s and '80s, looking at the display of stylized violence in them through Phillip Brophy's definition of "horrality" (a mix of horror, textuality, morality, and hilarity). She focuses on how Entertaining Comics (EC) in particular helped shape Romero's aesthetic and peculiar sense of humor and of the grotesque in zombie (as well as other films, such as *Creepshow*, 1982). Chera Kee contextualizes the influence of EC books and paints a wider picture of intertextuality, in which Romero's first film acts as stimulus to infuse new life in Marvel comics and beyond. She analyzes EC style in framing stories and how Romero makes it his in *Night*'s shots, as well as how comics zombie stories emphasized what was wrong with the living, much like Romero's films. Kee carefully delineates the history of zombies in comics from pre-censorship EC and imitators to post-code Marvel's evolution of zombies into muscular dead "heroes" and "zuvembies."

Gloria Pastorino establishes a parallel with the treatment of othered American Indians in Western films and Romero's zombies, showing how the innovative director, in creating a new genre, dialogues with existing popular ones. Pastorino specifically looks at how Westerns changed in the 1950s, reflecting Cold War politics, and how Romero's zombie films after *Night of the Living Dead* incorporate a new aesthetic of violence developed by Sergio Leone, Arthur Penn, and Sam Peckinpah in the Vietnam War years. Angela Tenga examines the relevance of "Last Night stories" in zombie narratives written after Romero's seminal film that, in turn, inspired films and TV series. These stories are not simply a means to get to know the characters better, but specific ways to connect universal devastation with personal experiences, revealing what is left of the human in a zombie apocalypse. Tenga examines how it is a typical first-person narrative that turns the person telling it into a custodian of experiences of a past that cannot return as well as a builder of new, shared experiences. In that, it is typical of zombie narratives and present in *Night* as well. Fulvio Orsitto (with a contribution by Gloria Pastorino) looks at how Romero initiated a cultural phenomenon in Italy that, while inspired by the American director, gave rise to a plethora of zombie and zombie-adjacent films in the 1970s and early '80s. The most important hybrid sub-genres are the cannibal, which is also exploited by auteur Pier Paolo Pasolini and partly indebted to "mondo"/snuff films, and the zombie proper, which also has ramifications in sexploitation, detective, and historical films. Albeit at times far from Romero's sensibility, all these films are still indebted to him. After a long hiatus from the mid–1980s to the mid–2010s, Orsitto shows how young Italian directors in the third millennium are returning to the zombie genre in the way that Romero intended it: quirky, with a political subtext and no happy ending.

Bruce Peabody addresses the rarely examined status of the state in Romero's films, arguing that the zombie apocalypse highlights both government inadequacy and critical functions it needs to perform. Surveying Romero's six *Dead* films, he identifies four distinct forms of political community: broken states (weak or failing versions of traditional governments), semi-states (new, incomplete, and sometimes distorted forms of rule), false states (that are morally or functionally bankrupt and sometimes dystopian), and dream states (imagined utopias that hint at new forms of politics). Cammie M. Sublette looks at racial inequality and stereotypes in America examining Jordan Peele's *Get Out!* (2017), vis-à-vis its inspiration, *Night of the Living Dead*. While not a zombie film per se, *Get Out!* shows the exploitation of black people whose brains are literally removed and "cannibalized" by white people, combining both pre- and post–Romero zombie traditions. Through a close reading of both films, she articulates the complexities of characters' interactions, underscoring how the issues raised by Romero's film are still unresolved fifty years later. Benjamin Isaak Gross looks at the writings of eighteenth-century philosopher Jean-Jacques Rousseau to reinterpret the nature and meaning of Romero's criticism of modern society and consumerism in *Dawn of the Dead*. According to Gross, Romero offers a thoroughgoing and damning critique of the shortcomings of classical liberalism, the tradition of political thought associated with a commitment to private property, free markets, the rule of law, and an emphasis on individual rights. In the course of this criticism, Romero offers us a picture of what it means to be fully human. Finally, in the conclusion to this volume, Bruce Peabody documents and interprets the rising popularity of zombies as a mass culture phenomenon and subject of academic interest. He goes on to make the case for why we can consider Romero to be a driving force in the zombie Renaissance (and a deserving focus of a book-length treatment). The essay concludes by offering a final set of reflections on the Romero legacy, looking at a number of enduring motifs and themes that can be traced to the director, including his complex but unflagging embrace of humanism.

All essays in this volume examine ways in which Romero has contributed to political awareness through his zombie films and has influenced generations of filmmakers, making zombies the perfect versatile vessel for today's political concerns. All in all, Romero-inspired films in the third millennium do not exorcise fears: they normalize them, since the state of exception has become our life and we, like Voltaire's Candide, are ready to accept that, since this is the best of all possible worlds, "zombies" and what they represent are a reality with which we must cohabitate—but it's not going to be ok….

Notes

1. Romero himself was puzzled by the phenomenon, as he told Peter Keough in 2010: "I don't get it. It's sort of an easy makeup job, I guess, for Halloween, but it doesn't always happen on Halloween … you just want to say 'get a life.' I don't know. I mean, it's great fun. I went to the one in Toronto and it's great and these people are so dedicated … Some of the makeup is great, some of the walks and stuff that they do is worthy of Lon Chaney. But *why* is that fun? That's like a, some kind of new happening. I can't quite identify it." In Keough, "Interview" with George "Romero." In Williams, *George A. Romero. Interviews*, 174. To shed some light, see, among others, Sarah Juliet Lauro, "Playing Dead: Zombies Invade Performance Art … and Your Neighborhood." In Christie and Lauro, *Better Off Dead*, 205–230; Chera Kee, "I Walked with a Zombie: Performing the Walking Dead." In Kee, *Not Your Average Zombie*, 150–165; Emma Austin, "Zombie Culture: Dissent, Celebration, and the Carnivalesque in Social Spaces." In Hubner, Leaning, and Manning, *The Zombie Renaissance in Popular Culture*, 174–190; Simon Orpana, "Spooks of Biopower: The Uncanny Carnivalesque of Zombie Walks." In Lauro, *Zombie Theory*, 294–315; Phillip Mahoney, "Mass Psychology and the Analysis of the Zombie: From Suggestion to Contagion." In Boluk and Lenz, *Generation Zombie. Essays on the Living Dead in Modern Culture*, 113–129; John Morehead, "Zombie Walks, Zombie Jesus, and the Eschatology of Postmodern Flesh." In Paffenroth and Morehead, *The Undead and Theology*, 101–123; Simone Do Vale, "Trash Mob: Zombie Walks and the Positivity of Monsters in Western Popular Culture." In Canini, *The Domination of Fear*, 191–202; Sara Sutler-Cohen, "Plans Are Pointless; Staying Alive Is as Good as It Gets. Zombie Sociology and the Politics of Survival." In Moreman and Rushton, *Zombies Are Us*, 183–193; John Vervaeke, Christopher Mastropietro, and Filip Miscevic, *Zombies in Western Culture: A Twenty-First Century Crisis*.

2. Dendle, *The Zombie Movie Encyclopedia*, 1–2.

3. See: Peabody, "Explaining the Paranoid Style in American Politics: System Disjuncture and Narratives of Fiction." In Sokolon, *Flattering the Demos*, 87–110.

4. Data found, among other sources, on the Pew Research Center website March 2017 report "Most Violent and Property Crimes in the U.S. Go Unsolved" (https://www.pewresearch.org/fact-tank/2017/03/01/most-violent-and-property-crimes-in-the-u-s-go-unsolved/) and the October 2019 (Five Facts About Crime in the U.S." (https://www.pewresearch.org/fact-tank/2019/10/17/facts-about-crime-in-the-u-s/), which compiles data from the U.S. Department of Justice, FBI reports and the Bureau of Justice Statistics. Violent crime includes offenses such as murder, rape, robbery, and assault, which declined by 51%, while property crime declined by 54% in the years between 1993 and 2018. According to the author of the articles, "Only about half of the violent crimes and a third of the property crimes that occur in the United States each year are reported to police. And most of the crimes that *are* reported don't result in the arrest, charging and prosecution of a suspect, according to government statistics."

5. Forster's film follows the disaster sci-fi model, where the resilience and perseverance of one brave person takes humanity back from the brink of total annihilation (à la *Armageddon*). Max Brooks' novel, upon which the film is based, is less triumphalist and has very little to do with the film. A cure is found but after ten years of war and ten years later millions of zombies are still active. Brook is a true fan of Romero's work and sees zombies as a disease, as a possible allegory for many modern-day preoccupations, as he declared in several interviews. "As far as books, the one that inspired me more than anything is *The Good War* by Studs Terkel. It's an oral history of World War II. I read when I was a teenager and it's sat with me ever since. When I sat down to write *World War Z*, I wanted it to be in the vein of an oral history. As far [as] movies, obviously the works of George Romero have inspired me deeply. However, the *Return of the Living Dead* movies have set the genre back to the dark ages. They cheapen zombies, make them silly and campy. They've done for the living dead what the old *Batman* TV show did for *The Dark Knight*." In *Eatmybrains*, 20 October 2006, https://www.eatmybrains.com/showfeature.php?id=55.

6. Much has been written about parodies and the idea of "splatstick" (splatter and slapstick) in zombie comedies, notably by Linda Badley, "Zombie Splatter Comedy from Dawn to Shaun: Cannibal Carnivalesque." In McIntosh and Leverette, *Zombie Culture*, 35–53; see also: Pifer, "Slacker Bites Back: *Shaun of the Dead* Finds New Life for Deadbeats." In Christie and Lauro, *Better Off Dead*, 163–174.

7. Sontag, "The Imagination of Disaster," 42.

8. *Ibid.*, 65.

9. Towlson, "Rehabilitating Daddy. Or How Disaster Movies Say It's Ok to Trust Authority," 12.
10. Baudrillard, *America*, 91.
11. In 2004 Romero moved to Canada, where he found more artistic leeway and creative freedom. He became a dual citizen in 2009. Not coincidentally his characters want to move north, to Canada, in hope of salvation.
12. When the film came out it was slaughtered by *Variety*, which condemned the "pornography of violence" and the "unrelieved orgy of sadism" of the film, casting aspersions on filmmakers and filmgoers who would enjoy such a film and calling for a Supreme Court ruling over such filth (*Variety*, October 16, 1968). If the reaction nowadays may seem excessive, it is worth mentioning that in 2017 Netflix "complied with a written demand from the German Commission for Youth Protection (KJM) to remove *Night of the Living Dead* from service in Germany only. A version of the film is banned in the country" (*Netflix*. Environmental Social Governance, 2019, 6).
13. In the 1990 remake directed by Tom Savini and produced by Romero, Ben becomes a zombie and Barbara manages to survive, snapping out of her initial shock very quickly and becoming excellent at fending for herself. Savini plays up the actions of the redneck militia at the end of the film, making them relish in the overkill of zombies, who are not just burnt on a pyre but also used as target practice once lynched. Those images become a staple in Romero's post-9/11 films, in which the value of the humanity that survives zombie attacks is constantly called into question. Even Barbara's last action is to shoot in the head the unpleasant and cowardly Mr. Cooper, who had saved himself by hiding in the attic, after shooting at Barbara and wounding Ben to death.
14. The father of Francine's unborn child, Stephen, and Peter's best friend and fellow national guardsman, Roger.
15. The remake of *Dawn* by Zack Snyder leaves basically no survivors, since the four who make it on the boat only find zombies on nearby islands and, therefore, either die of hunger or eaten. This film, victim of the post-9/11 "It's gonna be all right" syndrome (useless phrase uttered by a bitten character who lets the other four go on the quay just before shooting himself), was not produced with Romero's cooperation (unlike the remake of *Night*) and it completely lacks the original's humor and punch.
16. Not coincidentally November 2nd, the day of the dead, since the film begins with the protagonist, Sarah, looking at a calendar where all the days in October have been crossed out.
17. For an analysis of our appearance-obsessed society, it is worth mentioning the British five-episode TV series *Dead Set* (2008), which broadcasts the end of the world in a *Big Brother* set, where the last people alive are the—already brainless—protagonists of the TV reality show. The series obviously pays homage to Romero in several scenes and leaves no hope of survival in a world where no one seems to be worth saving.
18. Simpson, "The Zombie Apocalypse Is Upon Us! Homeland Insecurity." In Keetley, *"We're All Infected,"* 29.
19. Bishop, *American Zombie Gothic*, 26.
20. Dendle, *The Zombie Movie Encyclopedia*, 9.
21. *Ibid.*
22. Brodesser-Akner, "Max Brooks Is Not Kidding About the Zombie Apocalypse," The New York Times, 21 June 2013.
23. Khan, "Preparedness 101: Zombie Apocalypse," *CDC*, 16 May 2011.
24. Schweitzer, *Going Viral*, 16.
25. *Ibid.*, 158–159.
26. See also Riley, "The E-Dead: Zombies in the Digital Age," for a comprehensive discussion on the dissemination of millennial zombies. In Boluk and Lenz, *Generation Zombie*, 194–205.
27. Schmeink, *Biopunk Dystopias*, 216.
28. Derksen and Hudson Hick, "Your Zombie and You. Identity, Emotion, and the Undead." In Moreman and Rushton, *Zombies Are Us*, 14. Sarah Juliet Lauro and Karen Embry talk about zombies as a posthuman "swarm organism" in "A Zombie Manifesto: The Nonhuman Condition in the Era of Advanced Capitalism." *boundary 2. An International Journal of Literature and Culture*, 35:1, spring 2008, 88.
29. Lowenstein, *Schocking Representation*, 10.
30. *Ibid.*
31. Wetmore, *Post-9/11 Horror in American Cinema*. 159–160.
32. Agamben, *State of Exception*, 2.
33. *Ibid.*, 1.
34. "Patriot Act." Accessed October 6 2019. https://www.eff.org/issues/patriot-act.
35. Dahlia Schweitzer argues that the show is not really about zombies, as proven by the fact that in the first episode they appear (after the first scene with the little zombie girl) only after 23 minutes and they are absent from the titles of the first two seasons. She argues, "it quickly becomes clear that the walkers are not the real danger. The show provides, instead, an examination of humanity's propensity for aggression and destruction.... the healthy and noncontagious people are the real threat." In Schweitzer, *Going Viral*, 184.
36. Keough, "Interview with George Romero," 174.
37. *Ibid.*, 173.

14 Introduction

38. Keetley, "We're All Infected," 1.
39. Ibid., 7.
40. Bauman, *Liquid Times*, 96.
41. The episode goes one step farther, implying that there is an idyllic, bucolic past to be recovered in the dystopian societies of Season 9, since our favorite characters take an ancient plow and a colonial wagon from the museum, symbols of rebirth in a new country and agrarian toil to conquer the new land.
42. Anderson, *Imagined Communities*, 141.
43. Ibid.
44. Hogle, "Foreword." In Bishop, *American Zombie Gothic*, 3.
45. Schmeink, *Biopunk Dystopias*, 225.
46. Bishop offers the most comprehensive history of the phenomenon, albeit by no means the only one, in the first two chapters of *American Zombie Gothic*, "Raising the Living Dead. The Folkloric and Ideological Origins of the Voodoo Zombie," and The Return of the native. Imperialist Hegemony and the Cinematic Voodoo Zombie."
47. Romero's attempt at a vampire film, *Martin* (1978), deals more with Catholicism-induced neurosis and psychological problems than with actual vampirism.
48. Waller, *The Living and the Undead. From Stoker's Dracula to Romero's Dawn of the Dead*, 321.
49. Thoret, *Politique des zombies. L'Amerique selon George A. Romero*, 13. "La *zombication* [est un] processus de transformation qui évoque une renaissance monstrueuse—chaque humain mordu meurt puis renaît sous une forme altérée"—my translation.
50. Pagano, "The Space of the Apocalypse in Zombie Cinema." In McIntosh and Leverette, *Zombie Culture*, 71–86.
51. *Warm Bodies* (both Marion's novel and Levine's film) preceded *iZombie* for the idea that eating one's brain makes a zombie re-live the dead person's experiences.
52. In each season functioning zombies, who retain their basic personality as ethical or non-ethical people, with all the defects that living humans have, can be identified with discriminated groups in our society.
53. Engelhardt, *The End of Victory Culture*, 137.
54. Ibid., 215.
55. As he told Tony Williams in "An Interview with George and Christine Romero," In Williams, *George A. Romero Interviews*, 137.
56. As he told Denny Fisher in "George Romero on *Bruiser*, Development Hell, and Other Sundry Matters," "That's where it all came from. I mean the sixties is King and Kennedy and all that anger." In Williams, *George A. Romero Interviews*, 130.

Splat Panel Shocks

Romero, EC Horror and Innovation

EMMA AUSTIN

George Romero is widely hailed as forging the modern zombie narrative, in no small part due to his willingness to upset filmmaking conventions and take on startling, if not shocking, new dramatic themes. Robin Wood, among others, points to Romero's own commentary on the need for "revolution" within the cinematic worlds he creates: the "total disintegration of society is the necessary prerequisite for new growth."[1] Beyond displaying social collapse, Romero communicates and foments his revolution with relentless, subversive and mischievous depictions of violence, factors that may explain the lasting impact of his horror films as a whole, both beyond his lifetime *and* in a way that was visible to contemporary commentators. Gregory A. Waller gives context to this observation, noting that since the 1970s, "What horror films offer … is the representation of violence—violence embedded in a generic, narrative, fictional, often highly stylized, and oddly playful context."[2] Similarly, Phillip Brophy identifies this violence as a hallmark of what he calls "Horrality—horror, textuality, morality and hilarity,"[3] an understanding of contemporaneous horror which is self-referential and self-conscious. Those working in this generic framework are obsessed with the telling *and* showing of the horrific, playing to the audiences' awareness of the artifice and long history of these constructs, coupled with the visualization of horror enabled by changes in physical horror effects (and a relaxation in censorship) of the 1970s and '80s in America.[4] For both Brophy and Waller, Romero was a significant contributor to this new horror of the 1970s, his work positioned as a distinctive departure from his cinematic predecessors.

However, looked at in a different light, Romero's use of horror genre traditions indicates a much less innovative stance, with his repeated motif of creation through destruction influenced by an enthusiastic adaptation of familiar, longstanding popular horror culture tropes.[5] This approach is supported by Romero's own stated position on his influences and directorial intentions: "[It] is a celebration of shlock, not in the negative sense … [I am] very pleased with it: that is what my art is…. I love popular form cinema. I have loved it all my life."[6] Thus, notwithstanding the director's undeniable creativity and innovation, a defining element in Romero's work is his celebration of inherited traditions—specifically, his appreciation (and reimagining) of popular horror, science fiction films, and comics of the 1950s, notably the Entertaining Comics (EC) horror titles. In particular, as his *Dead* films developed over time, he responded to his own experience with

EC narratives by incorporating more gore effects and violence to add visual shock to his films, but also through developing more nuanced narratives.

This discussion begins by positioning how Romero's *Dead* films developed, establishing the initial notoriety and resonance of *Night of the Living Dead* (1968) with its reference to and divergence from established popular cultural influences from horror to science fiction to comic books. The second section offers a more focused and detailed appreciation of aesthetic and narrative framing in specific EC stories to show how, in the EC horror tradition, Romero's zombies shocked audiences with their horrific appearance, but also operated as embodiments of ironic humor and retribution in dark morality tales about American society. EC's bold use of saturated color and narrative tension when considering the undead body is particularly worth noting as a dominant influence on Romero's zombie film work. We can then trace developments from these initial influences, to the distinct manifestations found in Romero's later films that arguably focused much more heavily on transferring grotesque imagery and dark irony from a comic book aesthetic to a cinematic platform. This context enabled Romero's thematic concerns about zombies to emerge in a nuanced and multi-layered form, facilitating his influence on newer generations of zombie authors. This may form an ironic part of a Romero legacy: he mined meaning from previous media depictions to enable new transmedia texts, which in turn became "classics," which in turn instigated a new generation of inheritance, reverence, and innovation. In this way, an important part of the Romero legacy is his providing of both seminal source materials and an example of creative borrowing, sly reference, and reconfiguration. While Chera Kee's essay in this volume considers Romero's innovations with reference to William Seabrook and the challenges posed by the Comics Code Authority, this essay takes the paranoid films of the 1950s and literary works like Richard Matheson's *I Am Legend* as its starting point. I then move into a sustained analysis of the ways in which these sources and the EC horror comic culture helped create a distinctive architecture and aesthetic of shock that Romero inherited, developed, and extended to his contemporary imitators and the artists who followed him.

Positioning Night: Paranoia, Pessimism and Confinement in Popular Horror Culture

The critical and commercial impact of *Night of the Living Dead* is well established. *Night* is often identified as the film that changed the face of horror films in America[7] and its ongoing prominence within genre histories is testament to its strength as an entertaining and allegorical text—no matter how much the production team have denied intentional political or social commentary.[8] Crucially, the film also explicitly speaks to popular trends within American horror in the 1950s and '60s. *Night* was innovative, but we should also evaluate and celebrate it as a homage to popular film and horror culture.

Some of this tribute was practical rather than strictly artistic or creative. As the director and production team have all commented, horror was the cheapest type of film to make and many stylistic choices, such as location and filming style, were the result of budgetary restrictions and attempts to entice an audience with familiar cinematic violence (even if it was ultimately rendered in somewhat shocking form).[9] That said, Romero regularly acknowledged filmic and stylistic influences in his storytelling that both continued and diverged from established genre convention. In an interview with Richard Porton he responded to the question about these influences:

> Romero: Half of it is parasitic and the other half is instinctive. A small percentage of it is thoughtful.
> Q: Given your admiration for directors such as Welles and Michael Powell, I have the impression that you didn't start out with the intention of being pegged as a director of horror movies?
> Romero: I never did. Of course, I loved horror films. I grew up with EC comics and, when I was a kid, they re-released the Universal Famous Monsters.... I had this weird mixture of seeing these beautifully staged Gothic films, while the next day I would go to see *The Thing* or *The Day the Earth Stood Still* or some other paranoid vision.... I saw everything and came up with this very curious mixture of styles.[10]

The paranoid visions Romero is referring to are science fiction invasion narratives of the 1950s. Drawing on these, the narrative of *Night* identifies radiation to be a factor potentially responsible for the propagation of monsters, as did several early science fiction and horror films of this era. Moreover, in Romero's ongoing portrayals of the destructive and distant behavior of loved ones (who are now zombies) we can also trace overtones from William Cameron Menzies' *Invaders from Mars* (1953) and Don Siegel's *Invasion of the Body Snatchers* (1956), which also depicted the strange new behavior of former friends and lovers who have become "infected." Like Romero's ghouls, these earlier characters are rigid in their movements, seem to have undergone some form of "undeath" or control of the brain by aliens, and no longer recognize social or familial links or, indeed, emotions.

In addition to these points, *Invasion of the Body Snatchers* bears close similarities to *Night* in its mostly pessimistic tone and in the ambiguity of meaning with respect to what the films' threats represent and encompass.[11] More generally, in depicting a mass of zombies, *Night* shows stylistic and dramatic similarities with both *Invasion* and Edward Cahn's *Invisible Invaders* (1959) in exhibiting the undiscriminating scale of the infection or invasion. However, despite the ultimately grand scope of the calamity facing society, both Romero and Siegel's films underscore the loss of family and social ties as the most immediate, visceral, and threatening aspect of the dawning horror.

Beyond these creative sources and themes, *Night* can be traced to another notable influence: the perilous isolation of individuals found in works such as Richard Matheson's novel *I Am Legend* (1954) and its first film version, Ubaldo Ragona and Sidney Salkow's *The Last Man on Earth* (1964). Mark Jancovich typifies Matheson's style and concerns as being "preoccupied with the male anxieties of the 1950s, although he does not necessarily endorse these anxieties.... Normality is always relative within his fiction and, usually, it is monstrous. For these reasons, his fiction displays a general concern with paranoia, loss of control and estrangement."[12] In *The Last Man on Earth*, the undead seek to destroy the last survivor, who has barricaded himself in his suburban home. The attacking creatures bear startling resemblances to previous zombie and sci-fi incarnations and include friends and family members. This, of course, points to an obvious parallel with *Night's* besieged farmhouse and the eventual fate of its characters, especially in terms of the geographical and emotional isolation they suffer. Several years before conceiving *Night*, Romero wrote an allegorical short story, "Anubis," following the main premise of Matheson's novel, but making his monsters flesh-eaters. This would later form the basic plot for *Night*. The influences of Matheson and *The Last Man on Earth* can also be seen in some of the details and dramatic choices that define Romero's initial zombie film. In a scene from

The Last Man on Earth, the undead vampire-zombies converge mindlessly on the protagonist's home, beating the front with sticks while moaning his name. While *Night's* zombies cannot vocalize actual words, their intent and manner in attacking the farmhouse are nearly identical to this earlier cinematic imagery. It is in this shared siege that we can trace symbolic and visual links between the two films.

In these and many other ways, *Night* pays homage to previous movements and developments in horror and science fiction narratives. However, Romero's genre alterations and innovations are also important. Unlike many of the horror and suspense works that Romero gestures to, in *Night* there are no enduring heroes, only bickering, failed humans and, sometimes, fleeting moments of bravery or dignity. In *Night* and in Romero's subsequent films, there is also no hope in the rescuers, who in the end do not discern between the living and the undead. This bleak pessimism is assisted by Romero's use of location filming that emphasizes a washed-out farmland locale, which Elliot Stein refers to as a "flat murky ambiance … the ramshackle American Gothic landscape."[13] The shadowy *mise en scène* of the farmhouse and its environs underscores notions of escape and containment: Barbra's panicked run to the farmhouse and the dark garden at night into which the zombies keep appearing all feature the outside as a space or medium associated with threat, so that all that remains for the protagonists is confinement within. This confinement is both symbolic and physical: the trapped characters feed off each other's fear and hostility, leading to bad judgments and the final overtaking of the house by the undead.

It is also a definite visual choice. Romero spends time establishing the space of the living room and basement, since this is where the most dialogue, hence character revelation, takes place. As in earlier science fiction and horror films that featured safe domestic spaces, such as *Invaders from Mars* and *The Last Man on Earth*, American lower-middle class normality is established in the "home as haven."[14] This also serves as a careful dramatic build-up to the inevitable siege and invasion of the farmhouse by zombies. As *Night* progresses, the earlier shots of the interiors from bright, level, slightly distanced camera angles become off kilter, with faces in close up to emphasize the proximity of the budding threat. The editing also becomes faster and more menacing, letting us know that the contained space of the house has become a trap—critically captured in the final shot of the invasion sequence with Ben sitting alone in the cellar, waiting for morning (and, unwittingly, waiting for his murder). This is part of the dark irony in the film, since Harry, the histrionic would-be alpha male, claimed that the cellar was the best place to wait and was overruled by Ben and the others. The darkness of tone and substance is completed when Ben is killed by his long-awaited "rescuers."

This bleakness of story, alongside the now-famous scenes of unflinching flesh eating, marked *Night* as breaking with previous horror film narratives, providing at once a familiar but uncomfortably changed setting for the audience. Romero was explicitly engaging in that genre referencing seen as a hallmark of the new horror of the 1970s by Brophy, but at the same time, he was also introducing into cinema a newer form of graphic visual gore. These visualizations referenced another popular horror format of the 1950s, explicitly cited by Romero as another one of his influences: *Night* had "a nostalgic quality which recalls [both] the horror films and the EC comic books of the fifties, and this was contributed to by our intentional use, in some cases, of outrageously clichéd dialogue."[15] The links to some of these comic book aesthetics and narrative constructs plays out in both *Night* and the later *Dead* films, as the balance between showing gore and sustaining narrative is arguably a structural concern for both EC horror comics and Romero's ever-evolving zombie films.

The EC Comics Tradition and Horrality: Structure, Framing and Narrative Influences

Several commentators have discussed links between Romero and EC comics, notably Phillip Brophy in his seminal article on "horrality."[16] During what he terms "a small 'golden period'"[17] of horror film production starting in the 1970s, a new direction in the aesthetics and intent of certain contemporary horror films appeared, consciously referencing and reworking previous generic hallmarks. This new wave of horror was based upon "showing as opposed to telling ... [and was] strongly connected to [portrayals of] the destruction of the body"[18] which we see in the graphic gore of *Night*. It also importantly relied on "the cinematic realization of the textual organization of the comic book" and comics' unapologetically comedic aspects.[19] As noted, Romero consciously relied upon a comic tradition of intermittent "clichéd dialogue" as well as dark, ironic endings. Brophy clearly delineates Romero's later *Dawn of the Dead* (1978) and *Creepshow* (1983) as examples of horrality in their deliberate melding of the "macabre with the hilarious."[20] More generally, these are films that "recklessly copy and re-draw their generic sketching" by relying on past, cognate work. In this way such productions can be considered as "saturated fictions" where the "importance is the textual effect ... the contemporary Horror film knows that you've seen it before; it knows that you know what is about to happen."[21] In applying this argument to Romero, it is clear that his later zombie films rest on the audience's awareness of his previous zombie films (after all, despite their discontinuity, the *Dead* series represents arguably the longest running zombie narrative in film). Moreover, consistent with Brophy's conception, Romero uses specific narrative and thematic framings, explicitly referencing what had once been a popular and influential creative form: the EC horror comics of the 1950s.

As Stephen Sennitt argues, there were literally hundreds of horror comics available by 1953, but the most influential were the ec horror comics that started in 1950.[22] *Tales from the Crypt* (1950–1955), *The Vault of Horror* (1950–1954), and *The Haunt of Fear* (1950–1954) have come to typify this period of popular horror culture. The simplicity of the narratives alongside their bold visuals fueled the appeal of EC horror comics, hailed by several horror authors of film and literature (including Stephen King) as crucial inspiration for their own work. These comics were comprised of a selection of short horror stories, introduced by a monstrous "host" (such as the Crypt-Keeper or Old Witch), and featuring a "Letters" page through which EC published reader comments and responses to the comics. The individual EC titles were advertised and promoted with vivid and colorful covers, featuring a full-page "splash" illustration of a moment of horror that might (or might not) be part of the narrative within. While some stories were set abroad or in the past, the majority were placed in recognizably American settings, again linking EC to the contemporary topics and milieus depicted in U.S. horror and science film and fiction in the 1950s, including the works of Robert Bloch, Ray Bradbury and Richard Matheson. The tone of many of the stories is darkly humorous, with a notable reliance on twist or shock endings, often accompanying morality tales to warn against greed, destructive relationships, crime, and violence. Hoberman and Rosenbaum particularly note the repeated EC motif of destruction meted out in small group structures, sometimes families, a precursor to the domestic disintegration portrayed in the paranoid science fiction films mentioned earlier, as well as Romero's zombie films.[23]

The influence of 1950s EC horror comic culture is an acknowledged facet of Romero's work, not only through his participation as part of the teenage demographic who devoured the comics, but also in being swept up in the wider creative influence of popular horror culture generally, and horror comics in particular. Hoberman and Rosenbaum identify a "tight storyboard structure" in the comics, leading to paced, punchy short stories that were later mimicked in a variety of contexts, including by the American International Pictures (AIP) Edgar Allan Poe horror film series.[24] Williams makes an even stronger and broader case for EC's influence, noting the narrative structure, images of the decaying dead, "punch endings" and a "satirically satisfying" tone of the comics (where critiques of America combine with "graphic imagery") must surely have "contributed to scenes in later Romero films."[25]

EC stories featured a variety of monsters established in previous film genre narratives: werewolves, vampires, mad killers, and scientists. In particular, EC demonstrated a marked taste for depicting monstrous and reanimated bodies. Appearances of what we would now call zombies are a regular occurrence, formed as vengeance-driven undead creatures or voodoo-created monsters. For example, the *Vault of Horror* story "Till Death" (1952) focuses on the reanimation of a plantation owner's wife by his loving workers in a clear revival of sensationalist voodoo narratives present in American horror culture by the 1930s onwards.[26] Alternatively, vengeance stories such as "Graft in Concrete" (1952) focus on the physical state of the zombie, juxtaposing their fragmented, faded, decaying bodies against the lurid colors and settings of the living. This story, among many others from EC, is set in a recognizably contemporary American setting, but with no rationale offered for the appearance of the undead. They simply erupt into "normal" life, with their appearance used as a foreground and background threat in simplistic morality tales. The parallels here with Romero's zombies are clear.

The EC comics rely on cinematic techniques in their depiction of images, especially through the use of discrete panels as establishing shots, in framing characters' reactions, and through close-ups (especially of the returning dead). The most obvious and prominent devices EC horror titles employed to preview narrative gore and terror was through comic book covers which were brightly colored "splash" (full-page) pages, sometimes highlighting a key moment of a narrative. The covers captured a moment of realization of terror for the characters, with the fantastic source of danger highlighted and readily identified. In horror terms, it might be useful to think of these "splash" as "splat" images, where images of the grotesque, gore, or moments of heightened terror are crucial in delivering the promise of fear. We can see direct links between these comic covers and film posters, which offer looming terror, while, more importantly, suggesting both the depths of monstrous revelation and even critical moments when suspense and narrative give way to visual realization and shock—and hence release—for both the characters and audience. Here it is worth considering some specific examples from EC comics in greater detail to demonstrate the authors' and publishers' compositional and narrative choices designed to induce shock—particularly in those pages and stories that feature the undead.

Johnny Craig's cover for the *Vault of Horror* No. 18 (April–May 1951) is an excellent place to start: a couple embrace in the foreground, but the man's attention is drawn to the well (carefully labeled "Wishing Well") in the background, from which a dripping corpse is emerging, reaching for him. The man's terror is undercut by the rhapsodic expression of the woman waiting for his kiss. The juxtaposition of budding romance and dawning horror is ironic, and the conveyed shock through a perception of threat adds to a scene deeply marked with emergent tension and disequilibrium.

This presentation of shock is mirrored in many of the introductions to the EC stories, which drive towards a visual or emotional high point in the narrative. All EC stories have a narrator to introduce the title and context of the story, and to break down the fourth wall, thereby establishing complicity with readers. The stories begin with a quick visual and textual introduction to location and mood, with the promise of terror delivered with ominous character reactions or the hint of the monstrous. For example, "Till Death" begins with three panels: the introduction by the narrator (Vault-Keeper), with his speech bubble overlapping a second large panel on the left that takes up two thirds of the page and shows a male character on a red background, sweating with terror, holding a smoking gun. The third panel, clearly separated in time and space through a white gutter, then directly addresses the reader: "You stand ... staring anxiously out over the glittering, restless waters of the Carribean [sic] Sea."[27] The structure here is simple, a promise of drama and a careful presentation of character, location, and emotion to start the story, through careful compositional choices.

In a similar vein, the early framing of threat and the reactions of characters in Romero's films follow the same established comic-book and horror conventions. The use of saturated colors in the opening sequences of both *Dawn* and *Day*, for instance, seems to be a direct quotation of EC "splash" pages, as will be discussed later. A conventional horror narrative device is also making audiences aware of a background peril before the characters are, for instance in *Night* when a zombie enters the house in the background while Barbra lies stupefied in the foreground. Romero also relies on instances of shock and suspense that EC used to sell comics: the so-called "splat" moments highlighting the eruption of gore, shock, or terror at a critical narrative juncture. Both Romero's *Dawn* and *Survival of the Dead* (2009) feature these episodes in their narratives with graphic images

Panels from "Graft in Concrete" (*Vault of Horror*, Vol. 1, #26, August 1952). The focus is on atmospheric description, counterpointed by the tight framing of fear in the panels.

of exploding undead heads. In EC comics, we find splat moments in the cover pages and introductory framing images, but it is also a motif found in the narratives themselves. In "Till Death," the final image is a splat panel featuring the main male protagonist, his eyes opening wide as he returns as a zombie after committing suicide (to escape his zombie wife). The readers here can enjoy the shock value conveyed through the ironic fate of the main character, and also through a foregrounding of the horrific that dawns on both readers and the fictional protagonist at the same time. This approach reverberates in Romero's work repeatedly: through undead hands which grasp though the window at camera level in *Night*; with the child zombies plunging through the door in *Dawn*; and with the crowds of zombies who reach out to grasp characters throughout the film series, particularly in *Dawn* and the ending of *Day of the Dead* (1985).

Even *Diary of the Dead* (2007) a stylistic departure from Romero's other zombie films, emphasizes the framing of the sudden emergence of fear when the hand-held camera pulls to the left or right, or looks up, and a zombie is suddenly brought into startling focus. This is a visual equivalent of a dramatic "stinger shock," where the reaction of the character mimics our own sudden recognition of danger and is a key facet of all horror texts. However, it is particularly important in comic-book narratives, which preview the underlying threat through covers, ghastly narrators, the framing of panels, and narrative pacing, only to let this threat erupt onto the characters.

The background atmosphere of looming threat in both EC comics and Romero's work is facilitated by our familiarity with the conventions of the horror narrative, the "Horrality" of knowledge, shock, and then release. In EC stories, such as "The Chips are Down" and "Graft in Concrete," the artists and writers restrict zombies' presence to key moments while keeping readers keenly aware of their shadowy menace. In both stories, the undead initially appear in a splat page that forms the introduction to the stories, clearly juxtaposed against the living perpetrators of crime. This follows a familiar narrative structure that juxtaposes two jarring entities (the living and the dead) and promises future terror and visual gore. Notwithstanding this beginning, the undead then do not appear until the beginning of the dénouement. In "The Chips are Down" we see a rotting hand clawing out of the ground five panels before the story's end, and in "Graft in Concrete" the undead emerge on the final page. In both comics, the intervening panels and narrative have clearly set up the conflict of the living characters and their (im)moral stances, foregrounding the necessity of punishment—which the reader knows from the first page will come inevitably and through the claws (and mouths) of the undead. In other words, EC zombies are an unseen background threat, allowing the dialogue and characterization to play out in the intervening pages. The reader expects the undead to erupt at some point and can anticipate their violence on the living to be enacted through visually grotesque representations. This is markedly similar to the narrative dynamic in Romero's zombie films: he sees the zombies as exerting background pressure or danger and brings them forward, selectively, to underscore tensions amongst his human protagonists or other critical plot developments and narrative action. As he explained, "My films are about the humans. The zombies in my films are the annoyance … the films are more about human foibles and misbehavior and mistakes" that ultimately make the undead "annoyances" truly lethal.[28]

In *Night*, we can trace the pattern of danger, escape, and then re-ascending tension. The peril posed by zombies is visualized, then placed in the background (pushed aside by flaring tension amongst the combative humans), and then reintroduced so we can experience

Panels from "Till Death" (*Vault of Horror*, Vol. 1, #28, December 1952). Note the emphasis on decay, difficult to colorize but emphasized through the emerging skeleton, and the husband's reaction.

the redoubled dread of the undead menace layered on top of the human conflict. This double-tension recurs throughout Romero's zombie films. The idea that the Romero films are concentrated on the humans and their transgressions is an interesting one, since it allows us to trace another link with established EC representational strategies. In the EC narrative tradition, few people escape their fates: only those characters deemed morally worthy survive, although there are also endings where everybody is destroyed. All of the comic stories, especially those featuring zombies, rely on clearly framed locales where conflict is unavoidable: in marriage, friendships, or in business relations. The threat or the building antagonism is played out either in panels focusing on dialogue and thoughts or in the claustrophobic locations and interiors, where the panel layout emphasizes a squeezing of physical space that forces characters to confront one another—a visual choice where individuals are in almost suffocating proximity. The release of this tension is offered through physical escape from the predicament or setting, or, more usually, through violence.

A key example is contained in the story "Hook, Line and Stinker" about the vengeance visited on a man who uses fishing as a cover for his unfaithfulness to his lover, patiently awaiting him at home. The only two locations offered are the crowded interior of a home, with a mounted trophy fish prominent in the background, and a brief sequence of panels in a hayfield where Stanley's unfaithfulness is revealed. This latter episode triggers a confrontation in the house, with the final conversation framed by the windows and walls that visually morph into bold yellow and red blocks. The ensuing "outrageously clichéd dialogue," as Romero put it, emphasizes the emotional and mental state of the characters as they reach a breaking point. The panels are small and crammed together to capture the rising tension, with the available space dominated by facial emotions. As the tension rises further still, the panels become larger, communicating a sense of emerging violence: now body gestures instead of expressions are emphasized to show the tipping point for antagonists and protagonists. Romero's films follow a similar arc, where the conflict of personal motivations under pressure causes verbal fights, and then either resolution or (usually) physical and violent escalation.

Following this EC comics approach, a crucial dramatic element in Romero's zombie films is whether characters remain trapped or are willing to move beyond a confining location. The director combines setting and dialogue to create a space for building pressure, negotiation, and emotional release. In this way, the back and forth verbal conflict in the tight living room of *Night* runs parallel with the ongoing cycle of hostility and détente between Stephen and Fran in *Dawn*, symbolized by their battle over a television set that Fran switches off in their (small) hidden flat. In *Day*, the overt hostility between Rhodes, Sarah, and Dr. Logan is exacerbated by their confinement in a cramped, subterranean research facility. In *Diary, Land of the Dead* (2005), we find claustrophobic settings and sometimes freighted conversation in the close confines of a Winnebago van, an armored personnel vehicle, and a boat, respectively. Romero's small physical spaces, captured with closer camera shots, offer heightened attention to dialogue and quickened emotional responses—the fear and hostility of those jockeying for power and attention. *Diary* emphasizes an even smaller filming space through the first-person perspective of Jason Creed's camera, literally re-framing the world through his own lens, capturing what he sees as important and excluding everything else. For both the audience and many of *Diary*'s characters, Creed's control of the frame leads to building tension, as we (and they) strive to expand the scope of what is visible, especially with our knowledge that the zombie danger is omnipresent. Indeed, Creed's partial view is ironically criticized through the cause of his death: he is killed because of his lack of vision to see the zombie threat outside the frame of his camera.

While generally more nuanced than the EC stories, Romero's moralizing also involves broadly drawn and somewhat one-dimensional figures. Romero's characters certainly can and do develop over the course of his films, but they often display initial core attributes that mark their suitability for survival—or eventual destruction. It is clear that there are specific character types who are doomed, especially men who put groups at risk because of their own need for authority (such as Dr. Logan in *Day* or O' Flynn in *Survival*). These figures resemble not only the ill-fated characters in EC stories, but also Richard Matheson's protagonists: men whose anxieties lead to paranoia and an ultimate loss of self and social control. Their blindness to the realities of survival against their own concepts of identity and power is, however, still more forgivable than those characters explicitly positioned as evil or morally blank, a frequent attribute of characters in EC comics. Their crimes (whether adultery, theft, greed, or selfishness) invite retribution, often delivered in a form that is ironically linked to their misdeeds or personality (such as the fisherman Stanley's ultimate fate as a mounted trophy in "Hook, Line and Stinker"). In Romero's *Dead* series, such an extreme exemplar of amorality is found in Paul Kaufman in *Land,* who meets an ironic end worthy of an EC tale, killed because of his reliance on a limousine, a symbol of his opulence and contempt for others.

As Romero's sometime collaborator Stephen King notes, the idea of moral justice may be one of the key hallmarks of the horror comic books: "EC Comics were the last gasp of romanticism in America.... The scales were always put back in balance, even if it meant that this decomposing, rotting corpse had to get out of the ground and go after the people who killed him."[29] In the EC narrative tradition of justice, the world is either going to remain a cruel place with horrors undefeated, or those who have caused pain are punished through horrific incidents that echo their own misdemeanors. The husband in "Till Death," after trying to drown, shoot, and burn his decaying zombie wife, is turned into a zombie to go through the same process of decomposition—alongside her skeletal, but still reanimated remains. It is clear that Romero, in most if not all of his zombie films, follows this EC tradition of ironic justice for human sins for those he judges especially guilty. The decimation of the motorcyclists in *Dawn* is triggered by their unwelcome incursion into the mall, but Stephen also dies due to his greediness and aggression. Both Rhodes and Logan in *Day* die in the underground bunker that is supposed to keep them safe. The ironies, stark moral judgments and darkness in *Night of the Living Dead*, the 1950s science fiction films, and EC comics are present throughout every one of Romero's zombie films. Repeatedly, even minor sins and character flaws are the basis of the characters' undoing and demise. "Horrality" is evoked through the horror—and potential grim hilarity—of undeath, the ultimate leveler in Romero's zombie society.

EC Splat Panel Shocks: Gore, Color, Effects and the Zombies in Dawn

Night of the Living Dead established gore and physical effects as visual and narrative highpoints of terror within a moralistic narrative. Overall, Romero claimed, the intention was "to make [*Night*] as much of a metaphor as it was a thrill ride" and it is straightforward to trace the use of influences from 1950s genre films and EC comics.[30] *Dawn of the Dead* continued this legacy from EC Horror comics, but also relied on a more concerted use of physical make-up and gore, extended sequences of zombie destruction, and creative collaboration with talents like Dario Argento (who co-wrote and helped to score the film) and Tom Savini (the special effects virtuoso in *Dawn* and *Day*). It is important to remind ourselves that ten years passed between *Night* and *Dawn*, allowing a variety of interpretations of the zombie to play out across this span, most notably in Spanish, Italian, and American horror films. Crucially however, Romero retained some important references from *Night* and beyond. The influence of EC Comics was clearly identified by contemporary commentators: critics and Romero admirers alike noted the change of emphasis between his first two zombie films: the "straightforward punchiness of *Night* [exchanged] for something closer to a frolicsome comic-strip tone"[31] as embodied by *Dawn*'s "mixture of wit and horror."[32] We can extend these observations by considering the composition and visual representations in Romero's second iconic zombie film. As noted previously, among other parallels, both EC comics and Romero pay close attention to dramatic sequences that highlight confined spaces, the visually grotesque, and the sudden eruption of fears shared by characters and viewers alike. But looking closely at *Dawn* reveals other crucial areas where we can see the continued influence of EC comics, especially in Romero's use of color, gore, and representational choices in depicting zombies and dead bodies, which in turn cemented his position as a director of "Horrality" identified by Brophy in the 1980s.

The distinctive visual style that played out in the pages of EC comics is arguably one of the most important factors in establishing its enduring cultural impact and admiration by critics. As Grant Geissman notes, EC artists were encouraged to promote their own singular style, were credited for their work (unusual in the industry at the time), and were given specific stories that best suited their artistic approaches.[33] This emphasis on creative craftsmanship had several effects: particular artists became identified (in the company *and* by readers) with specific visual trademarks and emphases, such as close-ups of grotesque imagery, as was the case with Graham Ingels. Creative freedom also meant artists could adapt dialogue boxes, depending upon what layout worked best for the overall visual impact and thrust of their stories. Some EC artists, such as Jack Davis, favored bold lines and simpler art styles in character portrayals and backgrounds, to allow for impactful moments of action in smaller panels. For all of these artists, the use of color was key: EC comics relied on the bold impact of its front covers to generate sales. In addition, EC used contrasts in coloring as signifiers of conflict, and expressions of emotional turmoil.

In this regard, we can clearly link the EC use of extremes of color to the opening sequence of *Dawn of the Dead,* where Fran awakens from a nightmare to a new and all-too-real terror. The close-up of her face, wedged against the saturated orange-red corner of a wall, while the title of the film appears in bold white letters below, focuses our attention on her somewhat disembodied face as a study in fear. Only as the camera pulls back do we connect Fran, and the film to a particular location, a hectic television station where the deteriorating situation of the zombie apocalypse is becoming clear. Similarly, the opening nightmare sequence of *Day of the Dead* situates a slumped Sarah within a featureless, disorienting space. The stark white concrete room is bordered on the floor by a thick black line, similar to the lines of a comic book panel. She looks over at a calendar fastened to the far wall, which has each of the thirty-one days of October marked off (an important date in horror lore and an oblique reference to the popular 1978 *Halloween* film[34]). When she touches the colorful calendar image (a pumpkin field in saturated orange, with some ambiguous and possibly sinister figures wandering in the distance), dark hands shoot out of the wall to grab her. She then wakes up to find herself flying over a town in a helicopter, where the reactions of her fellow passengers indicate tension and despair. In both *Dawn* and *Day* (1985) the initial image of isolated, discombobulated terror is brought into sharper relief with the use of saturated color and careful visual framing, previewing a lingering promise of fear throughout the rest of the narrative, in a manner similar to the EC stories.

Aside from its reliance on the arresting use of colors, another notable hallmark of EC comics was its frequent and creative depictions of the breaking down of the human body (as trophies, fragmented body parts, or as flattened, bloated or shredded objects). These portrayals of decomposition were part of the medium's willingness to go "further than contemporary horror films, and featured beheadings, eviscerations, gouged eyes and so on, in gleeful detail … [somewhat leavened or softened] … by the wit of [the accompanying] storytelling and … superb artwork."[35] In particular, the emphasis is frequently on using dead bodies, staring heads, and reanimated corpses in the context of "shock" or "splat" panels, to center and accentuate the emotional reactions or both readers and the comics' characters.

This focus on a startling reveal of dead bodies, especially through close-ups on heads and images of dismemberment or decay, is also a crucial part of Romero's *Dawn* and the later *Dead* films. Here, the diminished bite of the Motion Pictures Production Code (which weakened considerably in the 1960s and was formally abandoned in 1968, the year *Night* was released) and changing social attitudes to representations of violence allowed Romero to go further than anything seen in the pages of EC (or on the silver screen). Hence, in *Dawn* we see a close-up of a zombie biting a woman's neck (with generous arterial spraying) in an apartment building, the decapitation by helicopter blade of a zombie at an airfield, and a bloody, sustained, and chaotic final confrontation between the zombies and bikers. Again, part of Romero's signature style is to soften or at least distance us from this onslaught of violence through humor and absurdity. Thus, even as we see *Dawn's* mall bikers running riot, dispatching countless zombies, and having their own flesh torn and eaten, Romero interjects moments of the gang striking the zombies with cream pies, spraying pressurized seltzer into their faces, and a gang member taking a break from the mayhem to check his blood pressure.

Brophy's idea of horrality is central here, as Romero emphasizes the breakdown of the body through color and effects, showing and telling through the destruction of the undead body how, in turn, society is breaking down. But unlike the EC comics he does this explicitly through blood: the bright red fake blood in *Dawn* is repeatedly splattered across the pale spaces of the mall and contrasted with clothes. This emphasis on blood can be explained by the involvement of Italian horror director Dario Argento in *Dawn's* production, as his films use gore extensively. However the idea of saturated color and contrast is also part of an EC tradition: the gray blue-green of the skin of the zombies bears similarities to the tones used in some of the EC stories, which continually use saturated contrasts of light and dark and color to draw attention to key aspects of the horrific.

Following *Dawn*, Romero pursued a more focused use of decomposition and bodies breaking apart in his next zombie film, *Day of the Dead*. However, this followed his explicit homage to EC in the episodic film *Creepshow* (1982). As Romero explained,

> Steve King and I, as long as we'd known each other, would talk about movies and the old EC comics. Steve bought me some original panels and a couple of books. I had a couple of original Jack Davis paintings and so we were sitting around and decided to do "Creepshow."[36]

Following a serial, comic book model, *Creepshow* offers a series of short narratives (written by King) that draw continuously from the plotting and creative trappings of the EC horror comics of the 1950s. *Creepshow* includes the Creep, a decomposing "host" acting as an amalgamation of the supernatural narrators of the horror comics. Moreover, some of the individual stories contained in the film invoke the vengeance ethos of the earlier comics. In "Father's Day," for example, a tyrannical patriarch returns from the dead to slaughter his equally unappealing family, while "The Crate" sees a monster in the crate used to dispatch one character's horrendous wife. Stephen King himself plays the character Jordy Verrill, in a vignette that references his own popularity as a horror author, while also underscoring the EC ethos of vanity, stupidity and greed as punishable characteristics. When Verrill tries to dig up a "meteorite" to sell, the object infects him leading to the grim titular result: "The Lonesome Death of Jordy Verrill." As Brophy noted, *Creepshow* "puts cinematic language at the service of the comic-strip"[37] to deliver a product with "incredible variation in tone of each of the five stories, ranging from the farcical to the horrific."[38] Visually, Romero utilized colored filters and extreme camera angles to imitate EC comics' bold aesthetic. Within the *Creepshow* stories themselves, Romero framed certain shots with bold outlines, mimicking the panels of a comic book. This is especially evident in the splat panel reveals at the end of the stories, including the frozen image of the "cake" (a severed, frosted head bedecked with candles) and the onlookers' horrified response contained in the film's first story, "Father's Day." The frozen end shot of "Father's Day" is then transformed into a comic book panel complete with speech bubbles.

Clearly, we can see the impact of anthology horror films (collections of stories brought together by a central premise or theme) in *Creepshow*. But the shifting tone of the linked narratives, which always come back to a final framing through a comic book panel, clearly positions this film as an extended consideration of horrality as well. The film is about showing and telling the influence of EC on modern producers of horror, centering on Romero, Tom Savini, and Stephen King's status as horror icons. *Creepshow's* short sharp splat shocks are an explicit and self-conscious discussion of legacy and innovation within popular horror culture of the time, the inventive "horrality" of gore effects showcasing the grotesque, and a reference to the influential popular culture of the film producers' adolescence—especially the enduring legacy of their beloved EC comics.

Still from *Creepshow* (George A. Romero, 1982). The saturated color, focus on the decapitated head, and splat panel framing all indicate the influence of EC comics—as well as offering an iconic, horrific ending.

Conclusion: A Comics Legacy?

Despite a notable decline in comic book sales since the last decades of the twentieth century, the links between comics and other media formats is at least as important now as it was for Romero when he started filmmaking.[39] Extensive comic book adaptations of Romero's work exist, from direct translations of films (the 1982 graphic novel *Creepshow* recreated the short stories of the film) to reinterpretations. The 1991–1992 *Official Night of the Living Dead* comic book series coordinated by Tom Skulan offers a "prelude" that sees a U.S. "mission control" exploding the returning satellite briefly mentioned in *Night*.[40] The series then recreates the entirety of the film, using a painterly, expressionistic style of black and white artwork as the narrative unfolds. As the situation worsens, the artwork changes: the panels drop to become angular and distorted, or disappear entirely, reflecting the chaos of Romero's final sequences in the farmhouse.

The 2004 graphic novel adaptation of *Dawn* by Steve Niles and Chee is markedly different, working in a colorful, simple art style, and condensing Romero's second zombie film, with little variation from key sequences, dialogue and representations. Through these and other media, it appears that the Romero films have a sustainable life away from their initial forms and that comics and film traditions continue to nurture one another. Notably, comic book issues have been used as promotional materials with Romero-inspired Blu-ray releases: *Day of the Dead: Desertion* Issue 1 was one such example, alongside the one-shot *Dawn of the Dead: Hotel Muerte* for the 40th-anniversary soundtrack release by Goblin, the Italian band that provided the soundtrack to *Dawn of the Dead*.[41]

Romero also had direct authorial input into zombie comics, as a writer for *Empire of the Dead* (2014–2015) which was published by Marvel, and the DC comic series *Toe Tags* (2004–2005), which featured the mini-series "The Death of Death" also written by Romero. In this last creation, a talking zombie protagonist attempts to come to terms with his new condition, while facing various threats to himself and his allies. Romero here is clearly returning to his interpretation of the zombie as sympathetic—a characterization generally ignored in the comic book adaptations of his work, but, as Chera Kee depicts, a tradition running through 1950s horror comics. In fact, the myriad and sophisticated ways in which Romero played with zombies' capacity for moral superiority, group cohesion, and basic decency (in contrast with their human adversaries) marks his biggest departure from his original inspiration in EC comics, where the zombies were, in vengeance narratives, simply a force for ironic justice. It is perhaps fitting that in the later part of his career Romero worked within comic books as well as film, coming full circle from his early love of EC to his own authorship of horror comics.

While beyond the scope of this essay, it is also appropriate to note in this context Romero's acknowledged impact on video game content, design, and appearance. Many game designers have incorporated his signature stylistic and thematic flourishes. As Susana Pajares Tosca notes, in *Resident Evil Code: Veronica X* the game

> makes full use of the well-defined fear-inducing style conventions of horror movies: the subtle but disquieting music, the sounds of steps, the moans of the zombies.... The cut-scenes have cinematographic quality, and during the game the player loses control of her character once in a while in order to allow for surprise effect scenes that are often quite terrifying.[42]

While Tosca does not link these features directly to Romero, this essay has developed the case that these and other narrative and dramatic techniques owe much to both the great zombie director and the artistic traditions that shaped his aesthetic. Moreover, many video games (and their creators) offer a more direct and explicit tribute. Thus, in the *Call of Duty: Black Ops Escalation* expansion pack, the director (playing himself) makes a cameo in the game, and the overall "zombie story line was inspired by Romero."[43] As the game's director explains in no uncertain terms, the expansion pack is our "tribute to the legendary George Romero, who truly defined the zombie genre and whose incredible work has been such an inspiration to our team."[44] Indeed, game creators across the industry echoed this sentiment in their statements about the director following his death.[45]

As a descendant of the visually popular horror narratives of EC comics, Romero showed his mastery of the tactics of the "splat panel" and the aesthetics of popular horror culture, a language of textual excess embodied by the new horrality found in 1970s horror films and later. In both EC comics and Romero's zombie films, the need for shock imagery was linked to narratives exploring human foibles in contemporary American society. Romero moved away from the saturated color of EC texts after *Creepshow*, but his work retained the EC traditions of cultivated irony and shock, which he blended with his signature style and developed into a broader, deeper interrogation of the monstrous. In turn, his works have inspired retellings that reproduce the horrality of *Night* and *Dawn* particularly, for newer generations of directors and comic book writers—and so the intertwined legacies of horror comic books, EC, and Romero continue as an integral part of popular horror culture generally and zombie texts in particular.

Notes

1. Wood, "Neglected Nightmares," 32.
2. Waller, *American Horrors: Essays on the Modern American Horror Film*, 6.
3. Brophy, "Horrality—The Textuality of Contemporary Horror Films," 3.
4. Ibid.
5. This is not to claim that Romero's zombie films (and horror work more generally) reference the existing genre in a uniform manner. We should adopt Brophy's analogy of "handling the films themselves like freshly severed limbs: objects both on their own and obviously fragmented." They can be read both as individual works, and as an overarching series that develops and discards earlier ideas when needed—a body of work that can be fragmented or joined together. Brophy, "Horrality—The Textuality of Contemporary Horror Films," 4.
6. Romero in Jones, "George Romero," 40.
7. See for example Newman, *Nightmare Movies*, Gagne, *The Zombies that ate Pittsburgh: The Films of George A. Romero*, and Waller, *American Horrors: Essays on the Modern American Horror Film*. The influence of *Night of the Living Dead* on zombie film in general is charted in Austin's PhD thesis "A Strange Body of Work: The Cinematic Zombie."
8. Surmacz, "Anatomy of a Horror Film," 16.
9. Surmacz, "Anatomy of a Horror Film," 15; Simon, *The American Nightmare*, Russo, *The Complete Night of the Living Dead Film Book*, 14.
10. Porton, "Blue Collar Monsters," 2. The Universal Famous Monsters refers to the iconic horror films released by Universal Studios during the 1930s and 1940s.
11. See McGee, *Invasion of the Body Snatchers, Chapter Six*.
12. Jancovich, *Rational Fears: American horror in the 1950s*, 30.
13. Stein, "The Night of the Living Dead," 105.
14. Bishop, *American Zombie Gothic*, 121.
15. Romero in Russo, *The Complete Night of the Living Dead Film Book*, 12.
16. Brophy, "Horrality—The Textuality of Contemporary Horror Films," 3.
17. Ibid.
18. Ibid.
19. Ibid., 8.
20. Ibid., 12. The films by Amicus Productions (a British film production company) that Brophy refers to are the horror films that include: *Dr. Terror's House of Horrors* (Francis, 1965), *Tales from the Crypt* (Duffell, 1972), *Vault of Horror* (Baker, 1973) and *From Beyond the Grave* (Connor, 1974). All of these use a framing narrative to link shorter horror stories together within the film, hence the term portmanteau or anthology horror.
21. Ibid., 5.
22. Sennitt, *Ghastly Terror! The Horrible story of the Horror Comics*, 11.
23. Hoberman and Rosenbaum, *Midnight Movies*, 120.
24. Ibid., 117.
25. Williams, *The Cinema of George A. Romero*, 24.
26. Bishop, *American Zombie Gothic*, 13.
27. Craig, Gaines, and Feldstein, "Till Death," 1.
28. Conterio, "Interview with George R Romero." Accessed November 12, 2018. https://medium.com/@mconterio/george-a-romero-interview-4c16169f56e0.
29. King, in Gagne, "Creepshow," 21.
30. Romero in Curnette "There's No Magic: A Conversation with George A. Romero." Accessed November 12, 2018. https://thefilmjournalblog.wordpress.com/category/rick-curnutte/.
31. Combs, "Review of Zombies," 33.
32. Rubinstein, "Romero Rubinstein 'Knights' for UA-overseas; producers Detail other Deals," 6.
33. Geissman, *Foul Play! The Art and Artists of The Notorious E.C. Comics*, 46.
34. The film begins on the eve of All Saints' Day and ends, aptly, on the Day of the Dead, November 2.
35. Sabin, *Comics, Comix and & Graphic Novels: A History of Comic Art*, 67.
36. Conterio, "Interview with George A. Romero." Accessed November 12, 2018. https://medium.com/@mconterio/george-a-romero-interview-4c16169f56e0.
37. Brophy, "Horrality—The Textuality of Contemporary Horror Films," 12.
38. Ibid.
39. Bacon, "Are Marvel & DC Comics Really Close to Failing?" Accessed March 4, 2019. https://screenrant.com/marvel-dc-comics-sales-failing.
40. Skulan, *Night of the Living Dead: Prelude*, 1–2. Much like the 30th anniversary version of *Night of the Living Dead* (Russo, 1999) which had extra scenes added to the film, including a reason for the "cemetery zombie" to be present, the comic explains the body at the top of the stairs in the farmhouse, and the attacks that drove the other characters to seek refuge in the house. In this, the ongoing efforts by John Russo to build on

the success of *Night* are visible—beyond those of Romero, who seemed content to let others reframe his work, including in Tom Savini's remake of *Night of the Living Dead* in 1990.
 41. Rustblade, "Dawn of the Dead—Double Cd + Comic Book + Poster."
 42. Tosca, "Reading Resident Evil," 213.
 43. Gaudiosi, "Night of Living Dead."
 44. *Ibid.*
 45. Phillips, "Games industry pays tribute."

No Grave Can Hold Them

Night of the Living Dead and the Rise and Rebirth of Zombies in Comics

Chera Kee

The story of zombies in popular American media is often framed as the story of two creative men. At the very beginning, in 1929, there is adventurer-turned-novelist William Seabrook, and in 1968, there is George A. Romero. Seabrook is credited with introducing the zombie into American pop culture while Romero is credited with transforming the once-docile creature into a threatening cannibal. While this narrative of the zombie's birth and subsequent reanimation is true, it often overlooks the myriad cultural influences that played a part in the zombie's journey from pitiful slave to ravenous corpse. In other words, while Romero's introduction of the flesh-eating zombie in 1968's *Night of the Living Dead* (1968) was trailblazing, Romero's work also needs to be appreciated within the context of the creative work he was engaging with: *Night of the Living Dead* and the rest of Romero's zombie oeuvre cannot be divorced from their ties to a wide array of influences.

In 1929, Seabrook published a book about the time he spent in Haiti called *The Magic Island*. Ostensibly a travelogue about "voodoo" and Haiti's culture, *The Magic Island* also contained a chapter about the one thing Seabrook supposedly saw that truly shocked him: the zombie. He told readers that the zombie was "a soulless human corpse, still dead, but taken from the grave and endowed by sorcery with a mechanical semblance of life."[1] Stories of zombies had circulated throughout the Western world since before Haiti became a nation in 1804, but this was the first time the zombie reached a wide audience. *The Magic Island* was a popular hit, soon spawning a host of zombie stories in magazines, on the radio, and in film. These stories contained *slave-style* zombies, which "arise out of folklore and stories about Haitian Vodou" and borrow heavily from Seabrook's descriptions.[2] These zombies may or may not be dead bodies, but they have lost their free will and serve a zombie master who typically possesses magical powers.

Thirty-nine years after *The Magic Island*, a newscaster in a low-budget horror film reported that the dead were returning to life to kill the living—but they weren't just killing the living, they were "eating the flesh of the people they kill."[3] It was a watershed moment for zombie cinema, as it marked the rise of a new kind of zombie: the *cannibal* zombie. The film was *Night of the Living Dead*, and in it, filmmaker George A. Romero imagined the undead not as pitiful slaves bowing to the will of a zombie master but as creatures compelled by a drive to consume human flesh. In the wake of *Night of the Living*

Dead, filmmakers imagined the cannibal zombie as "a resurrected corpse, and unlike its slave-style cousin," the cannibal zombie couldn't "be cured or rescued from its fate."[4] Moreover, while slave-style zombies in film typically look like the living and bear no obvious marks of their zombiness,[5] cannibal zombies are usually decomposing corpses that are clearly marked by the zombie state.

While the advent of decomposing cannibal zombies in film may have seemed like a radical take on the zombie character, they weren't entirely new. Not only were there precedents for decomposing corpses in earlier films,[6] but many of the zombies filling the pages of 1950s horror comics were decomposing corpses bent on revenge, coming back from the dead to dole out justice. In fact, some of these zombies were so gruesome that by the mid–1950s, concerns about the impact these kinds of characters had on children, not to mention the violence and gore accompanying them, motivated comics publishers to create the Comics Code Authority in 1954 to self-censor. One of the first things they prohibited was the zombie. Even when the Comics Code was relaxed in the early 1970s, the ban on zombies remained. These were dangerous creatures, it would seem.

Yet, in many ways, the damage was already done. George A. Romero and his associates were always very open about their love of pre-code horror comics of the 1950s,[7] especially the Entertaining Comics (EC) titles, and the role that these played in shaping *Night of the Living Dead* and Romero's later work.[8] Not only is the visual style of *Night of the Living Dead* punctuated with episodes that are reminiscent of comic book iconography, but several of the film's plot points seem to mimic the EC style of horror storytelling, with its dark humor, cynical views of American society, and especially its love of twist endings.

This interplay between comics and film would come full circle in the 1970s: at the beginning of the decade there was a new influx of horror comics. The zombie was experiencing a renaissance in pop culture more generally, due in large part to *Night of the Living Dead*, and Marvel Comics wanted to cash in, so they sidestepped the censorship. Taking advantage of the fact that rules about zombies didn't apply to magazine-sized titles,[9] Marvel published *Tales of the Zombie*, which revived a 1950s character known as "The Zombie." Elsewhere, to further circumvent censorship, Marvel introduced mindless creatures called "zuvembies." In both cases, however, the creatures were a combination of the cannibal-style zombie popularized by *Night of the Living Dead* and the more traditional slave-style zombie.

At first glance, then, it might appear that Marvel was taking an old-fashioned approach, simply dressing up slave-style zombies as their cannibalistic cousins; yet Marvel's experiments paralleled what was happening across media. While *Night of the Living Dead* upended decades of generic conventions, zombies didn't change overnight. Rather, artists spent the better part of the next decade playing with the ideas Romero introduced, trying to figure out how this new kind of zombie was going to work—just as Romero, in his own way, played with ideas introduced in the 1950s and '60s in shaping his zombies.

In this essay, I explore *Night of the Living Dead*'s place within the larger trajectory of zombie media, and in particular the ways in which the film's legacy is tied to zombies in comic books. My approach complements and contextualizes the analysis offered in the previous essay, in which Emma Austin examines the specific visual and narrative elements of EC comics that Romero utilized in his work and the ways in which conventions shared by both Romero and horror comics continue to influence horror today. Here, my aim is to place Romero's work within a larger historical and creative framework. Analyzing the ways in which pre-code horror comics of the 1950s influenced *Night of the Living*

Dead and how it, in turn, influenced zombies in comics in the 1970s, I argue that we need to consider the role comic books played in shaping Romero's seminal film and in turn, the role that film played in helping shape comics of the next decade and beyond: in thinking about George A. Romero's legacy, it is important to consider the ways in which his films fit into a larger intertextual system that continually works to keep the past alive.

While Romero's love of comic books—and their influence on his filmmaking style—is clear in many of his films, *Night of the Living Dead*'s specific historical place is important to consider. It appears after over a decade of comic book censorship and then helps initiate a rise in zombie-themed texts, including comic books. As a zombie film uniquely situated in-between the rise and fall of pre-code horror comics in the 1950s and the rise of horror comics in the 1970s, and as a film that was explicitly influenced by comic books, *Night of the Living Dead* can thus act as a guide for considering the interweaving ways in which zombie texts in a variety of media influence each other and the part Romero played in connecting some of these disparate lines together. Romero's zombies are undoubtedly made up of his own signature elements, but they are also, self-consciously, an amalgam of (aesthetic, moral, and functional) zombie types that pre-dated the director's seminal works.

Pre-Code Horrors

The first modern American comic books emerged in the mid–1930s, and by the late 1930s and early 1940s, the superhero genre was all the rage. But in the immediate post-war period, superhero stories seemed to be wearing a bit thin and other genres, such as romance and war, saw a boost in their readerships. As the 1940s progressed, crime titles became very popular, and over time, crime publishers "added elements of horror and terror to keep reader interests high."[10] There were horror elements in comics before this: superhero comics, for instance, might co-opt horror villains; other titles included literary adaptions of classical horror stories like *Frankenstein,* and horror images or storylines might make their way into detective or suspense stories, but there weren't any consistent stand-alone horror titles just yet.

However, in the period between 1947 and 1949, horror titles started appearing, and bit by bit, they caught on. Still, it wasn't until EC's entry into the market in 1950 with *The Haunt of Fear, The Vault of Horror,* and *The Crypt of Terror* (later *Tales from the Crypt*) that a full-fledged horror boom began. To put the boom into perspective, Jim Trombetta observes that "[o]f the eighty million comics that were released each month in the United States and Canada during the early fifties, a quarter were horror comics," meaning that from 1950 to 1955 dozens of horror titles were appearing on newsstands each month.[11] EC's horror comics are the best remembered of the boom, yet Trombetta reminds us that their titles only accounted for about three percent of this output.[12] Still, as much of the horror of the period tried to piggyback on the EC style, it's worth understanding just what made EC titles tick.[13]

EC comics tended to be written with a lot of dark wit, and other publishers soon followed suit. Horror author R.L. Stine recalls reading the horror comics of the 1950s as a child, noting, "The stories were ghastly and gruesome. They were written with something new to us: a wonderful combination of humor and horror."[14] Many horror comics of the 1950s were known for their gallows humor and grisly puns, but beyond the playfulness in these stories, there was a rebellious tone that often challenged Cold-War era values: in the horror comics of the 1950s, especially those trying to copy the EC style, evil was real, and while it might exist in the form of a traditional monster, it was just as likely to reside in the police department, the judiciary, or at home with one's parents. Nothing was safe from the biting critiques offered up in these comics; all aspects of American life were shown to be potentially corrupt. Given the EC preference for what they called "punch" endings (shock or twist endings), horror comics were far less comforting than other genres of comic books, showing that sometimes the boogeyman got the last laugh.

Zombies were popular figures throughout the horror boom, appearing in numerous stories and on countless covers, but Stephen Banes observes that they "were caught between the ... voodoo slave shufflers of the '30s and the ... insatiable Romero gut-munchers of the late '60s—controllable puppets vs. creatures capable of mass destruction."[15] The EC story "Zombie Terror" illustrates this middle space and, in particular, the ways that comic book zombies were diverging from their cinematic counterparts.[16] Like many zombie films of the era, "Zombie Terror" is set in the Caribbean and ties zombiism to some sort of "native" magic not unlike voodoo. However, anticipating many of the horror comics that were to come, these zombies are out for revenge, something you wouldn't have necessarily seen on cinema screens: unlike slave-style zombies, which ostensibly were under the control of a master, these zombies had wills of their own and used it to track down the men who killed them.

Moreover, while many zombies on cinema screens of the 1930s, '40s, and '50s were mute creatures, in comics, zombies could be quite talkative. Richard Hand observes that zombies in 1930s and '40s radio dramas were sometimes the voiceless, slow-witted slaves that audiences would have been familiar with on cinema screens but "in some cases the radio medium dictated that the living dead had a surprising degree of consciousness, with zombies able to think and talk."[17] Radio dramas were a strong influence on early horror comics,[18] so it makes sense that the undead in 1950s horror titles might likewise be able to think and talk.

For the most part, from the 1930s through the 1960s, the zombies in American cinema looked much like the non-zombies to the point where it was sometimes hard to differentiate between the living and the undead. Decomposing pre-code comic book zombies were thus far different from what one could see in other visual media of the time, and most likely sprang from a number of different sources. For instance, the undead on radio dramas were sometimes presented as decomposing corpses. Hand notes that while some of the undead on radio airwaves were physically untouched by their zombie state, others were harbingers of "the explicitly decaying living dead in pre-code horror comics or the zombies of the George A. Romero generation of 1968 and beyond."[19]

Tony Williams connects the EC style of the 1950s to the fact that "Many EC Comics artists had ... undergone military service."[20] This begs the question of how the realities of war and the dead bodies many soldiers had seen in World War II and the Korean War might have contributed to the prevalence of decomposing corpses in EC titles and elsewhere.[21] Perhaps the rotting corpses of the 1950s comics were a relic of war.

American pulp magazines may also have played a part in the physical appearance of pre-code zombies. The pulps were the direct forerunners of comic books, and Paul Douglas Lopes notes that over time, given the fact that many comic book publishers and artists worked in the pulps and frequently borrowed genres and storylines from pulp magazines, the more exaggerated and violent imagery of the pulps found its way into comics.[22] It makes sense, then, that the zombies of these comics were not only decomposing corpses, but in the finest pulp tradition, they were often in an advanced state of decay (see fig. 1). The decomposing corpses of early horror comics thus might have been a serendipitous meeting of pulp conventions, wartime memories, and popular descriptions conveyed through radio horror.[23]

With physically untouched zombies, as opposed to zombies that are decomposing, the terror of zombification revolves around slightly different concerns: in those zombie stories where the body remains untouched, to become a zombie is chiefly about a loss of control over one's mind: individual will is turned over to a master who can do with the zombie what they want.[24] In tales where the zombie is also physically altered, the fear is further tied to bodily decay. In both cases, there is a loss of identity but with decomposition, physical markers of health and youth are stripped away as well. Yet in many 1950s comic books, this is counterbalanced by giving the zombies a great deal of control otherwise. While there were comic book zombies who were under the sway of a master, many of the decomposing corpses of 1950s horror comics were active agents without masters directing them, which worked to invert and transform the typical fears associated with the zombie.

Even with their horrifying visages, many of these comic book zombies were vehicles for justice. In films of the 1930s and '40s, a zombie master might create zombies in order to seek revenge, and this theme was repeated in horror comics. Yet, zombies in comics could also act of their own accord to seek justice and right past wrongs and, unlike the zombies forced to work for zombie masters on screen, these zombies were often on the side of the moral good, trying to rectify the sins of the living. For instance, in the 1954 *Eerie* story "The Thing from the Sea," Eddie Murray returns from the dead to seek revenge on the man who killed him. This sort of story was common in 1950s horror comics as the murdered often came back to life to find those responsible for their deaths (fig. 1).[25] In these comics, then, bodily decay isn't always accompanied by a subsequent loss of control but rather it is the physical marker that wrong has been done to a body. Moreover, in stories like "The Thing from the Sea," where gruesome, physically-altered zombies come back from the grave, the zombie's appearance may spark fears of bodily decay but its appearance is also part of the fun: the gruesome physical body of the zombie becomes part of its arsenal against those who wronged it; the zombie's body becomes a weapon in its campaign to terrorize and then punish the guilty.

Hand observes that the zombies' associations with justice in these 1950s horror comics meant that readers could find a sense of "empathy" with them, as the stories often revealed a far worse monster: "the living, breathing human being," (an idea that would be subsequently reflected in the films of Romero).[26] In many ways, while the zombies of these early comics were horrific in appearance, they were not the bad guys. They might be scary, but they weren't a threat—unless one was guilty. As such, there was a sympathetic quality to them.

One of the possible reasons that similar sorts of decomposing zombies were not seen in American films during the 1940s and '50s was the Production Code Administration, which had stringent rules about violence and horror in American film. Given the dynamism of the comic book medium and the fact that each publisher was left to their own devices in terms of what to publish, comic books could show a grislier form of the undead than films could. Unfortunately for comics publishers, the popularity of crime and horror titles in the early 1950s, as well as the violence and gore contained within,

Figure 1: Zombie Eddie Murray seeks out the man who killed him. Wood, Wally (p & i). "The Thing from the Sea," *Eerie* #16 (June-July 1954), Avon: 4.

drew the wrong sorts of attention, and comic books quickly became a target for calls for censorship.

By 1954, in the wake of Senate subcommittee hearings—as well as Fredric Wertham's book *Seduction of the Innocent* (1954), which linked comic books to a host of evils including juvenile delinquency—it was clear that the industry was going to have to cave to calls for censorship or face possible government intervention. So, in 1954, the Comics Magazine Association of America (the industry trade group) formed the Comics Code Authority to allow publishers to censor content starting in 1955. The code prohibited "excessive violence" and stipulated that comics could no longer promote "disrespect for established authority."[27] Good had to triumph over evil, and "All scenes of horror, excessive bloodshed, gory or gruesome crimes, depravity, lust, sadism, [and] masochism" were no longer allowed.[28] With a particular eye on horror comics, the Code stated that "Scenes dealing with, or instruments associated with walking dead, torture, vampires and vampirism, ghouls, cannibalism, and werewolfism" were no longer allowed, and the use of the words "horror" or "terror" in comic book titles was prohibited.[29] As the last nail in the coffin, "gruesome illustrations" were prohibited as well.[30] As Bradford Wright notes, "Even by the conservative standards of the time, the code was extremely restrictive."[31] It effectively spelled the end of horror comics: many titles ceased publishing, and many publishers closed shop in the wake of the code's implementation. Other titles shifted genres or toned down their horror. Those titles that did remain, in Wright's estimation, "championed without criticism American institutions, authority figures, and middle-class mores."[32] But honestly, there weren't many horror titles left.

In the wake of the code, though, some publishers refused to let horror die and, as early as 1957, some were trying to reprint heavily edited versions of pre-code horror stories. But it was the publication of *Famous Monsters of Filmland* in 1958 that truly started to change the course of horror publishing.[33] Focused on horror films from the silent era up through the contemporary moment, the magazine was filled not with fiction but with production stills and articles that celebrated horror movie make-up, special effects, and behind-the-scenes stories—especially from classical horror films of the 1930s and '40s. It spawned a number of imitators and by the early 1960s, publishers were wondering if it might be possible to imitate the success of these magazines by using a similar nostalgia-driven tactic: reproducing pre-code horror stories in magazine-sized titles, as magazine-sized titles weren't beholden to code rules.

Nothing succeeded until the publisher of *Famous Monsters*, James Warren, introduced *Creepy* in 1964. *Creepy* was an adult-oriented black-and-white magazine-sized title that followed the traditional anthology format of pre-code horror comics[34] featuring "EC-style stories" and an EC-style storyteller named Uncle Creepy.[35] After *Creepy*'s success, Warren followed it up with the sister titles *Eerie* and *Vampirella* and, like *Famous Monsters* before it, *Creepy* spawned a number of imitators, most of these titles featuring reprints of pre-code horror stories. Thus, in the 1960s, two trends were apparent in horror magazines: one, there was a (often retrospective) focus on horror films, as in magazines like *Famous Monsters*, and two, there was an effort to bypass code restrictions with comics reprints, which meant re-running material from early 1950s horror comics, sometimes several times over.

Of course, nearly a decade after they had first appeared, the content of the pre-code horror titles didn't seem as outrageous anymore. In the wake of the horror spreading across American film screens, which was becoming more violent and bloody thanks to the death of the Production Code Administration, as well as growing social unrest and the Vietnam war, pre-code horror stories seemed quite tame by comparison. Horror in film was also becoming more cynical and pessimistic and, while horror in 1960s comics might have seemed to stagnate—because so much of it was focused not on producing new content but in reproducing content from other mediums or comics content from the pre-code era—it's worth noting that, at least in terms of the reprinted material, the pre-code horror comics were *already* cynical and pessimistic, so the reprints served to reinforce the trends seen elsewhere in horror at the time. Thus, the birth and revival of 1950s pre-code horror was able to indoctrinate two generations of Americans into a type of horror that was slowly starting to appear on film screens across the nation.

George A. Romero's Comic Book Style

Talking about his relationship to the 1960s horror magazines, and in particular *Eerie Publication's Weird*, comic writer and artist Stephen R. Bissette says,

> These were also precursors to the modern horror movies and literature to come. The first time I felt in a movie theater the way I had in my bedroom when I first read "Black Death" was when I saw *Night of the Living Dead* on the big screen…. Now, I'm not saying *Weird* was as good as *Night of the Living Dead* … but I am saying *Weird* and its clammy "the world's gone to shit" brand of horror was one of the few pop harbingers of what was just around the corner. Myron Fass and his shoddily printed pre-code reprints groomed and prepared cursed readers like me for where George Romero took us all in 1968 and after.[36]

While Bissette may have felt somewhat prepared for *Night of the Living Dead,* many cinema goers were not. The film turned not only the zombie genre but horror films in general, on their heads. Not only did it seem to re-write the zombie character and introduce a black protagonist—something that was unheard of up until that time—but unlike most previous mainstream horror, the lead characters died. While some of the revenge stories in pre-code comics showcased central characters who met their demise, in classical horror *cinema* the protagonists never died. *Night* helped change that expectation. Thus, while the film might have provided a "happy ending" in that the posse is shown fighting back and winning against the zombies at the end, the overall tone is nihilistic: no matter what anyone at the farmhouse does, they can't survive, and this sort of cynical tone was something that would be picked up by horror films as the 1970s progressed.

The relationship that Bissette draws between *Night of the Living Dead* and the 1960s horror magazines can also be stretched to pre-code horror comics. In the preface to *The Complete Night of the Living Dead Filmbook* (1985), George Romero states that *Night of the Living Dead* "has a nostalgic quality which recalls … the EC comic books of the fifties."[37] In several interviews, Romero commented on EC's influence on his films, and scholars and critics have likewise made the connection. Paul Gagne, for instance, has observed the ways in which *Night of the Living Dead* seems to mimic the look of EC comics, pointing out that the "use of action within stationary camera angles … is a lot like a comic-book artist's use of panels."[38] Kyle William Bishop likewise notes how in Romero's films "action is presented through a series of carefully framed and largely silent images."[39]

The film contains several shots that seem to evoke a comic book style. First of all, *Night of the Living Dead* is shot in academy ratio, giving it a more square-looking frame than most mainstream films of its time.[40] Also, while Romero does include camera movements within his shots, he is more likely to cut between actions, which contributes to the comic book feel of certain scenes, as he almost creates a "gutter" for viewers.[41] For instance, right after the first zombie attack in the graveyard, after Johnny has been killed, there is a low-angle medium shot of Barbra looking down at her brother and the zombie,[42] a cut to a close-up of the zombie looking up at her, and then a cut back to her reaction. There is no establishing or master shot to begin this sequence to delineate who is where,[43] nor do the actors' sightlines match; rather, in rapid succession, Romero provides (but also controls the scope of) everything the viewer needs to know, much as it might have played out in a comic book in three panels: the frightened woman looking, the zombie looking back, and the woman's reaction. Romero's editing in the scene disrupts classical continuity conventions by placing "gutters" in moments where typical film editing would show reactions and help delineate space.

Tony Williams also draws a tight line between the "punch" endings of the EC horror comics and the fates of *Night's* teenage characters Tom and Judy, observing that "viewers identifying with Tom and Judy soon receive a nasty shock reminiscent of the best O. Henry climaxes in the original EC comics strips" as the young lovers die.[44] Moreover, while not as humorous as some of Romero's later films, *Night of the Living Dead* also nods to the EC tradition of dark humor, especially in the zombie feast after Tom's and Judy's deaths. Not only did the gore from this scene shock audiences in the 1960s—much as the gore in pre-code horror comics did for readers in the 1950s—but the horror of what is happening is underscored by its absurdity: two zombies fight over a bit of intestine as another zombie happily munches on body parts. In pre-code horror comics, these sorts of images would have been played for (uncomfortable) laughs but in *Night of the Living Dead* there is no wise-cracking Crypt Keeper to soften the blow, making the scene that much more shocking.[45]

Yet, it is the thematic connections between *Night of the Living Dead* and 1950s horror comics that are critical to understanding how Romero's zombies both resurrect and reimagine the zombies of the 1950s. As a general rule, the pre-code zombies weren't cannibals but both they and Romero's undead are decomposing corpses. There is also a sense of realism at work with these zombies: as I discussed earlier, unlike slave-style zombie films, which typically presented the undead as physically unchanged, pre-code horror comics often showed the ravages of decomposition in a startlingly realistic fashion.[46] In keeping with this sense of realism, many horror comics were also set in mundane, everyday American spaces, contrasting the seeming ordinariness of American life with the evils lurking just below the surface.

Night of the Living Dead's filmmakers also strove for a realistic look and feel.[47] In *The Complete Night of the Living Dead Filmbook,* John Russo asserts "a *believable* picture only attains believability when it adequately mirrors what people call *reality*—In other words, what *feels* real in their own lives."[48] The film was shot on location, and beyond its initial premise—that the dead are somehow rising from their graves to eat the living—there is little fantastical about the story. The actors are unpolished, unglamorous amateurs, and the zombies themselves are realistic: while they are the dead reanimated, they aren't mutated into unbelievable forms. Part of the horror of the film, in fact, lies in how *ordinary* the undead seem: as they walk around the farmhouse, it is clear that these are regular people wearing suits and dresses. Their bodies speak to rather ordinary deaths: some wear toe tags or hospital gowns; at least one is nude. In many ways, this speaks to their humanity. For all the ways in which these zombies are cannibals, they are also the kinds of people you'd meet on the street in any given day: the boy next door or the lady at the post office (fig. 2).

Figure 2: Zombies as everyday people (*Night of the Living Dead*, Image Ten, 1968).

This ordinariness is also what gives pre-code horror comics and *Night of the Living Dead* their narrative bite. Both present American life without flinching away from the less-than-admirable aspects of contemporary society: in "The Dead Will Return," a *Vault of Horror* story from 1950, for instance, the reader learns that marriage isn't a sacred institution as a wife and her lover dispose of her husband's body (which will just not stay gone). In *Night of the Living Dead*, viewers witness bickering and in-fighting amongst the living from nearly the beginning. In neither instance is the world an uncomplicated place where good always triumphs over evil. Robert Alpert observes that "*Night of the Living Dead*'s social satire focuses on the misplaced, cultural belief that we can fully understand and wholly control our environment."[49] The EC horror comics often offered up similar commentary: the murderers in "The Dead Will Return," for instance, think they can control a dead body but soon find out otherwise, and the EC oeuvre was full of animated corpses who proved just how little control the living really had, in the same way as the irrepressible corpses in *Night of the Living Dead* do.

Even if the zombies of *Night of the Living Dead* aren't seeking justice the way that many of the pre-code zombies were, there is a similar single-mindedness to their drive to pursue and eat the living, a focus that upsets and exposes the fecklessness of human behavior and the rifts in human conventions and institutions. In both the film and the comics, the dead act as pursuer and the living as pursued but, whereas in the pre-code comics a narrative justification is given, as in "The Dead Will Return" with its dead husband coming back to avenge his own murder, in *Night of the Living Dead* no such explanation is given.

This too speaks to another shared characteristic: the ultimate source of zombiism isn't clear in either. In slave-style zombie narratives, there was almost always a locatable cause for zombiism: a potion, a machine, or a magic spell. However, in the pre-code horror comics that didn't focus on slave-style zombies, typically no cause for zombification was given. It was as if injustice itself reanimated the dead. In *Night of the Living Dead* while there is a possible explanation given as to what has caused the zombie phenomenon (a radioactive satellite), it isn't a definitive reason, nor is it repeated in Romero's subsequent films. Instead, many living characters in Romero's later films contemplate the possibility that the zombies are some sort of retribution for the sins of humanity.

The EC comics were written in the wake of World War II, during the Korean War (1950–1953). *Night of the Living Dead* appeared in the midst of the Vietnam War (1955–1975), and this may have partially driven this sense that zombies act as visceral reminders of the sins of the living. It is certainly true that EC head William Gaines and George Romero were both unafraid to use their art to assess American society. Bradford Wright reports that Gaines used his comics, "to critique, satire, and subvert entrenched American values and institutions at a time when few other voices in popular culture did so."[50] While George Romero and the other filmmakers responsible for *Night of the Living Dead* were always quick to note that there were elements of the film that had been read as political that were pure happenstance (such as the casting of Duane Jones as Ben), Romero also conceded that there was a conscious political bent to the film (and its successors).

Choices of medium and genre may have also given these creators great license to be critical of American culture. The choice of horror, which has historically been viewed as a genre of the lowest common denominator, may have allowed both the horror comics and *Night of the Living Dead* to sneak up on some viewers. Plus, for Gaines, working with comics—which have long been associated with children and noted for their disposability—may have allowed his social and political critiques to fly under the radar; many may have missed them simply because they were housed in "children's" media or because they were coming from talking skeletons and floating ghosts. In both cases, there is also the relative freedom that the artists had. Gaines was the head of EC comics. He liked thoughtful, critical horror, so he could publish it, especially as he was publishing these stories before the Comics Code. Similarly, Romero and his fellow filmmakers were making an independent film largely on their own, so potential oversight was at a minimum.

Yet, for all of the ways in which both the pre-code comics and *Night of the Living Dead* were produced by political rebels who chafed at authority and held an unflinching light up to the American way of life, in both instances, there is also a sense of returning to the status quo or at least to some moral equilibrium. In those pre-code horror comics where zombies acted as avenging angels, the zombies reanimated in order to right past wrongs and put the world in its proper place again. Even if the ultimate evil in these stories ended up being the living instead of the undead, the message was still that the bad would be punished. In essence, these stories were morality tales encouraging their readers to stay on the straight and narrow. While *Night of the Living Dead* is a bit more nuanced in its message, implicitly questioning the righteousness of the status quo, a number of subsequent films inspired by it use zombies and zombification much as pre-code comics did: as tools to punish the wicked and return us to the status quo.

In Romero's own *Day of the Dead* (1985), for instance, the ultimate survivors are those who are the most reasonable, while the exaggeratedly evil and misogynistic Captain Rhodes is torn limb from limb by zombies. Similarly, in *Land of the Dead* (2005), an army of the undead helps to overthrow the corrupt regime of Fiddler's Green and zombies kill its leader Paul Kaufman (Dennis Hopper), opening up at least the possibility of a more just future. Similarly, in Thom Eberhardt's *Night of the Comet* (1984), the good teenagers survive a comet-borne zombie virus while the group of unethical scientists who terrorize them eventually become zombified. Even in Andrew Currie's *Fido* (2006), the titular zombie is a loving father figure to the protagonist Timmy Robinson, protecting him from both bullies and the morally corrupt security chief, who ends up being zombified and put to work for the ZomCon company. By the end of the film, Fido helps to restore the Robinson's nuclear family.

These examples point to a trend that one can see generally in the pre-code comics, *Night of the Living Dead,* and a great deal of zombie media that has come after: it is the living, and not the dead, who are most often shown to be the true villains. As Hand observes, with the coming of the dawn in *Night* "the undead suddenly seem pathetic and vulnerable."[51] In Hand's estimation, this may be what fosters a "sense of sympathy" with them that "can be traced back to the moral justification of the 1950s zombies and the purity of their vengeance. The zombie may be terrifying, unsettling, and disruptive but it is never as evil as the living."[52] Of course, this is particularly underscored by Ben's death at the hands of the posse at the end of *Night of the Living Dead*,[53] but it even holds true for the 1990 remake of the film (written by George Romero) where Barbara—who in this version survives the night—looks around in horror at the living survivors of the zombie assault: they represent the worst kinds of toxic masculinity, and she is now stuck with them.[54]

In the pre-code horror comics, the zombies were judge, jury, and often executioner, but there was a clear sense of them respecting the line between guilt and innocence.

Night's zombies are indiscriminate in their killing and, moreover, so are the living. In fact, the zombies come across as somewhat more sympathetic or fathomable in their killings than the posse at the end of the film because we know that the zombies are only following the drive to eat. The posse, on the other hand, should be able to determine who to kill and who not, yet they shoot Ben. It is somewhat ironic that *Night*'s twist ending—Ben's death at the hands of the posse—would fit so well within the pages of an EC horror comic because it takes the underlying EC premise that justice can be served (even if it is by the undead) and shows it to be untenable.

The Zombies Return

Over time, the cannibal zombie featured in *Night of the Living Dead* came to be the predominant kind of zombie in U.S. media and the 1970s, in particular, were a fertile time for experimenting with this new zombie premise as filmmakers tried to capitalize on the movie's success. Bob Clark combined slave-style voodoo rituals with cannibal zombies in 1972's *Children Shouldn't Play with Dead Things*, and he created a variation on "The Monkey's Paw" with zombies in *Deathdream* in 1974. Nazi zombies appeared in 1977's *Shock Waves*, and George A. Romero returned to the genre with 1978's *Dawn of the Dead*.

But beyond the influence *Night of the Living Dead* had on zombie films, its popularity also helped reinvigorate the walking dead in comics. By the 1970s the comics industry realized that the Comics Code needed to be updated and a new version was introduced in 1971. The code relaxed its regulations on monsters and, as horror and monster magazines had been gaining traction in the late 1960s, publishers were eager to start producing horror. Paul Douglas Lopes reports that, "By 1974 horror, mystery, and monster comic books were second only to superhero comic books in the 250 titles that appeared that year."[55] Unlike the 1950s boom where horror comics were published in anthologies, though, this horror boom also saw horror superhero characters emerge, like Ghost Rider and Swamp Thing, whose stories would continue issue to issue.

Zombies were becoming a hot commodity in the early 1970s following the rising cult success of *Night of the Living Dead*, but they were still off-limits in comic books. As the revised code stated:

> Scenes dealing with, or instruments associated with walking dead ... shall not be used. Vampires, ghouls and werewolves shall be permitted to be used when handled in the classic tradition such as Frankenstein, Dracula, and other high calibre literary works written by Edgar Allen Poe, Saki, Conan Doyle and other respected authors whose works are read in schools around the world.[56]

As zombies did not have a literary antecedent, they were considered too low brow for comics audiences.[57] So what was a publisher to do? Marvel quickly figured out two workarounds to the zombie problem. The first was to do what publishers had been doing throughout the 1960s and use the magazine-sized format, which was still outside of the code's purview. The second was to get creative by playing with the zombie concept.[58]

For their magazine-sized entry into zombidom, Marvel revived a zombie character created by Bill Everett in a stand-alone story in *Menace* #5 from July 1953. In the original story, the zombie had no name but in his new form he was Simon Garth, a businessman killed and then revived via voodoo to become "The Zombie." His magazine, *Tales of the Zombie*, ran for ten issues from 1973 to 1975.[59] The title followed a voodoo theme and, beyond the Simon Garth stories, it included reviews and retellings of classic and recent zombie or voodoo-related films, articles related to voodoo and witchcraft, short pieces of fiction, and stand-alone comics, some of which were reprints of pre-code horror material.

In addition, *Night of the Living Dead* actually made appearances in a few issues of *Tales of the Zombie*. In the first issue in July 1973, Tony Isabella penned an article entitled "The Sensuous Zombie," which traces the zombie's appearances in films from the 1930s onward. In it, Isabella remarks,

> The latest attempt to bring the zombie to the silver screen is the 1969 [sic] shocker NIGHT OF THE LIVING DEAD. In this controversial film, some pseudo-scientific happening has caused all unburied corpses to be revitalized with a craving for human flesh. The film specializes in grusomely [sic] detailed deaths and monsters and it is this detail that first brought the film to the public eye. Critics panned it for the same reason they would later call it one of the greatest horror films ever made. It is a frankly scary film. It terrorizes you. You undergo a journey to Hell and back.[60]

In the third issue of *Tales of the Zombie*, Don McGregor provides a review and retelling of *Night of the Living Dead*. Later in the same issue, Gerry Boudreau reviews Romero's film *Code Name: Trixie*, better known as *The Crazies* (1973) and compares it to *Night*.

Beyond the explicit mentions of *Night of the Living Dead*, there are several other hints as to its influence on *Tales of the Zombie*. "The Thing from the Bog!," a stand-alone story from the first issue, ends with a crowd of zombies surrounding a murderer. While the notion of zombies-as-vehicles-for-justice is a pre-code concept, the story makes it clear that this has less to do with the zombies seeking justice and more to do with them no longer being under the control of a spell: they are compelled to attack the man, and the imagery of a group of zombies massing around a living being seems very reminiscent of *Night*.

Still, it might be in Simon Garth's penchant for violence that *Night's* influence is most acutely felt. In pre-code comics, the violence zombies might do often happened off-page. The threat was implied but not shown. In slave-style zombie films, zombies typically weren't the source of violence. They might be ordered to advance on someone by their master, but their menace rarely went beyond standing around and looking threatening. In *Tales of the Zombie*, this is not the case. In the first three issues alone, Garth kills a dog by slamming its body against the ground, shoots a man in the head, slams another man into an iron fence, strangles a snake to death for several panels, and strangles a woman in a mercy killing before throwing her body into the ocean. While this can't be directly attributed to *Night of the Living Dead*, it is clear that by the 1970s—in part because of the influence of *Night* on horror more generally—even voodoo-inspired zombie stories were upping the violence and gore.

In many ways, Simon Garth was an amalgam of zombie styles.[61] Given *Tales of the Zombie*'s voodoo theme, Garth had characteristics of the slave-style zombie: the character was revived and later controlled via voodoo. Yet, he was also a decomposing corpse and, when he wasn't being controlled by a master, he had free will and spent his time trying to protect his daughter from the forces of evil. Garth was thus a zombie who seemed to encapsulate traits from slave-style, pre-code, and cannibal-style sources. This was even addressed in the series' third issue in January 1974 when the editors wrote,

> this particular zombie is a *lemon*. Unlike your garden variety walking dead, Simon Garth's corpse can think to a limited extent, and there are certain things he can feel—though none of

them happen to be physical. Garth's curse, then, is perhaps far more terrible than any zombie's before him, for he is, in a way … *half-alive*. For though his body and soul are most assuredly dead, some nameless element of intelligence still dwells within him. He is unfeeling—but horrifyingly *aware*! He can act on his own volition unless the Amulet of Damballah prevents it. And therein lies the true terror of this Man Without a Soul.[62]

Garth's inability to inhabit his zombiness fully, then, seems to derive from Marvel's need to create a protagonist who can act on his own as the story dictates, providing a continuity of character across issues. It also fits the era well: in the wake of *Night of the Living Dead,* artists and filmmakers were grappling with just what a zombie was, and many were taking elements from Romero's film and putting them together with elements from the earlier slave-style tradition. It wouldn't be until after Romero's *Dawn of the Dead* that things would settle, and the cannibal zombie would be firmly entrenched as the most popular modern conception of the zombie.

Yet, this melding of styles is also reminiscent of what we see in pre-code zombie comics, where zombies could possess the traits of slave-style zombies while also being talking, decomposing corpses bent on revenge. In fact, in Marvel's original 1953 story, the zombie is a decomposing corpse with a full head of dark, close-cropped hair and tattered clothing open at the chest. His hands are skeletal, and his nose is gone, so he is clearly decomposing but he isn't as gruesome as some of the other comic book zombies of the era. The 1970s version is much the same, albeit with longer hair. However, the new Simon Garth is also incredibly strong and well-defined for a zombie (fig. 3), and on the *Tales of the Zombie* covers, Garth is always bare-chested, with his arm and chest muscles on display. In fact, Mike Howlett states that he "always found the original horror from Marvel in the '70s to be more superhero in nature than horror.… Zombie Simon Garth, for being dead, sure looked like he was in pretty damn good shape."[63] It seems that with *Tales of the Zombie,* Marvel was trying to get in on the horror boom and taking advantage of the rising popularity of zombies, while doing it in a very Marvel way; hence, Garth's zombiness was almost always subsumed by his superheroic, or anti-heroic, identity.

This is why it is also worth speaking about Garth's humanity. While the character can be violent and he can be used for malevolent purposes when a bad guy controls his amulet, he is also heroic, and he spends most of the series trying to protect his daughter, Donna. The arc of the series is such that ultimately Garth is able to succeed in making sure that his family is safe and his reward for this is the grave: to lie down and die, assured that his family doesn't need him anymore. It is a bittersweet end and thus, much like the zombies in *Night of the Living Dead*, or even those zombies seeking revenge in pre-code comics, Garth is at once a threatening figure and a tragic one.

Simon Garth, however, wasn't the only zombie in Marvel's arsenal. The second kind of zombie that Marvel introduced in the 1970s was a clever work-around of code rules called the *zuvembie*. The zuvembie was originally created by Robert E. Howard in the short story "Pigeons from Hell," published in 1938. Marvel co-opted the name in the 1970s to be able to have zombie adversaries in situations where it seemed appropriate, i.e., in storylines with voodoo themes or voodoo-inspired heroes or villains. The zuvembies appeared in Marvel titles throughout the 1970s and 1980s until the ban on zombies was lifted by a code revision in 1989.

Like Simon Garth, zuvembies had their roots in voodoo and, like so many slave-style zombies, zuvembies were the tools of a villainous master. In *Strange Tales* #171, which came out in December 1973, for instance, that master is Baron Samedi, who is working for A.I.M.

Figure 3: Simon Garth, a very well-defined zombie (Gerber, Steve [w] and Pablo Marcos [a]. "Voodoo Island," *Tales of the Zombie* #2 [Oct. 1973], Marvel, 5).

48   Beyond the Living Dead

(Advanced Idea Mechanics), an organization of supervillains, to take over an electronics plant in Haiti. Baron Samedi captures the superhero Brother Voodoo and explains how the zuvembies are created: after kidnapping locals, and "persuading" them to join his cause, they are given a brief session with a machine that drains their minds. As Baron Samedi crows, "Imagine it...—a mindless, emotionless army totally obedient to its master's commands."[64] Later, Brother Voodoo is able to free the zuvembies and they transform back into normal men. Thus, the zuvembies have much more in common with traditional slave-style zombies than they do with Romero's cannibal-style undead.

This speaks to the ways in which zombies of this era were caught between traditional slave-style renditions and newer cannibal versions of the zombie inspired by *Night of the Living Dead*. When the zuvembies are introduced at the beginning of the issue, they appear in a cemetery and look like decomposing corpses. They have hollow eyes and torn clothes but, like Simon Garth, their bodies are intact and even muscular. When the zuvembies are freed by Brother Voodoo, their "zombiness" disappears (fig. 4). As the narration relates, when Brother Voodoo destroys the machine controlling them, "each of them clutches at his face in sudden, searing pain—only to lower his hands a mere instance after—to reveal a new man."[65] The artists seemed to want to have their zombies both ways: as decomposing corpses and as slave-style zombies who weren't really dead.

Figure 4: Zuvembies, before and after (Wein, Len [w], Gene Colan [p], Frank Giacoia [i], "March of the Dead!" *Strange Tales* #171 [Dec. 1973], Marvel: 6 & 30).

These zombies also point to the differences between regular comics and magazine-sized titles in the 1970s. Whereas Simon Garth could be much more violent than his pre-code counterparts, due to code restrictions, the zuvembies couldn't even be real "zombies," let alone participate in the kinds of violence available to Garth. Yet, one way in which the zuvembies do seem to fit with the more modern conception of the zombie, as introduced in *Night of the Living Dead,* is that they are group creatures. Zuvembies don't really exist as individuals, unless an important character is turned into one. Rather, they are creatures of the mass. In *Strange Tales* #171, for instance, as Brother Voodoo fights a horde of zuvembies, the narration informs the reader that the zuvembies are "like some inexorable inhuman tide … washing over the battling Brother Voodoo in seemingly endless numbers."[66] Later, they are described as a "mindless mob."[67] While groups of zombies existed before *Night of the Living Dead*, this sense of a mob of zombies coming to attack was most likely a direct result of the film.

The mini boom in zombies was short-lived. The horror comics market in the mid–1970s was crowded. Those publications that had kept horror comics alive in the 1960s were hurting and by the end of 1974 most of the market dried up. Not only did a number of smaller independents close up shop but Marvel started ending its horror titles as well. The second, brief, horror boom was over, but its impact would nevertheless continue to be felt as this moment in the 1970s set up an important precedent that continues in zombie comics today: contemporary zombies typically come in one of two forms. On the one hand, there are the zuvembie-type zombies, zombies that are used as background material or as adversaries in stories that focus on living protagonists, such as *The Walking Dead* (2003–2019). On the other, there are the Simon Garth–type zombies, featured in comics that focus on undead protagonists who are articulate and intelligent, such as *iZombie* (2010–2012).[68]

Marvel's zuvembies and Simon Garth wouldn't have been possible if it hadn't been for the 1960s horror publishers who made a point of keeping horror going in magazine-sized titles after the Comics Code nearly wiped it out. But also, the rising popularity of zombies in the 1970s, spurred on in no little part by *Night of the Living Dead*, paved the way for Marvel's mini zombie boom in the 1970s. This creates a somewhat circular narrative for zombies in comic books. The pre-code horror comics of the 1950s influenced George Romero's upending of the zombie genre in 1968 and his film, in turn, helped Marvel reintroduce the zombie into comics in the 1970s.

A Zombie Legacy

At the end of his book on *Night of the Living Dead*, Ben Hervey asserts that the film's influence is vast; *Night of the Living Dead* signaled a "turning point" in American horror.[69] If pre–*Night* horror was reassuring, telling viewers that good could triumph over evil, then after *Night*, there were no such reassurances to be found. This is especially clear in the typical depictions of zombies before and after *Night of the Living Dead*. In slave-style zombie films of the 1930s, '40s, '50s, and '60s, zombiism was usually a state from which one could be rescued: the spell wore off or the zombie master would be destroyed. There was a happily ever after to be had. *Night* challenged this idea. Not only was there no longer an escape from zombiism but even if one managed not to be infected, one still might not be safe. All bets were off.

In horror comics of the 1950s, readers could find both sorts of zombies. There were the typical slave-style zombies who might be rescued, but there were also the undead returned from the grave to pass judgment on the living. These zombies weren't rescued, but usually after their justice was delivered, they faded away. Romero took these conventions and twisted them, creating zombies that just kept coming, zombies that had no task to fulfill but were simply programmed to eat. Still, his zombies could be highly sympathetic: while there are hints of this in *Night of the Living Dead*, in Romero's later films, especially *Day of the Dead* and *Land of the Dead*, it is obvious as zombies become fully realized characters of their own.

Almost all zombies across media today are imagined as cannibals, but they are also quite often seen as sympathetic creatures: even the most ferocious zombie adversaries of series such as *The Walking Dead* can be revealed to be former loved ones and friends, and films like *Fido* and *Warm Bodies* (2013) depict zombies who can be more compassionate and humane than the living. While *Night of the Living Dead* was not the first piece of zombie media to offer up sympathetic zombies, perhaps one of the most profound of Romero's legacies in zombie cinema has been his ability to render the zombie as both victim and threat. Much in the same way that pre-code comics often imagined zombies as horrific monsters and harbingers of justice, Romero envisioned the undead as complex figures inspiring both sympathy and disgust, and this has been a trait that has slowly spread across zombie media.

In 2014–2015, George Romero wrote the comic book series *Empire of the Dead*. Set in the *Night of the Living Dead* universe, the limited three-act series follows rising tensions between the living, zombies, and vampires. In the first issue, Dr. Penny Jones tells a story about her older sister, who was saved by their zombified brother. His humanity—his ability to remember his love for his sister, even in the zombie state—is what has inspired Dr. Jones' research and what gives her faith that things might change. Her companion doesn't buy it; zombies are nothing more than predators to him. Throughout the series' run, as both of them are proven right, the idea that zombies are complex, contradictory creatures that might both chomp off your face and save your life seems appropriate. It's a legacy inspired in part by pre-code comics that *Night of the Living Dead* and Romero's other zombie films later ensured: zombies that terrify but that also elicit our sympathy.

Empire of the Dead illustrates how Romero's work becomes enmeshed into a larger matrix of cultural and artistic movements. It is an amalgam of a variety of previous zombie media, including Romero's own *Dead* films. Yet this doesn't make it derivative. Rather, it demonstrates how George A. Romero's work offers up continuations of earlier patterns as reinventions of them. In embracing work that was already circulating in American culture—like the EC and other horror comics of the 1950s—George A. Romero situated his *Dead* films into a larger tradition of zombie media where old concepts didn't necessarily die but have been reanimated by future generations. Hence, sympathetic slave zombies of 1930s and '40s films, as well as the justice-seeking zombies of 1950s horror comics, are reimagined as Romero's wandering undead: similar, but not quite the same. Yet, a sense of continuity remains.

At the beginning of this essay, I noted that the story of zombies in American pop culture is often framed as the story of two men: William Seabrook, who introduced the zombie to mass audiences and George A. Romero, who reimagined it. Despite their formative and genre-defining influence, we must appreciate these creators' creative and intellectual debts. We need to consider their achievements and vision within a larger context of the ways in which any given work may reinvigorate, remake, or reimagine earlier works. The history of zombies is a many-faceted web, not a straight line, and George A. Romero's work has ties to a wide array of influences, just as it acts as an influence on a number of subsequent works. His legacy thus can't be divorced from the artistic legacies that preceded him, just as zombie cinema in the wake of *Night of the Living Dead* can't be separated from Romero.

Notes

1. Seabrook, *The Magic Island*, 93.
2. Kee, *Not Your Average Zombie*, 8.
3. Romero, *Night of the Living Dead*, DVD.
4. Kee, *Not Your Average Zombie*, 10. While perhaps not technically cannibals, as they are usually the dead reanimated, common parlance describes these flesh-eating zombies as cannibals as they are (former) humans eating (living) humans.
5. While some zombies did look a bit different from the living—often they might be pale with large, unblinking eyes and a lumbering gait—the physical differences between the living and the undead were typically not as marked as they would be with later, cannibal zombies. In several films of the 1930s, '40s, and '50s, for instance, zombies do not look any different than the living, and it is only in their behavior that one can tell they are zombies. See, for instance, *Revolt of the Zombies* (1936), *King of the Zombies* (1941), *Revenge of the Zombies* (1943), *Voodoo Man* (1944), and *Teenage Zombies* (1959).
6. See, for instance, the bug-eyed zombies of *I Walked with a Zombie* (1943) or *I Eat Your Skin* (1964) or the corpses of *Invisible Invaders* (1959) or *Plague of the Zombies* (1966).
7. Pre-code horror comics are so named because they pre-date the Comics Code, which went into effect in 1955. While technically, *pre-code* could refer to any comic before that time, in discussing horror comics, it almost always means comics released between 1950 and 1955.
8. Tony Williams draws connections between EC comics and Romero's work in both *The Crazies* (1973) and *Dawn of the Dead* (1978), as well as *Night of the Living Dead* (see Williams, *The Cinema*, 24). George Romero also directed *Creepshow* (1982), which is as clear an homage to EC comics as ever was.
9. The dimensions of standard-sized four-color comics during the Golden Age (up through the 1960s) were 7 3/4" by 10 1/2," while black-and-white magazine-sized titles were 8 1/2" by 11." Modern comics are 10 1/8" by 6 5/8."
10. Nyberg, "William Gaines," 58.
11. Trombetta, *The Horror!*, 31.
12. Ibid.
13. Of course, many publishers failed to replicate the EC style and others only half-heartedly tried, as they were more interested in gaining readers with flashy covers than in trying to reproduce the quality of the EC stories.
14. Trombetta, *The Horror!*, 9.
15. Banes, "A Word of Warning," 7.
16. The story actually pre-dates the horror boom by two years, appearing in *Moon Girl* #5 in 1948.
17. Hand, "Undead Radio," 43.
18. In particular, the conventions of having a "host" like the Crypt Keeper is something borrowed from radio dramas, as is the anthology format of horror comics.
19. Hand, "Undead Radio," 44.
20. Williams, *The Cinema of George A. Romero*, 23.
21. A similar argument is put forth by W. Scott Poole, who explores the role World War I played in shaping modern horror in *Wasteland: The Great War and the Origins of Modern Horror* (Berkley: Counterpoint, 2018).
22. Lopes, *Demanding Respect*, 4.
23. Horror comics of the 1950s sometimes even used this bodily decomposition as part of the plot. In the 1952 *Vault of Horror* tale, "Till Death," for instance, plantation owner Steve's new bride, Donna, dies, so he uses voodoo to turn Donna into a zombie, and for a few days, everything is fine. Donna is her former beautiful self. But then Donna starts to rot, and the horror of this tale is centered on Donna's decomposition and Steve's inability to love his bride because of how badly she stinks (Craig, "Till Death").
24. Although, to be fair, this can have serious consequences for the body and there are a fair amount of classical zombie films in which the master's control has sexualized overtones. See, for instance, *White Zombie* (1932) or *Voodoo Man* (1944).
25. Wood, "The Thing from the Sea."
26. Hand, "Disruptive Corpses," 214.

27. "Comic Book Code of 1954."
28. *Ibid.*
29. *Ibid.*
30. *Ibid.*
31. Wright, *Comic Book Nation*, 173.
32. Wright, *Comic Book Nation*, 176.
33. Bissette, "Introduction," x.
34. Pre-code horror comics and anthology-style books feature a series of stand-alone stories in each issue rather than telling different episodes of the same story across issues.
35. Howlett, *The Weird World*, 9. Each of the EC horror titles had a "host" who would introduce selected stories. These hosts included the Crypt Keeper, the Old Witch, and the Vault Keeper.
36. Bissette, "Introduction," xvi.
37. Romero, Preface, 7.
38. Gagne, *The Zombies that Ate Pittsburgh*, 8.
39. Bishop, *American Zombie Gothic*, 100.
40. Academy ratio is 1.37:1 and was the standard format for the width and height of screen images for several decades, but widescreen formats were introduced in the mid-1950s and had taken over most studio productions by the time *Night of the Living Dead* was made. The most common widescreen ratios in use today are 1.85:1 and 2.39:1.
41. The gutter refers to the blank spaces between the panels in comics and, as Scott McCloud observes, "Comic panels fracture both time and space, offering a jagged, staccato rhythm of unconnected moments" that the reader will then connect in their mind (McCloud, *Understanding Comics*, 67).
42. For reference, a medium shot is a shot that captures the human figure from roughly the waist up, whereas a close-up captures the head or the head and shoulders (the camera is close-up to the subject it is filming). A low-angle shot is one where the camera shoots the subject from below.
43. An establishing shot is a shot that is typically used at the beginning of a scene to delineate space; similarly, a master shot is a shot of a scene that is wide enough to capture all of the actors and the action in its entirety. In either case, the shot is from far enough away to show all of the subjects in the scene and their spatial relationships to each other so that the viewer has a clear idea of the overall space.
44. Williams, *The Cinema*, 34.
45. Another similarity between Romero's *Dead* films more generally and pre-Code horror comics are the anthology-like feel they share. The horror comics housed stand-alone stories so that each issue was different and yet, each issue shared a title and typically the same artists and writers and tended to have a consistent tone. With Romero's "Dead" films, the same is true: while characters and locations are different in each of the films, there is a sense—especially with *Night of the Living Dead, Dawn of the Dead,* and *Day of the Dead*—that the audience is witnessing different episodes within the same narrative universe.
46. While some might suppose this goes hand in hand with a turn toward scientific zombie creation, as opposed to magic spells and potions, this isn't the case. Tying back to the zombie's roots in stories about Haitian Vodou, many slave-style zombie tales, in film and in comic books, rely on the notion that magic is used to create zombies; yet many others envision scientific devices. Therefore, while the zombies in pre-code comics were becoming more and more beholden to the natural forces of decay, this wasn't necessarily tied to science more broadly.
47. To be fair, while this may have been an artistic choice, it was also due to budget constraints.
48. Russo, *Night of the Living Dead Filmbook*, 117.
49. Alpert, "George Romero's," 17.
50. Wright, *Comic Book Nation*, 136.
51. Hand, "Disruptive Corpses," 223.
52. *Ibid.*
53. As I argue elsewhere, there is a way to read the film so that Ben has to die for a return to the status quo to take place: if the status quo is represented by hegemonic whiteness, then Ben, as a Black hero, is a threat and things can only return to "normal" if he is eliminated. Thus, the return to the status quo illustrates the systemic racism at the heart of "normal" society (see Kee, *Not Your Average*, 74–75).
54. For other examples of films that position the living (or at least many of the living) as the true villains, see *28 Days Later* (2002), *Dawn of the Dead* (2004), *Land of the Dead* (2005), and the *Masters of Horror* episode "Homecoming" (2005).
55. Lopes, *Demanding Respect*, 71.
56. "Comics Code Revision."
57. It is probably impossible to know whether those writing the revision truly thought that zombies lacked the sophistication of vampires and werewolves or were perhaps anxious that comic book zombies would begin to look like the zombies found in *Night of the Living Dead,* but the rule is compelling in that it isolates the lone New World monster from the acceptable list.
58. For a comparison of Marvel's 1970s zombies to their pre-code counterparts, see Kee, "Beware the Zuvembies."

59. A *Tales of the Zombie* annual appeared in 1975, and the character made sporadic appearances in other Marvel titles in the 1980s–2000s. He is also one of the main characters in *Marvel Zombies 4* (#1–4, 2009).
60. Isabella, "The Sensuous Zombie," 38–39.
61. See Kee, "Beware the Zuvembies."
62. "Mails to the Zombie," 29.
63. Howlett, *The Weird World*, 95.
64. Wein, "March of the Dead," 26.
65. *Ibid.*, 30.
66. *Ibid.*, 6.
67. *Ibid.*, 7.
68. *iZombie* actually features both decomposing, cannibalistic zombies and the beautiful (although still brain-eating) zombie Gwen Dylan as its protagonist.
69. Hervey, *Night of the Living Dead*, 119.

Blowing It All to Hell
Zombie Films as Allegorical Westerns

Gloria Pastorino

> I used to say they've never made a good western and suddenly along came *The Wild Bunch*.
> —George Romero[1]

In the late 1960s, George A. Romero and a group of friends spent a little over nine months creating a low-budget, largely self-financed film that changed the way zombies were perceived, initiated a cultural phenomenon, and transformed horror films by creating a threat too close for comfort. Twelve years earlier, *Invasion of the Body Snatchers* (1956) had depicted a frightful allegorical scenario in which enemies take over and modify the American way of life by replacing people with perfect emotionless replicas. With a retro black-and-white palette chosen more for artistic than budgetary reasons,[2] Romero turned the *Body Snatchers* menace of a hostile but elegant takeover into an act of brutal assimilation of existing humans via literal consumption, as the dead came back to eat the living, to sustain their new existence. In *Night of the Living Dead* (1968) the relentless enemy is a perversion of the familiar, a fearsome Freudian "uncanny"[3] that haunts people not as a private nightmare but as a collective threat that needs to be violently and collectively counteracted. However, Romero's ghouls[4] trigger individual, rather than collective, responses that suggest the inherent self-destructiveness of humans, who are unable to coalesce effectively against a common enemy without showing endemic societal problems through their own prejudices and egocentrism. Not only are humans incapable of setting aside their differences even on the verge of gruesome death, but the nature of the common enemy lends itself to polysemic political and sociological allegories that emphasize a rather callous disrespect for human life.

In his six zombie films, produced over a forty-year span, Romero's zombies act as catalysts for extreme courses of action that ultimately show the impossibility of winning against an enemy who is either not understood, or exploited for scientific experimentation, or used as free labor force. Fighting ravenous flesh-eating beings is the ultimate goal for the survival of the human species, but the living cannot help unleashing verbal and physical violence on each other, to the point of self-destruction when disagreements escalate to unsolvable differences of opinions.[5] Often in Romero's films, when people destroy the living dead they prove that not all of humanity is worth saving. With the exception of Romero's first film (*Night of the Living Dead*), his protagonists unleash their basest instincts on captured or incapacitated revenants, resorting to torture, mockery, gratuitous cruelty, and ruthlessness. In fact, what is common to all of Romero's zombie narratives is the othering of an enemy that is already othered by its hybrid nature of inhumanly resurrected dead human. Zombies are pure Id, only focused on sustenance through assimilation of living humans, but also the mirror-image neighbors who seemingly possess what we desire and thus attract our justified hatred (with unjustified cruelty), and the Orientalized[6] others who are deemed inferior, thus expendable, without any remorse.

Even though zombie attacks emphasize the problems of coexistence among the living at the micro (interpersonal) and macro (political) level, people with very little in common are forced to unite, even briefly, to fight the common enemy, creating unlikely alliances and destroying or eliding social divisions in existence before the threat of zombies. In this respect, Romero's films follow the well-established tradition of Westerns in which American "Indians"[7] cement white communities with shared hatred for an inscrutable enemy, whose existence manifests itself only in the constant threat they pose to settlers, and whose reasons are never (or seldom) taken into account. Just like zombies, Indians seem to be after the sole satisfaction of their base instincts, utterly disregarding the complexity of the supposedly superior civilization they aim to destroy. Indians speak in tongues and are monomaniacally obsessed with killing and scalping white men and women, so much so to seem to be as concerned with their deadly and relentless satisfaction of pleasures as zombies are. The myth of the savage, blood-thirsty Indian has roots that go back over three centuries and is backed up by copious literature to justify the genocide that allowed European settlers to appropriate native lands. According to Tom Engelhardt, more than five hundred often best-selling tales of settlers' captivity were published by the nineteenth century.[8] Mary Rowlandson's tale from 1682 was the first: "Thus were we butchered by those merciless heathen, standing amazed, with the blood running down to our heels ... like a company of sheep torn by wolves."[9] Her descriptions portray the same helplessness facing a feral and unfeeling enemy. Because of their enjoyment of a pure satisfaction of pleasure unencumbered by language, laws, and other people's judgment, Indians and zombies are truly free, albeit at a basic level. The zombies' pleasure[10] is rooted in destroying the living and, thereby, is a limitation of the right of the living to enjoy their assumed rights. The Indian other in Westerns seems to possess a similar privileged enjoyment of something the white man wants (land, mining rights, horses, hunting grounds, access to water, etc.) and seems to be a mixture of a "noble savage," guided by simple, un-nuanced precepts, and a brutal obsessive killer whose freedom limits the white settlers' God-given right to appropriate land. To that end, the Indians' *jouissance* has to be curtailed definitively and remorselessly.

Survival mode for protagonists of Westerns and zombie films alike entails eliminating the pressing, relentless threat by banding together, so that a new order may be established. This proves problematic in *Night*, where Ben, the main character, takes the lead from the very first moment we see him but cannot keep in control of events. Romero's subsequent five zombie films make it even clearer that zombies are a peripheral problem to the more pressing one of the inability to agree on what is the common good for living humans. Romero's films can be read as Westerns that combine the traditional model in which Indians are the othered enemies with the new 1950s and '60s model in which a lone fighter for principles and justice saves the town. Such men can be found, for instance, in *High Noon* (Fred Zinneman, 1952), *Shane* (George Stevens, 1953), *The Man Who Shot*

Liberty Valance (John Ford, 1962), *Gunfight at the OK Corral* (John Sturges, 1957), and *The Big Country* (William Wyler, 1958), not to mention the new kind of Western inaugurated by Sergio Leone with *A Fistful of Dollars* (1967). However, "the town" is usually lost, survivors have an expiration date, and humanity as is does not seem to deserve to be saved. This essay explores the way in which *Night* is linked to its main inspiration (Richard Matheson's 1953 novella *I Am Legend*) and to John Ford's 1956 *The Searchers* in the way that the hero is an outlier who ends up being rejected by the same body of people he tries to save. Zombies, vampires, and Indians are the othered enemy, but so are Vietcong in 1968 (when *Night* was released) and, to a certain extent, dissenting Americans, fighting for civil rights and protesting against the war. Whether intentionally or not, Romero's first film reflects the anger of its times and the following five zombie films are all indictments of specific aspects of American society and politics that can be read through a Western film lens.

Protecting from "Injuns"

Robert Neville's existence in *I Am Legend* is defined by his mission to kill all the vampires he can find during the day and protect his besieged house from their attacks at night. As the sole survivor of an incurable, mysterious plague that has transformed all the people it has killed into blood-thirsty vampires, he leads a lonely Robinson Crusoe–like existence, as the only pioneer left in this post-apocalyptic frontier. When he meets another survivor, Ruth, something instinctively tells him that she is not quite like him: he feels no attraction to her and doesn't like her smell, "like Gulliver returning from the logical horses."[11] Instinctively, he perceives her as "other," even though he does not know to which extent they no longer belong to the same species. By the end of the novel, it is clear that Neville is not an only-hope-for-humanity lone survivor but rather an impediment to the "new normal" society of hybrid, mutated vampires who have found a way to live with the disease. As he explains, "I'm the abnormal one now. Normalcy was a majority concept, the standard of the many and not the standard of just one man."[12] He has no allies in this new society and neither does Ben, the protagonist of Romero's *Night*. Their lone hero status makes them outliers, whose elimination is a necessity to guarantee the normal functioning of society.

While Robert Neville's death makes him (a scary) legend, Ben is an ironic casualty of the new society constituted to exterminate the living dead. In fact, the squads of redneck militia who are combing the countryside in the morning to exterminate and burn all the ghouls in sight do not differentiate between the living and the dead: they detect movement through the farmhouse window and assume that the man they see is undead, so they shoot him between the eyes. Whether they realize he is alive and black, from such a distance, is irrelevant: in their minds, he is expendable. In Deborah Christie's words, both in Matheson's novel and Romero's film "the surviving human is sacrificed because he represents a body that is simultaneously too similar and too different."[13] Ben turns from a Greek-tragedy doomed hero to a Pinter-esque character in a film that has the structure of a classical play respecting the Aristotelian unities of time, action, and place. The haphazard assembly of people in the isolated farmhouse bears a resemblance to Pinter's contemporaneous *The Homecoming* (1965), not so much in terms of plot but in terms of unpredictability of responses, once self-serving humans are forced into close-quarter coexistence. Ben's long night's journey into day inside the farmhouse forces him to combat hysteria, selfishness, possible bigotry, warfare inexperience, and attempts at his own life along with the outside increasing external threat of hungry ghouls. The living dead are immediately established as an enemy who can (and needs to) be sacrificed without hesitation. Their "sameness," their being all alike in terms of desire and appearance, makes them the perfect other, equivalent to the faceless, nameless enemy of all recent wars and of Western movies up to the 1950s, even though their biological similarity and physical proximity also makes them neighbors whose aspirations used to be our same ones. Romero has repeated in countless interviews that the living dead are us, they are our neighbors, "expurgations of ourselves ... beasts we have created in order to exorcise the monster from within us.... You can kill the monster, but your next-door neighbor may become him tomorrow."[14] This is also what happens in Matheson's novel, where Neville's most persistent attacker is his old neighbor and friend Ben Cortman, whom he would be reluctant to destroy, if he managed to capture him, not "to cut off a recreational activity,"[15] but also because Cortman keeps him connected to the life he once had. The clear enemies are outside, but the people on the inside resemble the ghouls in the way they are self-absorbed and focused only on obtaining their goal in a general lack of certainties, where all that seems familiar turns out to be a source of fear and destruction. The living dead resemble living humans but they cannot be trusted and the home, the supposed safe haven, proves inadequate to protect survivors. As Kyle William Bishop observes, "the dwelling becomes both a place of comfort and safety *and* a structure of imposition and menace.... The house of *Night of the Living Dead* fulfills another requirement of Freud's uncanny too in that it functions as a site that hides the repressed traumas and anxieties of society."[16] Seeking refuge in the house can only be a temporary solution, since it signals to zombies the presence of food inside, just as it does for the vampires in Matheson's novel. Likewise, in Westerns such as John Ford's *The Searchers* (1956) or John Farrow's *Hondo* (1953),[17] the isolated house is too exposed not to be the object of raids, while in Howard Hawks' *Red River* (1948), among others, the pioneers' caravans[18] arranged in a circle to create a barrier prove a poor defense against attacking Indians.

The isolated farmhouse belonging to the protagonist's brother, Aaron, in Ford's masterpiece *The Searchers*, is not the only point in common with Romero's *Night of the Living Dead*. Ford's film begins and ends with a now iconic establishing long shot: the door of a house opens on the desert of Monument Valley framing a woman's dark silhouette while she steps onto the threshold. As she moves out on the porch, the long shot encompasses the infinite southwestern sky and the unmistakable buttes,[19] while a man on a horse slowly gets closer. Ethan, a peculiar version of the prodigal son, has returned from the war in 1868, three years after its end, with some ill-gotten money and a chip on his shoulder about the racial promiscuity of his "Texican" land of origin he has fought to protect. Indians ("Injuns"), specifically Comanche, are the immediate threat and the attack on his brother's farm happens shortly after all the main characters in the story have been introduced. The house is burned to the ground while Ethan, Martin (a young man he rescued as a little boy from an attacked house),[20] an ex-Confederate Army Captain/Reverend, and a bunch of neighbors are away checking on suspicious Indian activity.

Unlike in Romero's film, the audience does not witness the fight: it just assumes it was brutal, given that the two adults and the son are massacred and the two girls are abducted. Spectators only witness the meeting of twelve-year-old Debbie with the Comanche warrior Scar in the family's tiny cemetery. As in all classical Greek tragedies,

58 Beyond the Living Dead

the obscene ("off scene") cannot be shown, but its effects are what determine the unfolding of the tragedy. The audience also doesn't see Ethan burying his possibly raped and tortured older niece, Lucy, abducted along with Debbie, or old Mose tortured by Scar: such events are too brutal to show, since they threaten precious white lives. The Motion Picture Production Code (or Hays Code, in use until 1968) prevented showing Ethan scalping Scar (killed by Martin and left in his teepee), but it allowed the camera to linger on the aftermath of the passage of the US Cavalry through a Comanche village, with bodies strewn everywhere, and the line of captive women and children corralled into a barn at the Army barracks. In 1956, this could not have failed to bring to memory horrors of deported and imprisoned people in POW and possibly also concentration camps all over the world.[21]

Clearly belonging to a different genre, Romero's film goes in the opposite direction, literally displaying guts and glory,[22] but the point of the story is the same: zombies and

The Big Country (top, 1956) is the acknowledged inspiration for *Survival of the Dead* (bottom, 2009), down to the details of the final duel between the two warring men who, in Romero's version, keep fighting in perpetuity once they are dead. As Romero admitted to Peter Keough in 2010, "I got all the department heads together and showed them *The Big Country* (1958) and said, "Let's do this," and we decided to go all the way with 2:35 [aspect ratio] and not mute the colors and you know, try to make it look like a Wyler-esque or whatever." In Williams, *Interviews*, 177.

"Comanch," as Ethan calls them, are enemies who do not deserve either pity or respect. One scene in particular stands out: when the first rescue group is in search of the two abducted girls, they find a Comanche buried under a rock. One of the men, in a fit of rage, throws a rock at him. Ethan asks him why he doesn't finish the job and shoots out both of the Indian's eyes. When asked by the Reverend what good that did to him, Ethan's reply is: "By what you preach, none. But what that Comanch [sic] believes: ain't got no eyes, he can't enter the spirit land."²³ The scene highlights Ethan's deep-seated hatred towards the enemy, whose humanity he recognizes and denies at the same time: knowing the enemy's culture allows him to kill him more effectively. Interestingly for a comparison with *Night of the Living Dead*, to annihilate (not just kill) the enemy, Ethan shoots through the head, destroying both the seat of the brain and the means for achieving vision in the

In turn, the second-to-last episode of the second season of the TV series *The Walking Dead* ("Better Angels," 2012) quotes Romero's *Survival*.

afterlife. Audiences are not shown the gruesome gauging of the dead Indian's eyes with bullets. As in most other Westerns, here, too, Indians attack in droves and are defeated or staved off in one scene by six armed men and in another by just two, confirming the idea of the numerically superior but militarily inferior attacker, relentlessly and obtusely coming, but easy to defeat if the effort is concerted.

There are Western elements in all of Romero's films, whether implicit or explicit (as in *Dawn of the Dead* [1978] where there are even Cavalry bugles ironically playing during a fight scene with marauders in the mall; or in *Survival of the Dead* [2009], whose declared inspiration is William Wyler's *The Big Country* [1958][24]).[25] Western films are part of Americana: they define the values that shaped American identity, provide morality tales, define the terms of the struggle to expand the frontier, establish the law, and create a (white) mythology of how the West was won. As Tom Engelhardt reports, "between 1910 and 1960, film critic J. Hoberman estimates, one quarter of all films made were westerns; and the western, which in the 1950s achieved a dominant position on the small screen at home as well, remained a particularly white genre (even though one-quarter or more of all late-nineteenth-century cowboys had been black)."[26] Even just a quick Wikipedia search reveals that between the 1950s and '60s about 200 different Western-themed series aired. Given the pervasive influence of Ford's *The Searchers*,[27] it is not unlikely (albeit unprovable) that some of the elements of this psychologically complex Western may have stayed with Romero. For sure, *Night* shares with it the idea of a house under attack, providing insufficient shelter to the people huddled inside (an idea which plays out, in some form, in every one of Romero's zombie films). In Ford's film, just before the massacre, Lucy realizes what is about to happen and begins screaming hysterically; her mother Martha slaps her to make her stop, just as Ben slaps hysterical Barbra in *Night* and then, paternally takes care of her and tucks her in as he fortifies the house. Debbie is found by Scar in the cemetery, she is taken and is "reborn" to her life as a Comanche (five years later, when finally found by Martin and Ethan, she will tell Martin: "These are my people!"[28]). Much has been written about the problem of miscegenation in *The Searchers*, still prohibited from screen depictions by the Hays Code in 1955.[29] It seems likely that one of the reasons why Debbie is eventually re-welcomed in white society is because Scar is dead and she has no children. Since five years pass from the abduction to the time she is found, once Ethan assumes that Debbie has become sexually viable for the Comanche his only instinct is to kill her, as if the "contamination" with another race had made her less than human. That is the meaning of the scene with the three once abducted women rescued by the Cavalry: Ethan, horrified and disgusted, tells Martin: "They ain't white anymore, they're Comanch!"[30] Ethan's advocacy for purity of the race (which includes fear of miscegenation) makes his reaction to Martin (who is one eighth Cherokee) and Debbie inhumane. To him Debbie is lost and we know from one of the opening scenes that she hadn't been baptized yet at the time of the abduction, so there is no salvation of any kind in store for her: she has become something else, something that was once human and part of his social fabric, but that now is othered, turned part enemy. If this were a zombie film, she would be considered infected, no longer white, part of the Indian horde and ready to become a blood-thirsty revenant at any moment; or else, in *I Am Legend* and similar 1950s narratives, she would belong to a totally different species.

In the final scene of *The Searchers* (which circularly quotes the iconic opening one) after having had a last-minute change of heart about killing Debbie, Ethan returns her to the white world, entrusting her to the parents of Martin's fiancée (Laurie) and Lucy's dead fiancé, almost as restitution for their loss. Once the contaminated girl and the "octoroon"[31] Martin are re-accepted into the folds of a white society that forgives their hybridity, recognizing their fundamental whiteness, Ethan becomes obsolete. The camera pauses on the long shot that encompasses the vast landscape beyond the dark threshold of the house as Martin and Laurie bypass Ethan to get in while he remains outside and turns around to walk off, alone, into the wilderness. He is, like Ben and Robert Neville, the remnant of a dying breed, who cannot be invited in and self-isolates from the newly reconstituted order of the film, where family and good values triumph in the end, setting aside racism and contradictions. Ethan's final scenes parallel Neville's instinctive rejection of Ruth, until he realizes that he is legend, as the only surviving member of a dead species. Novel and film came out two years apart, reflecting the ethos of a changing society, dealing with racially motivated social unrest. As Martin Winkler observes, also talking about Tom in Ford's later *The Man Who Shot Liberty Valance*, "Ethan and Tom are necessary to bring about the process of civilizing the country, but they cannot themselves make the transition from savagery to civilization, joining the new society to which the future belongs."[32] Moreover, by profaning the dead, Ethan has let his anger take him too far beyond what is allowed even in war (just as Robert Neville does in *I Am Legend*) and for that reason he cannot be part of a new society based on acceptance of differences. As systematic destroyers of the dehumanized enemy, Ethan, Neville, and Ben in *Night* are legend; once they have accomplished their tasks to the best of their abilities and have become no longer useful, they become disposable. Neville and Ben pay with their lives. Ethan does not need to die because Westerns are edifying myths (even though this particular one is fraught with contemporary political tensions) while dystopias offer a possible worst-case scenario of the disastrous consequences of human choices. The circularity of the film's opening and ending scenes, though, suggests that what happened during the film is part of a cycle of violence that is bound to repeat itself. There are no guarantees that the people now occupying a house similar to the first one are safe. Both of Ford's final Westerns, *The Searchers* and *The Man Who Shot Liberty Valance*, highlight the contradictions, racism, and lies intertwined with the myths upon which America is built, and look at the political tensions and the blood spilled to create the American identity.

"If you stay up here, Mister, you take orders from me!"

Trouble with the neighbors is already present in Romero's assessment of the limitations of the melting pot of 1968 in his first film, where he expands on Matheson's model in *I Am Legend* and creates tensions within the isolated farmhouse. The seven people who find themselves besieged in the house in *Night of the Living Dead* could not be more different: a scared young woman who has just witnessed the brutal killing of her brother, a take-charge black man of whom we know nothing, and five people who hide in the basement for the first third of the film. These are a couple of young lovers (Tom and Judy) and a family (the Coopers) with a sick eleven-year-old daughter who has been bitten by "one of those things."[33] The forced grouping leads to clashes of personalities, as two definite factions emerge, without having a clear upper hand or high moral ground: the first-floor domain and the basement's.

After Ben has secured all doors and windows to the outside, thirty-five minutes into the film, he listens with Barbra to a radio broadcast about the monstrous and vicious attacks happening all over the region. The advice given is to stay put and not venture out. As Ben secures more windows, the camera lingering on the basement door signals the threat of something lethal coming from within. The fact that living people, rather than ghouls, are hiding there turns out to be a different kind of threat that eventually leads to the death of all seven people. Mr. Cooper and Ben are immediately at odds: the former is convinced that minding one's business and not helping the two people upstairs (Ben and Barbra) was the best course of action: "we are locked in a safe place and you're telling me that we ought to risk our lives just because someone might need help?"[34] Mr. Cooper would much rather stay in the basement, defend only one door, and hope to be rescued, while Ben, who would have expected some form of collaboration from other living beings, argues that upstairs they have a fighting chance and a way out. The debate soon begins to echo a similar debate between isolationists and interventionists during the Vietnam War, in full blast in 1968. Tom's point of how "down in the cellar there is no place to run to. I mean, if they did get in, there'd be no back exit; we'd be done for!"[35] echoes contemporary rhetoric about the spread of Communism all over the world and, eventually, in the US, if nothing is done to stop it. Tom argues for the same "politics of containment" that Ben is proposing: "At least out here you'd have a fighting chance!"[36] News coming from the media do not help: a TV broadcast now advises to try to reach "rescue stations [provided] with food, shelter, medical treatment, and protection by armed national guardsmen."[37] When Ben and Tom plan a mission to fuel the truck and leave all together, Tom, once again, argues for the need to intervene in the war against the living dead, as he explains to Judy: "this isn't a passing thing, honey, we've got to do something and fast."[38] His good-bye is that of a soldier going off to war, because being safe here and now is not enough. The action taken is the beginning of the end, since Judy jumps on the truck on impulse, everything that can go wrong does, the lovers get barbecued in the exploding truck and eaten, and Ben is not let back into the house by Mr. Cooper, who eventually becomes the first victim of his own selfishness and mean spiritedness. This whole scene can be read as an allegory of the war in Vietnam; from disputes over intervention (passive resistance or active combat), to missions gone wrong and lives lost, to non-acceptance or neglect of veterans returning from the front.

The constant threat and the unlikely grouping of survivors is reminiscent of classic Westerns such as John Ford's *Stagecoach* (1939) where a prison fugitive, a prostitute, a drunken doctor, a whiskey drummer, a gambler, the pregnant wife of a soldier, a thieving banker, and a sheriff join the coach driver in a dangerous ride from Tonto, Arizona, through Indian-"infested" territory in 1880. With nothing in common, this odd group of people is forced to share close quarters and fight attacking Apaches, while overcoming their own ingrained prejudices, personal interests, and quirky personality traits. Some of the most common literary tropes are at play in this film: the golden-hearted prostitute who falls for the wronged unlikely hero; the kind-hearted sheriff who ultimately cares for the spirit, not the letter of the law; the renegade doctor who rises to occasion when it counts; the war-profiteering, corrupt banker who gets arrested in the end; and the gallant and nostalgic confederate soldier protecting the strong-willed but physically weak woman. Since it is a film made in 1939, while the world was entering a war that America would join two years later, it is important to show how these disparate people can come together to fight a common enemy, setting all differences aside in a country built on the myth of welcoming everyone. The ever-present menace of an Apache attack quickly turns into reality, forcing them all into a mad run through the imposing buttes of Monument

Valley, with, of course, Indians in pursuit. The latter are portrayed as bloodthirsty warriors, emotionless moving targets who are a constant menacing presence and need to be shot remorselessly. They keep coming after the stagecoach, shooting arrows and bullets, missing, for the most part, and dying in droves. The irony of there being platoons of soldiers roaming the country to seek out and kill them is lost on audiences witnessing the Indians' exceedingly violent and apparently unjustified attack of a peaceful stagecoach, which makes legitimate the need to exterminate them brutally.

Similar to the situation in *Stagecoach*, for other aspects, is the one in *Diary of the Dead* (2007), the fifth film in Romero's series that goes back in time to the same night of the first film and documents the escape of a few college students in a Winnebago through zombie-infested Pennsylvania. The Winnebago is the modern version of the stagecoach and tensions run high among students participating in the filming of a mummy/horror film as a class project. A similar haphazard grouping occurs, even though students are a much more homogeneous body and the professor acts as glue and stand-in father figure. The same sense of impending doom pervades this film, as the Winnebago provides temporary moving shelter from zombie attacks (as caravans in Westerns do too) and, especially, from living people's attacks. In fact, students are robbed by national guardsmen gone rogue, once again confirming that the problem of zombie attacks (or Apaches) is incidental when people cannot get along and decide on a common course of action. Of course, for the most part, at least until the end of the 1960s, Westerns are meant to be celebratory depictions of how the West was won and "real men" were made, so "justice," love, and the re-establishment of (white) law and order triumph when the enemy is either annihilated or defeated and decimated. At the end of *Stagecoach*, Ringo is pardoned by the sheriff and let go free, after killing the three men responsible for his family members' deaths. The law may not have been respected, but the law enforcer makes an exception since justice seems to have been served by a deserving man, who also fell in love with a redeemable saloon girl. In John Ford's films especially—and *Stagecoach* is a perfect example—the righteous triumph, the mean-spirited and corrupt are brought to justice, people get over their prejudices, and the law turns a blind eye to misdemeanors for the greater good of the community. In Romero's films, however, even when protagonists manage to escape and not be eaten in the five films produced after *Night*, their future is at best uncertain and at worst doomed to a slower but inexorable extinction. The re-establishment of order is short lived because the enemy keeps on coming by virtue of being a continuation of mortal humans who are bound to return from the grave.

Kill Thy Neighbor as Thyself

Living dead and Indians need to be de-humanized in order to be treated as disposable creatures and be killed remorselessly. The only way to achieve this goal effectively towards any enemy is to consider him sub-human; the othering of enemies is the only way to justify shooting them in the head, burning them, or smashing their skulls. Sadly, by 1968 it was clear that such methods were not extraordinary measures against an uncannily and fictional hard-to-defeat enemy, but common practices in Hitler's Reich, World War II, prisoner camps, Pol Pot's Cambodia, or during the Vietnam war. Interesting parallels have been made between the zombies' liminal status of life in death and Giorgio Agamben's discussion of "bare life" embodied by the concentration camps'

64 Beyond the Living Dead

Ben tries to keep zombies at bay with fire and a rifle in *Night* (top) as he, Tom, and Judy try a run for gas, just as the coach in *Stagecoach* tries to escape the horde of Indians in a 7-minute-long scene (bottom).

Zombie Films as Allegorical Westerns (Pastorino) 65

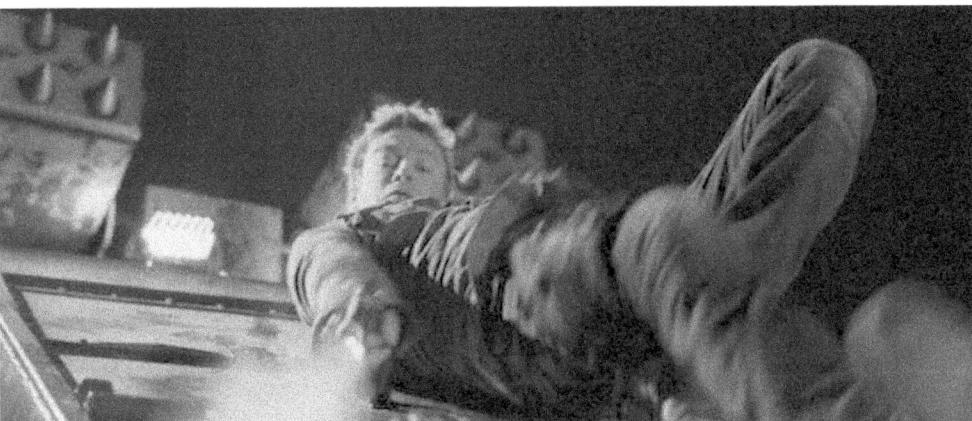

The quotation cycle comes full circle when Riley in *Land of the Dead* shoots zombies atop "Dead Reckoning" (bottom) as Ringo Kid shoots Indians atop the stagecoach (top).

Muselmann—the survivor who is barely alive, between life and death. Tyson E. Lewis, in particular, connects Agamben's thanatopolitics[39] to zombies who, by being deprived by the rituals associated with death (last rites, service, burial), "are mere materiality stripped of 'death' as a socio-symbolic event that defines *a life*.... Hence the strange numbness of audiences faced with images of mass graves—these bodies have been denied the dignity of death."[40] Watching zombies being killed causes no empathy, but rather a guilty pleasure in viewers and no remorse in killers. Romero made his first film in the middle of the controversial, seemingly endless Vietnam war, amidst protests and a mediatic barrage of images of death. Whether intended or not, it is hard not to view the multiplying living dead as stand-ins for the Viet-Cong, as many have noted. Particularly, the idea that only by killing the brain may zombies be destroyed for good and that burning them also fulfills the hygienic purpose of avoiding further contagion, brings to mind images of prisoners of the above-mentioned wars shot in the head at the edge of a communal tomb, burnt in ovens or collectively with either Napalm or atomic bombs. The horror of those images can only be offset by the rationalization that those particular enemies deserve that kind of death, that they belong to a different realm, and that they are not deserving of compassion. Romero's *Night* (and all subsequent films in the zombie genre) truly make the enemies "other" and emphasize their inhumanity in the very way they mindlessly destroy living humans. The gruesomeness of zombie attacks justifies the brutal response in an endless cycle of violence, where the audience is not spared the details of what the impact of bullets does to a human body (particularly the head) or of what actual dismemberment and disembowelment looks like, thus exposing the brutality of war as well. As Steven Shaviro argues, "these films literalize obscenity. In their insistence on cannibalism and on the dismemberment of the human body, their lurid display of extruded viscera, they deliberately and directly present to the eye something that should not be seen, that cannot be seen in actuality."[41] The obscenity of dismembered bodies matches the carnage taking place in Vietnam (minus the cannibalism, of course). Romero constantly denied having a pressing political agenda, even though his film is clearly a product of its times: "It was 1968, man. Everybody had a 'message.' Maybe it crept in. I was just making a horror film, and I think the anger and the attitude and all that's there is just because it was 1968."[42] Later he conceded that "the zombies could be the dead in Vietnam; the consequences of our mistakes in the past; you name it."[43] Karen Randell identifies specific moments in the film that reflect the link with the war, such as the American flag flapping over the cemetery in the opening scene, Barbra's shell-shocked attitude for most of the film, or the TV news reporter's reference to a "search and destroy operation"—Vietnam lingo that made it into the script written by the actor himself, whose day job was as a broadcaster in Pittsburgh.[44]

Regardless of the interpretation, the anger of the times is reflected in the interactions between the living and the remorselessness in killing the automata. The feeling of being under attack is constant and mirrors domestic tensions as well as the content of news coming from South-East Asia. The protagonists of *Night of the Living Dead*, barricaded in a farmhouse under siege, must defend themselves from enemies who keep coming at them, refusing to stay dead, presumably from underground tombs, just as the "all alike" Vietnamese enemies crept out of tunnels, seemingly motivated by a monomaniacal desire to destroy the better equipped American soldiers, relentlessly returning regardless of how ferociously and definitively they had been killed. Even the choice of a black actor to play the protagonist, as dictated by chance as Romero has always affirmed,[45] ends up being courageous in Lyndon Johnson's America, at war in Vietnam with an army desegregated only twenty years earlier, but where pacific racial coexistence or taking orders from men of a different race still proved difficult. Civil rights movements and riots, Martin Luther King's assassination a few months before the release of Romero's film, and Malcolm X's one three years earlier also make the choice of a black actor as take-charge protagonist particularly poignant. Ben is the only one who seems to know what to do, who boards up all possible entryways to the house, who devises a feasible plan and gives orders to stunned, uncertain, or downright hostile people. Race may play as much a part in Mr. Cooper's dislike to follow orders as wounded masculinity does. Regardless of the director's intentions, the end product shows a black man slapping a blonde hysterical woman, killing a white man who repeatedly puts Ben's life in danger, and being shot dead, in turn, by an all-white squad bent on killing everything that moves, in what ultimately looks like a lynching or an execution. Randell interprets this as

> friendly fire which reveals America's indifference to both internal and external forms of racial otherness as the film not only speaks to the context of America's overseas war, but the visual evocation of a lynch mob through the all-white gang of hunters and their vicious dogs who surround the farm house also exposes the dark undercurrent of internal Civil Rights–era racial tensions.[46]

The slap echoes a famous and equally shocking one in an Oscar-winning film of just a year earlier, *In the Heat of the Night* (Norman Jewison, 1967). In it, black Philadelphia Detective Virgil Tibbs, involved by chance in a murder investigation in Sparta, Mississippi, slaps cotton plantation owner Endicott after being slapped himself for daring to question him in relation to the murder. He becomes then the target of several chases by townspeople out to "teach the boy a lesson." The revolutionary impact and political implication of both slapping scenes (and Romero's feels like a direct quotation) cannot be overestimated. As Romero himself has remarked about the last scene of his film: "they look like a lynch mob ... a black man being chased by dogs was very much part of the average viewer's vocabulary."[47] Adam Lowenstein, in *Shocking Representation*, sees Ben's effectiveness as the take-charge man in the film as typical of characters in Howard Hawks' edifying films, "Teamwork and survivalist efficiency take such precedence in *Night* that Barry Keith Grant rightly detects a 'striking similarity to the adventure films of Howard Hawks.... As with, say, the cowboys on the Chisolm trail in *Red River* [1948] ... the characters in the living dead films are cut off from established codes and ethics, forced to survive on an existentialist precipice.'"[48] However, he sees the Hawksian group led by Ben as a failure, as opposed to the efficiency of the redneck militia at the end. There is no reconciliation between the Southern Chief of police and the assertive black man in the heat of Romero's *Night*.

"They used to be us"

Romero's othering, though, is not so much among living humans, but rather between the living and the revived dead, whose status as slow-moving and seemingly human killers makes them perfect targets of brutal executions that unleash pent-up fears and resentment. While *Night* seems to be an allegory of the war in Vietnam and the othered enemies mostly a non-descript army relentlessly launching attack after attack, subsequent films look at the living dead with a certain degree of sympathy when they become the target of excessive violence or ridicule. The nature of their sole desire makes them heinous, of course, but overkill should remind audiences that these enemies used to be human and a society that loses respect for the dead has long lost respect for the living as well. *Dawn* touches on this in the beginning, when two SWAT team members, Roger and Peter, meet as they are raiding a low-income building where residents have refused to turn in their dead to the National Guard. As they uncover increasing numbers of zombies and eliminate them, a Hispanic priest warns them: "When the dead walk, señores, we must stop the killing or lose the war."[49] More dead people means more living dead, so a tearful Peter is forced to shoot in the head a bunch of living dead huddled together in a basement. When Roger wonders why people keep the dead there Peter answers, "Because they still believe there is respect in dying."[50] However, once Peter and Roger take refuge in a shopping mall with pilot Steve and his TV producer girlfriend Fran, the humanity of the revived dead is forgotten and they are seen as walking targets, as in a videogame (something as new as shopping malls in the 1970s). "Infected" by consumeristic frenzy, the four protagonists find a gun store where they get armed to the teeth, with anything from hunting rifles to revolvers and cowboy hats and boots, as the soundtrack plays African animal noises and tom-toms. When Hells Angels–type bikers invade the mall and threaten their hard-won territory, instead of letting them take some useless items and letting them go, Steve reacts as a far West landowner who discovers cattle thieves on his land, engages in a shoot-out reminiscent of show-downs between settlers and Indians in several Westerns, and ends up losing his life.

The systematic appropriation of what used to belong to others is not just what happens with land in Westerns, but also seems to be the new normal of surviving humans living in the sanctuary city of Pittsburgh in *Land of the Dead* (2004). Looters aboard "Dead Reckoning" procure medicine, supplies, and also luxury goods for the community, while zombies live peacefully at the outskirts of civilization; it is their existence that is disturbed recklessly and disrespectfully by constant incursions (much like Indian lands were invaded and appropriated).[51] Once again, the living dead are used as target practice, killed for no reason and humiliated in their own habitat as well as in town, where they are used in freak shows, in amusement park dunk tanks, employed as gladiators in an arena reminiscent of *Mad Max: Beyond Thunderdome*, and made to participate in "Punch and Judy" shows for kids. A similarly cruel exploitation and overkill takes place in *Day of the Dead* (1985), where zombies are harvested from a corral at the end of an abandoned mine and used by "Dr. Frankenstein" for medical experimentation, not so much to find a cure, but to re-condition them using some residual memory of automated gestures buried in their brains. The dead outnumber the living 400,000 to one in this film and the mad scientist's goal is to get to a point when they can be tamed. While not a bad idea *per se*, the cruelty of vivisection, dismemberment, and electrodes placed on brains or torsos makes one wonder about the detachment, not just from a specimen but also from reality, needed to carry such experiments to term.[52] The realization that there are no limits to gratuitous cruelty is also explored in the *Blair Witch Project*-esque *Diary of the Dead*, a film constituted by the footage shot by directing student Jason Creed, a classmate, and eventually Jason's girlfriend Debra. Over images Jason had downloaded from the internet before dying, Debra quotes him saying that he thought he could help someone by recording what happens to his group. The footage shows "a couple of hometown Joes who went out to shoot targets but that day they used people, dead people, you know? just for fun. There was one target that was different from the rest: a woman, tied by her hair to the branch of a tree. The boys had this one set up just for kicks. They got out their favorite 12-gauge and…."[53] What Debra does not describe is shown: the face of the woman blown off and her body falling to the ground as her blue eyes keep watching us in a close-up, the upper part of her head still hanging by the hair. "Are we worth saving? You tell me,"[54] are Debra's last words and Romero's preoccupation since his first zombie film.

"They're blowing this town all to hell!"

The question of whether this humanity is worth saving lingers from film to film, as Romero develops his core ideas on what is wrong with the world we inhabit. Films, like any other form of art, express views on contemporary socio-political matters, even when they are period pieces like Westerns. Utopian and dystopian narratives provide direct criticism of their contemporary societies while suggesting possible solutions or worst-case scenarios. Romero's films are no exception: in creating modern apocalyptic myths that focus on what remains of humanity once stripped bare by extreme (in)natural selection, they provide a critique of the culture that generated them. Brian Henderson in his article on Ford's *The Searchers* uses Levi-Strauss' theories to explain how "the operation of a myth—both its construction from actual conflicts and its impact on audiences—always has to do with the time in which the myth is told, not with the time that it tells of. Thus, *The Searchers* has to do with 1956, not the 1868–73 period in which it is set."[55] As reflections on contemporary America, Westerns undergo remarkable changes from those made between the world wars (and right after World War II), and those made in the 1950s, '60s, and '70s, which reflect the tension of the Cold-War era, when the threat of Communism supposedly also came from within. The persecutory activities of the House Un-American Activities Committee (HUAC) proved that no one was safe, while spinning tales of the horror a Communist takeover of America would generate. As Tom Engelhardt observes, "the expenditure of energy involved in mobilizing the nation through constant infusions of fear and tales of horror led to exhaustion"[56] and eventually backfired through reprisals and demonstrations led by people who "did not look like the enemy."[57] This is reflected in films such as *Invasion of the Body Snatchers*, but also in a new kind of film Western, that no longer represents Indians as the overhanging, constant threat to the protagonists' well-being (although such scenarios still exist in TV series).[58] The enemy is no longer the mindless, relentless savage, but rather the white frontier society of men corrupted by local politics and private interests, possibly to the detriment of other neighbors (Mexicans). A 1950s film like *The Searchers* is, therefore, a problematic look back to simpler narratives where the enemy was easily identified because of its racial otherness. The new "other" then becomes what we reject of ourselves (or, as Martin Winkler argues, "Chief Scar is no less than Ethan's alter ego"[59]), an intruder who seems to possess what we want, or the neighbor who limits our liberty. Slavoj Žižek writes: "Since a Neighbour is, as Freud suspected long ago, primarily a thing, a traumatic intruder, someone whose different way of life ... disturbs us, ... this can also give rise to an aggressive reaction aimed at getting rid of this disturbing intruder."[60]

In 1952, *High Noon* changes the idea of the Western hero for a truly lone fighter, emphasizing the isolation of a man fighting for his ideas, pride, and dignity, and ultimately for the common good in McCarthy's America. Myths are debunked, especially that of uncompromising, staunch masculinity proposed by earlier films: the protagonist of *The Big Country* is a man from Baltimore, trying to bring peace to two feuding families in Texas; the weak drunken Sheriff in *Rio Bravo* (1959, and in the loose remake *El Dorado* made eight years later by the same director) needs to detox to be able to protect the town from bandits; the co-protagonist of *The Man Who Shot Liberty Valance* is a mild-mannered lawyer from out East, taking a small town and then a whole state out of the old age and into the future. In the 1950s, these are all valid models of how the West and, by extension, modern America is built on violence but also culture, reason, and more civilized ways of dealing with conflict and neighbors. The focus becomes the inability of humans to get along and the growing pains of modern democracy that involve a reassessment of priorities and the establishment of a new symbolic order. Stanley Corkin in *Cowboys as Cold Warriors* talks about the protagonists of these films as "morally correct and socially useful,"[61] expanding on the quoted words of John Lenihan: "Within the framework of the Western, a man had to do what he had to do with an instinctive, natural awareness of right and wrong. Fulfilling his personal code of honor also served society's best interests."[62] In Corkin's interpretation, such need for a savior goes hand in hand with the public's need "for the heroic gunman to deliver them"[63] in the MacArthur/McCarthy era. In this scenario, the Western is both a nostalgic look at simpler times, when "good" and "bad" are rather unnuanced categories (from a white settlers' point of view), and a means to reflect current politics. *The Magnificent Seven* (John Sturges, 1960) seems to portray Americans as "reluctant" paladins of lost causes, fighting to free some naïve Mexican *campesinos* from a mean Mexican bandit who steals all their crops, out of the goodness of their hearts, receiving no fee and exposing themselves to considerable personal danger and loss of life. Very little of the original film by Akira Kurosawa (*The Seven Samurai*, 1954) remains in this simplistic version of the story, except for the realization of the Pyrrhic victory of the warriors at the end, which, in the American context may be seen as an allegory of the military involvement in the Korean war. In Romero's films subsequent to *Night*, Pyrrhic victories are all that is possible: two or three characters may manage to save themselves (and no one else) but quite possibly for a limited time. In the 1960s the ethical certainties of the 1950s Westerns wane or, as Corkin argues, "the glorious days of moral clarity and uninterrupted growth had passed."[64] Ben in Romero's *Night* is an ironic version of the lone fighter of the above-mentioned films, whose moral stance is made problematic by the fact that he kills enemies without a second thought and ends up not protecting but rather killing (or abandoning to their fate) people he is supposedly helping. The premise is different, of course: he is a self-appointed leader of a group of people who are, like him, first and foremost intent on trying to save themselves. Much like Indians of classical Westerns, zombies then become just catalysts for the drama among characters to unfold, they are the plague people are escaping in Boccaccio's *Decameron*, and just like that plague they are lethal but incidental to the tales. Romero admitted it: "zombies are secondary … they're sort of like, annoyances … the stories are basically people stories."[65] What is pressing to him in 1968 is to represent the divisiveness of the country on matters that are central to (co)existence.

Two directors in particular revitalize the Western genre in the 1960s: Sergio Leone and Sam Peckinpah. Lee Clark Mitchell, in his *Westerns: Making the Man in Fiction and Film*, makes an interesting argument about how Leone's operatic "*Dollars* trilogy" (*A Fistful of Dollars*, 1964; *A Few Dollars More*, 1965; and *The Good, the Bad, and the Ugly*, 1966) "set the stage for Sam Peckinpah"[66] and

> made one aware of how much one needed to become exactly like the deadened landscape to survive, in the process of which personality itself is evacuated, transmogrified into a series of caricatures of western types. The most obvious instance of this, of course, is No Name himself … he seems deprived of life altogether.… Others also appear as little other than walking dead who only finally become active and recognizably alive when they are shot, left twitching in pain, released at last into a realm where movement and vitality are once again feasible.[67]

Whether Leone's films are parodies of Westerns, as Mitchell argues, is debatable; however, the stilted existence of No Name draws attention to the gratuitousness of the violence unleashed and to the bare bones of men's motives (greed, hunger for power, lust, humiliation of enemies). Leone plays with the conventions of the genre and he creates the first "living dead" of the Western genre in *A Fistful of Dollars*. In fact, in the iconic last duel of the film, No Name cannot die. He is shot six times by Ramón and each time he gets up taunting Ramón to shoot at the heart if he want to make sure one dies.[68] More importantly, after No Name has killed the five men of Ramón's posse he kills Ramón too in a fair, one-on-one duel. Ramón dies with bright red blood oozing from his mouth. One of his men, who tries to shoot our unlikely hero from a second-floor window, is shot by the owner of the Cantina and falls, his face a mask of blood. What Leone, unencumbered by Hays Code restrictions, sets up for Peckinpah[69] is also a special kind of gore: bullets no longer just leave a hole, but cause copious amounts of very red blood to spurt out. The effect, along with the impossibility to root for any of the characters, highlights the gratuitousness of violence while oddly desensitizing the audience to it. That is probably Leone's greatest contribution to the genre: violence engenders violence, escalating it to the point that it loses meaning.

Sam Peckinpah's 1969 *The Wild Bunch* unleashes even more violence in a story where there is no moral high ground. The bunch is made of outlaws swindled[70] by the very same Wells Fargo bank they rob, in a memorable 14-minute-long opening scene where the bloodiest moments are purposefully in slow motion, to appreciate the full impact of bullets on human bodies. They take refuge across the Rio Grande in Mexico during the revolution of 1913 and get involved with Mapache, "a thief who calls himself a general."[71] In *Gunfighter Nation*, Richard Slotkin sees the killing of General Mapache and his aids in the final scene as a tactical mistake akin to those committed with the counterinsurgency project in Vietnam. Peckinpah's "highly sophisticated understanding of the implicit connection between Mexico Westerns and the war in Vietnam"[72] is exemplified by the intrusion of the American bunch into the Mexican politics of Agua Verde; Mapache becomes "an adequate metaphor for the 'mission's' response to both Ho Chi Mihn and Ngo Dinh Diem." While such interpretation is plausible, it can also be applied to other films like *The Professionals* (Richard Brooks, 1966), for instance, where Americans get mixed into foreign (Mexican) politics in Westerns without having all the facts. However influenced by contemporary events as Romero and Peckinpah may be, what makes *The Wild Bunch* extraordinary is the absence of a symbolic order governing the actions of all characters in the film. According to French psychoanalyst Jacques Lacan, the symbolic, or the universal set of rules that shape human life (from language to cultural and behavioral conventions, to the law), is one of the structures of the human psyche that controls our lives. Through language, it is "the pact which links ... subjects together in one action ... founded on the existence of the world of the symbol, namely on laws and contracts."[73] In Peckinpah's film, thieves rob a bank of immoral thieves, who hire an ex-con and some ragtag bounty hunters and are ready to sacrifice the well-being of a town to capture bandits; running from the bank owner (not the law, which is conspicuously absent), they later get involved with a corrupt Mexican General equally loved and hated, and end up all getting killed in an epic carnage. No one is held responsible for anything, violence has no consequences, and no Lacanian "big Other" (symbolic order) creates any restraint. The violence unleashed from the very first to the very last scene of the film is unexpected and inordinately cruel, to the point that the film received an R rating (first time for a Western). It is worth re-quoting Mitchell's quote of David A. Cook's analysis in *Narrative Film*, which states how revolutionary the violence of *The Wild Bunch* was, since the director

> insisted for the first time in American cinema that the human body is made of real flesh and blood; that arterial blood spurts rather than drips demurely; that bullet wounds leave not

trim little pin-pricks but big, gaping holes; and, in general, that violence has painful, unpretty, humanly destructive consequences.[74]

Peckinpah makes it clear that the Wild West is not the ultimately positive myth it has been painted to be, but more often than not the reign of lawlessness in the complete absence of a symbolic order, where towns, symbols of civilization, are "blown … all to hell."[75] The leader of the bunch is hardly ever sure of the faithfulness of his men and accountability to any overarching big Other is not even an issue, not for the bunch, not for General Mapache, and not even for Wells Fargo.[76] Lawlessness reigns in a film that reflects the general feeling of living in times of political uncertainty both domestically and internationally. When comparing the photographs taken by Ron Haeberle and his testimony of the massacre at My Lai on March 16, 1968 (published in color on the pages of the December 1969 issue of *Life* magazine), the difference between the display of unrestrained violence in Peckinpah's film and of a real-life carnage seem minimal.

The remarkable difference in tone from *Night of the Living Dead* to *Dawn of the Dead* ten years later is in large part the product of the different aesthetic of violence portrayed in these films. Italian director Dario Argento, known for his psychological gory thrillers, particularly *Deep Red* (*Profondo rosso*, 1975), collaborated on *Dawn*, helping to turn an otherwise serious end-of-the-world scenario into a cartoonish display of special effects and dehumanizing violence.[77] In both films, slapstick comedy adds to the absurdity of situations in which humans waste their lives arguing or getting distracted, rather than fighting flesh eating creatures (what Steven Shaviro calls "marvelously tasteless sight gags"[78]). Blood in *Dawn* is copious and very red, as is in *Day of the Dead* as well, both to emphasize its fakeness and the remarkable wastefulness of humans, who in extreme circumstances abandon their allegiance to the symbolic order and end up resembling the living dead they are trying to stave off. One important difference, though, is that the masses of ever-increasing living dead act like an army, following a specific target univocally, while the living do not: they scatter, they follow individual base instincts or desires, and they refuse to acknowledge the importance of the symbolic order that, alone, cements societies and creates fully functioning individuals. The lingering on blood splatter, bodies riddled with bullets, exit wounds, and self-complacent portrayals of senseless, excessive violence are not the only things Romero has assimilated from Peckinpah's *Wild Bunch*: his five living-dead films after *Night* share a similar emphasis on the progressive loss of humanity of people who cease to consider the enemy human and cease to respect the life-shaping authority of a personal or collective big Other.

Romero's zombies are the catalysts for people's reactions once the glue that holds them together gets dissolved; each subsequent film reveals a specific cause for concern that creates situations akin to those of Peckinpah's *Wild Bunch* (carnages, wasted human lives, callousness facing death, etc.). *Dawn* (1978) denounces the excesses of consumerism identified in the novelty of the shopping mall—an abomination, a non-space that leads people to lose all sense of time walking down the windowless corridors of the cathedral of their new religion, worshipping a system in which everything is both indispensible and exchangeable/returnable, and where humans may very well be akin to living dead bent on satisfying their "need" alone. Shaviro sees zombies in this film as "simulacral doubles (equivalent rather than opposites) of living humans; their destructive consumption of flesh … immediately parallels the consumption of useless commodities by the American middle class."[79] Left to the sated enjoyment of all they ever desired (clothes, excesses of food, toys, videogames, guns, make-up, luxury goods, etc.) in the absence of a symbolic order, the four protagonists waste away, leading empty lives that make clear that the things marketed as absolute "must haves" are actually useless, or "kipple," as Philip K. Dick wrote in *Do Androids Dream of Electric Sheep?* in 1968. Fran, the character who voices her concern about what they have become, refuses Steve's marriage proposal, since in situations of total lawlessness institutions have no meaning. She also more closely resembles the dead when, playing with make-up, she looks exactly like one of the mall's mannequins used for target practice along with zombies. The distinction between humans, mannequins, which Shaviro calls "humanoid figures,"[80] and revived dead is completely erased in that image. *Day* (1985), at the height of Reagan hedonist years and the escalation of the Cold War, critiques both dehumanizing scientific experimentation and mad army responses on the verge of a possible nuclear war. In the film the army men are supposed to protect the three scientists looking for a way to deal with the zombie epidemic. Respect obtained with guns is not real respect, though, and the few army men led by a deranged Captain are a mockery of the law that only underscores its absence and the need to rebel against it.

Romero's last three films are made in relatively more rapid succession and are characterized by a much more somber color palette than the previous two, in which some levity is achieved through the brilliance of the colors and absurd situations that lighten the mood a bit. The self-destructiveness of humans who do not seem to have any redeeming qualities is the main concern of Romero's post–9/11 films. Each one denounces a different way in which the Western world has lost all decency, moral and ethical compass, and awareness of how social disparity, litigiousness, and media exploitation of suffering contribute to the spread of zombie invasions. *Land* (2005) looks at the disregard for the disenfranchised and the violation of the civil rights of anyone who does not belong to the richest 1 percent of the country; the rich and entitled who live in a mall-like ghetto ("Fiddler's Green, where life goes on"[81]), exclusive by nature and reproducing in post-apocalyptic times the anachronistic country-club segregation of times past. As all people who live in gated communities, the Paul Kaufmans[82] of this world (the Trump-like owner and CEO of the exclusive high-rise building) need the rest of society only insofar as it allows them to maintain their privilege. Once again, the army is in charge of border protection, but zombies outside the city have learned to fend for themselves, not even trying to reach the unjust and inhumane society of the living who are perfectly able to self-destruct without the aid of flesh-eating dead people, until the provocation from the living surpasses the limit and provokes them into action. Given the squalor of life outside Fiddler's Green, it is hard to feel empathy for the well-dressed men enjoying leisurely, sophisticated dinners, as the horde of zombies led by Big Daddy storms the mall. The situation parallels the one in *Dawn* where the biker gang invades the shopping center, but the philosophy is quite different. It is no longer about participating in the compulsive consumption of useless goods, but about class warfare and respect for human rights of the living dead too, who are portrayed as a sub-proletariat of sorts. *Diary* (2007) documents the obsession with rogue media reporting and broadcasting everything, editing and manipulating information in reality-TV mode[83]; the callousness of filming regardless of hurt feelings, fear, and dismay at killing beings that used to be human makes the directing student, Jason, worse than looters or zombies. Moreover, the official media twists and manipulates information, always looking for the most sensational angle to deliver news. In the opening scene of the film, the murder-suicide within an immigrant family in low-income housing is used to prove the social disruption

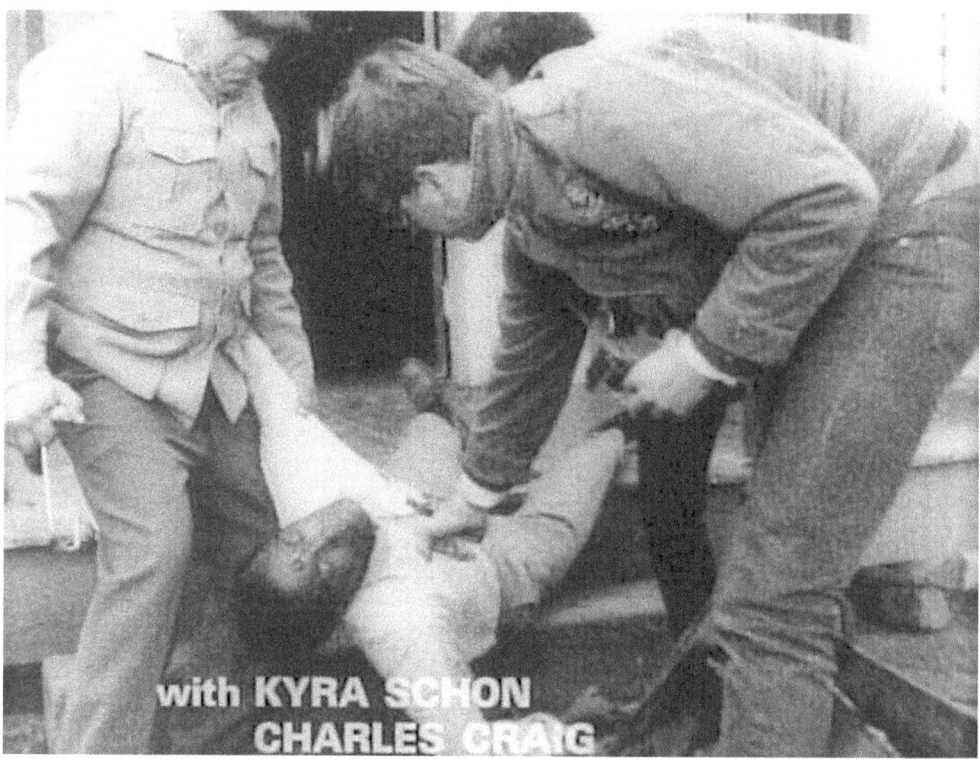

Night of the Living Dead's end titles (top) show Ben's body being dragged out in the open and set on fire; the action is shown through grainy stills that look like photographs from lynchings past. *The Wild Bunch*'s beginning titles (bottom) stop on postcard-type grainy stills as, among other things, a group of children tortures two white scorpions with fire ants and sticks and eventually set them on fire. The two sequences present eerie similarities.

caused by immigrants in "civilized" society, while we see the unedited bits that prove that they are revenants whose culture of provenance has nothing to do with the compulsion to eat humans. As Randy Laist notes, real-life disaster footage is mixed in the fiction of Romero's film and "the extradiegetic provenance of those images keeps one foot planted in the 'real world,' indicating a conflation of the fictional zombie outbreak and our own twenty-first century glut of televised catastrophes."[84] Finally, *Survival* (2009) alludes to

The copious brilliantly red blood splatter in *Dawn* (top) is reminiscent of the use of blood in *The Wild Bunch* (bottom). Interestingly, the massacre in the Mexican village of Agua Verde at the end of the film begins when Mapache purposefully slits Angel's throat instead of returning him to the "bunch" as promised. The arterial spray from Angel's severed carotid initiates a 6-minute sequence of unrestrained carnage.

never-ending conflicts that cause only self-perpetuating death and destruction; the feud between Muldoon and O'Flynn over what to do with zombies (train or destroy them) leads them to sacrifice living humans to satisfy their need to be right. Here, once again, order kept by guns does not foster respect and abidance by the rules of the big Other but obedience determined by fear. When asked if the old men's feud represented contemporary American Democrats and Republicans destroying themselves and the country, Romero commented: "I did think of that.... It could also represent Israel and the Middle East or the Senate. The whole world needs an anger management plan.... 'I don't remember who started this fight. But I'm on this side and I don't like you.'"[85] In all five films after *Night* the way of eliminating the enemy (living dead or disliked human) entails using the same excessive violence displayed in Sergio Leone, Sam Peckinpah, and Arthur

76 Beyond the Living Dead

Penn's films, later appropriated by slasher films at the end of the 1970s, or by overt homages to Romero such as John Carpenter's 1976 *Assault on Precinct 13*, which substitutes Los Angeles gang members for zombies. The living dead in Romero may be the othered enemy who can be killed remorselessly, but the ones who end up devoid of humanity are the living who have lost touch with the symbolic order and have become a wild bunch.

Notes

1. Nicotero, "Romero: An Interview with the Director of *Night of the Living Dead*," 32.
2. See, for instance, Ork and Abbagnalo, "*Night of the Living Dead*—Inter/view with George A. Romero," 4: "You shot in black and white ... was that by choice or was color too expensive? ROMERO: No, that was by choice. We could have had budget for color."
3. According to Freud's essay "Das Unheimliche" (1919), the uncanny is a strangely familiar experience, unsettling because not just strange but misleading. Recognizing something that may turn out to be what one did not expect is anxiety generating: in horror movies, for instance, a doll that comes to life (a life-like toy that becomes alive) or a house (by definition an intimate space, a shelter) that turns onto its inhabitants. In the case of zombies, a dead person who comes alive and wants to eat one fits in perfectly with Freud's definition—especially if the dead person is a family member: the familiar that becomes unfamiliar and threatening.
4. Romero did not call the living dead "zombies" until 1978 when he made *Dawn of the Dead* giving in to media pressure. Otherwise he defines them as "ghouls." He seldom referred to them as zombies even after 1978.
5. This happens in all of Romero's living dead films, with the exception of *Diary of the Dead* (2007), where only the dead kill or are (re)killed, even though the potential for murder in this film is present in more than one occasion and only barely avoided.
6. According to Edward W. Said's definition in his seminal book *Orientalism* (1978), that sees the Orient as the Western invention of a neighboring, subaltern "Other," mysterious, exploitable, and dismissible.
7. I purposely use the word "Indian" because "Native American" or any other politically correct term would be anachronistic here and just as inexact, since the first inhabitants of the American continent were people who identified themselves as pertaining to specific tribes (Cheyenne, Apache, Iroquois, Pawnee, etc.), cultures, and languages. In several Westerns they are called by their tribe's name, but in others the generic misnomer "Indians" is used.
8. Engelhardt, *The End of Victory Culture. Cold War America and the Disillusioning of a Generation*, 23.
9. Ibid., 215.
10. Pleasure that in Lacanian terms could be jouissance, or what goes beyond the pleasure principle, the surplus of enjoyment.
11. Matheson, *I Am Legend*, 126.
12. Ibid., 159.
13. Christie, "A Dead New World: Richard Matheson and the Modern Zombie," 80.
14. Seligson, "George A. Romero: Revealing the Monster Within Us," 78. Seligson's 1981 interview refers specifically to the 1978 film *Martin*, about an eighteen-year-old boy who believes he is a vampire, and makes references to other Romero films, including *Night of the Living Dead*. The idea that every human being has the potential for perpetrating violence is also explored in Romero's 1993 *The Dark Half*.
15. Matheson, *I Am Legend*, 108.
16. Bishop, *American Zombie Gothic*, 124.
17. *Hondo*, however, is a bit of a special case, since Mrs. Lowe's house is left alone by the Apaches with whom everyone else seems to be at war and is eventually protected by Hondo, a Cavalry man who has Apache blood. While being on the whites' side, facing the eventual end of the Apache once the General gets there, he comments that theirs was "a good way."
18. Caravans are stand-ins for the houses that pioneers eventually built on land taken from the Indians.
19. Of course, Monument Valley is in Utah, not in Texas where the film is set. The conflation of a gorgeous Southwestern place with the comparatively flat and featureless desert of Texas makes the outrage at "savages" "stealing our" beautiful land while taking our children and raping our women even greater.
20. Marty has been "adopted" by Aaron's family. Ethan's problem with him for the whole film is that he is one eighth Cherokee, even though he has been raised white.
21. Vast audiences would have been familiar with such images from World War II films, particularly POW ones such as Fred Zinneman's *Act of Violence* (1949), Lewis Gilbert's *Break to Freedom* (1953), or Billy Wilder's *Stalag 17* (1953). David Lean's *The Bridge over River Kwai* was made two years later (1957). The first, striking documentary on German death camps was 1955 Alain Resnais' *Night and Fog* (*Nuit et Bruillard*) but it was

probably not widely known in the U.S. Internment camps for enemy aliens existed in the U.S. as well, but it is unlikely that many people would have been familiar with their existence and modalities, even though from 1942 to 1945 over 120.000 people of Japanese ancestry, 11.000 Germans, and 200.000 of the 600.000 not yet naturalized Italians were sequestered in them. Nevertheless, images from WWII and, more recently, Korea were part of people's collective imaginary.

22. Steven Shaviro discusses at length how horror and pornography purposefully "violate social taboos, [...] desublimating" the acts they portray in order to create in the audience a physical reaction to the physicality seen on screen. Steven Shaviro, *The Cinematic Body*, 100.

23. Ford, *The Searchers*, DVD.

24. Tony Williams points this out several times, in his book *The Cinema of George A. Romero: Knight of the Living Dead* (2015, 223) and in his collection of interviews *George A. Romero: Interviews* (2011, 177 and 179).

25. A Wild West atmosphere pervades also the very successful series *The Walking Dead* (2010–), the new millennium product closest to Romero's idea of slow-moving zombies who besiege small communities of living humans trying to reconstitute society. Its protagonist, Sheriff Rick Grimes, from episode one wears a cowboy hat on his uniform and rides on horseback into a zombie-infested city among abandoned cars strewn on the freeway. As P. Ivan Young points out in "Walking Tall or Walking Dead? The American Cowboy in the Zombie Apocalypse," the series' storyline is "steeped in cowboy lore" (in Keetley, *We're All Infected*, 59) starting with Shane's name (Rick's police partner in pre-zombie times, doppelgänger, and anti-hero), which alludes to George Stevens' 1953 film, *Shane*. The series' search for a hero leads to the conclusion that "the American system fails as long as the culture of violence prevails" (*Ibid.*, 66).

26. Engelhardt, *The End of Victory Culture*, 34.

27. Brian Henderson in his article "*The Searchers*: An American Dilemma" (in: Eckstein and Lehman, *The Searchers. Essays and Reflections on John Ford's Classic Western*, 47) quotes Stuart Byron's article on the influence of *The Searchers* on filmmakers and quotes famous directors like Cimino, Scorsese, Spielberg, and Milius confirming how consciously or unconsciously scenes and frames from that film seeped into some of their most famous films.

28. *Ibid.*, DVD.

29. See, for instance, the articles in Arthur M. Eckstein and Peter Lehman's excellent collection *The Searchers. Essays and Reflections on John Ford's Classic Western*.

30. *Ibid.*, DVD.

31. Even though the term is typically reserved for people of African descent, it may also be used to refer to Indians in Central and South America. Given the racially charged discourse of the 1950s in the U.S., it does not seem inappropriate to refer to Martin as an octoroon as well.

32. Winkler, "Homer's *Iliad* and John Ford's *The Searchers*," 162–3.

33. *Ibid.*, DVD.

34. *Ibid.*, DVD.

35. *Ibid.*, DVD.

36. *Ibid.*, DVD.

37. Romero, *Night of the Living Dead*, DVD.

38. *Ibid.*, DVD.

39. See Giorgio Agamben's *Homo Sacer: Sovereign Power and Bare Life*. Stanford: Stanford University Press, 1998, for an in-depth discussion of politics that go against life through mass exterminations and genocide.

40. Lewis, "Ztopia: Lessons in Post-Vital Politics in George Romero's Zombie Films," 93.

41. Shaviro, *The Cinematic Body*, 99.

42. Quoted in Reed, "Rhetoric Goes Boom(er): Agency, Networks, and Zombies at Play." In Boluk and Lenz, eds., *Generation Zombie. Essays on the Living Dead in Modern Culture*, 233.

43. Wells, *The Horror Genre from Beelzebub to Blair Witch*, 80.

44. Randell, "Lost Bodies/Lost Souls: *Night of the Living Dead* and *Deathdream* as Vietnam Narrative," 70–1. Unlike most other people who identify zombies in *Night* as Viet-Cong allegories, myself included, Randell offers an original reading of zombies as returning veterans, as corpses either denied by American consciousness or lost in battlefields from which they never returned alive or dead. She identifies them as "symptoms of the anxiety of the loss of American life (rather than of the North Vietnamese)," 71.

45. See for instance the 1972 interview with Alex Ben Block (in: Williams, *George A. Romero: Interviews*, 10) where Romero maintains that they had "no preconceived notion as to the role being a black role [...]. It's not mentioned in the script at all." The same thing is reiterated in several interviews and is also present in the 2013 documentary by Rob Kuhns, *Birth of the Living Dead*.

46. Randell, "Lost Bodies/Lost Souls: *Night of the Living Dead* and *Deathdream* as Vietnam Narrative," 71–2.

47. Kuhns, *Birth of the Living Dead*, DVD.

48. Lowenstein, *Shocking Representation*, 162.

49. Romero, *Dawn of the Dead*, DVD.

50. *Ibid.*, DVD.

51. In "Colliding Modalities and Receding Frontier in George Romero's *Land of the Dead*," Outi J. Hakola

makes an interesting point on *Land* as a Western film, treating the zombified wilderness as the frontier looted by people living in Pittsburgh for the benefit of a self-serving minority, responsible for the impoverishment of the living within the fenced city. He argues that Romero reverses the genre's tenets: "Westerns celebrate civilization's emergence from frontier conflicts through the displacement from frontier morality by civilized morality. By doing the contrary, Romero challenges the Western's idea of the stable, invulnerable, and victorious role of civilization. The frontier, in the postapocalyptic world of the film, is no longer advancing and spreading the civilization, but instead receding" (140).

52. Sarah and the other scientist discover what has been going on in the mad "Doctor Frankenstein"'s lab, where he has detached limbs from specimens, since the lack of arms and legs makes them easier to control, kept heads alone, and even kept recently dead members of their group to feed his pet-zombie Bub as a reward for his progress. The experiments, though, look more like the ones performed on Jews by the Nazis than anything Mary Shelley could ever have imagined. The mad scientist with a plan is also reminiscent of real-life Dr. Mengele's fictional 85-time "cloning of Hitler" depicted in Franklin Schaffner's 1978 *The Boys from Brazil*.

53. Romero, *Diary of the Dead*, DVD.

54. Ibid., DVD.

55. Henderson, "*The Searchers*: An American Dilemma," 51.

56. Engelhardt, *The End of Victory Culture*, 128.

57. Ibid.

58. As Tom Engelhardt reports, "between 1910 and 1960, film critic J. Hoberman estimates, one quarter of all films made were westerns; and the western, which in the 1950s achieved a dominant position on the small screen at home as well, remained a particularly white genre (even though one-quarter or more of all late-nineteenth-century cowboys had been black" (34). Even just a quick Wikipedia search reveals that between the 1950s and '60s about 200 different Western-themed series aired.

59. Ibid., 153.

60. Žižek, *Violence*, 59. The concept is quite clear in Romero, "I never called them Zombies, though, I never thought of them as zombies…. To me they were dead neighbors." In Keough, "Interview with George Romero," 172.

61. Stanley Corkin, *Cowboys as Cold Warriors*, 148.

62. Ibid.

63. Ibid., 149.

64. Ibid., 211.

65. Keough, "Interview with George Romero," 173–4.

66. Mitchell, *Westerns: Making the Man in Fiction and Film*, 225.

67. Ibid., 233.

68. No Name is wearing a rudimentary bullet-proof vest: a large metal plate hidden under his poncho. Ramón actually shoots all six bullets at the heart but can't perforate the plate.

69. The Hays Code ceased to be in use in 1968, when it was replaced by the Motion Picture Association's rating code.

70. The booty turns out to be steel washers rather than gold.

71. Peckinpah, *The Wild Bunch*, DVD.

72. Slotkin, *Gunfighter Nation*, 594.

73. Lacan, *The Seminar of Jacques Lacan: Book 1. Freud's Papers on Technique, 1953–4*, 230.

74. Mitchell, *Westerns: Making the Man in Fiction and Film*, 250.

75. Pekinpah, *The Wild Bunch*, DVD.

76. An interesting coincidence is that *The Wild Bunch*'s beginning titles, with grainy stills of the protagonists riding into town wearing the disguise of Cavalry uniforms, look eerily similar to *Night of the Living Dead*'s ending titles, with grainy stills of the shooting squad standing over Ben's dead body. The graininess of the photographs make those moments part of history—a violent, hopefully past history, upon which the country (and myths) is born.

77. The most recent version of this cartoonish, gratuitous, and unrestrained violence can be seen in all Quentin Tarantino's films, and particularly, since we are talking of Westerns, *Django Unchained* (2012) and *The Hateful Eight* (2015).

78. Shaviro, *The Cinematic Body*, 101.

79. Ibid., 92.

80. Ibid.

81. Romero, *Land of the Dead*, DVD.

82. Kaufman in German means "merchant" and, incidentally, Kaufmann (with two "n"s) is a well-known name in Pittsburgh. The namesake owner of Kaufmann's Department Stores commissioned *Fallingwater*, a house designed by Frank Lloyd Wright, which encloses a stream and waterfall, along with trees rising through it—much like the greenhouse cathedral-like environment of the inside of Fiddler's Green. It is hard to think that Romero did not mean to have his own jab at the exceedingly rich and at how they choose to revel in unnecessary luxury, especially as the rest of the world is struggling to survive. By 1930, as America was hit by the Great Depression, Kaufmann had tripled his revenue from the Department store (earning 30 million

dollars vs. the 10 of 1912). Two years after *Land of the Dead* was made, as the world was hitting another great recession, "the number of billionaires in the U.S. multiplied forty times in the 25 years to 2007—whereas the aggregate wealth of the 400 richest Americans rose from $169 to $1500 billion," as quoted in Bauman's "Does the Richness of the Few Benefit Us All?" (104) in *A Chronicle of Crisis* (2017). Heartfelt thanks to Pennsylvania resident, scholar, and friend Martin Donoff for pointing out the Kaufman-Kaufmann connection.

83. It would have been interesting to see what Romero would have done with the 2016 presidential elections, in the age of navel gazing, selfies, tweets, "fake news," populism, and electoral manipulation.

84. Laist, "Soft Murders: Motion Pictures and Living Death in *Diary of the Dead*," 106.

85. Williams, "George A. Romero on *Survival of the Dead*," 183.

Dead Men Telling Tales
From *Night of the Living Dead* to *Zone One*

Angela Tenga

In the half-century or so since the release of George Romero's *Night of the Living Dead* (1968), its place in the evolution of zombie narrative has been studied extensively. Romero has been credited with creating a "formula" that would become a convention of later zombie narratives. The elements of this formula will be recognized easily not only by fans and students of zombie fiction, but by just about anyone with even a passing acquaintance with the genre. Kim Paffenroth provides an overview of these "basic characteristics of zombies [that] were laid out in Romero's first film"[1]: for reasons not usually specified, the recently deceased return from the dead and prey relentlessly on the living, consuming human flesh and infecting everyone whom they bite so that their victims, too, will rise from their graves; the risen dead are "autonomous beings, not under the control of someone else"; the living eventually learn that the only way to stop the risen dead for good is to destroy their brains; and the plotline follows the struggles of a small group of survivors, who battle the undead when they're not too busy trying to manipulate, dominate, and/or destroy each other.[2] Romero's later work adhered somewhat to this formula but also presented variations of it, and other filmmakers and writers have, over the past five decades, offered their own visions of the undead that depart, in various ways, from Romero's original model. Some of these later zombies can think, speak, plan, organize, and even win the hearts of adolescent females, as in Isaac Marion's zombie romance novel *Warm Bodies*. The classic zombie, though, and the one that still dominates in the popular imagination, is the original "ghoul" of Romero's seminal first zombie film: the inarticulate, single-minded walking corpse with an insatiable craving for human flesh.

Romero's legacy is unquestionable, but it goes beyond the popularization and near institutionalization of the set of storytelling conventions with which he has become so closely associated. One of the less-scrutinized aspects of Romero's work is the role of the embedded tale that *Zone One* author Colson Whitehead would call, forty-three years later, "the Last Night story": characters' personal accounts of the transition from their former lives to a life of running from the hungry dead.[3] What Romero created and Whitehead formally named is a narrative that emerges as a distinct function of the experience of sudden, traumatic change—a narrative that enters the psychological space inhabited by those who are struggling with a lost past, an excruciating present, and a fragile, uncertain future. This narrative, perhaps as much as any other element of the "Romero formula," has been an established feature of more than fifty years of zombie fiction. Romero's prototype of the Last Night story explores the possibilities of firsthand survivor narrative as a device that creates a sense of authenticity while emphasizing the perspective of the individual, who alone is capable of articulating a story that is, paradoxically, both conventional and personal, a singular expression of collective experience. Through its Last Night stories, *Night of the Living Dead* presents a type of survivor narrative that is particularly suited to the zombie apocalypse: stories that convey their tellers' private struggles to come to terms with widespread, devastating change that occurs seemingly overnight, stories that recognize the tenuous nature not only of individual lives but also of civilization and its productions, and stories that declare the fragile humanity of their tellers. Outside the diegetic framework, these stories can be further recognized as valuable expressions of character, sources of exposition, and opportunities for reader/viewer engagement. Moreover, the Last Night story signals a larger transition in human experience: no longer the authors, architects, and engineers of history, and no longer seeing their world through many of the lenses through which history traditionally has been read (such as economic patterns and technological advancements), humans either live from day to day as survivors, or they exit the human world as corpses or zombies. It seems, then, that before the term "Anthropocene" came into popular use to describe the current stage of geologic time as dominated by human impacts, George Romero created a story to mark its end.

A creative legacy is constituted through artistic responses, including imitation, repetition, adaptation, and renewal. *Night of the Living Dead* established a model of the Last Night story that would be featured not only in later cinematic zombie works, but also in written works about the living dead. Like the undead monster itself, the Last Night story has evolved through the imaginative efforts of Romero's many successors. Colson Whitehead, who cites George Romero's original *Dead* trilogy as a major influence on *Zone One*, comments in a *Time* interview on his own contribution to the zombie genre: "when you tackle a genre, you want to salute what attracted you to it.... You want to expand the territory and reinvigorate it; to add to the master zombie narrative."[4] Therefore, students of Romero's work can best understand his legacy through examination of how later writers and filmmakers, like Whitehead, have expanded and reinvigorated the territory that Romero first explored. This essay will focus on a set of print and video works whose Last Night stories not only reflect Romero's vision but also include significant innovations—works that represent both Romero's legacy and milestones in their own right. This study is grounded in the work that provides the vocabulary and conceptual framework for discussing the Last Night story: *Zone One*, in which Colson Whitehead explicitly recognizes, names, and defines the formal features of the convention that George Romero established implicitly, by his example, when he made the film that inaugurated the zombie subgenre of monster horror. Next, Romero's use of the Last Night story to develop character, provide essential exposition, and draw viewers into the fictional realm of his first *Dead* film will be considered. From there, a review of Richard Matheson's *I Am Legend*, an inspiration for Romero, will suggest that the theme of storytelling and specifically the loss of narrative authority can be located within this influential source. Following the line of influence further will lead to examination of those who incorporated and revised the classic Last Night story: Robert Kirkman's *The Walking Dead,* the graphic novel series on which one of the most successful zombie franchises is based, whose seriality allows the Last Night story to be situated within a broader context; Adam-Troy Castro's "Dead

Like Me," which extends the fictional world of *Night of the Living Dead* and incorporates an imagined Last Night story for the film's protagonist, Ben, in order to illuminate personal and social aspects of the zombie apocalypse; AMC's *Fear the Walking Dead*, in which one character's video recordings of survivors' Last Night stories become a way of preserving the voices of the apocalypse; Max Brooks's *World War Z*, a collection of interviews with survivors of "The Zombie War" that privileges unofficial, unauthorized narratives, often voiced by extraordinary and potentially unreliable narrators, including both the ethically and the mentally compromised; Isaac Marion's *Warm Bodies*, which complicates the idea of survivor narrative by proposing that zombies consume victims' experiences and feelings when they eat their brains, creating an articulate zombie protagonist who narrates a victim's Last Night story; and finally, Alden Bell's *The Reapers Are the Angels*, which offers a particularly bleak vision of the Last Night story as a dead-end tale situated between mutually unintelligible parties, raising questions about the possibilities of narrative in the conditions of a zombie apocalypse. Collectively, these works build on the convention that Romero established and refashion it, using their embedded stories to transform zombie narrative.

Locating the Last Night Story: Roots and Relatives

All Last Night stories are, to some extent, simple "before and after" statements about characters' experiences, but viewing them only on this level would be reductive. They are perhaps best appreciated in terms provided by the writer who gave them the label that granted them a life of their own: as Whitehead comments in a 2012 interview, *Zone One* "is about a survivor trying to adapt to the new world. There's a before and an after, and his world has been changed, damaged.... For me, the big tragedies—a terrorist attack, a tsunami—and the personal ones that no one knows about, the ones that you carry around, are of the same piece."[5] Whitehead's observation explains why the Last Night story is more than just a before-and-after comparison: it connects the individual and the universal, translating massive and potentially incomprehensible devastation into personal, understandable narrative units. In larger terms, then, the Last Night story is the zombie narrative's distinctive statement on human extinction.

The Last Night story occupies a position within cognate genres but distinguishes itself from its artistic relatives or peers as a specifically zombic phenomenon. One of these relatives has been studied by Wylie Lenz, who argues that the "contagious-voracious zombie" is less a "figure of relatively recent cinematic origin" than one best situated within "a long-established literary tradition: the apocalyptic plague narrative."[6] Certainly, the Last Night story of zombie narrative shares much, thematically and formally, with plague accounts that offer grim glimpses of swift and widespread death wrought by an enemy of mysterious origin. As Steven Zani and Kevin Meaux suggest, "the zombie film contains lessons already available in Giovanni Boccaccio's *The Decameron* ... or Daniel Defoe's eighteenth-century *A Journal of the Plague Year*."[7] Unlike these predecessors, however, the Last Night story is intensely personal. The tales of *The Decameron*, though attributed to individuals seeking refuge during the European fourteenth-century bubonic plague outbreak, do not focus on the experiences of these narrators; typically, they are designed instead to entertain or edify.[8] Defoe's *Journal*, while it directly addresses the plague experience, is broader in scope, presenting, as its full title indicates, "Observations or Memorials of the most Remarkable Occurrences, as well Public as Private, which happened in London during the last Great Visitation in 1665."[9] Zombie narratives typically (though not exclusively) showcase the struggles of individual survivor groups without necessarily casting a spotlight on the widespread or even global extent of the horror, although that scope, when not directly portrayed, is implied through the ubiquity of the Last Night story. The Last Night story insists, almost universally, on first-person narration of an individual's own experience: it sometimes touches on broader concerns, but its primary focus is what has happened to its narrator.

A closer analogue may be found in vampire narratives, in which a type of Last Night story may be told by survivors who are trying to escape or defeat the vampire. This is the case, for example, in Bram Stoker's *Dracula*, in which letters and journal entries written by various characters record their encounters with the undead count, and their collective insights reveal clues that enable the "Crew of Light" to overcome the menace of Dracula.[10] A more persistent variant of the Last Night story is the vampire's own tale of the circumstances surrounding his/her transformation. In screen narratives, this story is commonly rendered in flashback—as with that of Eric Northman in HBO's *True Blood* (2008–2014), for example.[11] This vampiric Last Night story often (though not always) elicits sympathy for the vampire by portraying him/her as a victim who did not choose this monstrous state (or chose it as a last-resort alternative to dying), and it typically reinforces the vampire's continued identity.[12] Many vampires are transformed at the point of death and exchange their human difficulties and finite lifespans for a more comfortable and eternal existence as undead predators. For example, Northman, a successful nightclub owner and sheriff within the local vampire community, was a Viking prince whose father's crown was wrongfully taken after his murder; mortally wounded in battle, Northman was nearly dead when the vampire Godric offered to change him.[13] The conventional Last Night story of zombie narrative performs more as a statement of disempowerment; a survivor in the zombie apocalypse generally looks back on a happier life and fears for the future. Further, while a vampire's Last Night story reiterates his individuality, the Last Night story of zombie narrative is commonly an expression of community: the narrator of a Last Night story explicitly acknowledges how precarious his/her own situation is while implicitly recognizing that those who hear the story share the same plight and have stories of their own—at least until they fall prey to the zombie horde and can no longer recall, much less relate, their stories.

The death of the ability to articulate personal and collective history is a fundamental fear expressed in *Night of the Living Dead* and later zombie works. Scholars from various disciplines have recognized the centrality of storytelling to the human experience. Jonathan Haidt, for example, notes that storytelling is a cross-cultural constant, that "every culture bathes its children in stories."[14] Jonathan Gottschall connects the modern storytelling impulse to that of our ancestors who told stories about "selfless heroes and shrewd humans ... the origin of the sun and the stars, the nature of gods and spirits, and all the rest of it."[15] One implication of the Last Night story is that, in a zombie apocalypse, storytelling might function less to glorify larger-than-life heroes and more to affirm the average person. In addition, storytelling might once again offer a way of explaining a world filled with monsters, mystery, and menace, a world that would perhaps be as incomprehensible to its human inhabitants as was the world of our earliest ancestors who invented stories to explain it. Richard Kearney proposes that through storytelling, humans become curators of their own experience and custodians of collective history:

> It is, in short, only when haphazard happenings are transformed into story, and thus made *memorable* over time, that we become full agents of our history. This becoming historical involves a transition from the flux of events into a meaningful social or political community.... Without this transition from nature to narrative, from time suffered to time enacted and enunciated, it is debatable whether a merely biological life (*zoe*) could ever be considered a truly human one (*bios*).[16]

As the quintessential storytelling unit that all survivors of the zombie apocalypse share, the Last Night story allows them to become what Kearney describes as "full agents of [their] history" who combine their individual tales into a collective narrative of loss and despair. The "haphazard" journey of the individual merges with those of other survivors into a recognizable pattern, forming a foundation for tightly knit social groups while also allowing for the existence of loosely bound communities of individuals who may tell each other stories and then go their separate ways—a survivor diaspora. Kearney further argues that narrative insists on the inclusion of both a storyteller and an audience, that "this crucially intersubjective model of discourse … marks narrative as a quintessentially *communicative* act."[17] In a zombie apocalypse, then, storytelling becomes a way of both preserving one's humanity and reinforcing the humanity of those to whom one's story is told. Further, it is a means of distinguishing one's human reality from the zombie state, in which identity, history, and narrative are erased.[18] The idea that a special genre of narrative would emerge in a zombie apocalypse adds a realistic touch to what many would view as a far-fetched scenario; as human survivors would adapt and evolve, so would their stories.

Whitehead's notion of the Last Night story formally recognizes narrative as integral to the human experience and self-consciously elucidates conventions of the tradition in which *Zone One* participates. In *Zone One*, we see the zombie apocalypse through the eyes of a member of a Manhattan "sweeper" team—a group of survivors who serve on a task force to destroy and dispose of zombies. The protagonist, whom the other characters have playfully nicknamed Mark Spitz because he can't swim, distinguishes among three versions of his Last Night story—the Silhouette, the Anecdote, and the Obituary, each appropriate for a different level of interpersonal contact. The exercise of discretion in the choice of which version to present allows for the use of storytelling in a measured way, be it as a shield—for example, to avoid revealing too much to a person whose intentions are unclear—or as a handshake—a version of one's story that more openly shares details. Mark Spitz observes, though, that "[a]t their core, Last Night stories were all the same: They came, we died, I started running."[19] By reducing the Last Night story to skeletal terms, Whitehead exposes its formulaic conventionality; however, the prominence of the Last Night story within his novel also highlights its importance. In *Zone One*'s final moments, protagonist Mark Spitz decides to end his life: "You have to learn how to swim sometime. He opened the door and walked into the sea of the dead."[20] With this act of self-destruction, Mark Spitz makes a closing nihilistic statement that is expressed through the language of the limitation that gave him his nickname, reversing the ability to swim from life-saving skill to death metaphor. In choosing to die, he indicates not only that his life is no longer worth living, but also that no version of his Last Night story is worth telling. His existence, identity, and subject status are obliterated; readers never even learn his real name.

In her reading of *Zone One*, Kelli Shermeyer proposes that "Mark Spitz represents his identity through a series of scattered small anecdotes … and the novel itself functions as Mark Spitz's Last Night story."[21] Shermeyer's interpretation expands the scope of the Last Night story to include narration of the circumstances of and/or leading up to a character's last night as a living, breathing, thinking human. In the case of Mark Spitz and based on the terms that he specifies, this story might best be articulated as, "They came, we died, I stopped running." Shermeyer's addition of this interpretation of the "Last Night" is useful because in many zombie narratives, there is no meaningful distinction between the "Last Night" as defined in Whitehead's novel—the passage from the pre-apocalyptic way of living into a life of running from the undead—and a character's last night of human life as it is generally understood. Many characters do not survive long enough, within the diegetic framework, to formulate Last Night stories that look back across a span of time, so the narrative itself can be construed as the story that they *would have* told. A zombie narrative that culminates in the death and/or zombie transformation of a protagonist who has no Last Night story in the *Zone One* sense constitutes, in essence, the Last Night story of that protagonist (and the countless others whose similar tales are never directly recounted).

Hearing the Last Night Story: Forms and Features

Both views of the Last Night story can be usefully applied to *Night of the Living Dead*, whose stories vary in length, tone, and complexity, each expressing the character of its narrator. The roles of story, narrative mode, and audience are most evident in the exchange between Ben and Barbra, who take refuge, independently, in what appears to be an abandoned farmhouse. Barbra, whose brother is killed by a ghoul in the opening sequence, is apparently overwhelmed by shock and grief when Ben arrives at the house. She becomes hysterical when she discovers a rotting corpse at the top of a staircase, and thereafter she is marginally functional and barely communicative, exhibiting a modicum of understanding when asked to perform tasks but not vocalizing responses or initiating conversation. Ben attempts to engage her in conversation but does not let her mental distraction deter him from the task of securing the house. He describes seeing a gasoline tanker beset by the risen dead and a diner surrounded by a horde just before he managed to escape: "I realized that I was alone with fifty of sixty of those things just standing there, staring at me. I–I started to drive I just plowed through them. They didn't move. They didn't run or—just stood there, staring at me.... They scattered through the air like bugs."[22] Ben provides a coherent, detailed account that weaves together events and his responses to them, and he does so while clearing dishes and a tablecloth from a table, then dismantling it so that its parts can be harvested for defensive uses. His ability to articulate and elaborate while maintaining a focus on the urgent task at hand marks him as what Kyle Bishop has called "a heroic icon of American pragmatism, hardly slowing down to let the gravity of his horrific situation sink in."[23] Barbra, in contrast, is dazed and childlike. While Ben is taking the table apart, she picks up the discarded tablecloth and begins folding it, their contrasting behavioral modes conveying varying (and gender-coded) abilities to cope and adapt. Ben views the table in the practical (and stereotypically masculine) terms demanded by the moment—as a resource needed for survival—while Barbra tends to the tablecloth in a rote, learned (and stereotypically feminine) way, giving it attention that belongs to a remembered way of life but that hardly seems suited to the current circumstances. After Ben finishes, she tells her story in simple terms and includes details that have more emotional than narrative value: "We were riding in the cemetery, Johnny and me. We came to put a wreath on my father's grave. And he said, 'Can I have some candy, Barbra?' And we didn't have any."[24] While telling her story, Barbra cradles the tablecloth in her lap and caresses it, attaching to it as a relic of a world that has very recently become archaic. She becomes increasingly agitated as she tells of the ghoul's attack, and Ben encourages her to calm herself; when she fails to do so and instead begins insisting that they must go look for her brother, he ignores her and continues securing the house until she tries to leave. He prevents her and tells her that her brother is dead. When she raises her hand and slaps him, he strikes her, taking charge of her fate and ending the exchange of stories.

Taken as a whole, the scene in which Ben and Barbra relate their Last Night stories renders character depth while highlighting the transactional possibilities of storytelling. Not only does Ben's account provide exposition that gives viewers a deeper understanding of the zombie crisis, but his aggressive response to the hysteria in which Barbra's story culminates establishes him as a self-appointed leader who will take extreme measures to do what he believes is best. Perceiving Barbra as mentally unfit, he concerns himself with her physical survival rather than her emotional needs. Barbra's account, in contrast, portrays not only her deteriorating and unstable mental state, but also her powerful desire to be listened to. Telling her tale is one of the last acts that she will take as an individual who has sovereignty over herself. The emotional impact of reliving the experience of the ghoul's attack is too much for her, and she loses control of her story and herself. When another group of survivors emerges from the cellar, Barbra's fate becomes a function of the power struggle that develops between Ben and Harry, the other group's leader. Arguing that the safest course of action is to hide in the cellar and bar its door, the only point of entry or exit, Harry opposes Ben's assertion that the house is suitably fortified and that having other exits is preferable, just in case its defenses are breached. The two quarrel, and when Harry announces that he's going down to the cellar, that he intends to bar the door and allow no one else to enter, and that he's "taking the girl with [him,]" Ben warns him to "keep [his] hands off her."[25] Harry leaves without Barbra, whose preference, if she has one, remains unspoken. Telling her Last Night story marks Barbra's transition from subject to object; not only does she cease to narrate her past, but she is no longer the author of her future, either.

Beyond the individual stories that characters tell, the entire film can be said to constitute a Last Night story in much the same way that Shermeyer views Whitehead's novel as the Last Night story of Mark Spitz. On the morning after the Night of the Living Dead, sole survivor Ben is shot in the head by a militia team that mistakes him for a zombie. Paffenroth characterizes this film as "overwhelmingly the most hopeless and depressing of all the Romero zombie movies, even though the others end with the total victory of the undead and the complete (or near complete) extinction of the human race."[26] Indeed, this somber ending appears to refuse the possibility of consolation, emphasizing instead the futility of human projects. The closing sequence, in which Ben's corpse is gathered up with meat hooks and added to the pile of bodies, expresses his transformation from active subject to inert object through a series of grainy stills. This sequence renders the de-personalization of death in an intensely personalized way. Moments become disconnected as death separates the individual from motion and speech. Fluidity and narrative belong to the living; both Ben and his story are lost.

The loss of voice and identity and the exclusion of the subject-self from stories told about it are central features of the work that inspired Romero's horror classic: Richard Matheson's *I Am Legend*. In an interview with Dan Yakir, Romero identified Matheson's novel as "the basis for a short story that in turn became the basis for *Night of the Living Dead*."[27] In *I Am Legend*, protagonist Robert Neville believes that he is the sole survivor of a devastating vampire plague. Each day he leaves his heavily fortified house to hunt vampires, distinguishing between two kinds: the "true vampires" or "living dead" and the ones "that [are] still alive."[28] He is unaware that some of these "living" vampires, or infected humans, have found a way to manage their disease and have formed a community where they live as another sort of "human." They send a woman, Ruth, to spy on Neville, the man who has been exterminating them; though initially mistrustful, Neville develops romantic feelings for her. After getting a blood sample from her, he promises to find a cure if she is infected. As he's examining the sample, though, Ruth knocks him unconscious. She leaves a note that reveals her true purpose and warns Neville to run before an attack force from her community arrives. When he fails to do so, he is shot, taken captive, and placed in a cell to await execution. In the last lines of the novel, Neville sees himself through the eyes of this new Other: "Normalcy was a majority concept, the standard of many."[29] He is now the Other who differs from everyone else. He muses that he is "a new terror born in death, a new superstition entering the unassailable fortress of forever."[30] Tracing Robert Neville's development from solitary survivor to genocidal oppressor to a sort of bogeyman, the novel also chronicles his evolving understanding of his own version of the Last Night story—not merely the point of transition from old world to new world, but the entire series of developments that lead him to recognize his misunderstanding of the new world. The fatal forces that bring him to ruin are, arguably, loneliness and chauvinism. Deprived of companionship and desperate to have someone to listen to his story, he instrumentalizes Ruth; to him, her purpose is to hear the narrative of his past and potentially to fulfill a role in the unfolding narrative of his future. It never occurs to him, however, that *he* is playing a role in *her* narrative. As Nicola Bowring suggests, the novel emphasizes "the *process* of alienation, becoming other, in losing … the 'I Am' of subjectivity."[31] In the end, Neville's personal self dissolves into a public self over which he no longer has sovereignty. His identity and his story are now the collective property of a society of new vampire-humans. Although Romero reimagined Matheson's vampires as "ghouls," he kept his focus on this central loss. By communicating their versions of the Last Night story—sketches that render character by bringing glimpses of individual "before" and "after" moments into a shared "now"—Ben and Barbra declare themselves narrating subjects, but like Robert Neville, corpses and zombies are objects that are narrated by others.

At a more basic level, the Last Night story is a commonsense feature of apocalyptic narrative; logically, survivors would be expected to exchange information about themselves and their experiences when they meet. These stories thus serve a straightforward narrative function by providing exposition and offering insight into characters. For example, in Robert Kirkman's graphic novel series *The Walking Dead,* a survivor group sits around a campfire on a snowy night, and protagonist Rick Grimes, a former sheriff's deputy, asks the other characters what they did for a living before the world fell apart.[32] Their responses reflect many of the features of Romero's Last Night stories and also illustrate a range of variations on that basic form. Most of the characters include mundane details about where they lived and how they sustained their lifestyles as well as more personal information, such as which members of their families they have already lost.

Because the zombie apocalypse is a long-term, ongoing phenomenon, survivors perceive their points of entry into that continuum differently, so the typical Last Night story describes the circumstances that, for the storyteller, mark the moment of departure from the old world. Some shared narratives (whether in *The Walking Dead* or elsewhere) omit explicit description of the Last Night in order to highlight other important narrative information.

In *The Walking Dead* graphic novels, this contrast is clearly seen in the stories of Dale, Glenn, and Jim. Dale is an older retiree who drives a camper, which he currently shares with two sisters, Andrea and Amy. Dale explains that he and his wife were on the road "when everything started happening," camping at a site that his wife "never left" (see figure 1).[33] He then describes finding Amy and Andrea stranded on the road and giving them a ride before joining up with the group. Dale's account is a fine example of a simple Last Night story, concisely presenting data in three stages—before the Last Night, the Last Night, and after the Last Night.

Last Night stories around the campfire in *The Walking Dead*.

Glenn's account, in contrast, presents only two stages, omitting the details of the Last Night to emphasize only his before and after information. A core character in both the graphic novel series and the AMC television adaptation, Glenn discusses his job as a pizza delivery boy, his problems with meeting his financial obligations, and his unsatisfactory relationship with his now-dead parents.[34] His account of what sounds like a very average life may surprise readers in light of his bold and heroic actions in an earlier scene in Atlanta, where he saved Rick from almost certain death. His acrobatic rescue included a jump across the rooftops of two adjacent high-rise buildings—a feat for which driving a delivery vehicle is not likely to have trained him. Glenn's story leaves his actual Last Night in obscurity to highlight more salient information: the contrast between his ordinary life before the zombie plague began and the extraordinary abilities that he has developed or discovered since then.

Finally, Jim's Last Night story consists of a single word: "Mechanic."[35] His account offers only the most basic answer to Rick's question, with no elaboration and no reference to his Last Night. It is a fitting response for his character, who seems traumatized and withdrawn. It is not until after the camp is attacked by a group of zombies that his backstory begins to unfold. While defending the camp, Jim becomes enraged, wildly beating a zombie long after it has been destroyed and accusing it of killing his family. He is bitten in the fight, and while he lies in bed, feverish, he reveals more of his story: "Boss at my garage.... First guy I saw attacked. He turned in a couple hours. No one's ever lasted more than a day ... not after being bitten."[36] In the end, Jim feels the zombie virus in his system and asks to be left behind in the hope of reuniting with his lost loved ones: "When I come back ... maybe I'll find—find my family.... Maybe they c-came back, too. Maybe we can be together again."[37] In Jim's Last Night story, readers can glimpse features of both Ben's and Barbra's from *Night of the Living Dead*. Like Ben, Jim focuses on a moment of shock and dawning recognition—the attack on his boss performing similarly to Ben's experience at the diner—and like Barbra's, Jim's story provides psychological insight about its traumatized teller. Jim's Last Night story, like his psyche, is fragmented; told in stages rather than all at once, his narrative merges his personal history with his present challenges. His inability or unwillingness to share his experience with the others around the campfire foreshadows his decision to withdraw entirely from the living and join the undead. He is unique in his decision to return as a zombie rather than be put safely to rest after his death by a merciful bullet in the head.

As these examples suggest, Last Night stories can be shaped in different ways to render character, situate events, and advance plot. Moreover, the contrasts among characters' Last Night stories suggest ways of reading both the stories and the storytellers. While Kirkman's Last Night stories share the fundamental features of Romero's, the serial nature of *The Walking Dead* allows for longer character trajectories, giving Last Night stories new meanings as characters evolve. For example, Glenn becomes a key figure in the survivor community over time, gaining status and respect from others. His Last Night story is recontextualized in light of his broader story arc, documenting his growth from an "everyman" figure with mundane problems into a leader who faces mortal danger repeatedly and overcomes extraordinary challenges. This feature of the Last Night story in Kirkman's series is consistent with Bishop's contention that "only the graphic novel has managed so faithfully to track the plight of consistent characters over a long period of time."[38] AMC's small-screen adaptation of *The Walking Dead* has also capitalized on the potential for serial narrative to develop character over extended plotlines, fulfilling Bishop's hope that "such a production … would finally give the zombie narrative the time it needs to map out the complicated human relationships that would result from a zombie infestation that ends normal society."[39] Although Romero could not chart such character evolution in his first *Dead* film, which spans a single night, he provided the original Last Night story that Kirkman adapted and expanded, deepening its meaning.

In Romero's first *Dead* film, the self-narrated Last Night story provides insight into character, but Adam-Troy Castro demonstrates how a character's imagined version of someone else's Last Night story can be equally revealing. His short story, "Dead Like Me," extends the Romero legacy by offering the perspective of a character who is not part of Romero's apocalyptic vision, but who inhabits a parallel imaginary space. The story is told by an unnamed narrator who, readers infer from details of his account, is the younger brother of Ben from *Night of the Living Dead*. The narrator notes, for example, that he had "wasted precious weeks combing the increasing chaos of rural Pennsylvania for [his] big brother Ben, who lived in Pittsburgh."[40] This remark identifies the narrator's brother by name and situates him within the undead geography of George A. Romero.[41] Structured as a set of guidelines for living undetected among the undead, the story includes the narrator's speculation about Ben's Last Night, adding an interesting postscript to what the audience knows of Ben's fate. The narrator says with confidence that his older brother, who had "always taken charge of every crisis that confronted him, and inspired others with his ability to carry them through," had surely "brought a whole bunch of naive trusting people down into his grave with him."[42] Although readers are privy to the authorial reverse-engineering that lies at the root of the narrator's musings, his description of his brother's likely fate—and the fates of those around him—recalls and extends Romero's bleak message. The narrator's view suggests disbelief in the possibility of reward for heroism, honor, virtue, or even effective action in the zombie apocalypse—a view echoed in his recollection of his lost "childish, shell-shocked hope that Ben would be able to make everything all right, the way he had when you were both growing up with nothing."[43] Although the narrator actually rather effectively reconstructs Ben's story, its narrative reach is, in diegetic terms, extremely limited: to avoid being detected and pursued by the undead, he now lives his entire life pretending to be a zombie, avoiding thought, memory, emotion, and reaction—sensations that would reveal to the horde that he is alive and mark him as prey. To maintain his cover, he also speaks to no one, so he will not immortalize Ben by spreading his hypothetical version of his big brother's Last Night story. Moreover, the narrator's contrasting descriptions of himself and Ben are personal musings that connect with larger social issues. Whereas he identifies his brother as "a leader [and a] fighter," he describes himself as "a follower, a yes-man, an Oreo."[44] His comment on race relations accords with Romero's racially charged depiction of Ben's "extermination" by an all-white militia. Unlike Ben, who would not accept a subordinate role, the narrator tries to fit into a white-dominated world, and when that world collapses, he adapts his behavior to fit in with the world of a new dominant group: the undead. Castro's story proposes that we may become the thing that we hate when we cannot vanquish it, as the narrator's pre-apocalyptic way of dealing with a racially divided world trained him for the voluntary sacrifice of his power of speech that renders him as inarticulate as a zombie.

Extending the Last Night Story: Preservation and Variation

Castro's "Dead Like Me" highlights the possibility of reconstructing Last Night stories about others, a potential (if not entirely reliable) means of memorializing the dead. The narrator's surrogate Last Night story addresses broader concerns about the functions and limitations of storytelling. The fear of losing one's story is, as anthropologist Ernest Becker proposed, part of the human dread of a meaningless death—or rather, a meaningless life. Becker argues that what humans fear "is not so much extinction, but extinction with insignificance."[45] One way that individuals may seek to secure their legacy is through stories told about them after they die. Matheson reflects on this idea in the figure of Robert Neville, who believes that he will be remembered as something supernatural, larger than life, powerful, and menacing—not as a hero, but as a monster. This view is mere speculation, however; whether Neville will be remembered for very long or even at all is unknown, situated beyond the boundaries of Matheson's novel. His final, self-enlarging fantasy of his future legendary stature may or may not be prophetic, but whether his vision is accurate or not, it reflects *his* desire for meaning and permanence. The range and longevity of one's narrative are key measures of the human perception of importance, and zombies embody the horror of storylessness and loss of legacy as much as they do any other human fear.

Colson Whitehead captures this problem eloquently in his invention of the undead category of "stragglers": zombies who stand paused in the midst of performing a mundane task on which they are eternally stuck. The sweeper team plays a game called "Solve the Straggler" whose goal is to reconstruct the straggler's life and death and thereby explain the significance of the task that it will never complete. For example, while clearing an office, the team finds a young man poised over a copy machine: "The straggler's right hand held up the cover and he bent slightly.... He peered into the glassed-off guts of the machine, as still as the dust."[46] The game begins when Mark Spitz proposes his theory: "Ned the Copy Boy enjoyed his job. Enjoyed it too much."[47] One of his two companions, Gary, counters with, "More toner, stat!" His other companion, Kaitlyn, seems to take the prize when she quickly offers three witty straggler quips: "'My God, it's full of stars.' And 'If we can identify whose gluteus maximus this is, we'll have our culprit.' Finally, 'I can see my house from here.'"[48] These humorous remarks give way to more genuine contemplations about how the straggler had ended up in that particular place: "Had he traveled miles, had he been here since Last Night? Had he worked in this office six incarnations ago, when it was an accountant's or dietitian's office?"[49] The game of Solve the Straggler highlights the fundamentally human need for story and suggests the psychological state of the survivors, whose desensitizing dark humor distances them from the death and destruction that surround them. Whitehead further attributes to the game the power to give the sweepers a sense of "mastery over a small corner of the disaster" and notes that of all the possible explanations for a straggler's condition, the "most frightening proposition was that he had no connection to this place, that this ... was simply where he broke down."[50] The novel identifies the disconnection of the individual from the story told about him as a source of horror. A person's potentially random placement at the time of death can generate spurious narratives that deprive the individual of his or her rightful story. Although the undead can no longer tell their stories or confirm the accuracy of any reconstructed account, humans still try to unravel their mysteries, or at least give their own lives meaning through their ability to recount tales. The attempt to restore the stragglers' narratives acknowledges the people that they used to be and comforts the living with the idea that perhaps, after they die in obscurity, someone will still want to know who they were.

This message is echoed in AMC's *Fear the Walking Dead* spinoff series through the character of Althea, nicknamed Al, who drives a SWAT van furnished with video equipment that she uses to record the stories of people whom she encounters. When her vehicle is stolen in the season-four episode titled "Weak," a very sick Al is desperate to get it back. She is so desperate that she lies to her traveling companion, June, about a nonexistent stash of antibiotics so that June will risk her life to retrieve the fictitious life-saving medication—and, more importantly to Al, her van. When the lie is revealed, an outraged June demands an explanation, and Al tells her that the van will "keep [them] breathing." Not satisfied, June presses her for the real reason, and Al finally admits why the van is so important to her. It contains something even more precious to Al than antibiotics: "The tapes, the stories I have locked in my van. That is all that's left of pretty much all the people I've ever interviewed. It isn't just other people's stories: it's the people I knew, the people I loved." Against June's protests, Al insists that she won't "leave *them* behind" (emphasis added).[51] The equivocal pronoun reference blurs the distinction between the recordings and the interview subjects—an ambiguity that essentially conflates people and their stories. Her deep attachment to the recordings fuses narrative and identity; for Al, leaving behind the recorded stories is a form of abandonment that condemns those who told them to a second (or perhaps even a third) death. Al knows their stories and could tell them herself, but recounting their stories on their behalf is insufficient: the recorded story preserves not just the memory of the image and voice of a departed loved one, but also the subject status of the storyteller, a status lost by all of Romero's original survivor group in *Night of the Living Dead*.

The zombies of Romero's first zombie film do not achieve subject status, though he explores the idea of zombie sentience in later entries in his *Dead* series. As Paffenroth notes, Romero was committed to "undoing the idea of unintelligent zombies, making their increasing intelligence the theme of… *Day of the Dead* and *Land of the Dead*."[52] The possibility of zombie subjectivity takes the Last Night story in a new direction in Isaac Marion's zombie romance, *Warm Bodies*. In Marion's novel, the Last Night story is preserved in an unusual way that complicates the ideas of both narrative and narrating subject. When the zombies of *Warm Bodies* ingest brain tissue, they experience the inner life of their victims—their thoughts, emotions, and memories.[53] The protagonist, who calls himself "R" because he cannot remember his full name, is a highly functioning zombie who lives in a community of the undead in an abandoned airport. While out on a group hunt one day, he kills a young man named Perry but saves his girlfriend, Julie, to whom he quickly forms a vicarious attachment through Perry's remembered feelings. R vows to keep Julie safe and comes to know more about Perry's life as he consumes his brain piecemeal, savoring the memories and emotions. Among them is Perry's recollection of his Last Night, when he and his father left their home in search of a safe refuge. Perry notices his father's white-knuckled grip on the steering wheel of his truck as they leave their world behind: "The gas station where I bought Coke slushies is on fire. The windows of my grade school are shattered. The kids in the public swimming pool are not swimming."[54] This vision of loss is completed when Perry asks if his mother will return from the dead and is told that his father ensured that she would not. When Perry asks why, his father replies, "Because she's gone. No one comes back. Not really.... Bodies are just meat."[55] Perry's Last Night memory, which denies the possibility of the true return of the (un)dead, also holds the key to R's transformation from zombie back to living human. Perry's father says that their memories of his mother "make her live" and that they get to keep "[t]he part of her that matters most."[56] As R eats more and more of Perry's brain, memories of his feelings for Julie transfer to R. He experiences love for her, and when she returns that love, he begins to regain his humanity. Perry's *Last* Night story is, in essence, R's "*First* Night story." His memory of his father's explanation of how they should keep his mother alive is instrumental in R's redemption, enabling him to recover the part "that matters most." After Perry dies, he lives on through R's acquired memories and emotions. R's recovery of his subject status is Perry's legacy.

Unlike R, most zombies do not recapture their humanity, just as Romero's first ghouls do not exhibit the possibility of regaining human consciousness or the power of speech. Zombie narrative is predominantly anthropocentric; zombies are part of the world of objects through which human subjects move. Bowring's analysis of *I Am Legend* argues, "The separation of self and world dies out at the point at which [Robert Neville] becomes a part of the fabric of narrative, of world, and ceases to view himself as an autonomous being, a 'self.'"[57] But vampire-human hybrids have stories and tell stories; zombies, in general, do not. Perhaps Robert Neville will in fact become, as he expects, a legendary monster to the new vampire-humans; perhaps they will invoke his name to induce their children to eat their dinners and go to sleep, and perhaps their children will tell stories about Neville to scare each other as they sit around a campfire. But zombies—at least the original Romero ghoul and those created in its image—have no campfire stories. In zombie fiction, the dissolution of the boundary between self and world is the death of narrative itself. That zombie narrative embeds the idea of stories as an emblem of humanity and selfhood is evident even in works that depict relatively little direct predation by the undead. Perhaps the most powerful example of this is the importance given to personal narratives in Max Brooks's *World War Z: An Oral History of the Zombie War.* The novel consists of a series of individual accounts recorded by an agent of the U.N. Postwar Commission after a global zombie outbreak nearly extinguishes humankind. In the introduction, the narrator explains that this work includes only about half of the total material that he gathered—the half that was deemed unsuitable for the official report because, as the chairperson informs him, the commission wants "clear facts and figures, unclouded by the human factor."[58] While the narrator honors the chairperson's wishes, he also places great value on the excluded material, arguing that it is precisely the human factor that "connects us so deeply to our past" and constitutes "the only true difference between us and the enemy we now refer to as 'the living dead.'"[59] When he emphatically protests, "we can't let these stories die," the chairperson suggests that he publish them separately in his own book.[60] His impassioned appeal indicates how deeply he connects narrative and humanity. To him, loss of story is tantamount to loss of humanity. The zombie horde, lacking speech, thought, and memory, is a self-less, unstoried collective.

With respect to institutional authorities, *World War Z* echoes and renews Romero's critique from *Night of the Living Dead*. When the day after the Night of the Living Dead dawns, the sun appears through haze and twisted branches, signaling the arrival of the first signs of human life: a news helicopter and a militia group traversing a field. These are the privileged but dubious voices that will narrate the Last Night. As an interviewer follows the activities of the militia, team leader Sheriff McClelland grimly and obliviously closes Ben's narrative at the film's conclusion: "Okay, he's dead. Let's go get him. That's another one for the fire."[61] For all intents and purposes, Ben is now no different from the "things" whose invasion of the farmhouse he barely survived, and what the public will hear is a narrative of victory. All the members of the survivor group have died, and with them their stories. No one will learn of Ben's against-all-odds survival of the undead onslaught, of his efforts to save Barbra and the small group of people who all sought refuge in the same farmhouse, of the series of unfortunate decisions, miscalculations, and interpersonal conflicts that brought death to them all, or of his wrongful execution. *World War Z* represents an attempt to recover such lost stories and, in a sense, "right" the wrong that closes *Night of the Living Dead*. The important content, the interviewer insists, is the "human factor" expressed through survivors' stories, especially the ones rejected by the commission. His collection recuperates the lost voice of the individual.

In the volume that results from the chairperson's suggestion, the narrator offers a full range of Last Night stories, presenting global experiences of The Zombie War. In so doing, he records not only the details of each person's account, but also the universality of the need for narrative. The novel includes interviews with those who rose to heroic levels—such as Kwang Jingshu, a Chinese doctor who encounters "Patient Zero" in New Dachang, a remote village in the Greater Chongqing municipality—as well as with those who exhibited rather unheroic traits, such as Breckinridge Scott, who used the zombie plague as an opportunity to turn fear into profit. "Breck" is a capitalist entrepreneur who unapologetically admits to developing and marketing a drug called Phalanx, which was an effective rabies vaccine but had no preventive or curative value with respect to the zombie virus. As documentation of the "human factor," all stories, regardless of their ethical implications, form essential components of the narrator's project because they portray an "unedited" range of human responses to cataclysmic events.

One of the most telling narratives in *World War Z* is that of Paul Redeker, the controversial author of the Redeker Plan, which entailed the deliberate sacrifice of a substantial portion of the population in order to save a smaller segment, including the government and military. His interview takes place in the facility where he has been institutionalized after some sort of breakdown that apparently caused him to dissociate from his true identity and adopt a new one named Xolelwa Azania. No precise diagnosis of Redeker's condition is given, but readers may infer that a trauma-induced psychological state set in after the adoption of his plan in his native South Africa and of similar plans in other nations (such as South Korea's Chang Doctrine and the Prochnow Plan in Germany). Although there is no indication that Redeker recognizes his inner self, he still tells the story of how that self disappeared after devising a plan that, in his view, was not entirely unjustified. He tells the interviewer that Redeker vanished after the authorities decided to adopt his plan:

> Even now, no one knows what really happened to him. That is when I stepped in, in those chaotic weeks when the Redeker Plan was implemented.... I understood his way of thinking better than anyone left alive.... Paul Redeker, an angel and a devil. Some hate him, some worship him. Me, I just pity him. If he still exists, somewhere out there, I sincerely hope he's found his peace.[62]

As Xolelwa Azania, Redeker can both rationalize his actions, now those of someone else, and experience, at a safe psychological distance, remorse for the deaths that resulted from the plan that he created—just as those who destroy the zombies that used to be family members, friends, and neighbors might require a defensive buffer in order to survive.

Redeker can simultaneously pity the man who engineered a carefully calculated and controlled genocide and characterize him as a "heartless monster."[63] The interviewer does not express an opinion of Redeker, allowing the man's own self-judgment to speak for itself. Redeker's account adds another dimension to the idea of the Last Night story because it suggests the priority of story over self: even if Redeker was indeed a monster, his narrative survives after his psyche is fragmented and he ceases, on some level, to exist. He performs as narrator of a story in which he appears as a mere technician, not an architect, and although he loses himself, at least he does not lose his story.

As frightening as the prospect of loss of story is, the scale of the zombie apocalypse entails a further horror—the absence of audience. With potentially no one left to listen to one's tale, storytelling loses the humanity-defining communicative purpose cited by Kearney, and narrative becomes the proverbial tree falling in a forest devoid of human ears to hear the sound it makes. This problem plays a central role in Alden Bell's *The Reapers Are the Angels*, which repositions the Last Night story to explore the relational possibilities of utterance and audience. Set in the American South, the novel presents the tale of Temple, a teen protagonist who has spent her brief life in a postapocalyptic wasteland dominated by the living dead. She is a lone wanderer and a warrior, confident in her ability to master any difficulties that she encounters in her travels. She has few memories of a world without zombies and has effectively been an adult for most of her sixteen years, fending for herself, fighting her own battles, and finding her own way in the world. Because she knows no other way of life, her transitional moment is not the arrival of the monsters that she most often refers to as "meatskins" or "slugs," but the "thing that turned her from one thing to another, from a human into an abomination."[64] This transformation coincides with the death of Malcolm, a boy who may have been her biological sibling—she is not sure—but whom she treated as a cherished younger brother or even as her own child. Malcolm was attacked while Temple was distracted, absorbed in scrutinizing blueprints on the walls of the office of a factory warehouse, which to her are "testimonials to the faith in the power of human ingenuity to shape something out of nothing."[65] It is a moment of childlike wonder with a very adult cost. Temple refers to this incident as "her biggest sin of all."[66] She is riddled with guilt for the lapse, blaming herself for his death and feeling that she is likely beyond redemption, that "there was evil in her and that no action however grotesque or unholy could be ill suited for the thing she had become."[67] Temple shares her secret burden with none of the people with whom she develops relationships in her travels. Instead, readers hear the account that she relates in a chance encounter with a woman who speaks no English and cannot understand the story that Temple tells. So profound is her need to unburden herself that it doesn't matter that her words are unintelligible to her audience—indeed, it is perhaps *because* they are unintelligible that she is able to tell the story at all. For Temple, utterance alone suffices; the idea of audience, like the idea of story, evolves under extremity. Bell's novel reconstructs the Last Night story as the moment when meaning is lost. For Temple, in effect a child of the zombie apocalypse, the "official" last night—the moment when "[t]hey came, we died, [and] I started running"—arrived before she was old enough to have clear, specific memories. Her Last Night story represents instead her transition from meaning-making subject to empty object. Although she is able to experience moments of pleasure and wonder, she loses the ability to connect emotionally with other humans, such that even her story must be told in a distanced way, to someone with whom she has an insurmountable linguistic barrier. Her Last Night story conveys the horror of lost humanity as the persistent need to narrate, even in a non-communicative context. With only the numberless dead as its unfailing audience, story itself acquires a fragile, empty, and even zombic quality. It is emptied of its interpersonal function and transformed into a solipsistic activity whose cathartic value touches only the teller—a tragic drama of soliloquies only, with no dialogue, a confession without hope of absolution.

The "Last Night" Tradition: Unseen and Undead

Since *Night of the Living Dead*, zombie narratives have inherited and reshaped George Romero's legacy in many ways, borrowing and transforming key themes and structures, including the Last Night story. That said, perhaps the most surprising thing about the ongoing adaptation of the Romero-inspired Last Night story is how much it has settled into the narrative background. Despite its widespread presence, the Last Night story has persisted and evolved in an almost unseen way, a convention that was nearly invisible until Colson Whitehead named it. Since its first appearance in *Night of the Living Dead*, the Last Night story in its various incarnations has occupied an important and dynamic place in zombie narrative, expressing the human need not just to narrate, but also to be narrated. The Last Night stories reviewed here reflect a range of styles and media, from film and prose to graphic narrative and television, but in all cases, storytelling functions as a self-constituting activity whose loss empties the human of its meaning. From the killing of *Night of the Living Dead*'s unrecognized hero to the suicide of *Zone One*'s protagonist, zombie fiction has framed the horror of human extinction not as the mere death of a once-dominant species, but as the loss of its stories. At the same time, zombie narrative expresses a deeper fear that even our cherished stories, and, by extension, our lives, lack meaning—that, as Macbeth says in the final act of Shakespeare's drama, "Life's but a walking shadow, a poor player/ That struts and frets his hour upon the stage/ And then is heard no more. It is a tale/ Told by an idiot, full of sound and fury, / Signifying nothing."[68]

Notes

1. See Paffenroth, *Gospel of the Living Dead*, 2–5.
2. Ibid.
3. Whitehead, *Zone One*, 2011.
4. Townsend, "Colson Whitehead's Pop Culture Zombies."
5. Colbert, "Colson Whitehead's Monsters."
6. Lenz, "Toward a Genealogy of the American Zombie Novel," 98.
7. Zani and Meaux, "Lucio Fulci and the Decaying Definition of Zombie Narratives," 100–101.
8. Boccaccio, *The Decameron*.
9. Defoe, *Journal*.
10. Stoker, *Dracula*.
11. "Never Let Me Go," *True Blood*, HBO, 19 July 2009.
12. Analogues for this type of story exist in zombie narrative as well—for example, in Marc Price's 2008 film *Colin*, which follows the activities of a possibly semi-sentient zombie protagonist and closes with a flashback that depicts his last living moments, allowing viewers to glimpse his lost humanity.
13. "Never Let Me Go," *True Blood*, HBO, 19 July 2009.
14. Haidt, *The Righteous Mind*, 328.
15. Gottschall, *The Storytelling Animal: How Stories Make Us Human*, xiii.
16. Kearney, *On Stories*, 1–2.
17. Ibid., 3.

18. It is not universally true that zombies lose all cognitive ability, as some zombies, even in the Romero canon, retain memories and their ability to speak, but this has not been the norm in zombie fiction.
19. Whitehead, *Zone One*, 112.
20. *Ibid.*, 259.
21. Shermeyer, "Systems Die Hard," 127.
22. Romero, *Night of the Living Dead*, DVD.
23. Bishop, *American Zombie Gothic*, 116.
24. Romero, *Night of the Living Dead*, DVD.
25. *Ibid.*
26. Paffenroth, *Gospel of the Living Dead*, 43.
27. Yakir, "Morning Becomes Romero," 60.
28. Matheson, *I Am Legend*, 27.
29. *Ibid.*, 159.
30. *Ibid.*
31. Bowring, "Richard Matheson's *I Am Legend*: Colonization and Adaptation," 130.
32. Kirkman and Moore, *The Walking Dead*, Issue 5, 12.
33. *Ibid.*
34. *Ibid.*, 13.
35. *Ibid.*
36. Kirkman, Moore, and Rathburn, *The Walking Dead*, Issue 6, 6.
37. *Ibid.*, 12.
38. Bishop, *American Zombie Gothic*, 206.
39. *Ibid.*, 206–207.
40. Castro, "Dead Like Me," 370.
41. In an interview with editor John Joseph Adams on his web site for *The Living Dead*, Castro has confirmed that he has "always believed the protagonist to be the weaker younger brother of Ben, the doomed lead of the original *Night of the Living Dead*" (http://www.johnjosephadams.com/the-living-dead/author-bios/interview-adam-troy-castro/).
42. Castro, "Dead Like Me," 373.
43. *Ibid.*, 370.
44. *Ibid.*, 373.
45. Becker, *Escape from Evil*, 4.
46. Whitehead, *Zone One*, 80.
47. *Ibid.*
48. *Ibid.*
49. *Ibid.*, 81.
50. *Ibid.*
51. "Weak," *Fear the Walking Dead*, AMC, 2 Sept. 2018.
52. Paffenroth, Gospel of the Living Dead, 6.
53. R is not unique in the zombieverse. For example, the returned dead of the *iZombie* graphic novel series and CW television adaptation also acquire insights about the minds and lives of the deceased when they eat brains. The publication of both the first *iZombie* graphic novel and Marion's *Warm Bodies* in 2010 and the release of the big-screen adaptation of Marion's novel and premiere of the *iZombie* television series in 2013 and 2015, respectively, appear to be part of a trend toward increasing interest in sentient zombie protagonists in the second decade of the new millennium.
54. Marion, *Warm Bodies*, 29.
55. *Ibid.*, 30.
56. *Ibid.*
57. Bowring, "Richard Matheson's *I Am Legend*: Colonization and Adaptation," 137.
58. Brooks, *World War Z*, 2.
59. *Ibid.*
60. *Ibid.*
61. Romero, *Night of the Living Dead*, DVD.
62. Brooks, *World War Z*, 139.
63. *Ibid.*
64. Bell, *The Reapers Are the Angels*, 190.
65. *Ibid.*
66. *Ibid.*
67. *Ibid.*, 192.
68. Shakespeare, *Macbeth*, V.5.24–28.

The Night of Spaghetti Horror
The Flesh-Eating Frenzy of Italian Zombies and Cannibals

FULVIO ORSITTO *and* GLORIA PASTORINO

Less than one year after George Romero's *Night of the Living Dead* premiered in Pittsburgh, on October 1, 1968, the flesh-eating contagion started spreading within Italian cinema. Initially, the infection hit *auteurs* like Pier Paolo Pasolini who, on August 30, 1969, screened *Porcile* (*Pigsty*, 1969) in the small Friulian town of Grado.[1] Then, it infected more commercial filmmakers, who took their inspiration from Romero and ran with it, reinterpreting Romero's cinematic invention of flesh-eating undead beings in distinctive anthropological, psychological, or pseudo-erotic ways, amply exploiting gory possibilities. Pasolini, a prominent poet and novelist, is the first Italian intellectual who "decided 'to divest' himself of high culture"[2] and invest in a popular domain like cinema. Inspired to change his means of expression by his assessment that literature had become too self-centered and elitist, Pasolini tightrope walks between the *auteuristic* approach[3] and entertainment, making films characterized by a distinctive, and almost oxymoronic, combination of depth and levity.[4] Although perhaps peripherallly influenced by Romero's zombies, Pasolini's *Porcile* is important insofar as it shows for the first time on Italian screens the eating of human flesh, rather than a mere allusion to it.[5] On the other hand, in purely commercial cinema, Romero's watershed film clearly changed the way in which the eating of human flesh was displayed in Italian cinema. In fact, all pre–Romeroesque Italian zombie depictions follow the classic repetition of the master/slave dynamic established by Victor Halperin's archetypical *White Zombie* (1932), avoiding any depiction of flesh-eating acts and their consequent gruesome effects. After *Night of the Living Dead* opened the door to a new world of gore, flesh-eating is represented in very graphic terms in the two horror subgenres that end up glorifying it. The first one is the cannibalistic subgenre, which mainly shares the iconoclastic violence of Pasolini's flesh-eating images, totally ignoring his subtleties and overall discourse on Italian society. Cannibal films push to the extreme tropes already present in the so-called "mondo" subgenre, a category that incorporates a handful of exploitation documentaries showing exotic customs and taboo behaviors from around the world. The second subgenre is the Romero-derivative zombie film that mainly aims at shocking the audience and making as much money as possible at the box office.

Even in commercial cinema, however, the constant presence of death evident in both above-mentioned subgenres may be interpreted in metaphoric terms, given that this kind of obsessive representation of death in the Italian cinema of the 1970s and early

1980s evokes a fear of death of Italian cinema itself. One cause of such fear is surely the economic crisis caused by the rising competition of unregulated, privately-owned television channels and new ways of fruition of the cinematic product such as the VHS.[6] Other causes of people's reluctance to leave their homes to go to the cinema were the elevated cost of new-release tickets (*prima classe*) for the average family and the actual, pervasive fear caused by the violence of the so called "lead years." In fact, in the period that goes from the bombings in Piazza Fontana in Milan (1969) to well into the 1980s, after the devastating bombing of the train station in Bologna in 1980, Italians lived in fear of being blown up, or arrested without probable cause and detained indefinitely (since the law allowed it), or kidnapped, or caught in violent demonstrations. Films got "domesticated," by bringing entertainment inside the "domus" (spectators' homes), as well as by empowering viewers by giving them a remote control for TV sets and VHS players to manage their own fruition of films. The main consequence of this domestication of the film product was that a good share of people would go to movie theaters to watch films that could not be broadcast on TV because so violent and taboo-breaking not to be screened or even distributed on VHS (as such, they were often labeled as "nasty films" and banned in several countries).[7] Cannibal and zombie films exorcised fears by offering outlandish and exotic scenarios and diverted audiences' attention from the politics of the day. Their box office success insured that Romero-inspired (or adjacent, like cannibal films) products continued to be made, progressively becoming more about spectacle than content.

In the two decades following *Night of the Living Dead*, Italy produced a huge number of undomesticated (and, possibly, undomesticable) films, which followed the path to shock audiences showed by the American director, eventually leading to extreme consequences. The human flesh-eating frenzy charactering Italian zombie and cannibal films constitutes a case study worth analyzing within a larger discourse on Romero's influence on other directors and cinemas. In spite of Lucio Fulci's notorious motto "Violence *is* Italian art!,"[8] the depth and explicitness of the violence informing the Italian cinematic depictions of death since the 1970s are undoubtedly indebted to Romero's visually groundbreaking *Night of the Living Dead*, which forever changed the standard of what could be shown to spectators (at least at the movies). Showing (dead) people banqueting on just killed human entrails opened the door to even more gruesome images in Italian films. Special effects took a page from Romero's book of low-budget filmmaking and used animal parts to illustrate the most graphic flesh-eating scenes. As Romero recalls, "One of the investors later on was a butcher, and that's where we got the intestines. He brought them out to the set and we said, 'That's great.'"[9]

Eating Human Flesh: Auteuristic and Commercial Approaches to Cannibalism

In *Night of the Living Dead* and in the subsequent five zombie films he made, Romero perverts the idea of cannibalism, turning it into an infusion of life-in-death. In fact, flesh eating is regenerative of death, not of life, as is normally the case explained in several anthropological studies on cannibalism. According to Peggy Reeves Sanday,

> Cannibalism is a complex human image with many meanings. As a practice it may simply be a response to famine or enter into the transformation and social formulation of psychic energy. In many cases, ritual cannibalism physically enacts a cultural theory (of order and chaos, good

and evil, death and reproduction) that enables humans to regulate desire, to build and maintain a social order. As a symbol of chaos, cannibalism is equated with all that must be dominated, controlled, or repressed in the establishment of the social order. Evil is projected onto enemies, animals, the cosmos, or harbored as a basic human instinct. In ritual cannibalism, the victim becomes the symbol of evil—the living metaphor for chaos, which must be dominated in the interest of social well-being. As a life-giving symbol or a symbol of order, ritual cannibalism physically regenerates social categories by transmitting vital essence between the dead and the living or between the human and the divine. Society is reproduced in the social power that these rites confer and in the reaffirmation of the social hierarchy.[10]

A literal act of anthropophagism can be easily charged with ulterior meanings and symbolism. Maggie Kilgour argues, "cannibalism as an image is related to the breakdown of certain notions of identity and language,"[11] specifically those that emphasize the condition of communion, which she defines as "benign symbiosis."[12] From this perspective, "the cannibal, long a figure associated with absolute otherness and used to enforce boundaries between a civilized 'us' and savage 'them,' may in fact be more productively read as a symbol of the permeability, of instability, of such boundaries."[13] The state of communion reached when the eater incorporates the eaten (in many cultures even gaining his/her strength) exceeds the binary logic of savage vs. civilized, and implies an intrinsic sublimation in "a more complicated system of relation, in which it becomes difficult to say precisely *who* is eating *whom*."[14]

Given the existence of various kinds of cannibalism, the association between this phenomenon and alterity is even more inaccurate than it may seem at first.[15] Despite its taboo nature for Westerners, the eating of human flesh is such an ancestral behavior that it may occur in anyone, given the right conditions (to avoid death from starvation, for instance). This kind of anthropophagism dictated by the need to survive dates back to the habits of *Homo erectus*, *Homo habilis*, and *Homo neanderthalensis* and is still present in some indigenous cultures, where the basic need for proteins has been substituted by culturally codified and accepted rituals. Obviously, forms of cannibalism which are not forced by hunger or part of cultural rituals, are not condoned or accepted by any culture, and are usually exhibited by serial killers or very disturbed individuals.

The flesh-eating act shared by cannibals and zombies offers a link with consumerism. In his thorough study on contemporary consumerism seen as invader and colonizer of human subjectivity, Marlon Xavier notes that as a "ubiquitous image in the contemporary cultural industry, especially in the United States, the zombie symbolizes an extreme image of the *consumer* as a product of consumerism."[16] As many critics have noted, this observation cannot be better exemplified than in George Romero's *Dawn of the Dead* (1978), in which an American shopping mall becomes the site of battles between zombies, human "survivors," and eventually a gang of bikers. These fights also serve as a melodramatic metaphor for "theoretical disputes over the nature and value of consumerism,"[17] which have effectively created a consumerism debate. As Stephen Harper deftly summarizes,

> On one side of this debate, a host of unrepentantly Marxist critics have described the baleful impact of capitalist production on those whom it exploits and the depoliticizing effects of commodity fetishism on consumers. On the other side, postmodern ethnographers and sociologists have argued that consumerism empowers capitalist subjects by granting them a limited, but politically important space in which to live out utopian fantasies of autonomy.[18]

This happens both to the four protagonist survivors of *Dawn* and to the zombies who keep trying to enter the mall. In fact, the four forced friends, once they have secured the perimeter of the mall and eliminated all zombies inside, live out both the fantasy of a happy family in a completely furnished apartment and their individual fantasies in the multiple scenarios offered by the shops and department stores in the mall (throwing away money in the bank, dressing up like cowboys after having staged an actual frontier-type battle with undesirable zombies, playing all the arcade games they want for free, wearing all the clothes they could not afford, putting on elaborate make up and having free access to accessories and perfumes, learning how to ice skate, shoot, etc.). The way in which the four give free rein to their dream of having everything money can buy turns them into a product of consumerism that makes them similar to their undead counterparts, who keep returning to the mall out of instinct. As Peter says, "They are after the place. They don't know why; they just want to be in here."[19] The need to return to the mall adds another layer of automatism to the zombies' already automated desire to eat living human flesh to survive, thus including consumerism in the essential acts governed by the Id. The line between the living and the undead gets blurred, since the four humans at times seem just as brain dead (in front of a TV set or videogames) or as mannequin-like (when Fran puts on make-up that makes her look like a doll).

Cannibalism is not just the product of tribal cultures; even in western society, one may maintain that everything and everyone is food to be consumed. As Stephen Harper puts it, "every consumer is reducible, in the last analysis, to cannibalism. The present work relationships, as well as the relationships between people—social, political, and economic—are still basically cannibalistic. Those who can, 'eat' others through their consumption of products, or even more directly in sexual relationships. Cannibalism has merely institutionalized itself, cleverly disguising itself."[20] Romero's fourth zombie film, *Land of the Dead* (2005), illustrates precisely this instance, offering a post-apocalyptic scenario in which a representative of the overly rich 1 percent of the world population, Kaufman, lords over an impoverished mixture of living and undead humanity, cannibalizing their physical and mental resources, exploiting both in a similar dehumanizing fashion, and considering them expendable and existing just for the entertainment of the elite. The film actually serves as a microcosmic allegory of our contemporary world, where almost half of the population lives on less than $2 a day, cannibalized by the 1 percent and the middle class (which in the film could be represented by that portion of the living that is not completely impoverished, while the rebelling zombie masses outside of the walls of the city are the dispossessed and disenfranchised).

Metaphorical cannibalism, as well as literal flesh eating, is present in all of Romero's films, from the very beginning: *Night* may very well be seen as a patriarchal cannibalization of women (Barbra, the little infected girl's mother, and Judy have very little say in the decisions made), of "uppity" blacks, or of metaphorical enemies reminiscent of those fought in Vietnam. *Dawn* has variously been studied as an allegory of consumerism, which literally eats up humans, transforming them in self-perpetuating shopping addicts. *Day of the Dead* (1985) shows the dangers of both a cannibalizing type of science that stops at nothing to carry out dehumanizing experiments and of military rule (in both cases maniacal alpha males metaphorically cannibalizing everyone under them end up being eaten). As stated, *Land* is the representation of the cannibalistic exploitation of the masses by an unfeeling oligarchy. *Diary of the Dead* (2007), much like *Dawn*, shows the perils of a self-cannibalizing mechanism: the obsession with filming everything because only what is recorded is "real." Finally, *Survival of the Dead* (2009) depicts the obsessive desire of an island's patriarch to keep his living-dead family members and friends from his same "clan" (which can be seen as an allegory of political factions) around until a way to tame, teach, and train them to eat anything other than humans is found, killing outsiders and transforming them into zombies, effectively cannibalizing the rest of humanity and condemning it to extinction.

Flesh-Eating in Auteur and Commercial Cinema: From Pasolini's Metaphors to Exploitation Films

Although *Porcile* openly displays the eating of human flesh, Pasolini inserts cannibalism into the narrative mostly for its metaphorical potential, echoing the allegory of American society in Romero's *Night*. Pasolini's allegory of Italian society is less overt,[21] but nonetheless visible. To the attentive eye, his criticism of the Italian "economic miracle"[22] is blatant and continues in his subsequent films through the juxtaposition of a mythical past (often idealized—especially in the so-called "trilogy of life" films)[23] with a decaying present that shows its brutal cannibalistic tendencies towards this prior era, in both historical and cultural terms.

In *Porcile*, Pasolini inaugurates themes that will recur in other films dealing with anthropophagism. The binary dialectic (also present in *Night*) between "us" and "them," for instance, emerges in this case at the ontological level from the very structure of the film, divided in two parallel episodes juxtaposed by the montage: the first taking place in contemporary Germany and the second set in a generic medieval past. In turn, these two episodes offer a binary dialectic: the contrast between fathers and sons in the contemporary episode, where the discourse on anthropophagism is developed by Pasolini in metaphorical terms and we witness the association between consumerism and cannibalism.[24] A slippage occurs here, though (as it will in an episode of *The Walking Dead* that quotes this scene): this time man does not eat man, but man eats pig and (at the end), pig eats man.[25] In the medieval episode, on the other hand, in the contrast between the group of cannibals and other individuals anthropophagism is not metaphorical. Characters are what they are: some are cannibals, some are not. Man eats man. Literally. And even though Pasolini's approach to gore is quite distinct from Romero's, given his avoidance of any kind of hyper-realistic orgy of blood and entrails, what happens here is visible and clear. Words are unnecessary and almost completely absent, while in the contemporary episode they flow in order to deceive and mislead both the characters and the audience. The film ends in the present, with a reference to a most horrific and sadly real metaphorical cannibalism. The protagonist's father looks at the camera inviting the audience to ignore the ambiguous liaison between his son and the pigs that devoured him, as well as his own ambiguous involvement with the Nazi party, for which he "once supervised the 'devouring' of concentration camp victims."[26] It can be argued that if Romero was the first one pushing the envelope in terms of what could be shown to cinema audiences, Pasolini demonstrated that even in the Italian conservative society of his time similar results could be achieved.[27] Even though their message and social criticism were aimed at different "worlds," both directors walked a new path to shock that spectators were eager to follow.

In commercial cinema, anthropophagism becomes a common visual trope in many Italian films (and co-productions) made during the 1970s and '80s. The narrative of these explicitly violent films revolves around cannibalistic acts being practiced (along with torture, rape, and many other gratuitous acts of graphic violence) by native tribes from the South American and, at times, Asian rainforest. There is no holding back on any kind of shocking detail, especially those depicting violence towards animals (something that makes these films full-fledged snuff movies). At first, one may think that since this is the only "real" act of violence perpetrated at a living being's expense—while all others were simply staged for the spectators' benefit—its presence was crucial to increase the film's perceived realism.[28] In fact, as Mark Bernard reminds us, Italian cannibal films "blend documentary realism with fictional filmmaking by narrativizing footage of actual animal slaughter at the service of an imagined story."[29] However, at a closer look one easily notices that even these real acts of violence are not improvised, but carefully pre-planned by filmmakers for the audience and the story's supposed benefit. Moreover, as highlighted by Jay Slater, these Italian film productions are characterized by the inaccurate depiction of "jungle savages, with non-specific tribal backgrounds" and ignore the reality of tribal cannibalism as "part of religious and battle rites," merely focusing on the exploitation of anthropophagism as a plot device "that allows a group of actors to devour the cast in an orgy of special effects."[30]

The Italian cannibal subgenre's roots can be found in the mondo subgenre, which consisted of a handful of exploitation documentaries (or shockumentaries) made in the early 1960s[31] that showed exotic customs and genuine taboo behaviors from around the world. Given that these films showed (but did not actively solicit or condone) actual human executions, they often bordered on the "snuff" subgenre. Mondo movies mostly "consisted of bizarre and sensationalist footage from around the world and anticipated the cannibal film by including footage of wildlife"[32] but also "tribal rituals and culinary grotesquery."[33] Cannibal films, while following this approach, also rely on "Rousseau's idea of the noble savage," often turning anthropophagism into "a cathartic act, to punish the bad bwana and re-establish those laws of nature broken by the white man."[34] In fact, "while many read the cannibal film as a savage deconstruction of the colonial voyeurism of mondo movies, others do not see the films as a significant improvement from their predecessors,"[35] to the point that Shipka claims that the Italian cannibal film merely replaced the "'your culture sucks' mantra of the mondo movies with an 'every culture sucks' attitude."[36]

As a subset of the mondo subgenre, typically cannibal films show mondo filmmakers or anthropologists from a Western country going to jungles and rainforests and entering into some sort of conflict with native tribes that retaliate by way of murderous and anthropophagic behavior at the Westerners' expense. Ironically, these films were also informed by an anti-imperialist attitude since, on many occasions, Westerners were the first ones to perpetrate extreme cruelty and violence upon the natives (who were merely reacting by inflicting the same behavior). Rarely anthropophagism was shown being practiced (behind closed doors) in modern urban centers, such as in *Emanuelle e gli ultimi cannibali* (*Emanuelle and the Last Cannibals*, directed in 1977 by Aristide Massaccesi, aka Joe D'Amato[37]), or in Mediterranean islands, such as in *Antropophagus* (filmed in 1980 by the same director). One of the most influential directors of this subgenre is Umberto Lenzi, who arguably started the whole flesh-eating frenzy in commercial Italian cinema in 1972, with his *Il paese del sesso selvaggio* (*The Country of Savage Sex*, aka *Man from Deep River*, aka *Sacrifice!*). He would later come back to even more shocking descriptions of anthropophagism with his *Mangiati vivi!* (*Eaten Alive!*, 1980) and, especially, with *Cannibal Ferox* (1981), "Lenzi's final cannibal film and one of the last in the cycle."[38]

Worldwide known for his cinematic cannibalistic exploits—and still admired by modern filmmakers such as Quentin Tarantino and Eli Roth, who had him play a cameo role in his 2007 *Hostel: Part II*—Ruggero Deodato innovates the subgenre by enriching the complexity of his film plots with meta-cinematic elements, which convey an ineffable sense of *mise en abîme* that strikes the educated viewer even more than the usual animal killings. In fact, while his 1977 *Ultimo mondo cannibale* (aka *Last Cannibal World*; aka *Cannibal. The Last Survivor*; aka *Jungle Holocaust*) is mostly remembered for its realistic feel,[39] it is *Olocausto cannibale* (*Cannibal Holocaust*, 1980) that truly "exemplifies the fantastic imagination of Deodato as a filmmaker."[40] Using the meta-cinematic pretext of a film within the film (or, more accurately, of a documentary found after its authors are dead), Deodato's work initiates the so-called "found footage" subgenre, which includes (among others) films like *The Blair Witch Project* (Daniel Myrick and Eduardo Sánchez, 1999), *Paranormal Activity* (Oren Peli, 2007), *Cloverfield* (Matt Reeves, 2008) and, of course, Romero's *Diary of the Dead*. This film differentiates itself from other examples of the cannibal subgenre, thanks to the unprecedented hyperrealism of certain images which assault the spectators with an extraordinary violence that is far from the fake-educational tone of the mondo movies. Deodato, however, does not forget his mondo ancestors, paying homage to these filmmakers when he juxtaposes Riz Ortolani's oneiric music to extremely violent images (making the audience feel the same bewildering effect typical of mondo movies), and including a sequence from a pseudo-mondo film entitled *The Last Road to Hell*, which displays a firing squad at work. However, as Slater reminds us, "the executions are real, and the footage was most probably borrowed from the shelves of Jacopetti and Prosperi themselves,"[41] the inventors of the mondo "shockumentaries." An incredibly successful film that almost destroyed its director's career, *Olocausto cannibale* is fascinating because it represents a certain mood permeating the Italian cinema of those years and because, even without the *auteurist* context in which *Porcile* was framed, it still associates cannibalism with consumerism. Moreover, it is deemed "a phenomenal Italian exploitation picture, containing more thought and ingenuity than in any other film in this subgenre,"[42] and can be considered "the first film bold enough to suggest that the stuff we see on the news is every bit as staged as what's shown in the cinema."[43] This is a key concept that informs Romero's cinema as well, particularly *Diary of the Dead*, where the protagonist's girlfriend finds and broadcasts the original footage of zombies coming back to life, unmasking the manipulation of the truth of the previously broadcast Fox-type news on the violence endemic in communities of undocumented Hispanics.

Several Italian directors dabbled with the cannibal subgenre, trying to hybridize it with other subgenres such as sexploitation, mondo thrillers, and even war films.[44] However, the most obvious blending of subgenres is the one between cannibal and zombie films. A case in point is Bruno Mattei's 1981 *Virus—L'inferno dei morti viventi* (*Hell of the Living Dead*), a gruesome Italian variation on post–Romeroesque zombie genre, which uses stock footage of a documentary titled *New Guinea, Island of Cannibals* (filmed in 1974 by Akira Ide) just to make the audience believe that the research facility in which the zombie contagion begins was actually in New Guinea. Another combination of cannibals and zombies takes place in Marino Girolami's 1980 *La regina dei Cannibali* (*Zombi[e] Holocaust*), which features a team of scientists who become victims of a mad doctor performing experiments on both the living and dead. This time the story unfolds on a Pacific island, and the researchers have to escape not only from the doctor's zombies, but also from the local cannibals. The storyline is clearly reminiscent of Romero's *Day*, in which Dr. Logan (nicknamed "Dr. Frankenstein" by the soldiers) ruthlessly dissects zombies and also recently dead members of the group of soldiers, scientists, and civilians hidden in the underground bunker, whom he feeds to his almost domesticated zombie protégé "Bub."

Intraspecies and Interspecies Acts (Cannibals vs. Zombies)

Zombies were first described in William B. Seabrook's 1929 book about Haiti, *The Magic Island*, as "soulless human corpses resurrected by black magic and ordered to perform menial tasks for their new Master."[45] In cinema, the repetition of this master/slave dynamic has characterized the representations of zombies from Victor Halperin's 1932 *White Zombie* until 1968, the year of George Romero's groundbreaking *Night of the Living Dead*.[46] As a consequence, until Romero's film, zombies were nothing more than an exotic variation of the Golem, the anthropomorphic creature made of inanimate matter that inhabits many legends of Jewish tradition and folklore, who also serves its master. As part of a somewhat contained group (insofar as they are incapable of reproducing themselves), zombies were summoned and then used by villains to achieve their mischievous goals. Spectators and critics alike often defined these generic living dead "as 'flesh eaters,' 'ghouls,' 'cannibals' or 'zombies.'"[47] Romero himself did not call his creatures zombies (instead of ghouls) until *Dawn*, when he gave into a popular interpretation of his films that caused the conflation of his undead with the traditional enslaved zombies. However, strictly speaking, "a ghoul is defined as a creature that robs graves of its corpses and devours them,"[48] while the word cannibal is not appropriate either, since "in *Dawn of The Dead*, TV scientists explain that cannibalism, in the true sense of the word, implies an intraspecies activity"[49]—and zombies never prey on each other.

Among the most striking features of post–Romeroesque zombies is the fact they answer to no master—a characteristic informing all of Romero's films, with the possible exception of *Land*, where they follow their own zombie spiritual leader, Big Daddy, to fight the humans who keep disturbing their peace and destroying them. Not belonging to a contained group, they often become part of uncontrollable hordes, multiplying themselves fairly quickly by biting their victims, or even just by infecting them with their blood. As a consequence, one might ironically argue that the sexual revolution of the late 1960s somehow hit the zombie world as well, if not by sexualizing the living dead, at least by turning them into creatures capable of reproducing themselves in a non-pleasure generating but necessary act (an interesting distortion of said revolution, one might add). As a substitute of the sexual act, the bite still implies the exchange of bodily fluids. However, what is most conspicuous is the fact that while cannibals perform an intraspecies act, biting and eating members of the same species, assimilating them, both in a literal way (by digesting them) and in a metaphorical one (assimilating their supposed "power"), zombies, as flesh-eaters, perform an interspecies act, biting and, eventually, eating members of their species but in a different stage of life (i.e., not dead yet). The ultimate consequence of this flesh-eating act (technically not anthropophagic, because it does not imply a man eating another man, but a reanimated corpse eating a living human being) is not assimilation but the reproduction of the zombie species and, taken to its logical extension, the extinction of humans.

Finally, said rapid and uncontainable spreading of the zombie contagion characterizing post–Romeroesque narratives has turned these creatures into perfect villains, true icons of modern otherness or, more specifically, symbols of the dark side of modernity, precisely because of their uncontrollability. This is even more visible in zombie films made after 9/11, because today's living dead perfectly evoke the fear of an "other" that we cannot really define or understand, who looks like us while being different from us (a fear some scholars consider a consequence of the crisis of multiculturalism).[50] In fact, Romero's zombies are characterized by a hybrid status, which perfectly exploits their human proximity (since they used to be us) but also their alterity (which evokes our most repressed inner Freudian Id, that is: the uncontrollable urge to eat in order to survive—tamed after millennia of Super-Ego's efforts to shame it as taboo behavior but, evidently, still inside us).

Post-Romeroesque Italian "Zombi" [sic]

Louis Paul maintains that "cinematic offspring like zombie films … and even rip-off genres that consisted of Italian versions of internationally financially successful films from other countries would virtually inhabit as many available screens worldwide that could contain them."[51] However, it took more than a decade after Romero's *Night of the Living Dead* for truly post–Romeroesque zombies to appear in Italian commercial cinema and then invade screens worldwide. In the meantime, Spaniards such as Armando De Ossorio[52] and Jorge Grau[53] brought the living dead to European screens, alternating the attempt to bring something different and more extreme to the table[54] with the wish to pay homage to Romero's masterpiece. For instance, in De Ossorio's second installment of the Templars' saga, there is a long scene in which the protagonists, hidden in a church to elude the creatures, have to decide if they want to use a car as a means to escape, which echoes the discussion in *Night* about filling the truck up with gas to leave the farm house.

In the mid–1970s, even when Italian productions conveyed depictions of the living dead that were finally breaking the master/slave archetype, they still avoided contemporary settings, as in the only film Aristide Massaccesi made using his real name (rather than the Joe D'Amato pseudonym): *La morte ha sorriso all'assassino* (*Death Smiles on the Murderer*). In this 1973 feature, which adds elements of the *giallo*[55] subgenre to the mix, the story unfolds in the early 1900s, and revolves around an undead woman, Greta, who has been brought back to life by her brother using an ancient Inca potion. As a zombie, Greta has several peculiarities, like the fact that she can talk and interact with other characters without been spotted as undead, given that she can decide to hide her skeleton-like face when needed.

Things changed dramatically toward the end of the decade, with zombies beginning to inhabit contemporary narratives soon after Romero's second zombie film, *Dawn*. As Stephen Thrower recalls:

> *Dawn of the Dead* had been bankrolled as an American/Italian co-production, with Romero's producer Richard Rubinstein forging a deal with Italian horror specialists Dario and Claudio Argento. *Dawn* hit Italian cinemas first, on 1 September 1978, but Rubenstein was unable to snare an American release until 20 April 1979, nearly eight months later. This was due to serious problems with the US ratings board, the MPAA, who indicated that there was no way *Dawn of the Dead* would secure an "R" certificate without massive cuts. As a result, Romero's film had difficulty securing a stateside distributor.[56]

In Italy, however, Romero's *Dawn of the Dead* was widely distributed in 1978 and proved extremely successful at the box office, earning more than 80 million lire in its first six-week run and paving the way for a 1979 that became "a revitalising year for Italian horror," with Lucio Fulci being "the director most responsible."[57] As Stephen Thrower reminds us:

> Flagrant imitation of American hit movies was a long-standing characteristic of Italian popular cinema, and yet it's wrong to paint the relationship as purely parasitical. The commercial impetus may have been to copy, but once the money was in place there was room for maverick creativity and imagination. What's more, detractors of the so-called "spaghetti horror" often neglect to mention that the process was one of cultural cross-pollination, a two-way street.[58]

Although Lucio Fulci's hit *Zombi 2* (*Zombie Flesh-Eaters*, 1979)[59] was misleadingly marketed by its Italian distributor as a sequel to Romero's *Dawn* (distributed in Italy and in France as *Zombi*), the film was actually informed by imagery other than Romero's. As Fulci himself states: "I wanted to recapture the moody atmosphere of witchcraft and paganism that must have been prevalent when Europeans first settled in the Caribbean during the 1700s. That's when the concept of zombies—human slaves brought back from the dead—first became popularly known to western civilization."[60] As the director admits in another interview, his main source of inspiration happened to be Jacques Tourneur's 1943 *I Walked with a Zombie*, rather than Romero's film, where zombies are "alienated creatures who live on the fringes of society," concluding that "*Dawn of the Dead* is a political movie, a great movie, but different from my *Zombi*."[61] If anything, the exotic setting of his film aligns him more with the cannibal sub-genre than with Romeroesque zombies.

Fulci's film also "drew upon older horror imagery (from Hammer's 1966 *Plague of the Zombies* and the Val Lewton horrors of the 1940s), pointing to the redundancy of any simple notion of an 'original.'"[62] Last but not least, Fulci's zombies—"far more revolting and putrescent than Romero's—exuded a foreboding reek of Death beyond the cerebral allegory of the American hit. Whether conceived as a 'rip-off' or not, the film turned out to have its own quite unique identity."[63] Moreover, to use Thrower's words:

> there is a distinction to be made between Fulci's approach to the gruesome and Romero's. In *Dawn of the Dead* the violence, however shocking, is remarkably clean, well-defined: and the ghouls are, almost without fail, nothing more than pasty-faced versions of their old living selves. This ironically feeds Romero's allegorical preoccupations. His zombies have to represent *something*, in the name of either political or (in the case of a zombified Hare Krishna devotee) frivolous irony. Too much decay and they would—horror of horrors!—become indistinguishable from each other. [...] Fulci's cadavers dispense with the conceits of allegory and perambulate around as Dead Things.[64]

After *Zombi 2*—besides Marino Girolami's already discussed awkward attempt to mesh the cannibal and zombie subgenres in *La regina dei Cannibali* (1980)—comes Umberto Lenzi's 1980 *Incubo sulla città contaminata* (*Nightmare City*), another groundbreaking Italian variation on post–Romeroesque zombies. A major figure in Italian exploitation films (with a couple of previously discussed seminal cannibal films under his belt), Lenzi revolutionizes the pace of the narrative and, more importantly, of the zombies. On the screen there are now hordes of running infected that pre-date by a couple of decades the fast zombies featured in Danny Boyle's *28 Days Later* (2002) and Juan Carlos Fresnadillo's *28 Weeks Later* (2007), but also in Zack Snyder's remake of *Dawn of the Dead* (2004), and Marc Forster's *World War Z* (2013), to name four of the most successful recent zombie films. Although Lenzi maintains that *Incubo sulla città contaminata* should not be added to the zombie subgenre, but rather labeled as a "radiation sickness movie"[65] with some kind of anti-military and anti-nuclear moral, the violence, strength and speed of the infected, along with the extraordinary special effects make this a hard-to-forget film in terms of Italian "zombie."[66] In fact, as Louis Paul puts it, the film's zombiefied masses that run "bearing with them axes, guns, pieces of wood, furniture and anything they can use to pry apart the human body"[67] are memorable. Lenzi's film is also a precursor of the 1990s fast-spreading-virus disaster films (such as Wolfgang Petersen's 1995 *Outbreak*) or mysterious disease ones (such as Todd Haynes' 1995 *Safe*), which have become popular in the new millennium as well, in the pandemic virus variation (like Steven Soderberg's oddly prophetic 2011 *Contagion*) as well as its allegorical zombie version (in the above-mentioned fast-running zombie films, but also in the series *The Walking Dead*).

Andrea Bianchi's 1981 *Le notti del terrore* (*Burial Ground: The Nights of Terror* aka *The Zombie Dead* aka *Zombi Horror*) was also characterized by a mild social commentary. Accidentally reanimated by a professor at an archeological site, a group of zombies attacks the rich and depraved guests of an old mansion in the Rome countryside. The close-up shots of the rotten corpses are masterfully alternated to the sex scenes that involve the guests and, more importantly, to the disturbing Oedipal scenes between a teenager and his mom, conveying a bland—but fascinating—critique on the decadence of the *bourgeoisie* (this film's signature shot shows the zombified son biting off his mother's nipple). Peter Dendle defined it "a high-impact, somber dirge that sustains tension mercilessly and wastes little time on plot and circumstance."[68] He also adds that, even though it may seem a cheap clone of *Zombi 2* (to the point of being marketed in some countries as *Zombi 3*), Bianchi's film actually improves some of Fulci's strong points,[69] such as zombies' intelligence and skills, which in this film seem to be heightened, since they are able to decapitate people with a scythe and to use axes to break through doors. Even more interesting is the fact they are smart and patient enough to pose as monks (hiding their rotten faces and hands) before feasting on one of the characters.

In terms of sexploitation, Joe D'Amato would repeat what he had done with respect to the cannibal subgenre, titillating spectators' inner desires with a few "sexy zombie" titles as well, such as *Le notti erotiche dei morti viventi* (*Erotic Nights of the Living Dead*, 1980)[70] and *Porno Holocaust* (1981), both using "non–Western locations as a 'primitive' backdrop to depict juxtapositions of explicit sex scenes with extreme acts of violence."[71] Besides the graphic images (in terms of both sex and violence), what emerges in these peculiar zombies films is also, in Xavier Mendik's words, "the director's repeated focus on a past act of illicit desire that provokes horror and violence within a present-tense setting," which lends itself "to the notion of 'the return of the repressed' that has been advanced by psychoanalytic interpretations of the creative work."[72] These films too are precursors of a trend that has become popular in the new millennium, with films such as Marcel Sarmiento and Gadi Harel's *Deadgirl* (2009), or comedies such as the New Zealander Peter Jackson's *Braindead* (1992), Andrew Currie's *Fido* (2007), or Jeff Baena's *Life After Beth* (2014), among others.

The golden period of Italian "zombi" films continues thanks, once again, to Lucio Fulci and his so-called "Gates of Hell" tryptic. The first installment of this unofficial trilogy, *Paura nella città dei morti viventi* (*City of The Living Dead* aka *The Gates of Hell*, 1980), eludes the (now) classic post–Romeroesque depiction of zombies, proposing a more supernatural kind of approach that, on the one hand pays homage to H.P.

Lovecraft's writings, and on the other is intertwined with the *giallo* subgenre (given the presence of *giallo*'s archetypical investigative reporter's figure). The film opens with a séance during which one of the participants has a vision of a priest's suicide. The medium leading the ritual warns everyone about the imminent arrival of an obscure evil force. Later the audience will discover that this suicide (which took place in the village of Dunwich)[73] had opened a gateway to hell through which the living dead will come into our world on All Saints' Day.

The second film of this ideal triptych is ...*E tu vivrai nel terrore! L'aldilà* (*The Beyond* aka *7 Doors of Death*, 1981), whose authentic Louisiana locations—and the haunted house/hotel trope—make the story more relatable to an American audience while, at the same time, evoking the already mentioned "moody atmosphere of witchcraft and paganism"[74] visible in *Zombi 2* and ultimately harking back to the African roots of zombie legends. Fulci's penchant for the supernatural here is mixed with the Southern superstitions pervading the narrative, creating a film in which zombies' presence is tied to black magic rituals but also to the Catholic concept of Hell. Arguably this director's masterpiece, *L'aldilà* mixes horror genres' imagery; in Dendle's words, "very ancient and badly damaged, the hotel zombies are corrupt in the extreme. They are more like ghosts than zombies in their nebulousness and caprice, appearing only when a character is alone, and retreating mysteriously after a single, conscientiously planned encounter."[75]

Quella villa accanto al cimitero (*House by The Cemetery* aka *Zombie Hell House*, 1981) concludes Fulci's unofficial zombie trilogy presenting the audience with a film that alternates gory details to atmosphere and mood and, more importantly, with even more mixing of horror tropes (from the haunted house to the mad doctor, from the creature in the basement to the living dead). Taking advantage of its New England's authentic locations, at first the film "feels uncomfortably like a barefaced Italian imitator of Kubrick's *The Shining*."[76] As John Kenneth Muir recalls: "To wit: a sensitive little boy is physically warned (in this case by a girl inhabiting a photograph) not to travel to a haunted house. However, he must go, because his family will be living there for six months (in *The Shining* it was for the winter). And, not unexpectedly, the house itself boasts a terrible history of tragedy, murder and death."[77] Later on, when the story unfolds, Fulci's inventiveness becomes more evident through a strategy of hybridization that renders this film rather unique. There are no hordes of zombies, but rather a Civil War doctor named Freudstein—a combination of Freud and Frankenstein, that needs no further comments. A "ghoulish murderer" who has managed "to prolong his own life with the creative use of corpses,"[78] like many monsters in postmodern horror films, Freudstein blurs boundaries by definition. He is obviously a living dead but, as his name suggests, a highly "educated" one, who can also avail himself of psychic powers, and seems to have found the secret of eternal life—but not eternal youth. In Ian Olney's description he is: "A tall, gaunt, weirdly insectoid zombie who, dressed in a surgeon's smock, murders unsuspecting victims in order to obtain their life-sustaining body parts, he challenges a number of the binary oppositions—animate/inanimate, human/non-human, life/death—upon which our understanding of the natural order is based. Moreover, he defies the clear-cut distinctions made in classical horror films between good and evil, normal and abnormal."[79]

In these three films, which arguably constitute the peak of the Italian zombie subgenre, it seems evident that, rather than merely using Romero's template, Fulci decided to hybridize it with a profoundly Italian imagery—arguably "forged from the rich, bloody iconography of Roman Catholicism"[80]—and crossbreed it with Pagan rituals and superstitions, and Gothic literary and cinematic influences alike. The result is at the same time decadent and sophisticated, rotten and defined, gory and classy—certainly less political, but more abstract and evocative than Romero's. In conclusion, to use Thrower's words, "For lovers of the grisly and macabre, 'Lucio Fulci' will always be a name to savour. […] his deliberately goading approach ('Violence *is* Italian art!') makes him an uncomfortable fit for mainstream acceptance."[81] Nonetheless, albeit becoming notorious for bloodshed, "he also achieved subtler effects. A melancholy lyricism in the face of mounting dread characterizes these marvelous Gothic horrors."[82]

Romero-esque Renaissance in the Third Millennium

Without lingering on the many other (less interesting) zombie depictions that inhabit Italian commercial cinema in the 1980s[83]—which contribute to bringing the subgenre close to total extinction at the end of the decade—and glossing over the feeble resurgence of the 1990s (characterized by numerous unrelated titles re-released as various *Zombi* sequels by T-Z Video for a quick cash grab),[84] the subgenre stays dormant until the new millennium. In our post–9/11 world, when terror becomes harder and harder to define and explain because enemies may come from within and are almost impossible to predict and contain, the living dead have become once again a "living" allegory of our times—a very effective one that favors the spreading of zombies (or zombie-like figures) on all possible screens and media surrounding us. Romero himself led the way by making three films post 9/11 that have even stronger (albeit perhaps less nuanced) socio-political messages.

More recently, in Italian culture, zombies have also become a means to depict and (possibly) analyze through a different lens one of the most relevant topics in contemporary Italian society, culture, and politics: the immigration phenomenon. A film that shares Romero's need to expose political and societal flaws is Luna Gualano's 2018 *Go Home—A casa loro*. In it, an inexplicable zombie outbreak spreads through a group of right-wing protesters in front of a suburban Roman reception center for undocumented migrants, after they attack and kick to death a young man, part of a neighborhood counter-protest. Enrico, the only neo-Fascist survivor, is forced to seek shelter in the center he wanted to dismantle among the very individuals he sought to expel from the country, while zombies outside keep banging on the center's doors and rage on. To stay alive, he must pretend to be one of the left-wing sympathizers and interact with some of the guests of the center: he shares a meal, plays soccer with a boy (Alì), gets defended from a zombie by a tall and muscular African man (Ibrahim), and stands watch to protect a bitten Italian man who volunteers at the center from other guests who would like to kill him. As the film progresses, he seems to begin to understand the value of human solidarity. However, the admittedly Romero-inspired film does not offer easy consolatory epiphanies aiming to prove that if people only got to know one another they would get along beyond racial, religious, and cultural differences. When the wounded Italian and a bitten Arab turn zombie and all hell breaks loose, Enrico manages to run around with Alì, protected by a mallet-swinging Ibrahim, who, steps from the exit, offers himself as bait to the horde of incoming zombies so that the other two can save themselves. Enrico, cowardly to the bitter end, throws Alì to the horde to escape. Once outside, with a smile on his face, his skull gets smashed from behind by a badly bitten (but not yet turned) Ibrahim, who thus avenges the boy's and his own imminent death.

Luna Gualano explains how she had hoped that the film would be obsolete by the time it was released, but proved still very relevant a year after starting the project. Welcomed by some comments on Facebook along the lines of "meglio zombie che negri" (better zombies than blacks) the film is a perfect metaphor of the kind of blind hatred toward the "other" that is still feeding Italian right-wing rhetoric. The center for migrants is both a home to defend, like in Romero's *Night*, and a large space like the shopping mall of *Dawn*, that attracts hatemongers as the mall attracted shoppers. Guests of the center fight among each other, as any group of survivors does in all of Romero's films, prompting the same question of whether this is the kind of humanity worth saving. Zombies here are both the metaphor of an Italian society full of ignorance, scared of whoever may look different, and of intolerance at all levels, as the quote from Henry Ward Beecher at the beginning of the film attests, "Nothing dies so hard, or rallies so often, as intolerance." Interestingly, the first zombie outbreak happens soon after Enrico picks up a stone and hits the young man who falls to the ground becoming an easy target for the murderous right-wing horde: violence cannibalizes all the living in the film and flesh eating becomes a means to achieve assimilation—both literal, through digestion, and symbolic, through the elimination of the Other. A brutal allegory of the current Italian cultural and political situation, this film seems to highlight how hard it has become nowadays to negotiate a space for diversity to exist and be, at least, tolerated—let alone be accepted.

Notes

1. This screening represented in fact a "piratesque" act (to echo Pasolini's words), given that the film was also among those presented at the Venice Film Festival—an institution created by the fascist regime in the 1930s that Pasolini's subversive and disrespectful behavior meant to criticize for being obsolete. In metaphorical terms, one might argue that the fact that Pasolini added a screening of his film to be held simultaneously to the one in Venice was also a "cannibalistic" (or "self-cannibalistic") act, meant to nullify the main screening of his film and his chances to win the Festival.

2. Viano, *A Certain Realism: Making Use of Pasolini's Film Theory and Practice*, 48.

3. Since the mid-1950s, the influential journal *Cahiers du Cinéma* started publishing essays by French film critics, who will later become directors, giving birth to the French New Wave movement. They proposed a new approach to films studies that focused on the role played by film directors. They distinguished between directors who were actually informing their works with their own *weltanschauung* and, as such, had actually acquired the status of *auteurs* of their films and those who were merely *metteurs en scène* (i.e., those who were just translating a screenplay onto the screen). By so doing, film critics and directors like, among others, François Truffaut (who used this terminology as early as 1954) and Alexandre Astruc (who contributed to the *auteur* theory with his *caméra-stylo*, i.e., camera-pen, notion), dramatically empowered film directors, giving them the same intellectual status of literary figures (the only difference was that film *auteurs* were using cameras, instead of pens).

4. Content-wise, Pasolini's films play like cinematic essays, especially for their heavily structured social analysis and critique. In terms of form—while he shares the rejection of classic montage and acting with various avant-garde's directors—unlike, for instance, French New Wave directors, he steers clear of film genres, presenting the spectators with films that are almost impossible to categorize (and are hence called Pasolinian). As a consequence, the uniqueness of his films is given by the unresolved dichotomy between the approach of a highly sophisticated intellectual who wanted to communicate with a larger audience using a popular means of expression in a way that, however, was (mostly) misunderstood by the same spectators he wanted to reach. Outraged by the popularity of some of his own films, he abjured them on more than one occasion, stating that they had been cannibalized by the film industry, and had become successful for the wrong reasons.

5. Moreover, the anthropophagic acts displayed by Pasolini often evoke a form of metaphorical cannibalism that permeates all of his following films and that constitutes his interpretation of what was happening to Italian society in the 1960s and '70s. In Pasolini's view, the mass culture spreading throughout Italian society since the 1960s, with its promotion of consumerist models of life, was a new and dangerous form of Fascism threatening to cannibalize all pre-industrial aspects of Italian culture (that is, archaic habits connected to agriculture, but also regional languages and peculiarities), homogenizing and, ultimately, metabolizing all differences in order to promote a new culture of fake tolerance for the sake of better "product placement." Speaking

of tolerance, Pasolini himself states: "I do not believe that nowadays' tolerance is real. It was decided from above: it is the tolerance of consumerist power, which needs an absolute formal flexibility in people's lives, for individuals to become good consumers. An unscrupulous, free society, in which couples and sexual needs (heterosexual ones) are multiplied, is accordingly avid for consumer goods." Pasolini, *Scritti corsari*, 259. My translation.

    6. In the mid-1970s, Italians changed their perception and fruition of the audiovisual product in general. Until that point the Italian film industry was the largest in Europe, with a higher number of spectators than the English, German, and French industries combined (according to Miccichè, "Introduction," in *Italian Cinema of the Eighties*, 9). However, in the middle of the decade the new wave of technological innovations opened the door to television channels that, for the first time, appeared as a valid alternative to the state channels' monopoly (see: Cianfarani, "Society, Market and Industry." In *Italian Cinema of the Eighties*, 13). The consequential increase in entertainment offerings, provided for free by these new private networks, inevitably induced a profound change in the habits of Italians, giving life to "one of the most significant social and industrial phenomena of recent years" and provoking "new patterns of social behavior" (*ibid.*). Moreover, in 1976 the Constitutional Court sanctioned the legitimacy of private local channels, freeing the airwaves and opening the door for access to various frequencies, disregarding the fact that, unlike other Western countries, Italy had never passed any type of legislation in this matter. The consequences of this decision would naturally be felt in the years to come, and if Sorlin declares that, in reality, "broadcasting deregulation extended to most developed countries in the 1980s," it should not be forgotten that Italy allowed for a real "far west" situation in the second half of the 1970s, in a general frame dominated by an absence of rules that favored a television development that was nowhere else "as rapid and unsupervised as in Italy" (Sorlin, *Italian National Cinema. 1896–1996*, 145). Hence, it is precisely during these years that the crisis of Italian cinema began, while "private broadcasters expanded to levels inconceivable in the other Western industrialized nations and decisively, although not single handedly, brought the recession to a head," to the point that "in just a few seasons what had been the second-largest film market in the West, preceded only by the United States market, was reduced by over two-thirds" (Miccichè, "Introduction," 9). However, the fact that the Italian film industry was entering a period of crisis does not imply that people were less interested in the film product. The most radical change, in fact, was happening on the level of fruition of films with the various private networks that were preparing to mount a process of cannibalization of the Italian film archive without precedent. Secondly, the film-product was about to be cannibalized by another technological innovation that would bring entertainment straight to Italian homes (and far from theaters): the Video Home System (VHS). It was the diffusion of the home video market that delivered the *coup de grâce* to the traditional model of cinematic fruition, initiating a decrease in theatergoers and profoundly changing the habits and tastes of spectators. Finally, scholars like Mary Wood believe that the fear of internal terrorism rising in the Italy of the 1970s (which had made spending time in central areas of Italian cities and towns a somewhat dangerous experience) contributed, along with the expansion of televisual offerings, to the transformation of cinema fruition "from a collective social experience to a domestic experience" (Wood, *Italian Cinema*, 23).

    7. This is akin to what happens today when viewers can choose among a plethora of TV channels and films streaming on internet entertainment services such as Netflix, Amazon, Hulu, etc., thus going to theaters mainly to see spectacular and adventure and sci-fi blockbusters.

    8. Quoted in Thrower, *Beyond Terror. The Films of Lucio Fulci*, 11.

    9. Block, "Filming *Night of the Living Dead*: An Interview with Director George Romero." In Williams, *George A: Romero: Interviews*, 10.

    10. Reeves Sanday, *Divine Hunger: Cannibalism as a Cultural System*, 214.

    11. Kilgour, *From Communion to Cannibalism: An Anatomy of Metaphors of Incorporation*, 194.

    12. *Ibid.*, 122.

    13. Guest, *Eating their Words. Cannibalism and the Boundaries of Cultural Identity*, 2.

    14. Kilgour, *From Communion*, 15.

    15. It must also be pointed out that, from a conceptual perspective, the cannibal's mindset may not be as exotic and peculiar as one may think. Keith Allan and Kate Burridge, for instance, highlight the presence of numerous (and common) micro acts of cannibalism in our daily lives, such as the practice of organ transplants, the use of human tissue (like placenta) in pharmaceuticals, and even the act of fingernail biting (Allan and Burridge, *Forbidden Words: Taboo and the Censoring of Language*, 188). In Alexandra Heller-Nicholas's view, "Hinging as it does on transubstantiation (where bread and wine are said to become the blood and body of Jesus Christ)," even "the Roman Catholic Eucharist has a long critical history of being compared to cannibalism" (Heller-Nicholas, "Cannibals and Other Impossible Bodies: *Il Profumo Della Signora in Nero* and the Giallo Film." *Scope: An Online Journal of Film and Television Studies*, 22).

    16. Xavier, *Subjectivity, the Unconscious and Consumerism*, 285.

    17. Harper, "Zombies, Malls, and the Consumerism Debate: George Romero's *Dawn of the Dead*," *Americana: The Journal of American Popular Culture*.

    18. *Ibid.*

    19. Romero, *Dawn of the Dead*, DVD.

    20. Harper, "Zombies, Malls, and the Consumerism Debate: George Romero's *Dawn of the Dead*," 82–83.

21. Also because one episode takes place in contemporary Germany (and can only be linked to Italian culture through the general discourse on Nazi-Fascism) and another one is set in a generic medieval past stripped of any possible Italian vestiges.

22. With the expression "economic miracle" (aka "economic boom") mass media, economists, and historians refer to a period in Italian history that lasted approximately two decades (from the early 1950s to the end of the 1960s), during which Italian economy changed from being based mainly on agriculture to rapidly becoming a key player in the industrial arena. This epochal change caused enormous alterations to Italian (and regional) culture(s), to the point that—in Pasolini's view—dialects and "peasant culture" (representing Italy's past) ended up being forgotten, if not totally obliterated in the process.

23. With this label, film historians refer to a triptych of films Pasolini directed in the early 1970s: *Il Decameron* (*The Decameron*, 1971), *I racconti di Canterbury* (*The Canterbury Tales*, 1971), and *Il fiore delle Mille e una notte* (*The Arabian Nights*, 1974). The literary sources on which these films were based were totally re-interpreted by Pasolini, to the extent that more than filmic "adaptations" these motion pictures are to be considered cinematic "re-creations." Finally, the term "trilogy of life" symbolizes the triumph of vitality that characterizes all three films, conveyed by Pasolini through the continuous showing of (often naked) bodies, and that has suggested film historian Millicent Marcus the coinage of the expression "writing with bodies" (Marcus, *Filmmaking by the Book. Italian Cinema and Literary Adaptation*, 136).

24. The display of anthropophagism in films transcends Italian cinema and is shared by American cinema and by the Latin American film movement called "Third Cinema," which often uses cannibalism as a metaphor to convey social and political commentaries. In Brazil, for instance, many films of the so-called "tropicalist" subgenre (which also emerged at the end of the 1960s) are modeled after the *Manifesto Antropofago* written by Oswald De Andrade (a cornerstone of 1920s Brazilian modernism). This movement and the filmmakers inspired by it in the late 1960s share—according to Glauber Rocha in "The Tricontinental Filmmaker: That Is Called the Dawn"—a very clear social and political agenda, given that both advocate "the creation of a genuine national culture through the consumption and critical re-elaboration of both national and foreign influences." In Johnson and Stam, *Brazilian Cinema*, 82. This way the indigenous culture is kept alive by literally devouring the cultural influences of the colonizer, so that rather than being overwhelmed, it ends up devouring "what is positive and useful according to its needs, and spits out the rest. In some cases, eating your oppressors becomes the ultimate assimilation of their power, an act of political and military revenge," as Totaro says in "Porcile," in Slater *Eaten Alive! Italian Cannibal and Zombie Movies*, 39. Consequently, one could argue that sometimes cannibalism is also a tribal (and alternative) form of consumerism, as Joaquim Pedro de Andrade confirms stating that cannibalism "is an exemplary mode of consumerism adopted by underdeveloped people," in "Cannibalism and Self-Cannibalism." In Johnson and Stam, *Brazilian Cinema*, 82.

25. In this regard, it must be noted a recent (and unequivocal) homage paid to this *Porcile*'s scene visible in "The Well," the second episode of season seven of *The Walking Dead*, where we can see (with another slippage) pigs eating "walkers," as zombies are called in this extremely successful television show.

26. Totaro, "Porcile," 41. Hence, "though not as inflammatory, one can see how *Pigsty*, with its scatological satire of the Nazis and the bourgeoisie, looks ahead to Pasolini's final film, the infamous *Salò*." Ibid., 41.

27. Pasolini's cinematic works after *Porcile*—namely, the already mentioned "trilogy of life" films and *Salò* (1975)—were metaphorically cannibalized by commercial cinema. The "trilogy" unintentionally spawned a subgenre named "decamerotic," which only focuses on the exploitation of those same naked bodies of the past that Pasolini wanted to celebrate (forcing him to write a public "abjure" his trilogy). *Salò* in particular, although being considered by many critics the most "unconsumable film" ever made (to echo the *auteur*'s words), ends up being cannibalized by commercial cinema, involuntarily inspiring the "Nazisploitation" subgenre, which waters down Pasolini's criticism towards totalitarian regimes and just shows gratuitous torture acts on a generic Nazi-Fascist background (often even in concentration camps). In the ultimate effort to defeat commercial cinema's attempt to taint and consume his "pure" representations of bodies of the past—generating countless exploitation films that he considered nothing more than consumerist excrements—in *Salò* Pasolini brings said excrements directly on the screen (breaking many other visual taboos along the way). Unfortunately, this final and desperate effort to make a cinematic product the Italian film industry system could not cannibalize, digest, and defecate was destined to fail as well.

28. It must be pointed out that while many animal killings were introduced as such into the films' narrative, many others were edited into presumed cannibalistic scenes, so as to trick the audience into believing that the flesh natives were eating was actually human. In this context, one cannot avoid remembering how a similar thing happened (also for budgetary reasons) in Romero's *Night of the Living Dead*.

29. Bernard, "'The Only Monsters Here Are the Filmmakers': Animal Cruelty and Death in Italian Cannibal Films." In Paul, *Italian Horror Cinema*, 193.

30. Slater, "The Cannibal/The Zombie." In *Eaten Alive! Italian Cannibal and Zombie Movies*, 12.

31. Such as *Mondo cane* (*A Dog's Life*, 1962), *Mondo cane n. 2* (*Mondo Insanity*, 1963), and *Africa addio* (*Africa: Blood and Guts*, 1966).

32. Bernard, "The Only Monsters," 193.

33. Hughes, *Cinema Italiano: The Complete Guide from Classics to Cult*, 289.

34. Curti and La Selva, *Sex and Violence. Percorsi nel cinema estremo*, 290. My translation.

35. Bernard, "The Only Monsters," 193.

36. Shipka, *Perverse Titillation: The Exploitation Cinema of Italy, Spain and France, 1960–1980*, 124.

37. It must be noted that, since the 1950s, Italian directors have often disguised themselves under pseudo-Anglicized names, hoping to market their films more easily to international audiences (a case in point is Spaghetti western's father Sergio Leone who, before achieving worldwide success, used to go by the name of Bob Robertson).

38. Paul, *Italian Horror Film Directors*, 149.

39. Which was perhaps given by Deodato's claim that it was shot "using real flesh and blood cannibals." Cited in Paul, *Italian Horror Film Directors*, 111.

40. *Ibid.*

41. Slater, "Cannibal Holocaust—Review by Jay Slater." In Slater, *Eaten Alive! Italian Cannibal and Zombie Movies*, 109. However, it must be noted that in *Olocausto cannibale* images are freed from the weight of the mondo genre's typical voice-over and often seem to evoke the ghost of Pasolini's *Salò*, especially when they emphasize certain voyeuristic aspects inherent to the seventh art (in this respect, one might compare the vision of the documentary made by the group of explorers of the film within the film, with *Salò*'s torture scenes, presented to the audience through a set of binoculars). Deodato's film is entirely played on the thin line between fiction and (a supposed) reality, between the documentary on various indigenous tribes made by the protagonists of the film within the film, and the subsequent revelation that they used to manipulate all these scenes. Actually, the protagonists of the film within the film go even further, entering the space of the documentary only to weaken even more its authenticity by pretending to be outraged by the incredible violence of the natives.

42. Slater, "The Cannibal/The Zombie," 14–15.

43. Kaufman, "Cannibal Holocaust—Review by Lloyd Kaufman." In Slater, *Eaten Alive! Italian Cannibal and Zombie Movies*, 105.

44. Among the numerous Italian directors who dabbled with the cannibal subgenre, it is worth mentioning the work of those who tried to hybridize it with other subgenres. This path has been followed, for instance, by Sergio Martino, who highlights the voyeuristic aspects of both mondo and cannibal films, offering the audience a remarkable sexploitation film that takes advantage of the iconic body of former Bond-girl Ursula Andress, in his *La montagna del dio cannibale* (*Slave of the Cannibal God*, 1978). It was however Joe D'Amato (*né* Aristide Massaccesi), who pushed the envelope in terms of what can be shown to the audience even further, directing films like *Emanuelle e gli Ultimi Cannibali* (*Emanuelle and the Last Cannibals*, 1977), *Papaya dei Caraibi* (*Papaya, Love Goddess of the Cannibals*, 1978) and *Orgasmo nero* (*Black Orgasm* aka *Voodoo Baby*, 1980), which all mix cannibalism and sexploitation, foreshadowing his later career as a porn film director. The blend with mondo movies, on the other hand, continues until the very last epigones of the subgenre: Michele Massimo Tarantini's 1985 *Nudo e selvaggio* (*Massacre in Dinosaur Valley* aka *Cannibal Ferox 2* in the UK), and Antonio Climati's 1988 *Natura contro* (*The Green Inferno*); while in *Schiave bianche. Violenza in Amazzonia* (*White Slave*, aka *Cannibal Holocaust 2: The Catherine Miles Story*)—co-directed by Mario Gariazzo and Franco Prosperi in 1984; in *Italian Horror*, Louis Paul observes: "the waning Italian mondo and cannibal film genres [...] are turned into a *giallo* thriller" (280). The cannibal subgenre is also hybridized with the war film genre in Anthony M. Dawson's (*né* Antonio Margheriti) 1980 *Apocalypse domani* (*Cannibal Apocalypse* aka *Invasion of the Flesh Hunters*), which opens with a flashback to the Vietnam War, and later displays soldiers who, once infected, "use weapons as a means to rip their victims apart, making it easier to tear the flesh and organs from their bodies" (*Ibid.* 167). Even Ruggero Deodato contributes to subgenres' crossbreeding with his 1985 *Inferno in diretta* (*Cut and Run*), by mixing elements of the thriller with the exploits of an unlikely cannibal army controlled by a corrupt Colonel.

45. Slater, "The Cannibal/The Zombie," 17.

46. Even in Italian cinema, pre-Romeroesque depictions of zombies merely repeat the master/slave dynamic. A case in point is a film directed in 1964 by Giuseppe Vari: *Roma contro Roma* (*Rome Against Rome*, aka *War of the Zombies*), which hybridizes the horror and "sword and sandal" genres but ultimately, in terms of representation of the living dead, relies once again on the master/slave archetype. Hence, this story of a corrupt Roman politician who (helped by a wizard) resurrects an entire Roman legion to take the Empire is nothing more than a "colorful but minor contribution to both the horror film genre and the heroic adventure sagas from which its origins sprung" (Paul, *Italian Horror*, 18), in spite of John Drew Barrymore's presence in the leading role. More interesting, at least for its Gothic atmosphere, is Massimo Pupillo's 1965 *Cinque Tombe per un medium* (*Cemetery of the Living Dead* aka *Terror-Creatures from the Grave*). However, this film's living dead, victims of an ancient plague summoned by the villain, are nothing more than a complement to the main narrative, centering around the performance of horror genre's icon Barbara Steele. Nonetheless, in Roberto Curti's words, this was "perhaps one of the most popular Italian horror films of the decade abroad" (Curti, *Italian Gothic Horror Films, 1957–1969*, 150). Finally, it is also worth mentioning the first filmic adaptation of the Richard Matheson book *I Am Legend*, a 1964 American-Italian co-production titled *The Last Man on Earth*, co-directed by Ubaldo Ragona and Sidney Salkow, starring horror icon Vincent Price. In fact, although the creatures present in the narrative are more similar to vampires than zombies, in the film they are definitely zombie-like in the way they walk (whereas in the novella they move at regular human speed) and,

as a cinematic trope, they anticipate and foreshadow Romero's living dead. Another interesting example of a creature sharing both vampires' and zombies' characteristics is the "jiangshi," popular in Chinese folklore and protagonist of the famous *Mr. Vampire* franchise, which consisted of a total of five motion pictures, all directed by Ricky Lau between 1985 and 1992 and which contributed to the success of the so-called jiangshi subgenre, very popular in Hong Kong during the 1980s.

47. Slater, "The Cannibal/The Zombie," 17.
48. *Ibid.*
49. *Ibid.*
50. See Giuliani, *Zombie, alieni e mutanti. Le paure dall'11 settembre a oggi.*
51. Paul. *Italian Horror*, 33.
52. De Ossorio began his saga about Knights Templar coming back from the dead as revenants in 1972 with *La noche del terror ciego* (*Tombs of the Blind Dead* aka *The Blind Dead*), followed by three official sequels: *El ataque de los muertos sin ojos* (*The Return of the Evil Dead* aka *Return of the Blind Dead*, 1973), *El buque maldito* (*The Ghost Galleon* aka *The Blind Dead 3*, 1974), and *La noche de las gaviotas* (*Night of the Seagulls* aka *The Blind Dead 4*, 1975).
53. In 1974 Grau directed a hybrid blend between the Sci-Fi genre and the zombie subgenre titled *No profanar el sueño de los muertos* (*Let Sleeping Corpses Lie* aka *The Living Dead at Manchester Morgue* aka *Don't Open the Window*), which has been recognized as "the most effective and disturbing Spanish film of the period" (Kay, *Zombie Movies. The Ultimate Guide*, 83–84).
54. Exemplified by Grau's attention to gory details, especially in a cult scene, unfortunately, not present in any remaining print of the film, in which a zombie eats an eyeball.
55. The so-called *giallo* film subgenre is an Italian hybridization of the thriller and horror genres, informed by detective, psychological, and at times even supernatural elements, mixed with sexploitation and a strong slasher component as well. The use of the Italian adjective "giallo" (yellow, in English) to label this peculiar mix however has a literary origin, given that it was the most common color of mystery novels' covers in Italy since 1929 (when the Mondadori publishing company decided to launch a new line of books with this kind of cover to promote detective and mystery stories).
56. Thrower, *Beyond Terror*, 15.
57. *Ibid.*
58. *Ibid.*
59. Fulci's film actually earned modestly at the national box office but made more than 30 million dollars worldwide, opening the door to an epic wave of Italian "zombi."
60. Fulci, interviewed by Jim Winorsky in *Fangoria* #8, October 1980—cited in Thrower, *Beyond Terror*, 19.
61. Know, *Reel Terror. The Scary, Bloody, Gory, Hundred-Year History of Classic Horror Films*, 239.
62. Thrower, *Beyond Terror*, 15.
63. *Ibid.*
64. Thrower, *Beyond Terror*, 32.
65. Kay, *Zombie Movies*, 111.
66. In fact, regardless of Lenzi's claim, this film was marketed, at least in Greece, as *Zombi 3: Efialtis stin poli*, even though its plot has nothing to do with neither Romero's nor Fulci's films.
67. Paul, *Italian Horror*, 148.
68. Dendle, *The Zombie Movie Encyclopedia*, 29.
69. *Ibid.*
70. According to Dendle, here D'Amato "seems to confuse 'eroticism' with abundant sex, and besides that, the entire concept of combining scenes of lovemaking with a zombie massacre presupposes a strange sort of mood to begin with." *Ibid.*, 64.
71. Mendik, "Body in a Bed, Body Growing Dead: Uncanny Women in Joe D'Amato's Italian Exploitation Cinema." In *Cinema Inferno: Celluloid Explosions from the Cultural Margins*, 124.
72. *Ibid.*
73. Dunwich was also the setting of H. P. Lovecraft's 1929 eponymous novella *The Dunwich Horror*.
74. Thrower, *Beyond Terror*, 19.
75. Dendle, *The Zombie*, 23. In the continuation of his analysis, Dendle adds that "In one memorable, scene these zombies assume an unparallel, sinister dignity when they surround blind Emily (Keller), staring at her while she screams for mercy—not advancing or attacking, just staring." *Ibid.*
76. Muir, *Horror Films of the 1980s*, 251.
77. *Ibid.*
78. *Ibid.*, 252.
79. Olney, *Euro Horror. Classic European Horror Cinema in Contemporary American Culture*, 53.
80. Slater, *Eaten Alive! Italian Cannibal and Zombie Movies*, 17.
81. Thrower, *Beyond Terror*, 11.
82. *Ibid.*, 12.
83. Including, but not limited to, films like *Zombi 3*—which epitomized the unfortunate return of Lucio Fulci to the zombie world (an effort co-directed with Claudio Fragasso in 1988)—and Claudio Fragasso's *Oltre*

la morte (*Zombie 4: After Death*, 1988), but also Claudio Lattanzi's *Uccelli assassini* (*Zombie 5: Killing Birds* aka *Killing Birds—Raptors*, 1987).

84. This is the case of films like *Zombie 3: Return of the Zombies* (a 1973 Spanish production originally titled *La orgía de los muertos*, aka *The Hanging Woman*—directed by José Luis Merino); *Zombie 4: A Virgin Among the Living Dead* (a 1973 French production originally titled *La nuit des étoiles filantes* aka *Christina, princesse de l'érotisme*—directed by Jesús Franco); *Zombie 5: Revenge in the House of Usher* (directed in 1983 by Jesús Franco); *Zombie 6: Monster Hunter* (a 1981 Italian film by Joe D'Amato originally titled *Rosso sangue* aka *Absurd* aka *Antropophagus 2*—being a pseudo-sequel to D'Amato's own *Antropophagus*); and *Zombie 7* (which is, in fact, none other than Joe D'Amato's 1980 *Antropophagus* aka *The Grim Reaper*).

From Fiddler's Green to Juiced Up Islands

The State of the State in Romero's Zombie Narratives

BRUCE PEABODY

The public watching George Romero's zombie films instinctively senses what critics and scholars have long insisted and what the director himself has freely conceded: his work is openly political.[1] As Michael Ryan and Douglas Kellner note, Romero is part of a "leftist use of the monster motif" which draws "attention to particularly monstrous aspects of normal society" and criticizes "conservative values and institutions from the police to the patriarchal family to white supremacism" rather than reinforcing the status quo.[2] In the same vein, R. Colin Tait argues that zombie movies in general have always been a "staging ground for political issues" and that *Night of the Living Dead* (1968) in particular "has long been considered one of the most overtly political films of its era."[3] The zombie scholarship that has flowered over the past two decades has thoroughly explored the politics embedded in Romero's portrayal of gender, race, and class, as well as the director's persistent but shifting interest in topical controversies, from the generational and cultural strife of the 1960s to the dangers posed by new media to our personal autonomy and relationships.[4]

But for all its creativity and fecundity, the increasingly crowded field of zombie studies has something of a blind spot in its scholarship on Romero's politics. Relatively few works systematically examine the director's expressed attitudes towards the state—that is, towards different forms of governance and organized political rule.[5] This essay attempts to address this deficiency by studying the configuration and significance of Romero's various "zombie states."

Readers might regard this project with skepticism for several reasons. First, one could argue that the rise of the living dead, at least on the mostly uncontrollable scale that follows *Night*, seems antithetical to the operation of the state. Wherever it occurs, the mass ascendance of the dead implicates government failure. As Kim Paffenroth tells us in *The Undead and Theology*, "the outcome in almost all zombie fiction and films is an apocalypse, an end of the world as we know it: an end of 'civilized' life and the ushering in of an indeterminately long age of barbarism, terror, and violence."[6] Vampires, ghosts, and werewolves can coexist alongside human communities, but the zombie apocalypse ushers in a dramatic landscape inhospitable to traditional governance. In the context of a world beset with reanimated corpses, and perpetual threats to Romero's protagonists (from the dead as well as the living), focusing on the director's implicit commentary on the various forms government might assume may seem like a rather narrow or abstruse interpretive stance; it's a bit like studying the architecture of the farmhouse in *Night,* rather than the roiling interpersonal dynamics within.

But while the outbreak of zombies connotes dysfunction in all sorts of human institutions, their persistence inevitably calls for organized political responses, even if these assume somewhat different forms. Max Brooks's *World War Z* is a sustained examination of how the spread of "zack" hordes is ultimately contained with new (and ancient) institutions and ideas about politics.[7] Less overtly, George Romero is also interested in the contributions, misdeeds, and omissions of the state and its officials. Indeed, over the course of his six zombie films, Romero outlines a range of different government arrangements and imagined political communities. These appear as weakened, reborn, and distorted institutions familiar to us (the federal government, police, National Guard) as well as through more evolved and even utopian forms. Engaging in a survey of these political associations is useful not only for tracing the long reach of the Romero's influence (since countless other works replicate and play with his varied depictions of the state), but also for thinking about his distinctive contributions to how we conceive of the limits, and necessity, of political institutions in the twenty-first century. And in the director's more speculative moments, we can catch hints of new and emancipatory forms of political organization he seems to admire.

All this said, there is a second reason students of Romero might give scant attention to the state. The official institutions of government appear to be somewhat outside the director's central thematic interests, particularly his emphasis on diffuse and sometimes uncoordinated social sources of injustice.[8] As Steven Shaviro notes, Romero seeks to uncover "the *hidden* structures of our society in the course of charting the progress of its disintegration."[9] This draws his gaze away from the formal instruments of political and legal authority to more diffuse sites of power and conflict: media control rooms, traditional (and often patriarchal) relationships, longstanding historical antagonisms, and economic inequality.[10] According to Kim Newman, in the *Dead* films, "American society is cast in the role usually given to an individually hatable character"; the villain is not government *per se* or even its agents.[11] Thus, Romero's thoroughly studied portrayal of "consumerism gone mad"[12] in *Dawn of the Dead* (1978) is not the direct result of government choices or commands, but an extension of our "commodified identity" and an expression of his protagonists' bourgeois dreams from their pre-zombie lives. More specifically, Romero seems more concerned with what political theorist Iris Marion Young (among many others) has identified as "structural injustices" which emerge

> when social processes put large groups of persons under systematic threat of domination or deprivation of the means to develop and exercise their capacities, at the same time that these processes enable others to dominate or to have a wide range of opportunities for developing and exercising [their] capacities.... Structural injustice is a kind of moral wrong distinct from the wrongful action of an individual agent or the repressive policies of a state.[13]

Fran's refusal to be turned into a subordinate "den mother" (in *Dawn*), the casual racism of Steel and Rhodes in *Day of the Dead* (1985), and Big Daddy's status as a member of the proletariat (with a sparking class consciousness) in *Land of the Dead* (2005) all support this interpretation, and underscore the zombie director's absorption with broader, systemic political questions rather than with the missteps and misdeeds of government specifically.

But conceding this point does not undermine this essay's rationale. After all, Romero himself indicated that his broad social criticism does not preclude targeting the state: "if I can take a jab at the media or the church or the government, I can't let it go by."[14] Moreover, while governments are not the sole creators of the structural injustices referenced by Young (and omnipresent in the movies of Romero), the state can obviously contribute to the development and perpetuation of these inequities. Thus, the ascriptive beliefs about race and gender expressed by characters in *Day* can be traced to prevailing attitudes in pre-zombie society, but, significantly, they are uttered by members of the military, a government institution with a checkered history of promoting equality. Similarly while misinformation about the dead is spread by many sources in Romero's films (including, notably, a media that is presented as somewhat reckless), national and local governments contribute as well. In sum, while not insisting that government is the single or even primary source for our social ills, Romero signals that it is definitely part of the problem.

Finally, we might note that the director's examination of wider structural social problems is closely informed by his understanding of the state insofar as his portrayal of the collapse of government and the proliferation of human suffering creates a critical position for rethinking our interpersonal relations, ranking of substantive values, and for imagining wholly new societies. In Romero's films (and in many of the creative works he has inspired) our attention is directed "less on containing the zombie apocalypse [than] understanding the new complexities emerging from a zombie aftermath in which bare life and community economies must be redefined."[15]

After the (Zombie) Flood: Four Forms of Political Community

As indicated, the standard zombie narrative presumes the weakness or deficiency of the state.[16] Presumptively good governments maintain law and order, limit unauthorized violence, and check the spread of contagions. The rise of the undead marks spectacular political failure along all of these dimensions. In the film *28 Days Later*, when an incredulous Jim insists that "There's always a government. They're in a bunker or a plane,"[17] he is bluntly informed "there's no government. No police. No Army."[18] The pressure and urgency of dealing with throngs of the dead are so immediate that longer term worries, such as facilitating state action or (re)forming government, are set aside. As Brooks explains, "When the living dead triumph, the world degenerates into utter chaos" and political organizations and personnel are either destroyed or exiled.[19]

But while the menace of the dead is ubiquitous in Romero's films, their presence does not extinguish all claims to leadership (legitimate or otherwise), the prospect of continued community, or the need for justice.[20] Indeed, with few exceptions, the moments of greatest peril for Romero's protagonists are brought on by careless, selfish, or iniquitous humans rather than zombies acting on their own.[21] The imperative of politics, as an endeavor fundamentally about regulating conflict between persons, is never far at bay. Romero is never willing to surrender his stories entirely to the dead, to entropy, and the total cratering of human capacity and achievement—what the political philosopher Thomas Hobbes memorably described as a "war of every man, against every man" in which there is no culture or "Society ... [but only] continual fear, and danger of violent death."[22] Romero does not offer up a "nihilistic vision of hopelessness," but instead presents us with survivors who have demonstrated both the attributes (planning, recourse to reason, courage, moral judgment, compassion) that make self-rule possible and the shortcomings (jealousy, self-interest, misjudgment, prejudice) that make government necessary.[23]

Ultimately over the six *Dead* films, Romero teases out four different forms of political community that emerge in the midst and aftermath of the zombie apocalypse. First, at various points, the director portrays manifestations of the old (weakened and even repudiated) political and governing order (what we might call "broken states"). Second, Romero introduces new and incomplete forms of rule, often representing exaggerations or distortions of specific political values or principles ("semi-states"). Third, the director gives us morally or functionally "false states" such as the dystopian Fiddler's Green. Fourth and finally, Romero gestures to a series of purported or imagined utopias ("dream states"). These idyllic visions are fragile and somewhat unformed, but they offer the promise, albeit fleeting, of a more complete and enduring form of governance or self-rule.

Identifying and describing the contours of these four rough forms of political community helps us better understand Romero's political architecture and the ideals he champions. Over the course of his films, the director confronts the omnipresent horror of the dead without embracing a conservative yearning for the previous social and political order, a liberal extension of state power, or a survivalist libertarianism. This essay's survey of the state of the state in Romero's zombie films reveals an iconoclastic critical perspective that targets ideology more than politics, while pointing to both important features of governance and civic life and intractable problems.

Broken States: The Old Order in Disarray and Retreat

Starting with *Night,* according to Gregory Waller, Romero "offers a thoroughgoing critique of American institutions and values" by revealing "flaws inherent in the media, local and federal government agencies, and the entire mechanism of civil defense."[24] At a minimum, the abundance of lethal (and rapidly reproducing) zombies is antithetical to sociologist Max Weber's famous contention that states are distinguished by their ability to exercise "a monopoly of the legitimate use of violence."[25] Furthermore, in apparent repudiation of Weber's account, a substantial proportion of the violence Romero depicts involves private citizens engaged in (sometimes mistaken) self-defense or aggression. In this way, each onscreen impaling, gunshot, and explosion (not to mention the director's countless more creative forms of zombie destruction) signals the retreat and failure of the traditional state.[26] In both *Night* and *Dawn*, official law enforcement agents work alongside private "volunteers" and "rednecks"—who do most of the actual zombie killing.

In addition to this implied condemnation by absentia, Romero's films offer more direct criticism of the old, familiar (and weakened) state. The U.S. government and its agents (especially the military and law enforcement) are late to arrive to crises and uncertain how to proceed once they do appear. As the broadcaster in *Night* intones, in the face of the dead, the "reaction of law enforcement officials is one of complete bewilderment."[27] Throughout the *Dead* series, citizens get information about the zombie outbreak, and how to respond, from newscasters or private citizens rather than government agents. As *Night* unfolds, Romero tells us that "the president has called a meeting of his cabinet to deal with the sudden epidemic of murder which has seized the eastern third of this nation."[28] But we are later informed that since "convening, this conference ... [the government] has not produced any public information."[29] *Diary of the Dead* (2007) extends this theme of a feckless, out of touch, and ineffective Washington by bringing us a press report that the "president continues to monitor the situation from his ranch and ... he asked the American people to remain vigilant."[30]

Even when the traditional state makes a more tangible appearance it is usually depicted as weak or unequal to the crushing challenges posed by the zombie apocalypse. As Crocket puts it in *Survival of the Dead* (2009), the National Guard "added more than our fair share to the body counts, but it didn't do any good."[31] In *Day*, Rhodes's insistence that "there have to be survivors in Washington"[32] is met with derision, reflecting doubts about the national government's competence and, perhaps, its very existence. In still other portrayals, the state's shortfall is irrelevance more than weakness: it is simply focused on the wrong things and unable to handle crisis triage. Again in *Day*, John laments the government's failure to avert past and present "disasters" and instead focusing on bureaucratic data collection and storage of business and tax records, defense department budgets, and immigration and census reports.[33]

Even more condemning, Romero's films contain a number of examples of official and traditional government policies that are wrong-headed and dangerous. As the horrific events in *Night* unfold, reporters speculate that the government itself may be responsible for the rise of the flesh-eaters. Perhaps the dead are mutants, reanimating because of contamination triggered by a Venus satellite explorer which "was purposely destroyed by NASA, when scientists discovered it was carrying a mysterious, high-level radiation with it."[34] Similarly, *Dawn* opens with a chaotic Philadelphia TV station broadcasting inaccurate government reports about supposed "rescue stations" that have actually been infested with the living dead. As Francine, Stephen, Roger, and Peter make plans to escape, they are accosted by police who accuse them of theft and threaten them with violence, even as these officials also seem to be abandoning their duties. Later, the OEP (presumably the Office of Emergency Preparedness) announces "by command of the federal government" that citizens must leave their homes "no matter how safely protected ... or well stocked"[35] to move into central locations—once again jeopardizing public safety, this time by creating what amounts to a convenient buffet for the dead. And, of course, in *Night,* the auxiliary presence of police cruisers, uniformed deputies, a presiding sheriff (who issues the deadly command), and attack dogs, gives an official imprimatur to the murder of Ben, even if it is nominally at the hands of a volunteer. Here, as in so many moments in Romero's body of work, the director offers a series of nested and overlapping critiques: the posse's killing of Ben is not only immoral and shocking on its own, but raises doubts about its ability to discriminate friend and foe. And, of course, the manner and nature of the killing is evocative, pointing "to the way U.S. soldiers were operating at the same time in Vietnam (they use helicopters and call their work a 'search and destroy' operation)."[36]

Government ignorance spills over into active malfeasance in *Diary*. The film opens with breathless news coverage of a man who shoots his zombie-infected child and wife (who subsequently reanimate). A local chief of police later dismisses the incident as merely an attack carried out by illegal immigrants in which the two attackers were "mistakenly pronounced dead"[37] before they rose from their gurneys. Debra notes that film clips of the episode have been "re-cut" and distorted. "The media were lying to us, or the government was lying to them. They were trying to make it seem like everything was gonna be all right."[38] Even when officials with the Department of Homeland Security concede that something is amiss, raising the national security threat level to orange, they still downplay the rise of the dead as mass psychosis triggered by an emergent virus.

Romero's sustained representation of failed and flawed government action reflects longstanding skepticism in the public about our leaders, institutions, and their capacity to govern.[39] Interestingly, these attitudes of political mistrust began to take a stronger hold in the late 1960s, in the same period when Romero first (re)launched the zombie cinematic franchise.[40] As Romero himself notes, his inspiration for *Day* drew from a perceived disintegration "of values of trust"[41] in a variety of institutions including the government.

Romero's Semi-States: New Forms of Authority and Tyranny

In addition to giving us numerous examples of how traditional political institutions are weak, inactive, and even deceptive, Romero's films also gesture to alternate forms of governance, made possible by the incursion of the dead and the retreat of the customary state. In the face of these developments, surviving humans band together and attempt to fulfill or shift traditional operations or functions of government.

Not surprisingly, many of these renderings are dark. *Day* gives us two fledgling semi-states, each of which are unstable and morally flawed. At the film's outset, we are introduced to an uneasy scientific-military partnership hidden within the subterranean Seminole Storage Facility. While the precise terms of this "operation" are unclear, it is part of a "rushed" plan in which military officers were ordered to protect researchers studying the physiology of the undead. While launched by "Washington," this desperate project is now self-contained and independent. The operation has a limited geographic authority and mission (to teach the zombies how to "behave"), but also a hierarchy with at least ostensible civilian control (the military figures including Captain Rhodes have been instructed "to facilitate the job of [the] scientific team"[42]).

In short order, however, this first version of a pseudo or semi-state gives way to another. After several of his soldiers die at the hands of captive zombies, Rhodes loses his patience with Dr. Logan's experimentation and promise of research "progress." Rhodes promptly redefines their mission as one of "war" rather than inquiry, and introduces his own autocratic form of rule. As he announces, in the future "nothin' happens around here without my knowin' about it! And anybody fucks with my command, they get court-martialed, they get executed."[43] Rhodes's reference to "command" and court-martial suggests he still wants at least the veneer of established military structures, while also seeking to erase any gap between his personal wishes and official commands. Moreover, his new "military operation" is aggressively anti-democratic, placing civilians at the command (and disposal) of the armed forces, rather than the reverse. Instead of being driven by scientific inquiry and a specific civic mission, Rhodes merely announces that "we're gonna get the hell out of here and leave you [Dr. Logan] and your highfalutin asshole friends"[44] behind. The (short-lived) new order is opposed to deliberation (Rhodes tells Sarah to "shut up and sit down" and promises execution if she persists in challenging

In *Day of the Dead* (United Film Distribution Company, 1985) Rhodes (Joseph Pilato) quickly wrests decision-making authority from a group of scientists and researchers.

his rule), evidence-based decision making, and to civilian control itself. More broadly, we can associate it with "unchecked militarism" and authoritarianism, combining its keystone ideological elements of "personalized" rule, dividing the world into "us vs. them" components (and vilifying outgroups), projecting strength (especially through violence), and emphasizing the breakdown of order.[45] Rhodes enacts or threatens harsh, disproportionate violence, demands unquestioning obedience, warns about incipient chaos, and marks himself and his soldiers as being opposed to others: zombies, scientists, Sarah (as the lone woman), and racial minorities.[46]

Both the scientific and military semi-states in *Day* are doomed because they lack legitimacy (even amongst supposedly loyal followers). The initial civilian-scientific mission unravels because Rhodes cannot see its payoff (and, on the contrary, laments the loss of five men in the course of protecting the researchers), and his subsequent authoritarian order lacks a reliable hierarchy and mission. When Rhodes orders Steel to shoot Sarah, the Private merely points a mocking finger at her. In the end, both operations fail to fulfill their ostensible purposes. Logan's research endeavors do not enable him to control Bub (never mind the other zombies) and Rhodes fails to provide order, losing his grip on Weber's proverbial monopoly of violence, even within the modest confines of the underground bunker.

Beyond *Day*, Romero's primary references to semi-states involve military and para-military organizations. In particular, he frequently introduces the National Guard, at first as an extension of the traditional state and then as a seemingly freestanding and even criminal enterprise.[47] By *Diary*, the Guard appears as a group of roadside bandits, robbing Jason, Debra and their friends and leaving them with nothing but weaponry. Here, what is arguably the state's defining trait—providing security—is inverted and perverted. The Guard endangers the group (stealing their food and supplies) while leaving them armed, so these private citizens can assume the signature governmental function of defense. As one of the victims of this robbery cynically notes, "They're not murderers, just thieves."[48]

The rogue National Guardsman persist as a self-contained and self-directing association in *Survival*. While their power, authority, and functions hardly replicate the kinds of services and form of rule we would expect from a stable and organized state, they demonstrate group loyalty, solidarity, and effective coordinated behavior including self-defense (against zombies as well as human hunters) and the capacity to requisition a ferry and armored truck. Although basically limited to the goal of group survival, by the film's end the collective remains relatively intact (certainly in comparison to the self-destructive O'Flynn and Muldoon clans), well resourced (they retain firearms and possession of the armored car that includes a cache of a million dollars), and capable of collective decision making (the cohort consciously chooses to quit Plum Island, despite its allure).[49]

False States: Dystopias and Shadow Orders

If any single plot thread ties Romero's six zombie films together, it may be the elusive search for a safe space, whether a secluded house, a shopping mall, an underground bunker, a self-contained luxury high-rise, an armored vehicle, or even a clunky Winnebago.[50] This idea is rendered explicitly and repeatedly in *Diary*, which offers Debra's musing that "as soon as the shit hits the fan, the only place you want to go is home."[51] But the idea of a haven from the dead can also assume a more enduring and organized form: imagined political and social communities that offer a more complete life than Romero's desperate semi-states, while still representing a radical departure from the traditional (and discredited) governance directed by national and state authorities.

Land of the Dead's Fiddler's Green serves as Romero's prototypical false utopia—a planned community custom-tailored for surviving the zombie uprising in comfort and elegance. Fiddler's Green is actually an enclave within a city or perhaps, more accurately, a kind of castle complex within a fortified medieval town. For its wealthy residents, the luxury high-rises seem to offer an ideal society and the protection of an ersatz state, specially designed to withstand the surrounding undead hordes. As an inviting infomercial informs us, the structure is guarded by geographic and "natural boundaries" (the confluence of three rivers), and "hand-picked members of its own private militia"[52] (not to mention an electrified fence and a buffer of thousands of defenseless poor clustered in the surrounding Uniontown).

Beyond enriching developer Paul Kaufman (and his Board of Directors), this post-apocalyptic refuge offers many services and functions otherwise associated with organized states. Kaufman provides defenses for both the city as a whole and, more specifically, his elite real estate complex. He has uniformed staff including personal henchmen, soldiers, and the crew of the armored vehicle, Dead Reckoning. More broadly, Kaufman has taken steps to ensure the perpetuation of his rule. After Cholo seizes Dead Reckoning and threatens Fiddler's Green, the ruler reassures his Board that "I've established outposts with food and supplies … that will support us.… Alternative sites have been chosen for us and our families as well as necessary support personnel."[53]

Indeed, we come to learn that Kaufman's entrepreneurship is as much political as it is economic and martial. As he tells us,

Paul Kaufman (Dennis Hopper) is an oligarch in *Land of the Dead* (Universal Pictures, 2005).

> It was my ingenuity that took an old world and made it into something new. I put up fences to make it safe. I hired soldiers and paid for their training. I keep the people on the streets away from us by giving them their games and vices. It costs me money! But I spend it because the responsibility is mine![54]

Kaufman's rule, and the arrangements that perpetuate Fiddler's Green, are not focused on the well-being of the population as a whole. The masses live in a "slum," short on medicine and other supplies, distracted by "games and vices," and kept in check by force. As Slack explains, Kaufman's "got his fingers in everything" and provides distractions like prostitution, gambling, drugs, and zombie arena combat as "a few cheap kicks so we don't go thinkin' too hard about why he's eating steak and the rest of us are lucky to get the bones."[55] Both Slack and her rebellious co-conspirator, Mulligan, want to resist and imagines turning the city into a "fit place to live in" for everyone.

In short, Kaufman's claim to rule calls to mind the inequities and "bread and circus" distractions associated with imperial Rome rather than the actions of a benighted oligarch. The short arc between the debased leadership of Rhodes and Kaufman is further suggested by their racism (Cholo is denied access to Fiddler's Green because of his unwanted status, a point driven home when Kaufman refers to him as a "fucking spic bastard"[56]), and the contempt for women shown in both of their worlds (in *Land,* Kaufman punishes Slack by throwing her into the zombie arena, and she notes that she was training to join the army until "somebody figured I'd be a better hooker than a soldier"[57]). By the end of *Land,* Kaufman's complete disregard for the masses is laid bare as he attempts to flee the city while the people remain behind, pinned between the advancing dead and the electrified city gates. The dream of a better life in Fiddler's Green is revealed to be a death trap.[58]

Dawn offers a more nuanced and seductive state of existence than that promised by Fiddler's Green: a relatively secure consumer cornucopia or "playground" nestled inside a suburban shopping mall.[59] To be fair, the presence of hundreds of hungry undead banging on the center's windows makes it a stretch to call this retreat a paradise. But given where Francine, Peter, and Stephen have come from (a chaotic and overrun Philadelphia), it is not surprising they describe their discovery in initially glowing language. As Roger says, "This place could be a gold mine."[60] After Roger discovers the keys that allow access to the various mall stores he describes them as "Keys to the kingdom."[61] Stephen brags to Fran about "all the great stuff we got" and announces that "This place is terrific!"[62] Later, when the group considers abandoning the mall for an uncertain trip north, Stephen objects that "we have everything we need right here." Peter also resists: "I've been thinking … maybe we've got a good thing going here. Maybe we shouldn't be in such a hurry to leave."[63]

While the mall with its earthly delights offers a version of what Gregory Claeys and Lyman Sargent have called the age-old "utopia of sensual gratification,"[64] it suffers from a number of problems. To begin with, its allure is not experienced by all of the Philadelphia refugees equally. While Fran perhaps enjoys some aspects of the shopping center (ice-skating and donning a mink coat) she is a steady voice of alarm, culminating with her warning that her comrades are "hypnotized by this place…. You don't see that it's not a sanctuary, it's a prison!"[65] Indeed, this suggestion that the mall is more reminiscent of the island of Calypso rather than the homeland of Ithaca is expressed by Fran's rueful comment that "I guess we forget about Canada, right?"[66] This sentiment is repeated in a sequence where Roger wonders "how the hell are we gonna get back," with Peter responding: "Who the hell cares! Let's go shopping!"[67]

Moreover, *Dawn's* characters "find no [lasting] joy or satisfaction from the mall's many pleasures" and it soon becomes a "symbol of their now essentially meaningless lives."[68] Romero erases the divide between the empty shuffling of the zombies, going through the motions of their former lives, and the desperate living shoppers.[69] Indeed, in the end the mall is inhospitable to even bourgeois pleasures (perhaps because the future is so uncertain): Fran refuses to get married to Stephen on the grounds that "It wouldn't be real."[70] Similarly, she—and the rest of the group—have trepidations about bringing her baby into the world. And even when Romero shows us a scene of Fran and Stephen sharing an intimate moment in bed, they stare away from one another vacantly. These and other scenes seem to give specificity to Francine's lament that "It's really all over … isn't it?"[71] Even when *Dawn's* protagonists carve out time and space that is not imminently threatened by living or dead foes, the existence is grim, depressing, haunted, and less than fully human. The "heroes' survival has become a parody of the vanished society rather than an outlaw alternative."[72]

Despite its openly satirical and dark dimensions, Romero's shopping oasis seems to offer at least the hint of something more substantial.[73] At its best, *Dawn* gives us a version of a "supreme society because the four humans inhabiting the mall come to share all things equally, have no visible conflicts between them, and enjoy safety from the physical threats contained outside."[74] Peter is a black man regarded as a political and social peer—his decisions and perspectives carry at least as much weight as anyone else's.[75] While the gender dynamics in *Dawn* are more complex, Francine "progressively assumes a genuine autonomy."[76] Once she is treated differently because of her pregnancy, she forcefully objects and informs the group that she won't be their "den mother." She insists on being fully informed about group discussions, and taught key survival skills, like how to fire a gun and fly the helicopter. Indeed, this last aspect of her empowerment proves crucial: following Stephen's death, she alone can fly the chopper, and thereby save herself and Peter, at least for a time. As Newman summarizes, "With a touch of hope, they fly off into the sunrise."[77] While an imperfect "sanctuary," without the trust, camaraderie, and self-mastery facilitated by *Dawn's* mall, the film would have ended earlier, and on a decidedly bleaker note.[78]

Survival conjures up another false utopia, although, like *Dawn*, it ultimately seems to offer something besides moral blight, at least at its outer edges. The path to Plum Island is as dangerous and unreliable as its bloody reality, dominated by an internecine clash of clans. "Captain Courageous" tells his naïve audience that they should "Follow the signs to Slaughter Beach" where they will receive a warm welcome at a location that is "small and under control." But once there, we only find another autocrat, the stubborn and self-righteous Muldoon, whose vision of surviving with the dead involves domestication. His claim to rule is only slightly less vicious than Rhodes's or Kaufman's, and is based on a similar perception of the social contract: his subjects should obey him, unquestioningly, because he has provided order and the means of subsistence. As Muldoon explains, "we got an obligation to protect ourselves and what's ours ... [and] what's mine is everybody's. I provide the bread and butter for people here."[79]

By *Survival's* end, the contract has been broken, and Plum Island is soaked in blood. But the film also sounds some ambiguous notes. As the movie ends, Crocket teasingly muses that "The reason we came out here is because we'd thought it would better than any place else. Still could be."[80] Romero's penultimate shot, of the dead devouring horse flesh, invites the possibility that Muldoon's fantasy might be possible after all. Zombies can be taught to eat animals rather than humans and so, perhaps, commensalism (which, etymologically speaking, refers to a literal sharing of meals) is possible. To be sure, the picture is cloudy: O'Flynn's zombie daughter seems to have a drive to eat *both* human and horse flesh, and Crockett, Boy, and Tomboy depart Plum Island rather than taking their chances with this brave new world. The image of zombies rending horses is hardly inviting, and one wonders if Romero is gesturing to his admitted roots, the book *I Am Legend*, in which a new strain of monsters replaces humanity.[81]

Dream States: Romero's Imagined Alternatives

Despite his sustained interest in politics, Romero does not aspire to be a disciplined state-builder, or even an organized political philosopher. Even the director's most developed regimes, like the plutocratic-military order in *Land,* are less than fully rendered. This artistic imprecision continues with his most impressionistic sketches of what we might call his "dream states." Unlike the false utopias (the mall), dystopian orders (Fiddler's Green), or flawed substitutes of traditional governments (Plum Island), Romero's aspirational dream states appear to be genuinely attractive.[82] Upon encountering these alternatives, which are, admittedly, shown only fleetingly and spun from the most diaphanous of materials, our first impulse is neither flight nor fight. Wood suggests that the helicopter escape in *Dawn,* complete with the knowledge that Francine is carrying developing life inside of her, is fragile but "exhilarating."[83] The movie is, he insists, "perhaps the first horror film to suggest—albeit very tentatively—the possibility of moving beyond apocalypse."[84]

Day of the Dead offers up two intertwined versions of a seemingly benevolent political association, both implicitly based on an easygoing and cooperative existentialism. After a tense confrontation with Rhodes, Sarah retreats to John and Billy's Winnebago, which they have affectionately dubbed "the Ritz" (they also call it "civilization" and "the last holdout"[85]). Here, laughing and smiling (for perhaps the only time in the entire film) and enjoying drinks, the three friends discuss the future (including their plans to leave the compound) and John's personal ethos (which entails abandoning the search for knowledge and attempts to master the world, in favor of enjoying simple, sensual pleasures). Indeed, the Ritz is a preview of a more fully realized escape: flight to a remote island where, John says, "we could start over, start fresh, get some babies. And teach 'em, Sarah, teach 'em never to come"[86] back to the authoritarian military base. John has floated this idea before; at the film's outset he suggests to his companions that they should fly to "an island someplace, get juiced up ... and spend what time we got left soakin' up some sunshine."[87] At the end of the film, when the dead have breached the Seminole compound, Billy tells John "We're countin' on ya to fly us to the promised land."[88] Indeed, the last shot of *Day* shows that Sarah and her friends may have reached this goal: the scene finds them resting on a sun-soaked beach, with seagulls as their only companions and John contentedly fishing for their next meal. Admittedly, some writers have dismissed this "promised land" as offering nothing more than "hedonist escapism."[89] Even more damning, the entire vision might be illusory; after all, *Day* depicts several vivid visions involving Sarah that turn out to be mere dreams. But even this possibility does not eliminate the film's tranquil island as a candidate or placeholder for an imagined paradise.[90]

Indeed, the allure of this isolated, natural setting exerts a pull across Romero's *Dead* series. In *Dawn*, the police who originally detain Stephen and Francine divulge that they are headed "down river" to "the islands" in their flight from the dead. *Survival*, too, banks on this concept—even if Plum Island itself turns out to be thick with animosity and bloodshed. For *Survival's* Boy, the draw of an island is that it stands as a "place where the shit can't get at us."[91] At several points in Romero's series, Canada serves as substitute for the island metaphor. As noted, Francine expresses disappointment when the group seems to have forgotten about the dream of heading north to Canada, and *Land's* Riley expresses the same longing.[92]

In Danny Boyle's *28 Days Later* (Fox Searchlight Pictures, 2002), Ben's (Cillian Murphy) dawning awareness that society has been transformed is framed by the abandoned Houses of Parliament.

Romero's Best Regime? Walking the Boulevard of Broken States

What do we make of this tableau of absent and broken government institutions, rotten new semi-states, and hazy "utopian"[93] dreams? Can we piece together a comprehensive picture of Romero's preferred or ideal form of governance from his dream states (and from the moral failings of the alternatives)? What general conclusions can we come to about how the director presents and evaluates the shape and scope of state power and (dys)function?

To begin with, as many writers have noted, the director rejects a commonplace response to horror: he does not express a longing to vanquish the dead merely to return to (or reinforce) the *status quo ante*. Romero provides no halcyon flashbacks, nor does he express longing for what the *Walking Dead* refers to as our "Days Gone By." Even the first few minutes of *Night*, before the protagonists or viewers can imagine a world filled with the living dead, are choked with atmospheric dread and a sense that something is amiss. George Romero is no conservative or traditionalist. Indeed, as Robin Wood explains, the very "premise of *Dawn* … is that the social order (regarded as in all Romero's films as obsolete and discredited) *can't* be restored."[94]

Given this backdrop, it would be reasonable to wonder if Romero veers in a more radical libertarian or individualist direction, taking up Henry David Thoreau's insistence "That government is best which governs not at all."[95] Jennifer Proffitt and Rich Templin see Romero's work as presenting a "persistent struggle between a strong liberal democracy and a more individual-centered libertarian worldview."[96] As Peter Biskind argues, unlike "centrist" vampires who operate within (and take advantage of) the prevailing social order, the modern zombies birthed by Romero "are extremists" who upend and discredit human institutions and even sociability itself.[97] Indeed, at some points across Romero's *Dead* films he seems to endorse a simpler, more natural, less interdependent existence. *Land's* Riley insists that he's "gonna find me a place where there ain't no people" at all.[98] After all, where every person is a potential infected, the fear of others is hardly surprising; as Roger warns in *Dawn*, "We've got to stay out of the big cities. If they're anything like Philly, we may never get out alive."[99]

While these comments do not target organized politics directly, as Aristotle reminds us "Every state is a community of some kind."[100] If Romero's humans are forsaking customary communities, it seems to follow that they are also abandoning traditional states. Noel Ransome claims that in *Day*, Romero favors the "holistic, separatist viewpoint" of John and McDermott, breaking from the government-oriented solutions of the other characters (the progressive liberalism of Sarah and Logan and the conservative emphasis on order of Captain Rhodes).[101] Over the course of Romero's films, even the dead seem to be lurching towards individuality and free will outside the strictures of an organized state.

But the strains of self-sufficiency and isolation in Romero's work only thread so far. The director's characters—even the most maverick humans (Riley, Crocket, John, Muldoon, and O'Flynn) and the most independent of the dead (Bub and Big Daddy)—are unavoidably social and cooperative. To be sure, Romero's dramatic personae are often distinct and even outrageous characters who bristle against convention and the authority of existing political orders and leaders. But they are not atomistic or isolated like Matheson's Robert Neville (or Jim at the outset of *28 Days Later* or Miss Helen Justineau in *The*

Girl with All the Gifts). Unlike other dystopian and fantastic works, Romero's free-spirited individuals are better off for their sociability and collective planning. They don't ultimately select "self-assertion" and "individualist will over social cooperation," negotiation, and compromise.[102] Even *Survival's* Riley, who longs for "a place where there ain't no people," departs, without irony, with two companions who will, presumably, help him survive and find his way. Anxiety over losing one's individuality may be "central to American culture," but this fear is not a central theme in Romero's films, where unconventional types proliferate amidst often disapproving antagonists and norms.[103] Moreover, in *Dawn's* secure mall, when Romero's characters are seemingly capable of unbounded autonomy (existing as what Robin Wood describes as "potentially free people, with new responsibilities of choice and self-determination"), they still face a crisis while clashing with other rugged individualists (the biker gang).[104]

If Romero's politics cannot be described as libertarian or survivalist, might we, alternatively, identify him as a multicultural liberal—with the state dedicated to safeguarding individual rights, maintaining access to democratic channels and institutions, and generally protecting and valuing collective identities and practices?[105] As Shaviro argues, across the Romero universe, the director's most sympathetic protagonists and most admirable groupings "seem to be groping toward a shared, democratic kind of decision making" that celebrates difference.[106] Similarly, other scholars have noted that in Romero's first three *Dead* films "cooperation (between races, sexes, family members) is privileged as an alternative to the mindless, self-indulgent greed of the Dead" (not to mention misbehaving and anti-social humans).[107] Dawn Keetley references the alliance between Big Daddy and a "white female zombie" to support the idea that *Land* encompasses a "recognizable 'multicultural liberalism'"—a broad recognition of difference that extends to the film's humans conceding that even the undead are the "same as us."[108] As Keetley elaborates, at "the end of the film, the humans and the zombies set off to establish their own separate 'place,' and while they appear to have no intention of living together, they will presumably tolerate each other."[109] More broadly, Romero offers the recurring and intertwined goals of overcoming human difference and working cooperatively as likely organizing principles for any brave new post-apocalyptic world we can imagine.[110] As *Day's* Sarah puts it, amidst the unrelenting strife within the Seminole Storage Facility, "Maybe if we tried working together we could ease some of the tensions. We're all pulling in different directions."[111] This familiar, liberal theme of strength and solidarity through diversity (and appreciation of difference) plays out in every one of Romero's films and forms the core of the aspirational communities he offers up, even in passing.[112] From *Night's* boarded farmhouse to the ragtag crew of Dead Reckoning and Crocket's rootless National Guard troupe, Romero celebrates myriad characters, lifestyles, and demographics, while providing regular suggestions that these individuals are safer, happier, and better together.

The filmmaker's racial politics are particularly interesting in this regard; while he has long claimed that Ben's status as a moral and strategic leader was unintentional, his subsequent work frequently links racial stereotyping with corrupt leadership (Rhodes and his lackeys, and Paul Kaufman come to mind), and his most harmonious communities feature strong minorities (as we see in *Dawn's* mall outpost, the trio of companions in *Day*, and *Land's* Dead Reckoning crew).[113] Big Daddy, a zombie who is also black, is a distinctive and even superlative moral figure whose appearance signals a shift in how Romero (and his protagonists) think about the dead. He displays autonomy, leadership, and compassion—far beyond the bounds of any of his fellow flesh-eaters but also, frankly, beyond what many of Romero's humans are capable of displaying. Big Daddy tries to push his fellow dead out of the path of Cholo's gratuitous spray of bullets. Even the white and privileged friends in *Diary* turn to a group of African American survivors who provide them with internet service, physical protection, gas, and other supplies.[114]

But this multicultural interpretation of Romero's preferred political stance—and views regarding the main objects of legitimate state power—explains only a portion of his concerns. Romero's protagonists are appropriately preoccupied with existential questions along with issues of equity and access. And he certainly does not furnish us with a clear picture of what is a multicultural approach to the living dead.

Can we, alternatively, take up Romero's recurring concern with economic justice and equity—and accurately describe *this* as his preferred target for state action? Is Romero a socialist? Countless critics and commentators have discussed Romero's arch attack on consumerism in *Dawn*.[115] Keetley argues, further, that Romero's films present zombies as a "propertyless" multitude threatening not just our lives and material goods, but the very identity of humans who strive to secure "land and property at any cost."[116] This vision culminates in *Land of the Dead's* "particular form of utopianism ... a liberal-socialist redistribution of resources" and a "shifting of private property (and land) from the few to everyone."[117] Of course, if this is Romero's preferred approach, it is in some tension with his recurring skepticism regarding state power. And even though *Land* gives us an army of poor humans and undead collectively assaulting "the luxury condo of the rich" (Fiddler's Green), Romero does not convey a sense that their alliance will continue. Even Riley's recognition that the undead just want a "place to go, same as us" sounds more bourgeois than revolutionary.[118]

Could Romero's ideal state be founded on a creed of pacifism? Beginning with the indiscriminately murderous officials in *Night*, Romero offers up a series of skeptical portraits of cops and soldiers. Conversely, he seems sympathetic to those who renounce violence, such as the SWAT officer Peter, who ends *Dawn* by leaving his rifle with the undead, before fleeing in the news chopper. Even Crocket and his band of free agent National Guardsmen mostly observe the climactic battle between Plum Island's fractured forces, before finally bolting from the island entirely. The inhabitants of the island paradise at the end of *Day* are a scientist, a helicopter pilot, and an electronics expert—arguably the three most peaceful figures in the entire film.

These portrayals, however, are balanced by Romero's white knuckle *realpolitik* and unhesitating embrace of self-defense: without a readiness to dispense regular and even indiscriminate violence, none of his protagonists would survive. Stated differently, there's no reason to think Romero is opposed to violence in all forms or even to official use of force. Indeed, in recounting his original short story that gave rise to the *Dead* series, Romero favorably describes a group of humans who control and cull the dead and maintain "law and order." Instead of being repugnant, these figures are where "we'll ultimately get our hope; those are the characters we'll be able to care about."[119] Overall, it seems fairer to conclude that Romero is opposed to militarism and authoritarianism, where claims to power (and the exercise of force) are tethered to "personalized" forms of rule rather than serving pressing human needs including legitimate public safety concerns.[120]

So: what do we make of this? Does Romero offer us *any* cogent vision of a preferred human society or give us a clear picture of what role the state should wield in forging a new and improved society after the zombie apocalypse has flushed away the old order? Exploring this topic requires some divination. As this essay has tried to make clear, while the filmmaker offers some fairly clear and recurring political critiques (involving such topics as militarism, tribalism, racial bigotry, and consumerism), it's not obvious he's got a consistent vision of the best state or regime, or an appetite for promoting specific governing institutions. The director's positive visions of post-apocalyptic survival are cloudy, at best (and in the case of *Day* may *actually* be a dream). As Wood tells us, in responding to questions about the prospects for and preferred direction of social and political change Romero provides "the most equivocal, guarded, and complex answer[s]."[121]

The explanation for this is partly structural. With the backdrop of a nearly constant zombie menace, Romero's created worlds give us a limited horizon for political possibility and sustained state action. Moreover, with few exceptions, the director's films do not offer continued story arcs or common protagonists, villains, or settings. Thus, his characters and their conflicts appear somewhat situational, ahistoric and instant, posing a challenge for making generalizations across films. Related, Romero constantly plays with new issues and narrative formats in his films (such as the personal histories his characters share in *Night*, the musical montages in *Dawn*, and the mediated video imagery of *Diary*), and he offers evolving portrayals of the dead. The shambling flesh-eaters of *Night* are very different from the purposeful and rebellious undead in *Land*. Both dramatically and thematically, then, Romero's *Dead* series resists systematic comparison, which is, of course, a tribute to the director's innovation and restlessness.

Romero's Non-Ideological Revolution: A "Vision of a Layered Society"

But another explanation for the director's political ambiguity (at least with respect to his preferred image of the proper role and priority of the state) is more fundamental: when all is said and done, George Romero, for all his interest in "social criticism,"[122] seems curiously non-ideological. On the contrary, as he explained, his films depict the toll of "going along with an ideal, which speaks to fanaticism or patriotism or whatever that causes war."[123] Robin Wood, in his seminal essay, "An Introduction to the American Horror Film," argues that the nature of the "apocalyptic horror film" is to destroy "the dominant ideology" of the times and to suggest that it can not be recovered and is, instead untenable "as all it has repressed explodes and blows it apart."[124] Romero's films reveal something further: the extreme shearing forces unleashed by the zombie apocalypse appear to be inhospitable to ideology more generally. The director himself has offered that "all of my zombie films are just sort of snapshots of the time they were made; I don't expect them to be much more than that"; even his trenchant social criticisms are "really just snapshots of what's going on."[125]

As documented across the critical scholarship, he refuses to pull any punches in his attacks against any number of belief systems (from consumer capitalism to patriarchal constructions of the family), but he does not seem comfortable offering a clearly rendered replacement. The fact that no demographic, economic, or social subgroup is spared pain and suffering in Romero's works further signals that we will find no easy answers or consistent, comforting belief systems in his universe. Instead, the director presents his political views through frames that are usually personal, metaphorical, and anecdotal.

Again, this is not to suggest that Romero is uninterested in ideology, but that the director's concerns are too eclectic and evolving to be fixed on any one belief system, even critically.[126] Thus, Romero considers the tensions between state-supported capitalism and socialism (and the related struggles of the Cold War) in *Day* and *Land*, without ever signaling that this is a privileged filter or frame for understanding U.S. or global politics. If anything, we can make the case that Romero seeks to understand and play with the interactions and cycles of ascendancy and repudiation of opposing ideologies. As Romero tells us in his interview with Dan Yakir, the original short story upon which the *Dead* series is founded deals "with a revolutionary society coming into being in the form of a zombie society."[127] Romero's story lays out three "parts" or phases of the relationship between the "operative society" of humans and "zombie society," with the final phase involving a "vision of a layered society" in which "the humans are little dictators" trapped in subterranean "bomb shelters" (like Rhodes in *Day*) who have to still interact with and superintend the world above in which zombies are mostly in control or "operative."[128]

We can see this interactive, layered approach to opposed belief systems (and their accompanying different claims to rule) in a number of Romero's films, with this dynamic clash often evincing a dialectic character.[129] In *Dawn* Shaviro notes, the "consumers' Utopia [formed by Francine and her male compatriots] comes to an end only when the mall is invaded by a vicious motorcycle gang: a bunch of toughs motivated by a kind of class resentment."[130] But the destruction and threat brought on by the bikers is ultimately essential in releasing *Dawn*'s protagonists from their empty consumptive stupor, and awakening them to flight and at least temporary moral freedom. Similarly, Newman tells us that Romero's original plan for *Day* was to show "the passing of the Living Dead plague and the establishment of an ambiguously utopian new normality after the overthrow of the repressive old order."[131] In the actual released film the audience squirms through a recurring clash between the militaristic and scientific worldviews of Rhodes and Sarah, resulting not in a victory of one over the other but in a literal and figurative retreat toward John's sybaritic "third way." Finally, as already documented, in *Land* the plutocrats of Fiddler's Green are opposed by the joint uprising of landless humans and dead, leading to a new world order in which—perhaps—zombies and humans can coexist.

In this interpretation, then, Romero is both critical of ideology and fascinated by its evolution and power, without obviously favoring one political and intellectual stance over another. Intriguingly, this claim actually secures his status as a revolutionary insofar as his films depict the implosion of the traditional state (and its attendant ideologies) alongside the frequent toppling of the replacement "false" and "semi-states" (and the vague promise of "dream states"[132]). Romero is a state-shattering force—again and again. As Wood puts it, Romero believes that the "total disintegration of society is the necessary prerequisite for new growth" and that disintegration certainly includes multiple versions of the organized state and its organs and agents.[133]

Beyond his iconoclasm (he smashes the state, its ideals, and its icons), Romero can be thought of as a revolutionary in his interest in revolutionary consciousness, and how we develop a point of view that challenges mainstream views and institutions. His apocalypse does not lead to a foundation in the rubble for casting a new state (or advance a preferred ideology). Instead, he produces a kinetic, charged environment which gives rise to numerous nascent case studies in how the awareness and interpersonal relations of his characters can be transformed when their familiar social and political order is taken away. Thus, in *Diary* Debra "faces down a competent, pragmatic black man ... who has organized his community" and through this dynamic we "see in embryo the types most likely to inherit the ruins [depicted] in *Dawn* and *Day*."[134] Similarly, Ryan and Kellner note that

134 Beyond the Living Dead

Dawn offers "a positive image of salvation or at least hope" in the form of a "black policeman relinquish[ing] his rifle to the Dead in order to escape with a white woman."[135] In these and other episodes, Romero invites us to consider how a transformation in prevailing institutions (concerning gender relations, the military, the purposes of science and progress) can lead to a transformation in our self-understanding, powers, and autonomy.[136] To put it differently, Big Daddy's budding critical awareness is something of a stand in for both Romero and his intended audiences.

Zombie States: What Are They Good For?

In the end, then, Romero's deployment of different zombie states reveals a revolutionary but non-ideological mind. But what does this treatment actually teach us about politics, and what he thinks states should do to remain legitimate and effective? First, Romero's attitudes about states seems to borrow from a classical concept in political philosophy: that each form of governance gives birth to its own peculiar citizens—with resulting distinctive problems.[137] As Aristotle puts it in *The Politics*, "the citizen under each different kind of constitution must also necessarily be different."[138] This idea is captured most baldly (and broadly) in *Survival of the Dead*, which tells us that "Lousy times make lousy people."[139] But it is also at the core of *Dawn's* critique of consumer capitalism, and *Land's* ruminations about the sapping effects of economic and political disempowerment. When Mike notes that Big Daddy and the other dead across from Fiddler's Green serve as simulacra, retracing their earlier existence and "pretending to be alive," Riley counters: "Isn't that what we're doing? Pretending to be alive?"[140]

Second, and more obviously, Romero's direct and implied portrayals of weakened, partial, and debased government institutions across his zombie films is revealing as a way to track his shifting political anxieties across five decades.[141] As Romero himself put it, "If there's something I'd like to criticize, I can bring the zombies out…. So I've been able to express my political views through those films."[142] While numerous scholars have focused on Romero's undead as metaphors for these worries about "current problems," we can access them even more directly by looking at the director's treatment of states.[143] Thus, the absent and irresponsible government of *Night* (a government that may have accidentally created the flesh-eaters and is at least complicit in the deaths of Ben and his companions) reflects disapproval of the U.S. government's role in the nuclear arms race and Vietnam War.[144] *Land,* issued just a few years after the 9/11 attacks, features a ruthless leader, Kaufman, who dismisses Cholo's demand to be admitted to Fiddler's Green on the grounds that "We don't negotiate with terrorists" and goes on to reassure his Board that Cholo will be assassinated.[145] Romero efficiently encapsulates both the paranoia and fear triggered by the 2001 attacks as well as stubborn misgivings about the government's response.[146]

In *Diary*, Romero explores how the state seeds widespread distrust through its incomplete and deceptive media narratives, a budding concern in the internet and infotainment age, and a specific apprehension triggered by real world events like the invasion of Iraq in 2003 and the discovery of a massive NSA surveillance program in 2005.[147] As noted, *Diary* also presents an interview with "Chief of Police Arthur Katz," who, either through ignorance or dereliction of duty, dismisses a zombie attack that initiates the film's action as mayhem "carried out by a bunch of illegal immigrants."[148] Debra is quick to call out Katz and notes that the footage of the attack has been edited in a way that shows that the government and media are "lying," to reassure the public. Romero reinforces these themes throughout *Diary*, mixing in actual footage of mishandled disasters like Hurricane Katrina.[149]

Beyond viewing the state as spinning political weathervane—pointing us to the trends and tensions that most engage Romero's attention "at a particular moment" in American history, the artist's varied treatments of government allows for a third and perhaps most interesting interpretation.[150] In both the failures and sketched promise of various political orders, Romero points to essential and unique functions of government (as opposed to other forms of social organization). The nature of the zombie narrative almost invariably contrasts the dead's absence of social organization with humanity's capacity (if not always success) to engage in collective action as one of its best tools for survival.[151] As Brooks tells us, "The truth is that zombies have no social organization to speak of. There is no hierarchy, no chain of command, no drive toward any type of collectivization."[152] In contrast, he notes, people "Working together, always together, has shown to be the only successful strategy for annihilating an undead army."[153] Thus, the range of failed and broken states in Romero's films actually highlights why government is needed; indeed, by illustrating what is core to the state's operations, we can also see more clearly its potential for overstepping its powers and creeping towards tyranny. This functional approach to understanding governance makes sense given Romero's disinterest in prescribing particular policies or providing anything resembling a detailed representation of the best regime.

So what does this orientation teach us about the essential operations of government in the teeth of the zombie invasion—and, presumably, in contexts far beyond? Most obviously, as discussed previously, Romero borrows a core concept from Weber: successful states are uniquely qualified to dispense "legitimate" violence, especially to instill order.[154] Political failure in this regard washes through all the *Dead* movies, but reaches something of a nadir in *Day of the Dead*, where Dr. Logan announces that government forces missed their opportunity to dispatch the dead when their numbers were manageable. Instead, "we let them overrun us…. We're in the minority now. Something like 400,000 to 1 by my calculations."[155] Of course, in addition to its failure in maintaining a monopoly of violence, Romero also shows us the devastating effects of *illegitimate* violence: Ben's murderer at the end of *Night*, the casual (and immoral) bloodletting of Rhodes and Kaufman, and the dueling patriarchs in *Survival* who transform Plum Island into bloodlands.

Of course, given Romero's anti-militarism, a Weberian approach to state power has discrete limits.[156] But the director also makes it clear that his fictional states have failed for a second reason: their inadequacy in helping distribute scarce resources effectively.[157] Indeed, when Dr. Logan dismisses the idea that the solution to the zombie threat is mass extermination, he notes "You haven't got enough ammunition, Captain, to shoot them all in the head."[158] The very same idea is echoed in *Diary* when Debra simply concludes that "There weren't enough bullets to stop them all."[159] This notion overlaps with political scientist Harold Lasswell's understanding of the state's vital role in deciding who gets what, when, and how.[160] Framed in this broad fashion, we see critical government lapses throughout the *Dead* series. Lasswell's definition of politics is central to the economic, land, and healthcare inequities that sully Romero's *Land* (as Newman puts it succinctly, the whole film is "an argument over how a society with limited resources should be run").[161] But this distributive problem also hovers over the challenges of media access in *Diary*, and the heated conflict over the resources and protection given to Dr. Logan and his research team in *Day*.

The third and final government function Romero gestures to involves the related task of social coordination, especially to secure public goods—beneficial projects and outcomes which are not readily obtained through private markets and decision making.[162] Although the National Guard is generally derelict in Romero's films, and while Kaufman's training and arming of soldiers and building of city fences is self-serving, these characters and activities point to plausible social needs, even where zombies aren't incipient threats. In addition, the public goods that governments can help promote aren't limited to matters of defense. While it turns out to be misguided and even macabre, the government-sponsored research compound in *Day of the Dead* seeks a coordinated scientific solution to the zombie menace.[163] As Sarah tells Rhodes, "if there was more cooperation [in this project], your men wouldn't have to risk their asses as often." The pressing nature of this element of governance is suggested by the long list of endangered public goods facing our new century: clean air; sustainable energy sources; a climate compatible with human flourishing; building institutions for containing pandemics; and protecting fisheries and other sources of food, among many others.

One Last Conjuring: Bad Moon Rising

In sum, reviewing and organizing the role of the state in Romero's works reveals political criticism and longing, numerous portrayals of outright failure, as well as select moments of transcendent aspiration. The director's catalog of misdeeds and failings by state actors and institutions also serves to highlight essential and non-transferrable government functions. But Romero's films also convey a prescient warning about system failure. The proper structure, form, and even successful operation of our government can only do so much when a society and its citizens are inert, distracted, or poisonously divided. As the political scientists Steven Levitsky and Daniel Ziblatt warn "fear, opportunism or miscalculation [can] ... bring extremists into the mainstream" of a political order.[164] When this happens

> Institutions alone are not enough [states and their] Constitutions must be defended—by political parties and organized citizens but also by democratic norms. Without robust norms [such as mutual toleration and forbearance], constitutional checks and balances do not serve as the bulwarks of democracy we imagine them to be. [Instead institutions] become political weapons, wielded forcefully by those who control them against those who do not.[165]

While these issues may seem rather remote from Romero's ruptured and entropic worlds, they run parallel to themes laid out in his last film, *Survival of the Dead*. Here, he directs us to observe that sometimes discord can't be sublimated or managed by politics; indeed, the instruments of the state can be weaponized, exacerbating divisions. As the director elaborated, with *Survival*

> The idea was to make a film about war or entities that don't die, conflicts, disagreements that people can't resolve, whether it's Ireland, or the Middle East, or the Senate ... that was the idea.... So I said OK, the best way to tell this story I think is to have a protagonist go to the island only to find out that it's in the middle of basically a war that won't die, between these two old guys.[166]

Here Romero tells us explicitly that O'Flynn and Muldoon are stand ins for combative states, locked in undying (and sometimes resurrected) disputes fueled by clashing ideologies, religion, hyper-partisanship, or cultural schisms.[167] As Romero put it in a different context, the movie is about "the same theme that I've been beating on forever. It's war, it's like enmities that don't die, people, even faced with huge game-changing event[s] still shooting at each other instead of addressing the problem."[168]

Romero's vision is not just comic and absurd, but terrifying. And, as usual, the director does not give us an easy way out. One might think that the prospect of species annihilation and the relentless terror of the dead would be enough to reconcile even long-simmering hatreds, at least for a time. The social psychologist Jonathan Haidt has argued that in societies where people cherish fundamentally different (or even inherently opposed) values and sources of identity, a foreign attack or an external calamity can bring them together.

> Human beings are pretty good at uniting to fight at whatever level is most important at a given moment. This is why every story about a team of warriors or superheroes features an internal rivalry, but all hatchets are buried just before the climactic final battle in which the team vanquishes the external enemy.[169]

But the last image ever conjured by Romero, *Survival's* two rivals locked in futile combat before a rising moon, suggests the limits of this unity through crisis narrative.[170] After all, what could be a greater threat than the prospect of the undead wiping out humanity? As Sarah puts it in *Day,* "We're in a desperate situation here! We need each other. Can't we just get along?"[171] The TV scientist sounds the same alarm in *Dawn* in trying to convince his audience that "This is not the Republicans versus the Democrats who've got us in a hole economically or we're in another war. It's more crucial than that. We are down to the line, folks.... We've got to remain logical.... It's that or the end."[172]

But in both *Day* and *Dawn,* Sarah and the scientist's pleas go unheeded. Indeed, throughout the *Dead* films, Romero shows us a grim alternative: that we can't get along, and that the state's structures and even our awareness of a genuine, desperate, mortal threat give way to our partisanship, to other strains of tribalism, to our belief that our ideals or way of life are superior to others. As John cheerfully opines in *Day:* "That's the trouble, Sarah. People got different ideas concerning what they want out of life."[173] In fact, the problem is deeper: what Romero warns against is not just our disagreements about the good life, but a haunting sense that the other side is our enemy. In the context of contemporary politics, scholars have identified "affective polarization" as "hostile feelings for the opposing party [that] are ingrained or automatic in voters' minds" and not tethered to policy concerns, ideology, or self-interest.[174] *Survival's* Crocket worries about the arbitrary spread of these primal, historical hatreds from leaders to followers, and across time and generations. His warning to Boy—"You and me might end up shooting at each other one of these days"[175]—is born not of animus, but a budding sense that the divisions that grip humanity are stubborn, inherited, and beyond the bounds of reason. "I was on the Flynn side from the beginning. So I just saw Muldoon as the enemy."[176] As Crocket's final voice-over warns, in "an us-versus-them world, someone puts up a flag, another person tears it down and puts up his own. Pretty soon, no one remembers what started the war in the first place, and the fighting becomes all about those stupid flags."[177]

Thus, the shattering end of *Survival* threatens to be ours as well: we may simply value our hatreds more than our self-interest and perhaps even our survival.[178] Of course, to the extent that zombie assimilation embodies what Skal has called "dysfunctional images of human connectedness" and widespread concern that "basic social contracts are in jeopardy," this theme has been with Romero from the beginning.[179] But at the end of the *Dead* series, and at the conclusion of Romero's career, we can better appreciate that for all the director's relentless critique of structural injustice and the failings of state and society, he also squarely targets We the People. "It's very easy to blame government or corporations or anything else but it's really our own responsibility. We must make decisions for ourselves. I'm not going to be a part of this or that."[180] Finding a path to healthful human assimilation, especially through a thicket of animosities grown by extremists and tended by political entrepreneurs, is an encompassing, daunting, and relentless task, much like dispatching armies of the living dead.

Notes

1. Romero has repeatedly acknowledged that his films were always interested in "social criticism," spanning such issues as the disintegration of the family, race relations, feminism, political tribalism, consumerism, our utopian aspirations, and many others. Vallan, "A Pinewood Dialogue with George A. Romero"; Williams, *George A. Romero: Interviews*, 47, 77.

2. Ryan and Kellner, *Camera Politica*, 179, 181.

3. Tait, "(Zombie) Revolution at the Gates," 62, 65.

4. For a small sampling of this scholarship, see Grant, "Taking Back the Night of the Living Dead," 220; Lowenstein, "Living Dead," 108–116; Skal, *The Monster Show*, 357; Tait, "(Zombie) Revolution at the Gates"; Wood, "An Introduction to the American Horror Film," 219; Greenberg, *Screen Memories*, 151; Hervey, *Night of the Living Dead*, 95–8; 107–118; Lightning, "Interracial Tensions in *Night of the Living Dead*," 22; Garrett, *A Long, Long Way*; Newman, *Nightmare Movies*, 270.

5. Some arguable or partial exceptions include Booth, "Organisms and Human Bodies"; Greene and Mohammad, *Zombies, Vampires, and Philosophy*; Hall, "Varieties of Zombieism"; Keetley, "Zombie Republic"; Keetley, *"We're All Infected"*; Lewis, "Ztopia"; Linnemann, Wall, and Green, "The Walking Dead and Killing State"; and Proffitt and Rich Templin, "Fight the Dead." Both Daniel Drezner's *Theories of International Politics and Zombies* and Henry Giroux's book *Zombie Politics and Culture in the Age of Casino Capitalism* include some analysis of government behavior in the context of our pop culture fascination with the undead, but neither treatment could be described as systematic examinations of the place of states in zombie works. Salazar and Healy, "We're all The Walking Dead" contains a brief but useful overview of some of the different political forms present in *The Walking Dead* television series.

6. Paffenroth, "Apocalyptic Images and Prophetic Function in Zombie Films," 148.

7. Brooks, *World War Z*.

8. Bishop, *American Zombie Gothic*, 15.

9. Shaviro, *Cinematic Body*, 83 (emphasis added).

10. In this way, Romero continues and gives additional form to a twentieth century horror tradition which acknowledges the degree to which hidden, unplanned (especially economic) forces are in control of our lives. Skal, *The Monster Show*, 169.

11. Newman, *Nightmare Movies*, 284.

12. Skal, *The Monster Show*, 309; Loudermilk, "Eating 'Dawn' in the Dark, 83; Harper, "Zombies, Malls, and the Consumerism Debate."

13. Young, *Responsibility for Justice*, 52.

14. Williams, *George A. Romero: Interviews*, 130.

15. Salazar and Healy

16. Bishop, *American Zombie Gothic*, 19 (the "classic zombie story…[involves] the apocalyptic invasion of our world by hordes of cannibalistic, contagious, and animated corpses").

17. Boyle, *28 Days Later*, DVD.

18. Ibid.

19. Brooks, *The Zombie Survival Guide*, 155.

20. In Romero's last three zombie films (*Land of the Dead*, *Diary of the Dead*, and *Survival of the Dead*) his characters evince some interest in money, suggesting that our social and political concerns extend to the economy (a point that is made explicit in *Land* when Cholo endangers himself and others to acquire a $1,500 bottle of alcohol—not for his own consumption, but to curry favor with Kaufman).

21. As Romero himself put it, "With my movies that's what it's about; it's about humanity making the wrong moves." Balfour, "George Romero Strives for 'Survival of the Dead.'" Indeed, as Romero's films progress,

dispatching the dead becomes an increasingly manageable task, a nuisance, and even a distraction. For example, in *Survival of the Dead*, Sarge "Nicotine" Crocket lets us know that zombies are "easy enough to kill." The film's climactic battle is between Muldoon and O'Flynn (and their allies), while the surrounding zombies serve mainly as cannon fodder. Romero, *Survival of the Dead*, DVD.

22. Hobbes, *Leviathan*, 101.
23. Ryan and Kellner, *Camera Politica*, 169.
24. Waller, *American Horrors*, 4.
25. Weber, *From Max Weber*, 78 (italics removed).
26. Peabody, "Uncomfortable Fictions."
27. Romero, *Night of the Living Dead*, DVD.
28. Ibid.
29. Ibid.
30. Romero, *Diary of the Dead*, DVD.
31. Romero, *Survival of the Dead*, DVD.
32. Romero, *Day of the Dead*, DVD.
33. Ibid. The insignificance of these past bureaucratic concerns (and the implication that our leaders have been unable to avoid "all the other disasters that interrupted the flow of things") prompts John to cast doubts on the latest government sponsored project: trying to study and tame the dead. As he puts it in uncompromising terms, "We don't believe in what you're doin' here, Sarah."
34. Romero, *Night of the Living Dead*, DVD.
35. Romero, *Dawn of the Dead*, DVD.
36. Ryan and Kellner, *Camera Politica*, 181. See also Higashi, "Night of the Living Dead."
37. Romero, *Diary of the Dead*, DVD.
38. Ibid.
39. Hetherington and Rudolph, *Why Washington Won't Work*.
40. Hetherington and Weiler, *Authoritarianism and Polarization in American Politics*.
41. Romero, *Day of the Dead*, DVD (extra audio commentary).
42. Romero, *Day of the Dead*, DVD.
43. Ibid.
44. Ibid.
45. Pegg, *Nerd Do Well*, 233; Sondrol, "Totalitarian and Authoritarian Dictators."
46. Among other examples, Rhodes and his subordinates establish a racial outgroup by referring to "spics," identify Miguel as "yellow" and threaten John's "black ass" and "jungle-bunny" head. George A. Romero, *Day of the Dead*, DVD.
47. The traditional armed services do not feature prominently in Romero's films. This may, perhaps, reflect Max Brooks's idea that "conventional doctrines of warfare" don't work against undead. Brooks, *The Zombie Survival Guide*, 42.
48. Romero, *Diary of the Dead*, DVD.
49. The nature of the economy in Romero's films is ambiguous. On the one hand it is difficult to imagine that the ex-Guard's million dollars will have much value in the context of a nation overrun with the dead (or even in Canada, their intended destination). On the other hand, in *Land of the Dead*, Cholo states that "all I care about is money" and he claims that the alcohol he steals can be traded for over a thousand dollars in Uniontown.
50. Harpold, "The End Begins," 156.
51. Romero, *Diary of the Dead*, DVD.
52. Romero, *Land of the Dead*, DVD.
53. Ibid.
54. Ibid.
55. Ibid.
56. Ibid.
57. Ibid.
58. In *Diary of the Dead*, Ridley's home, which initially looks so promising ("It's like what god might have built, if only he had the money") also ends up as a kind of death trap with Debra, Tony, and the Professor entombing themselves in the panic room with few prospects for long-term survival.
59. Bishop, *American Zombie Gothic*, 242.
60. Romero, *Dawn of the Dead*, DVD.
61. Ibid. The subsequent famous montage shows the group sampling and enjoying hats, watches, jackets, pants, candy, sports equipment, bread, cheese and sausages, spices, coffee, and videogames.
62. Ibid.
63. Ibid.
64. Claeys and Sargent, *Utopia Reader*, 5.
65. Romero, *Dawn of the Dead*, DVD.
66. Ibid.

67. *Ibid.*
68. Bishop, *American Zombie Gothic*, 148.
69. See Tait, "(Zombie) Revolution at the Gates," 62; Lowenstein, "Living Dead," 108–116.
70. Romero, *Dawn of the Dead*, DVD. See, generally, Gwyneth Peaty, "Zombie Time."
71. Romero, *Dawn of the Dead*, DVD.
72. Newman, *Nightmare Movies*, 272.
73. Here one might contrast Romero's mall with an even more fleeting false utopia—something like the Winchester pub in *Shaun of the Dead* (2004).
74. Bishop, *American Zombie Gothic*, 152.
75. Paffenroth, *Gospel of the Living Dead*, 62–66.
76. Wood, *Hollywood From Vietnam to Reagan*, 107.
77. Newman, *Nightmare Movies*, 273.
78. Indeed, Romero's original ending for *Dawn of the Dead* had Fran decapitated and the helicopter engine sputtering out of life. Smith, "Dawn of the Dead."
79. Romero, *Survival of the Dead*, DVD. Muldoon's suggestion that his political obligations covers the entire island, and effectively conflate his interests and his subjects' is reminiscent of arguments made by Thomas Hobbes. See Peabody, "What Thomas Hobbes Can Tell Us."
80. Romero, *Survival of the Dead*, DVD.
81. Kane, *Night Of The Living Dead*, 22.
82. By this standard it's not obvious what to make of Fiddler's Green *after* Kaufman is killed and the existing order overthrown by what amounts to what Scott Foundas and Tait have identified as a "class revolt." Foundas, "Diary of the Dead"; Tait, "(Zombie) Revolution at the Gates," 62. On the one hand, Romero seem to be giving us a popular revolution formed by two waves—the rebellion of the human poor and the assault of the semi-sentient (and righteously outraged) dead. On the other hand, it's not clear how or whether these groups can live in harmony, and, of course, Dead Reckoning hurriedly leaves the scene, not waiting to see how all this will play out.
83. Wood, *Hollywood From Vietnam to Reagan*, 107.
84. *Ibid.*
85. Romero, *Day of the Dead*, DVD.
86. *Ibid.*
87. *Ibid.*
88. *Ibid.*
89. Wood, *Hollywood From Vietnam to Reagan*, 294.
90. Shaviro has a bleaker interpretation. He sees, at the end of *Day,* that the survivors "have nothing to look forward to but an empty, eventless, nightmare-ridden time—or worse..." Shaviro, *Cinematic Body,* 103.
91. George A. Romero, *Survival of the Dead*, DVD.
92. World War Z reflects a similar idea—that Canada may be a partial escape from the walking dead. Brooks, *World War Z,* 122–130. It might be tempting to see Romero's own move to Toronto, and eventual decision to become a Canadian as well as American citizen, as signaling an alienation from the U.S. and a move towards Canadian politics and culture. But the director himself did not make this claim.
93. Keetley, "Introduction," ("In zombie films the utopian moment, the promise of hope, typically comes right at the end").
94. Wood, *Hollywood From Vietnam to Reagan*, 105.
95. Thoreau, "Civil Disobedience," 5.
96. "Proffitt and Rich Templin, "Fight the Dead," 30.
97. Biskind, *The Sky Is Falling*, 71. Further, Biskind claims zombie films like *WWZ* are "traditional centrist" insofar as the "institutions of authority work just fine" (76).
98. Romero, *Land of the Dead*, DVD.
99. Romero, *Dawn of the Dead*, DVD.
100. Aristotle, *The Politics,* 86.
101. Ransome, "How George Romero's Progressive Politics Gave Way."
102. Ryan and Kellner, *Camera Politica*, 235; Bishop, *American Zombie Gothic*, 23 (arguing that there are no "survivalist fantasies" in Romero).
103. Ryan and Kellner, *Camera Politica*, 293.
104. Wood, *Hollywood From Vietnam to Reagan*, 105.
105. Kymlicka, *Politics in the Vernacular.*
106. Shaviro, *Cinematic Body,* 87.
107. Ryan and Kellner, *Camera Politica*, 181.
108. Keetley, "Zombie Republic," 331.
109. *Ibid.* See also Morehead, "Zombie Walks," 106 (*Land* intimates "that zombies and humans might be able to co-exist in some fashion").
110. Ryan and Kellner, *Camera Politica*, 181.
111. Romero, *Day of the Dead*, DVD.

112. Mill, *On Liberty*, 37–8; Gutmann, *Democratic Education*, 33.
113. Shaviro, *Cinematic Body*, 87.
114. In a revealing aside, the black survivalists in *Diary* explain that they "stuck around" their garrison warehouse because after the National Guard and white citizens fled, they inherited real power "For the first time in our lives." Given the serious threat this group still faces from the dead, it's not obvious we can describe their outpost as a kind of black power utopia, but Romero at least sparks the imagination.
115. Keetley, "Zombie Republic," 330 ("*Dawn* has consistently been read as a critique of pervasive consumer capitalism, allegorized in the zombies' instinctive return to the mall" and "their bottomless drive to consume. See also Tait, "(Zombie) Revolution at the Gates," 69, Lowenstein, "Living Dead," 108–116, and Bishop, *American Zombie Gothic*,191–196.
116. Keetley, "Zombie Republic," 295.
117. Keetley, "Introduction," 5 (arguing that the zombies in *Land* are aligned "with the poor, oppressed, and racially marginalized" humans).
118. *Ibid.*, 14.
119. Williams, *George A. Romero: Interviews*, 48.
120. Sondrol, "Totalitarian and Authoritarian Dictators." With some parallel to the director's attitudes towards violence, Romero also criticizes science, or, more accurately, scientism (most explicitly in *Day*). But here too, he seems to be primarily aiming at scientific progress divorced from human needs, rather than systematic inquiry *per se.*
121. Wood, *Hollywood From Vietnam to Reagan*, 115.
122. Vallan, "A Pinewood Dialogue with George A. Romero."
123. Williams, *George A. Romero: Interviews*, 130.
124. Wood, *Hollywood From Vietnam to Reagan*,192.
125. Williams, *George A. Romero: Interviews*, 166.
126. When enthusiasts of *Night of the Living Dead* encouraged him to make a sequel he objected: "I don't want to just make another [film], I have to have an idea, I have to have something to say!" Myers, "Interview with George A. Romero."
127. *Ibid.*, 47.
128. *Ibid.*
129. Wood's famous essay, "An Introduction to the American Horror Film," also points to the importance of dialectic evolution in emphasizing the importance of the dichotomy between normality and the "Monster" and the relationship between the two.
130. Shaviro, *Cinematic Body*, 92.
131. Newman, *Nightmare Movies*, 283.
132. A case can be made that while Romero is a revolutionary he is not, as some scholars contend, radical, both because he does not adhere to a consistent "root" idea and due to his unwillingness to abolish conventional institutions altogether.
133. Wood, "Neglected Nightmares," 32.
134. Newman, *Nightmare Movies*, 576.
135. Ryan and Kellner, *Camera Politica*, 181.
136. Wood, *Hollywood From Vietnam to Reagan,* 107 (discussing Fran's gradual transcendence of "the role of female stereotype" and Peter's "separation from norms of white-dominated society and his parital exemption from its constraints.")
137. See Diamond, "Ethics and Politics," 77–8. Intriguingly, Romero has also connected his thinking with another idea from Ancient Greek philosophy: the notion that regimes give rise to new and distinct replacements, forming a kind of cycle of political death and rebirth. As Romero explained in a 2008 interview, "I always thought of the zombies as being about revolution, one generation consuming the next." Onstad, "Revolution Cycle." Hitz, "Degenerate Regimes in Plato's *Republic*," Diamond, "Ethics and Politics."
138. Aristotle, *The Politics*, 86.
139. Romero, *Survival of the Dead*, DVD.
140. Romero, *Land of the Dead*, DVD.
141. Bishop, *American Zombie Gothic*, 207; Franklin, *Politics and Film*, 16.
142. Romero, "10 Questions for George Romero."
143. Franklin, *Politics and Film*, 16.
144. Maddrey, *Nightmares in Red, White and Blue*, 122
145. George A. Romero, *Land of the Dead*, DVD.
146. Bishop, *American Zombie Gothic*, 9; Gillings, "We're Obsessed With Zombies."
147. Bishop, *American Zombie Gothic*, 202.
148. George A. Romero, *Diary of the Dead*, DVD.
149. Stevens, "Diary of the Dead."
150. Onstad, "Revolution Cycle."
151. Brooks, *The Zombie Survival Guide*, 17, 125.
152. *Ibid.*, 17.

153. Ibid., 125.
154. See generally, Skal, *The Monster Show*, 397 (arguing that important traditions in monster cinema "can all trace their lineage in one way or another to the cultural trauma of war").
155. George A. Romero, *Day of the Dead*, DVD.
156. Ryan and Kellner, *Camera Politica*, 191.
157. Peabody, "Uncomfortable Fictions."
158. Romero, *Day of the Dead*, DVD. This idea is omnipresent in Brooks's *WWZ*.
159. Romero, *Diary of the Dead*, DVD.
160. Lasswell, *Politics: Who Gets What, When, How,* ix, 264; Easton, *A Framework for Political Analysis*, 90–98; Baumgartner, "Main Objective: Don't Starve," 45.
161. Newman, *Nightmare Movies*, 574.
162. See the discussion of "public goods" in Olson, *The Logic of Collective Action*, 2.
163. The idea that Romero is interested in project organization and execution as a creative and political problem is supported by the observation that his own career was marked by frequent filmmaking challenges. Kohn, "George Romero Says Nobody Will Finance His Next Zombie Movie."
164. Levitsky and Ziblatt, *How Democracies Die*, 7.
165. Ibid.
166. Eggertson, "BD Sits Down with Zombie Maestro George A. Romero!"
167. As Romero puts it most broadly: "The whole world needs an anger management plan." Williams, *George A. Romero: Interviews*, 183.
168. Balfour, "George Romero Strives for 'Survival of the Dead.'" Dawn Keetley provides a fascinating complement to this analysis with her chapter on David Moody's "Hater" series. Keetley argues that Moody offers us a particular kind of zombies ("affective zombies") who possess "a stark rage that annihilates the complications of identity politics grounded in history and eviscerates consumerism as the measure of a successful self." Keetley, "Condemned to History by the Hate," 134, 143. While not explicitly tethering this idea to partisanship, many elements of her analysis could be effectively deployed to understand political divisions in the 21st century, especially insofar as many of these conflicts do not obviously serve the demographic or material interests of those affected.
169. Haidt, "We Need a Little Fear."
170. In *Survival*, the extent of O'Flynn's self-deception is revealed when he claims, "We're all on the same side, those of us living," when, in fact, his driving impulse throughout the entire film is to dispatch Muldoon rather than fret about the undead.
171. Romero, *Day of the Dead*, DVD.
172. Romero, *Dawn of the Dead*, DVD.
173. Romero, *Day of the Dead*, DVD.
174. Iyengar and Westwood, "Fear and Loathing across Party Lines," 1.
175. Romero, *Survival of the Dead*, DVD.
176. Ibid.
177. Ibid.
178. In this way, Romero's theme is similar to *The Walking Dead*'s concerns with "learning how to value collectivity and act collectively in the face of profound crisis." Salazar and Healy, "We're all The Walking Dead."
179. Skal, *The Monster Show*, 372.
180. Williams, *George A. Romero: Interviews*, 64.

"They're [Still] Coming to Get You"

White Liberals as the Zombie Horde in Jordan Peele's *Get Out*

CAMMIE M. SUBLETTE

Part of the black identity is the horror of America. There are things we are cognizant of because we have to be.
—Jordan Peele[1]

On July 16, 2017, the day George A. Romero died, Jordan Peele tweeted, "Romero started it," along with an image of gun-wielding Duane Jones as *Night of the Living Dead*'s (1968) Ben. Romero's death inspired Peele's tweet, concretizing what should have been obvious: Peele is deeply influenced by Romero. In fact, Peele's *Get Out* (2017) is a descendant of Romero's masterpiece in ways that have yet to be articulated.

These horror films have many things in common, including their incredible success. *Night of the Living Dead* earned over 30 million dollars internationally upon its release, which would look more like 213 million dollars in today's economy.[2] *Get Out*, as Rob Wile notes, was named 2017's most profitable film overall, with worldwide earnings of more than 250 million dollars, which translates into an astounding profit margin for a film that was produced and marketed for 4.5 million.[3]

While profitability is an important marker of success for the filmmaker hoping to direct another film, there are many other indicators of success as well. Both films have enjoyed many accolades and much critical acclaim. *Night* is hard to overestimate in terms of its influence. So impactful is this film, that in 1999, the Library of Congress added it to the National Film Registry, a space jealously guarded for only films deemed "culturally, historically, or aesthetically significant."[4] Fans, critics, and other filmmakers have argued that this film single-handedly transformed the horror genre, birthing the zombie film that has, in the twenty-first century, become so ubiquitous. While it is perhaps too early to assess the full impact of *Get Out*, the film has been hailed as being at the crest of a new wave of black horror films.[5] *Get Out*'s record-breaking critical acclaim includes nominations for Best Screenplay, Best Film, and Best Director in virtually every major American film competition and a good number of international film awards for 2017–18, culminating in Peele's Oscar win for Best Original Screenplay in 2018.

In addition, both *Night* and *Get Out* are horror films featuring black male protagonists. This alone should not be remarkable enough to link the films, but there are relatively few horror films with black protagonists. In an interview with Stephen Colbert, Jordan Peele joked that, at the time of its release, *Get Out* was basically the only black horror film in existence.[6] Other horror films featuring black leads are, indeed, hard to find but include *Blacula* (1972), *The People Under the Stairs* (1991), *Candyman* (1992), *Vampire in Brooklyn* (1995), *Tales from the Hood* (1995), *Haunted Mansion* (2003), Zack Snyder's remake of *Dawn of the Dead* (2004),[7] Snoop Dogg's *Hood of Horror* (2006), and most recently, *The First Purge* (2018), *Ma* (2019), and Jordan Peele's own most recent film, *Us* (2019). Moreover, of those few, half feature their black leads not as heroes but monsters, even if somewhat sympathetic monsters. Thus, as Peele notes, it's relatively easy to list the few horror films featuring a black hero[8] and even easier to list the subset that also avoids clichés and racial stereotypes. The protagonists in *Night* and *Get Out*, however, are distinct in that they are heroic if not flawless, avoiding racial stereotypes in their depictions except in those places where the stereotype—that black people are fearful of hypnosis, for instance, or that all black people know each other—goes deeper than mere stereotype, crystalizing into a significant plot-point with an acknowledged history.

In addition to being fully developed protagonists, both Ben (*Night*) and Chris (*Get Out*) are surrounded by white people, many of whom are needy or appear to mean them harm. Ben, incredibly quick-witted and determined, finds refuge from a zombie attack in an abandoned farmhouse, but his refuge from zombies is never peaceful, even when they are temporarily held at bay. Also seeking refuge in the farmhouse are six white people with a variety of emotional traumas and familial dysfunctions, and many of their traumas and dysfunctions quickly become Ben's problems to manage.

Barbra (Judith O'Dea), the first of his companions to reveal herself, given that the others are, early in the film, hiding in the house's basement, vacillates between terror and a near catatonic apathy. She has just witnessed her brother's attack by a zombie and seems, for the most part, incapable, and even infantilized by grief and terror.[9] Ben finds shoes for her, protects her from zombies and other people, talks to her and listens, and risks his life for her several times. He also slaps her—hard—when he thinks she is growing hysterical. His relationship to Barbra is one of the underlying tensions throughout the film, for while there is never a discussion of any romantic interest either might have in the other, there are moments when they are clearly running counter to 1960s taboos regarding interracial relationships. For instance, after she faints, Ben lifts her onto a nearby couch and then unbuttons her coat and loosens her garments. Though practical and caring, these actions still crash into taboos regarding interracial relationships, and they occur only a few minutes after he slaps her, thus building layers of taboo behavior into the film's narrative.

Race & Fear in American Horror

Romero claimed that he cast Duane Jones as Ben without considering his race and without changing the script once a black man was in the lead role.[10] Peele notes that the film's meaning shifted with that casting decision, whether or not Romero intended it: "All social norms break down when this event happens and a black man is caged up in a house with a white woman who is terrified. But you're not sure how much she's terrified at the monsters on the outside or this man on the inside who is now the hero."[11] Indeed, Barbra's behavior around Ben remains enigmatic. When her head lolls and she gazes at Ben in apparent traumatized horror, we wonder if he is the source of or merely the witness to her terrified aspect. As film critic Robert K. Lightning puts it, "for Barbra, Ben arouses a more immediate or equal fear to her fear of the dead."[12] The behavior of the other whites in the house is likewise ambiguously racially motivated; most notably, that of Harry Cooper (Karl Hardman), who challenges Ben's every action, seems inclined to shoot Ben if given the chance, and eventually attempts to sacrifice Ben to the zombies outside. As Peele notes, that Ben is a black man makes all the difference in the way we read the white characters' actions, and thus their terror and hostility remain ambiguously associated with the race of the man trying desperately to save their lives and his own. In "Guess Who's Going to Be Dinner," Barbara S. Bruce argues that although "race is represented ambivalently" in *Night*, the film nonetheless "gives full vent to the anxieties permeating late-'60s American culture ... engaging race-based expectations without offering the panacea of a Poitier-like hero or readily identifiable and, therefore, containable black stereotypes."[13] Indeed, even if Romero was not fully aware of the racial implications of the film he was making in 1967, Duane Jones most certainly was. He tells a story about driving home after filming one day, ride-sharing with an extra on the film, a white woman. Along the way, the two were chased by a group of white teenagers. Reported Jones,

> And then I looked back. One of them started brandishing a tire iron at me. And the paradox and the irony that I had been walking around brandishing a tire iron at ghouls all day long, and there was somebody brandishing a tire iron at me from a car but in absolute seriousness. And that moment ... the total surrealism of the racial nightmare of America being worse than whatever that was we were doing as a metaphor in that film lives with me to this moment.[14]

Alissa Wilkinson, writing for *Vox*, connects Romero's casting of Ben—and the ways such casting changed the meaning of the film—to much of the zombie genre's attention to race: "[*Night*] didn't just provide a template for social thrillers and zombies; it also inspired a subtle and important way of integrating race into those stories."[15] And, as Wilkinson notes in the lead for her article, "Without *Night of the Living Dead*, we wouldn't have *Get Out*."[16] Thus, whether it was his intention or not, Romero made a film that was also at least as much about race and racism in the United States as it was about zombies. This embedded social critique is not surprising. In *Zombie Cinema*, Ian Olney notes that "the leading theory seems to be that the dead resonate with audiences today because they embody contemporary fears and desires."[17] Kyle W. Bishop, likely the theorist most closely associated with this representational approach to zombie films, asserts, "During the twentieth century, most serious explorations of the zombie invasion narrative—that is, those tales following the generic formula established by George A. Romero with *Night of the Living Dead* (1968)—based their thematic essence on one key premise: the monsters represent humanity."[18] Jordan Peele recognized this and thus, when he made *Get Out* some fifty years after Romero's seminal film premiered, Peele more deliberately confronted racism head on as the monster that it is.

One of the ways that Peele adapts and updates *Night*, then, is by adopting versions of Romero's earlier characters but ultimately dropping their symbolic and political ambiguity. For instance, *Get Out*'s Rose Armitage (Allison Williams) compares to Barbra in a number of ways, but where Barbra's intentions toward Ben are never transparent, Rose's malicious intent ultimately becomes unequivocal. Both characters are wrapped in family narratives that are pivotal to the respective movies' plots—Barbra because of her central role in the film's opening, a scene that starts with a long drive in the country and ends with her brother's death at the hands of a zombie and Rose because *Get Out* is, on the surface, a story about her boyfriend meeting her parents for the first time. Both Barbra and Rose exude white privilege and pampering, though this is more apparent in Rose's case because we see her in her parents' home surrounded by the many excessive trappings of white affluence.[19] Both Barbra and Rose are close to the brothers who torment them, and both undergo radical personality shifts once these brothers are killed. In addition, like the relationship between Ben and Barbra, the one between Rose and Chris, although updated, still confronts the taboo of interracial relationships. And perhaps most importantly, both women seem, at various points in the respective narratives, to be responsible for the downfall of our protagonists. Rose's malevolent agency eventually becomes evident as well as heartbreaking: her treacherous role in Chris's imprisonment and torture is horribly vivid in a scene where she first digs for her keys in her handbag, apparently desperate to help Chris escape, and then, sickeningly, dangles them out of his reach, saying, "You know I can't give you the keys, right, babe?"[20]

Like Ben, Chris is a protagonist to be admired. He is resourceful, capable, and strong, and he is also kind and caring. The guilt he feels over his mother's death (due to his inaction when she failed to return home on the fateful night of her accident) weighs on him deeply, allowing Rose's mother to access this vulnerability and pull him into "the sunken place," a state of hypnotic suggestion that renders him paralyzed physically and tormented psychologically. Chris, like Ben, does not foolishly enter and stay in dangerous situations if he can help it, and both men appear to recognize the danger of being trapped with white people, no other black allies in sight. Where Ben refuses to hole up in the basement with white people, a space without windows or a second exit, until it is a last resort (and the white people are all dead, thus leaving him alone in the basement), Chris declines hypnosis by a white person, tries to keep his phone charged and thus his connection to the outside world (i.e., black people) intact, and remains aware and observant, asking questions of the Armitage family (and especially Rose) whenever he senses something is wrong. Chris also seeks black allies each time a black person shows up at the Armitages', and his alarm deepens in relation to their strange behavior and standoffishness (which, unbeknownst to Chris, is due to their "possession" by the Armitages and their wealthy white associates).

Peele gives Chris motivation to put himself in harm's way, for he follows love, agreeing to travel to the rural location in upstate New York, far from his home, friends, and the safety of the city. He agrees to do this in order to meet his girlfriend's parents and despite his concern that she has neglected to inform them of his race. Love or not, though, Chris maintains a degree of healthy paranoia throughout the film. In fact, once he meets Rose's family, Chris's paranoia builds. As soon as he and Rose arrive at the Armitage home, he realizes they employ a black maid, Georgina (Betty Gabriel), and groundskeeper, Walter (Marcus Henderson), both of whom behave bizarrely, to say the least, as well as seem like stereotypes of late nineteenth century black domestic laborers in the South, throwbacks to a segregated and perilous America. Dean Armitage (Bradley Whitford) attempts to assure Chris that though this employment situation "looks bad," these employees are really family. That does little to mollify Chris, for racist white Americans have long claimed a special familial connection to their slaves and later to their black employees, despite not treating them as equals, acknowledging their employees' *actual* families, or recognizing any identity of these "family members" outside of their employment status. In *Clinging to Mammy: The Faithful Slave in Twentieth-Century America*, Micki McElya writes, "Faithful slave narratives emerged from a long history of white denials of the legitimacy of black families and their emotional bonds under slavery. When celebrating the figure of the black mother, whites never referred to her own family, a deliberate silence that allowed them to ignore the coercion that helped make possible this intimate relationship between black female caretakers and their white charges."[21] Likewise, Kimberly Wallace-Sanders, in her book *Mammy: A Century of Race, Gender, and Southern Memory*, notes that the mammy is the most enduring of faithful slave stereotypes, for it does the most cultural work to excuse whites for the horrors of slavery. Wallace-Sanders writes, "Ultimately, the mammy stereotype that blurs our vision is an exceptional example of the fluidity of social memory as well as a testimony to the dynamic power of cultural manipulation."[22] Further undermining their claims to be non-racist liberals,[23] Rose's family is too eager to connect to Chris on a racial level, too eager to control him (particularly once he's put under hypnotic suggestion without having given his consent), and too eager to introduce him to their white friends, all of whom seem quick to blunder into racist micro-aggressions. Peele has noted that he wanted a heroic protagonist who isn't oblivious to the danger he is in but nonetheless has a reason to stay.[24] Thus, we see Chris's paranoia, anger, and fear warring with his love for Rose. Unlike Ben, whose paranoia, anger, and fear are also quite prominent but whose motive for remaining in the abandoned farmhouse appears to be almost entirely about the danger presented by the monsters outside, Chris remains despite the danger *inside*.

A History of Racist Violence

Given that both Ben and Chris are black men living in the United States, a country founded on slavery and still notorious for its racial inequality and violence against black men and women, whether the violence and inequality is set in the 1960s or the twenty-first century, they *should* be paranoid. In fact, if they are going to live through these nightmare experiences, it is their paranoia that will save them. As Peele notes, "theoretically, their racial perspective is the very skill that helps them.... The lead in *Night* is a man living in fear every day, so this [the zombie invasion] is a challenge he is more equipped to take on than the white women living in the house. Chris, in his racial paranoia, is onto something that he wouldn't be if he was a white guy and there was a similar thing going on."[25]

The fear of racially motivated violence is at the heart of the similarities between these films, which Peele highlights in many allusions to Romero's masterpiece. In addition to Peele's revision of Romero's leads, he also alludes to and often reinvents plot points, props, and symbolism from *Night*. Without the many other references and allusions, these details may seem like just more "Easter eggs" of American horror referenced slyly in the movie. (Fans have noticed a number of references to *The Shining*, for instance, which Peele has confirmed are intentional.[26]) However, the similarities between *Get Out* and *Night* are more than mere Easter eggs to delight fans, for these references build deep intertextuality between the two films, which Peele then uses as backdrop to his exploration of race in the twenty-first century zombie film. Thus, just as Romero's film begins with a long car ride in a rural location, so, too, does *Get Out* use a long car ride in the country as an establishing scene. In both cases, the dislocation of our central characters from the relative safety of the urban space sets the stage for the films' horror. The attempted escape of Ben, Judy, and Tom in Romero's film is mirrored by Chris's escape from the house at the end of *Get Out*: both escapes include a fire, the use of a rifle in a pivotal betrayal, and the deaths of two innocents (Judy and Tom in *Night*, Georgina and Walter in *Get Out*). Both films include phone trouble as a key plot point, since a lack of phone service makes it impossible to get help, further isolating our main characters from family and friends. In addition, both films use television as the means for delivering bad news to our heroes concerning the horrible reality of their circumstances. Both films feature a basement where a good deal of the trauma and horror unfolds (and where, to be sure, our main characters resist going). Also, both films feature mounted deer heads on the walls of the houses, with Peele imbuing these deer mounts with a good deal of symbolic meaning as they come to stand for the old monied white Armitage family while also becoming an instrument of the family's undoing when Chris uses the antlered buck head as a lethal weapon against the Armitage family patriarch. Finally, both films end by establishing themes of mistaken identity and the horrific ramifications they have for black men in America.

Much has been written about *Night*'s social commentaries on the turbulent 1960s, including its proximity to Dr. Martin Luther King, Jr.'s assassination just six months prior to the film's release.[27] The end of the film is particularly haunting in this respect, for, having survived the zombie apocalypse, Ben is promptly killed by a white sheriff-led posse, his summary execution jolting and horrifying, particularly when juxtaposed with the nonchalance of the white men doing the killing. Their motives are left uninterrogated, so viewers have no way of knowing if Ben's murder was a case of mistaken identity—i.e., if they actually believed him to be a zombie—or if the equation is more metaphorical: they killed him because they place as little value on the lives of black men as on the zombies. The film's greater context does little to clarify this point. For instance, before the killing, Sheriff McClelland (George Kosana) tells the white men around him, "You want to get about four or five men and some dogs. There's a house over here, and we want to go check it out."[28] Ostensibly they want to check out the house to be sure it's empty of zombies. As the posse moves toward the house, viewers recognize that this is the house Ben is in, so it seems likely that Ben will now be rescued. By the release of *Night*, horror films had already established the expectation that at least one member of our besieged group would survive.[29]

There is something hauntingly familiar and eerie about this posse, though, for they conjure the slave-catching posses of the eighteenth and nineteenth centuries, the lynch mobs that emerged in Reconstruction America and persisted through the 1950s, and even the groups of blended vigilantes and law enforcement officers that attacked civil rights protestors throughout the 1950s and 1960s. Framed within this historical context, the *Night* posse, in fact, looks more likely to harm Ben than save him, and when Sheriff McClelland mentions that the National Guard is due to arrive, that merely highlights the connections between this scene and the many scenes of white racism and violent abuse of power occurring throughout the 1950s and '60s. It is this historical context that first led Lightning to identify the killing of Ben in *Night* as a "symbolic lynching."[30] All in the *Night* posse are white men, including the sheriff, other law officers, men who appear to have been deputized for this "hunt," and two reporters. The men carry guns and restrain dogs on leashes. Like slave catchers of the antebellum South and law enforcement officials of the 1960s who used dogs to attack peaceful civil rights activists,[31] these men and their dogs appear ominously dangerous to Ben. Visually, too, they bear a striking resemblance to many of the men who are represented in lynching photos in such works as

Without Sanctuary, a grisly record documenting many of the photos taken as souvenirs by whites who attended and participated in lynchings in the United States.[32] The posse in *Night* look like a hunting party, which, as Amy Louise Wood notes, is the stance taken in a large number of lynching photos. Wood writes, "the photographic convention that the lynching photograph arguably most evokes is that of the hunting photograph."[33] Further, the very history of the motion picture is founded on such imagery of lynchings. According to Wood, early Edison films of the variety referred to as "cinema of attractions," short films that depended heavily on voyeurism and were often absent any real narrative plot, "included tourist scenes, panoramas, fires and other disasters, circus scenes, and sexually suggestive scenes, as well as lynching and execution films."[34] Although most of these early lynching films were "reenactments of western 'frontier' or southern-style vigilantism," Wood argues that Southern audiences nonetheless would have viewed them through the lens they most closely associated with lynching: that of black men by white mobs.[35] One popular lynching film from 1904 eliminated any such distance or reframing of Southern lynchings. Titled *Avenging a Crime; or, Burned at the Stake*, this was a film that reenacted the violent white Southern fantasy of lynching, featuring a stereotyped portrayal of black male violence against a white woman, followed by swift and violent retribution by a white mob.[36] An even earlier film, one released in 1898 by American Mutoscope and Biograph Company, contained actual footage of an execution of a black man in Florida, as W. Scott Poole records, and this particular prisoner, Wood believes, was Edward Heinson, a black man who was convicted of raping a white fourteen-year-old girl, a key feature of the mythology of black men that was used to buttress pro-lynching rhetoric.[37] This film, Wood notes, remained popular enough that it was still being shown in 1902. Arguing that the lynching of black men is sublimated across the entirety of American mainstream film history, Robert Jackson writes, "It is a process marked by the steady appropriation and reinvention of the key elements of the historical phenomenon of lynching in the modern South—the targeting of black men, the paranoia regarding white southern womanhood, the combination of randomness and ritual, the rippling implications for entire communities, the necessity of squaring extralegal acts with ideas of law and citizenship."[38] These deep roots to historical white violence against blacks haunt the end of *Night* and serve to foreshadow and frame Ben's death.

As the posse nears the farmhouse, we see Ben inside, the lone survivor of the zombie attack, exhausted from battling the undead during a sleepless night. He hears dogs and gunfire as the posse shoots at a now small group of zombies meandering about outside the house. Getting closer, the sheriff casually comments, "Somebody had a cookout here," referencing a burned truck, the site of a failed escape attempt made by the sympathetic young white characters, Tom and Judy, who died in the truck and were then consumed by zombies. Although there are no bodily remains depicted here, given the (for the time) shocking display of gore involved in the deaths and consumption of Tom and Judy by the zombies, the casual indifference to human suffering on display bodes ill for Ben. Further, the crass humor implying no discomfort with cannibalism links the posse and the zombies. The history of chattel slavery in the U.S., after all, is an allegory of consumerist cannibalism, human lives mercilessly chewed up and spit out. White Americans' post-bellum and segregationist attitudes often extended this inhumane treatment of African Americans—to the degree that jokes about cannibalism abounded in whites' references to the lynchings of African American men.[39]

As Ben emerges from the basement, slowly moving toward a window, the sheriff, still at some remove from the house, instructs a man standing near him, "All right, Vince, hit him in the head. Right between the eyes." He shoots, and Ben is hit with the bullet, violently flung backward and to the floor, where he remains, unmoving. The sheriff merely comments, "Good shot! Okay, he's dead. Let's go get 'em. That's another one for the fire."[40] We then see grainy still photos of white men standing around Ben's body, torturous-looking meat hooks in many of their hands. Ben is alone, vulnerable, and the white men appear threatening, mob-like. This imagery further links the scene to historical instances of the torture and murder of black men in the United States. Historian Leon Litwack notes that the specifics of the lynchings of black men in the nineteenth and early twentieth centuries in the United States often demonstrated extremes of "sadism and exhibitionism…. The ordinary modes of execution and punishment no longer satisfied the emotional appetite of the crowd. To kill the victim was not enough; the execution became public theater, a participatory ritual of torture and death, a voyeuristic spectacle prolonged as long as possible."[41] The mob of white men, meat hooks in hand, surrounds Ben's prone body and provides a subtext to Ben's death, aligning him with the thousands of innocent black men and women who were lynched in the United States.

The credits roll as we hear the sheriff's voice, cutting into the haunting music that plays until it is drowned out by a helicopter, a likely allusion to human rights atrocities in Vietnam that were coming to light as this film was made.[42] The last thing viewers see is a bonfire of bodies, Ben's body presumably part of the inferno, which is yet another link to lynching, as the burning of the body was frequently the grotesque finale to extremes of violence whites perpetrated on black men.[43] If the film was not about race until the end, at that point, it becomes a more transparent indictment of the violence enacted upon black men in the United States.

Similarly, in *Get Out*, the end of the film bears heavy allusions to contemporaneous atrocities against black men. In fact, in the 2019 documentary *Horror Noire: A History of Black Horror*, Jordan Peele says that the ending of *Night* inspired the ending of *Get Out*.[44] In the film's denouement, Chris does battle with the Armitage family, with each member attacking him after their own fashion, trying desperately first to keep him imprisoned in the house, and then kill him. He vanquishes all of them, save Rose, then flees the house as she begins firing a gun at him. After a series of mishaps and loyalty struggles involving the black Armitage employees who seem to be battling internally with the whites possessing them, Rose and Chris fight. In the original ending, Chris ends up on top of Rose, choking her, when the police roll up on the scene. Chris stands no chance and knows it. He bears the full weight of the stereotype of black men as sexual predators, facing police in America known to disproportionately use lethal force against black men and women.[45] He slowly stands, hands up, accepting his fate. Though they don't kill him, they arrest him, assuming he is the criminal rather than the victim. When we last see him, he is in prison, a wasted and haunted soul, all hope for his exoneration and freedom extinguished. In the revised ending, the one Peele ultimately decided to use in the theatrical/official version of the film, Rose again comes after Chris with a gun, but then Walter intervenes and asks Rose to give him the gun. It seems he will shoot Chris, but instead, he turns the gun first on Rose and then himself. Rose is still alive, gasping for air as a police car arrives, but this time, Chris is rescued, for the officer on the scene is none other than Chris's best friend and airport TSA officer, Rod Williams (Lil Rel Howery). Therefore, in this revised ending, Peele allows a small collective of black men to thwart the white throng in their attempts to imprison and enslave or kill Chris. As Yohana Desta writes in *Vanity Fair*, the original ending for the film was "impossibly bleak."[46] This original ending, therefore, was in keeping with *Night*'s ending, an ending that historically situates even as it updates dismal and violent ends for black men at the hands of whites. Desta quotes Peele's articulation of his reason for the revision: "'The ending needed to transform into something that gives us a hero, that gives us an escape, that gives us a positive feeling.'"[47] Thus, Peele provides his audience the hopeful conclusion denied Romero's audience. Although this more hopeful ending potentially undermines the social critique of the film, it offers its black audience some respite from the horrors of white racism that was missing in Romero's film: the empowerment our hero finds in black friendship and community.

Surrounded by White Zombies

Andy Crump, in a review for *The Hollywood Reporter*, likely comes closest to articulating the link between the two films, arguing that *Get Out* essentially reverses the horror of *Night*, pushing us closer to Ben's nightmare perspective in being surrounded not just by zombies, but also by so many potentially threatening whites.[48] Crump pays particular attention to the two films' endings, writing, "In 1968 as in the 2010s, watching men gun down Ben without considering the possibility of violence motivated by racism is impossible; countless instances of police officers killing unarmed black men and black teens in recent years … emphasize how much American society *hasn't* progressed in the last five decades."[49] Just two years before the release of *Night*, James Baldwin wrote,

> "I have witnessed and endured the brutality of the police many more times than once—but, of course, I cannot prove it. I cannot prove it because the Police Department investigates itself, quite as though it were answerable only to itself. But it cannot be allowed to be answerable only to itself. It must be made to answer to the community which pays it, and which it is legally sworn to protect, and if American Negroes are not a part of the American community, then all of the American professions are a fraud."[50] Indeed, this is the cultural background that inspired Peele's original ending to *Get Out*, a critical commentary on the dangers black men still face in the twenty-first century when the criminal justice arm of the American social contract, the police, kill so many innocent and unarmed black people, especially men. The import of Ben's monologue about facing down the zombies takes on new meaning by the end of *Night*: "I realized I was alone with fifty or sixty of those things standing there, staring at me."[51] Eventually, both Ben and Chris find themselves alone, grossly outnumbered by monsters lacking humanity.

What Crump misses, then, is that the whites were the zombies all along, and this is more transparently the case as Peele reimagines *Night*. Peele sees Ben's race as essential to his characterization, noting, "In *Night of the Living Dead*, he is the guy who is ready to fight zombies because he's been fighting white people off his whole life."[52] In fact, though, in *Get Out* there is no difference, as Peele directly conflates the monsters: whites are attempting to kill or consume the black people they encounter, and in as relentless and mystifying fashion as the zombies of Romero's film. Peele says of the impact at the end of *Night*, "that's nothing if it's a white dude,"[53] that applies doubly to *Get Out*.

What Romero insinuated via Ben's death at the end of *Night*, Peele makes direct and literal: whites want the bodies of blacks, and they will, if given the chance, devour and use them. This is the legacy of slavery—the appropriation of black bodies, black talent, black culture, and black art by whites who insist that racism is a thing of the past. Indeed, *Get Out* can be understood as an extension of *Night's* horrible premise. It is the aftermath of Ben's death, or, at least, had the original ending of *Get Out* not been scrapped for a lighter, more affirmative and hopeful ending—one allowing our hero to walk away from his brush with zombies—it's the conclusion we should have anticipated. You don't defeat the zombie horde in either its undead or racial forms. The initially mocking and oft-repeated line from Johnny to Barbra in *Night*, "They're coming to get you," becomes so much more sinister once we know that they are, in fact, coming to get her. A similar inversion occurs with Chris, for his paranoia, fed by his even more paranoid black friend, Rod, no longer seems paranoid at all once it is clear what the Armitages have been doing: kidnapping, hypnotizing, lobotomizing, and possessing the bodies of black people, extracting black brains and swapping them for white brains and thus achieving virtually entire mental, physical, and even spiritual control.

Recalling the origins of zombies in Haitian voodoo, a hybridized faith blending elements of West African and Christian religion during slavery, Peele revisits the horrors of zombification that, as Olney notes, "represented an extension in death of the bondage [slaves] suffered in life."[54] In an even more extensive analysis, Kyle Bishop details this history of zombies rooted in Haitian religious beliefs, concluding, "the zombie is a folkloristic manifestation of a colonial or postcolonial society's greatest fear: subjugation, marginalization, and enslavement."[55] Peele's vision of the absolute and horrific control of the black body by whites invokes this early imagining of zombification. However, Peele (like Romero) does not portray his black characters—even those "possessed" by whites—as the real zombie monsters. Instead, Peele equates zombies and whiteness. Like zombies, the white people we encounter in *Get Out* are a horde of apathetic, unthinking, and hostile cannibals, dead themselves and driven to consume the living. Natasha Patterson writes, "Critics and fans have credited Romero with changing the face of the zombie film from the earlier renditions of voodoo-inspired tales of the living dead and creating the splatter film."[56] Peele is once again transforming the zombie film, turning it back toward its origins in voodoo while also taking Romero's nightmare vision to its logical conclusion. As Peele's *Get Out* makes clear, zombies were always symbolic of other fears, and the monster of racism has been embedded in the zombie film all along.

Notes

1. Peele, "Jordan Peele *Get Out* Keynote." *2017 Film Independent Forum*, YouTube, October 23, 2017. Accessed July 1, 2018. https://www.youtube.com/watch?v=YnpDiuE8HJU.
2. Schweitzer, *Going Viral: Zombies, Viruses, and the End of the World*, 147.
3. Wile, "Jordan Peele's 'Get Out' Is the Most Profitable Film of 2017," *Money*, August 8, 2017. http://money.com/money/4891175/get-out-jordan-peele-most-profitable-movie-2017.
4. Macek III, "The Zombification Family Tree: Legacy of Living Dead," *Pop Matters*, June 14, 2012. https://www.popmatters.com/159439-legacy-of-the-living-dead-2495844721.html?rebelltitem=1#rebelltitem1.
5. Means Coleman, "We're In a Golden Age of Black Horror Films," *The Conversation*, May 29, 2019. https://theconversation.com/were-in-a-golden-age-of-black-horror-films-116648.
6. Peele, "Jordan Peele Crashed a 'Get Out' College Course."
7. Of this film, Brooks, in *Searching for Sycorax*, notes that Snyder follows Romero's "zombie trope of the cool, calm, and collected black male survivor ..., [but] he fails to extend these courtesies of presence and complexity of characterization to women of color" (6). This criticism could be applied to *Get Out*, as well.
8. Peele, "Jordan Peele Crashed a 'Get Out' College Course."
9. For an overview of critical studies of Barbra's characterization and gender in general in Romero's zombie films, see Natasha Patterson's "Cannibalizing Gender and Genre: A Feminist Re-Vision of George Romero's

Zombie Films." Patterson disagrees with critics who read *Night of the Living Dead* as sexist, but she is also not entirely convinced by readings of Romero's zombie films as feminist treatises.

10. Kuhns, *Birth of the Living Dead*, 2013.
11. Zinoman, "Jordan Peele on a Truly Terrifying Monster: Racism," *The New York Times*.
12. Lightning, "Interracial Tensions in *Night of the Living Dead*," *Cineaction*.
13. Barbara S. Bruce, "Guess Who's Going to Be Dinner: Sidney Poitier, Black Militancy, and the Ambivalence of Race in Romero's *Night of the Living Dead*." In *Race, Oppression, and the Zombie: Essays on Cross-Cultural Appropriations of the Caribbean Tradition*, edited by Christopher M. Moreman and Cory Rushton, 61.
14. Newby, "The Lingering Horror of *Night of the Living Dead*," *The Hollywood Reporter*, September 28, 2018.
15. Alissa Wilkinson, "George Romero Didn't Mean to Tackle Race in *Night of the Living Dead*, But He Did Anyway," *Vox*.
16. Ibid.
17. Olney, *Zombie Cinema*, 7.
18. Bishop, "Battling Monsters and Becoming Monstrous: Human Devolution in *The Walking Dead*," 73, in *Monster Culture in the 21st Century: A Reader*.
19. For more analysis of the Armitage home in *Get Out* and its symbolic representation of white affluence, see Sublette's "The House That White Privilege Built: Jordan Peele's *Get Out* and the Haunting Legacy of Plantation Slavery" in *Horror Comes Home: Essays on the Places Where Cinematic Terrors Dwell*.
20. Peele, *Get Out*.
21. McElya, *Clinging to Mammy: The Faithful Slave in Twentieth-Century America*, 80–81.
22. Wallace-Sanders, *Mammy: A Century of Race, Gender, and Southern Memory*, 131.
23. Importantly, Peele did not want the Armitage family to be overtly racist or for the story to unfold in the too-obvious red-state South, as noted in Butler's "Jordan Peele Made a Woke Horror Film." Like another of the film's influences, *Guess Who's Coming to Dinner*, this is a film that tackles white hypocrisy and white privilege by interrogating white liberal racism.
24. Peele, "Jordan Peele Crashed a *Get Out* College Course."
25. Zinoman, "Jordan Peele on a Truly Terrifying Monster: Racism."
26. Desta, "Five Chilling Things You Didn't Notice About Get Out the First Time Around," *Vanity Fair*.
27. Crump, "How 'Get Out' Puts 'Night of the Living Dead' in a New Light," *The Hollywood Reporter*. In addition, Branden Soderberg argues that while Ben's death "evoked the assassinations of Malcolm X and Martin Luther King Jr" upon the film's release, "now it recalls the murder of Trayvon Martin, Michael Brown, Tamir Rice, and Laquan McDonald, along with many others who died in police custody such as Eric Garner, Freddie Gray, and Sandra Bland."
28. Romero, *Night of the Living Dead*, DVD.
29. To be sure, many horror films by 1968 at least implied the deaths of one or more characters, but one or more main characters also survived. For instance, the movies *Creature from the Black Lagoon* (1954), *The Blob* (1958), *Psycho* (1960), and *The Haunting* (1963) all allow central characters to survive. The first two certainly put main characters in harm's way a good deal, and the last two include the dramatic deaths of the main female characters. However, the trope of the survival of at least one or more main characters in horror film was pretty solidly established by the time Romero made *Night of the Living Dead*.
30. Lightning, "Interracial Tensions," 29.
31. Parry, "Police Dogs and Anti-Black Violence," *Black Perspectives*. Parry also notes in this article the continued and disproportionate use of police dogs against black and Hispanic communities, including as recently as 2014 in Ferguson, Missouri, the site of the police killing of Michael Brown. In Ferguson, reported the Department of Justice, the use of police canines appears to have been about the punishment of suspects rather than as a protective deterrent against criminal behavior/violence.
32. *Without Sanctuary: Lynching Photography in America*.
33. Wood, *Lynching and Spectacle: Witnessing Racial Violence in America, 1890-1940*, 94. Also, it is important to note that the posse or hunting party, although commonly associated with lynching in the American South, was not the only type of mob. Wood's study looks more deeply at mass mobs' involvement in what have been called "spectacle lynchings." Historian W. Fitzhugh Brundage classifies the types of lynch mobs that perpetrated lynching atrocities in Georgia and Virginia according to the following types: "mass mobs, private mobs, terrorist mobs, posses, and unknown" in *Lynching in the New South: Georgia and Virginia, 1880-1930*, Illinois University Press, 1993.
34. Ibid. 116.
35. Ibid. 134.
36. Ibid. 137–138.
37. Poole, *Monsters in America: Our Historical Obsession with the Hideous and the Haunting*, 84. Wood, *Lynching and Spectacle*, 125–126.
38. Jackson, "A Southern Sublimation: Lynching Film and the Reconstruction of American Memory," *The Southern Literary Journal*, 107.

39. Examples of this cannibalistic lexicon used by racist whites in references to African Americans abound, but for one particularly haunting instance, see the postcard in *Without Sanctuary* referencing the 1915 lynching of Will Stanley in Temple, Texas. The front of the postcard bears an image of the hanging, charred remains of Stanley, a large crowd of white men surrounding the corpse, some assuming exaggerated postures but all posing for the photograph. The inscription on the back reads, "This is the Barbecue we had last night. My picture is to the left with a cross over it. your son Joe."

40. Romero, *Night of the Living Dead*, DVD

41. Litwack, "Hellhounds," 13.

42. Many critics and reviewers read *Night of the Living Dead* as a film alluding to the war in Vietnam, including Ian Olney, who sees the Vietnam War as the driving factor in Romero's transformation of the zombie narrative. See also Bishop, *American Zombie Gothic: The Rise and Fall (and Rise) of the Walking Dead in Popular Culture*, 14, 117.

43. Litwack, "Hellhounds," 14–18, in *Without Sanctuary: Lynching Photography in America*.

44. *Horror Noire: A History of Black Horror*, 2019.

45. Khazan, "In One Year, 57,375 Years of Life Were Lost to Police Violence: A New Study Find Police Killings Exact a Toll Greater Than Accidental Gun Deaths," *The Atlantic*. https://www.theatlantic.com/health/archive/2018/05/the-57375-years-of-life-lost-to-police-violence/559835/.

46. Desta, "Jordan Peele's *Get Out* Almost Had an Impossibly Bleak Ending," *Vanity Fair*.

47. Ibid.

48. Crump, "How 'Get Out' Puts 'Night of the Living Dead' in a New Light."

49. Ibid.

50. Baldwin, "A Report from Occupied Territory," *The Nation*, July 11 1966.

51. Romero, *Night of the Living Dead*, DVD

52. Peele, "Jordan Peele Crashed a *Get Out* College Course."

53. Zinoman, "Jordan Peele on a Truly Terrifying Monster: Racism."

54. Olney, *Zombie Cinema*, 16.

55. Bishop, *American Zombie Gothic*, 59.

56. Patterson, "Cannibalizing Gender and Genre: A Feminist Re-Vision of George Romero's Zombie Films," in McIntosh and Leverette, *Zombie Culture: Autopsies of the Living Dead*, 109.

Rousseau, Romero, and the "Sentiment of Existence"
The Search for Perfectibility in *Dawn of the Dead*

Benjamin Isaak Gross

While George A. Romero conceded that his zombie films are generally vehicles for political and social commentary, Kyle Bishop aptly notes that *Dawn of the Dead* (1978) is a particular "triumph" in using the dead as a critical metaphor.[1] Through inviting the viewer to differentiate zombies from humans, *Dawn* explores how elements of classical liberalism (understood in its "Lockian sense"[2] to include a commitment to private property, free markets, the rule of law, and an emphasis on individual rights) cause the living to act like the dead.[3] Other scholars have also identified this aspect of the film's social and political criticism, analyzing it with such tools as Marxist dialectical materialism.[4] However, so far, little, if anything, examines how the Genevan political philosopher Jean-Jacques Rousseau, himself a great critic of liberal society and culture, can help us understand Romero's second *Dead* film and the director's broader legacy. As we will see, Rousseau's work increased our self-awareness of our place in (and discomfort with) modernity, and his philosophy continues to shapes the way we talk, feel, think, and even complain about the world.[5] The purpose of this essay, then, is to show how Romero's *Dawn* brings to life elements of Rousseau's political philosophy, and, in particular, how it engages ideas, questions, and critiques that are fundamental both to Rousseau's theory and the development of Western political thought.[6]

To be clear, this essay does not argue that Romero read or studied Rousseau. Instead, it shows that Rousseau's work provides a cogent and revealing frame for organizing our thinking about *Dawn*'s implicit critique of classical liberalism. To support this thesis, the first section of this essay offers a more developed account of what modern political philosophy and classical liberalism are to help us understand the precise target and extent of *Dawn*'s (and Rousseau's) criticisms. Section two then sets out the details of this critique, describing the key differences between animals and humans in Rousseau's thought, a crucial distinction, as he thinks liberal society misunderstands what it means to be human. Applying these tenets of Rousseau's philosophy, I make the case that the zombies of *Dawn* are properly regarded as "animals,"[7] a distinction that allows us to understand better how Rousseau (and Romero) think about what it means to be properly human. This leads to the third section, which shows both Romero and Rousseau finding that humans can act like the "living dead" in liberal society (by leading a diminished and even slavish existence) without actually being zombies. The final section of this essay considers the obvious remaining question: how *should* we live more completely? Here, I sketch the common answer provided by both Rousseau and Romero. Both the great zombie film director and the philosopher call for a restoration of nature, that is, they long for humans to experience life outside the conventions and vices of liberal society and to escape its underlying ideology.

Modern Political Philosophy, Romero, and Rousseau

In *Dawn*, Romero explores and challenges ideas associated with the political philosophy of classical liberalism. In particular, as many prior scholars have noted, he shows how the chase for accumulation of property can result in a debilitating consumerism which robs the four protagonists (Stephen, Peter, Roger, and Francine) of their full humanity and blunts their imagination about what alternate lives they might construct.[8] As Kyle Bishop argues, "When given the chance to transcend the framework of a late-capitalist society in an environment that provides them with all their needs, the surviving humans of *Dawn* only attempt to recreate the lost structures of society and become fatally overwhelmed by the perceived need to own rather than produce."[9] More broadly, by envisioning what happens to humans when they survive a zombie apocalypse, *Dawn* invites the audience to participate in some of the central debates coursing through modern political philosophy.

What is modern political philosophy? There is no simple answer, as there are many variations.[10] This category or grouping of political thought is commonly traced to Niccolò Machiavelli, and at a minimum, shares the view that we should begin our study of politics by considering how humans are instead of how they ought to be.[11] This agreement is in contrast to classical political philosophy, which generally argues that humans ought to live in a specific manner, and requires us to identify a shared purpose, goal, or end of life for all humans that is inherent in nature.[12] To have a shared end means that there is one idea of "human" that everyone should attempt to become. In other words, there is a superior way of life that all humans ought to desire.

Modern political philosophy rejects this view. Instead of looking for a final purpose to determine how humans ought to live, the systematic projects of the "moderns" are to discover what our original nature is.[13] Upon knowing our original nature, moderns argue that we can create societies that are achievable instead of imaginary utopias. By building societies from an understanding of how humans are instead of how they ought to be, progress is possible. The bar of expectations regarding both what individuals and political orders can achieve, however, is lowered from a set of lofty moral aspirations to an acceptance of our base nature and what is possible.

Dawn enters this debate by indirectly challenging some of the assumptions of a school of modern political philosophy known as classical liberalism. Classical liberalism (often traced to the political theory of John Locke) holds that a coherent philosophy begins with an individual's self-interest in life, liberty, and estate (land and other property). This serves as the foundation for a political system that includes natural law, individualism, human rights, limited government, religious toleration, private property, the advancement of knowledge through science, and the separation of the public and private spheres.[14] L.R. Sorenson summarizes classical liberalism as:

Humans are by nature individuals. Man is not by nature a political (or social) animal. Human nature, not history or reason or choice or the greatest good of the greatest number, indicates the standard of political right. Political society is a human artifact in service of individual natural rights, and sovereignty is, therefore, limited. Natural law, discovered by human reason, is instrumental to natural right.[15]

By examining how humans are, classical liberalism contends that it produces a political system that correctly understands the aims (and potential) of man based on his actual nature.

One way to understand Romero's criticism of consumerism is to see it as a challenge to classical liberalism's assumptions about human nature. *Dawn* suggests that the Philadelphia survivors' focus on the natural pursuit of self-interest and estates results in an imbalanced consumerism that destroys their humanity.[16] Seeing how *Dawn* connects to ideas within Rousseau is important because Rousseau is the first to question explicitly the arguments of classical liberalism while retaining the premise of modern political philosophy.[17] He does not reject modern political philosophy but aims to correct it.[18] Although Rousseau has ideas about what healthy human life and government are, his ideals are not rooted in a final or singular cause of human existence and behavior.[19] Instead, his theories are rooted in how nature and society form humans.[20] As Drury explains, for Rousseau, people are "infinitely malleable" and their humanity "is acquired, not natural."[21]

For Rousseau, this observation can be both liberating, insofar as a properly ordered society can help us "become master"[22] of our fate, but it also helps explain how in liberal civil societies that form the wrong kinds of people, we are awash in a kind of "human sickness."[23] In *Emile*, Rousseau warns that the practices of modern medicine may revive the body, but this science is also part of what destroys our humanity: "What difference does it make to us that [doctors] make cadavers walk? It is men we need, and none is seen leaving their hands."[24] Rousseau's walking "cadavers" are proto-zombies. While the science (and culture) of classical liberalism can heal the body, it destroys the spirit within the body. Our timid calculations about how to avoid death extinguish the desire to live completely. Thus, Rousseau sets the stage for *Dawn*'s zombies and Romero's commentary concerning humans who imitate their hollow existence.

Animals and Humans—What Are Zombies?

Are the zombies of *Dawn* animals or humans? This may appear to be a silly question, but it is very important for understanding both the relationship between the living dead and Romero's human survivors and whether we might regard the film as a fundamental critique of liberalism. If zombies are humans, then their ceaseless desire to consume is a core aspect of their humanity; it may be a challenge to be managed, but it is not necessarily a problem to be eradicated. Viewed in this way, Romero's film may not be an argument against classical liberalism. Instead, the film could be a warning of what happens when natural limits of consumption, such as spoilage, no longer exist. Under this interpretation, the film would support ideas of classical liberalism that argue reason, society, theology, and government must inform and even restrict our uses of property outside the state of nature.[25]

Rousseau's *Second Discourse*, and particularly its thoughts on pity, instinct, and perfectibility, provides an argument of what it means to be a human being, and is therefore key to understanding how we should regard Romero's zombies. Through investigating each of these aspects in turn, I show that the application of Rousseau's ideas to *Dawn* should lead us to classify zombies as animals not humans. This allows us to conclude that neither Rousseau nor Romero accepts that the desire to consume is a core principle of human nature.

Pity

Rousseau argues that two principles exist in all humans by nature, "one of which interests us ardently in our well-being and our self-preservation, and the other of which inspires in us a natural repugnance to see[ing] any sensitive being, and principally our fellow humans, perish or suffer."[26] The principles of self-preservation and well-being (i.e., love of oneself) and pity exist in humans *prior* to reason. Of these two principles, he argues that a man feels love of himself prior to feeling pity.[27] To feel pity, a man must have social contact with another being that he associates with himself. This is why he principally feels pity when he sees his fellow humans suffer; he can see himself as a member of this species and thereby internalizes the pain and suffering he observes.

The principles of self-preservation and pity, however, can come into conflict. A person may have to induce pain on another to achieve his own self-preservation. In natural settings (before governments are instituted and societies formed), a man chooses to limit his pain on others because he selfishly wants to minimize feeling pity.[28] Rousseau argues that a man (before he enters civil society) will naturally choose to do no harm rather than to fight another human. Only if he is forced to choose between his self-preservation or feeling pity will a natural man harm another human.

Like Rousseau's "natural man," the zombies of *Dawn* lack reason.[29] But if zombies are natural humans in Rousseau's sense, then they should experience pity and not needlessly harm other humans. Judged by these standards, *Dawn's* zombies are clearly not human (or even pity-experiencing animals). Throughout *Dawn,* zombies are distinguished from humans by their lack of emotions. Halfway through the movie, a televised scientific expert warns, "We must not be lulled by the concept that these are our family members or our friends. They are not. They will not respond to such emotions."[30] Without emotions, zombies cannot feel pity.[31]

Even if this scientist's specific observation is incorrect, additional evidence from *Dawn* confirms that zombies lack pity for humans.[32] If zombies are humans resorting to cannibalism for their self-preservation, then pity should limit the amount of humans they eat to survive. *Dawn* depicts the undead as gluttonous and indiscriminate in their feeding. Zombies are not interested in minimizing their harm to other humans, as they do not consume the maximum amount of their victims before moving onto their next target. Their lack of emotion and pity supports the idea that they are not humans, judged by Rousseau's ideas.

Instinct

This conclusion is supported by a second argument. Rousseau claims that animals, by nature, follow their instinct. In his words, they are unthinking, programmed, and iterative "machines."[33] By this, he does not mean that animals are made of wires, processors, and other electronics. Instead, animals are creatures produced by nature with instinct.

An animal has instinct so it can achieve its self-preservation and continuation of its species. This is not to say that animals are limited to their instinct, as humans can domesticate them.[34] What is crucial is that animals do not consciously domesticate themselves. When animals are untouched by humans, only their instinct—that is "hardwired" by nature—rules over them.

While humans are similar to animals in many ways, Rousseau finds some differences. One of these is that nature gives a human the capacity for self-rule: "I perceive precisely the same things in the human machine [as animals], with this difference: that nature alone does everything in the operations of the beast whereas man contributes to his own operations in his capacity as a free agent."[35] Freedom allows humans to make their own choices. People do not have to follow instinct alone (if humans even have an instinct). While we generally desire self-preservation and reproduction of the species, just like animals, we are ultimately free to choose how we want to achieve these ends.

Again, *Dawn*'s zombies follow Rousseau's notions about animals in this way as well. In the film, we hear the scientist's voiceover describing what motivates zombies. We are told, "These creatures are nothing but pure, motorized instinct"[36] for the sole purpose of self-preservation. Of course, one might object that, contrary to this scientist's observation, it's *not* entirely obvious that Romero's zombies need human flesh to continue their existence (as a form of self-preservation); instead, they seem to persist regardless of whether they consume human flesh or not. But, at least in *Dawn*—as opposed to Romero's last film, *Survival of the Dead* (2009)—they lack the capacity to choose the objects of their desire (or to set aside hunger). Here, again, zombies physically appear to be humans, but a closer inspection of their instincts reveals that they are not.

Perfectibility

The zombies of *Dawn* also help us understand Rousseau's most critical idea regarding the difference between animals and humans. Man differs from animals because he gives himself his own ideal of perfection: "But, even if the difficulties surrounding all these questions should leave some room for dispute concerning this difference between man and animal, there is another very specific quality that distinguishes them and about which there can be no argument: that is, the faculty of *perfecting* himself."[37] The faculty of perfectibility is complex. In short, Rousseau is describing a self-directed freedom within a man to shape himself in the image of his choice. All other animals, without human intervention, are limited to the instinct nature provides them. Again, this does not mean that animals are unable to evolve; it only means that they are unable to self-direct their evolution.

This concept of perfectibility again corroborates the idea that the zombies of *Dawn* are animals. In the movie, the scientist says, "There are reports of the *creatures* using tools, but even these actions are the most primitive. The use of external articles as bludgeons and so forth—I might point out to you that even *animals* will adopt the basic use of tools in this manner."[38] To be sure, the actual creation of tools, rather than the mere use of existing objects, provides evidence of perfectibility; creating a tool requires a being to imagine something not given by nature, and, specifically, an object that improves a being's life. In creating tools, humans use their faculties of self-perfection. This is why Rousseau argues that the inventions of "link and hook," "bows and arrows," animal-skin clothing, and fire are people's first tools directly related to perfectibility.[39]

But as the scientist notes, the zombies in *Dawn* do not create tools; they only use them. The use of tools (or the mere mimicry of tool-makers) is not evidence of perfectibility—consciously striving to make a new ideal for a species. As Rousseau explains, some species of monkeys will gather around a fire built by humans and push kindling into it.

> [But] I neglected to examine whether the monkey's intention was in fact to keep the fire going or whether, as I believe, it was simply to imitate the action of a human being. However that may be, it is well demonstrated that the monkey is not a variety of man, not only because it is deprived of the faculty of speech, but above all because it is certain that its species does not have the faculty of perfecting itself, which is the specific characteristic of the human species[40]

Creating a fire, and then maintaining it, through one's own will is a demonstration of perfectibility. An animal can imitate a human by stoking a fire. This imitation is not perfectibility, as the faculty of self-perfection must come from within a being. Again, while zombies use tools in *Dawn* (such as eyeglasses, hockey sticks, and escalators), this is not evidence of perfectibility, which requires a self-willed historical evolution. We see this, for example, in the ways in which Stephen, Peter, Roger, and Francine's evolving needs reflect how they come to view the mall environment and its resources: as haven, consumer utopia, and ultimately as a confining cage.

Dawn provides an excellent visualization of Rousseau's concept of human (and animal) nature. Romero forces the audience to confront something that looks human but lacks essential human attributes. As Greg Garrett explains, part of what makes Romero's zombies disconcerting is that "they have affinities to us yet seem alien."[41] Romero's *Dawn* (unlike some of his later works) presents zombies as emotionless, purely instinctual, and lacking any demonstration of perfectibility. While zombies look like humans, they are not. Thus, we have good reasons to believe their incessant drive to consumption is connected to their distinctive animal nature and is not a core principle of humanity.

While Rousseau's political philosophy can help us to interpret elements of *Dawn*'s zombies and their limitations, it is not a perfect fit. For example, Francine wonders why the zombies come to the mall. Stephen suggests it is, "Some kind of instinct. Memory. What they used to do. This was an important place in their lives."[42] Arguing that zombies are coming to the mall because it was an important place while they were alive suggests some element of free will remains and that they can still recall (and maybe even long for) their former self-perfecting selves.

That said, the zombies of *Dawn* lack important features needed to support Stephen's claims. Despite their different clothing, haircuts, and outward appearance, all of Romero's mall zombies behave in an interchangeable manner. If some memory is driving this behavior, why are the zombies not congregating in the specific stores that were important to them? The crowd at Macy's is very different from the crowd at KB Toys. In *Dawn*, the zombies do not behave like free or perfecting individuals. Unlike, say, Bub in *Day of the Dead* (1985), who retains enough of a recall of his former military life to give Captain Rhodes an ironic salute, the zombies in *Dawn* are fungible husks.

Indeed, *Dawn* is keenly aware of what it means to be human and how zombies lack this humanity. While the zombies are emotionless, the humans often display emotion and concern for values other than instrumental survival. For example when Roger wonders early in the movie why those living in the apartment building kept their dead nearby despite the obvious risk of reanimation, Peter explains: "'Cause they still believe there's respect in dying."[43] Romero shows that humans, even when a creature threatens their own self-preservation, continue to display compassion. Although zombies act out of instinct alone, humans freely decide how to best survive the apocalypse, and even whether survival itself is the highest objective. This freedom allows the living to experiment with different ideals of perfection in the film in a way that the zombies never do. In this way, the movie does not appear to be suggesting a correction for or deviation from liberalism and its reliance on a model of a people who are "free to live autonomously, to choose and pursue their values for themselves."[44] Instead, it offers a dystopian view of how this ideal of perfection can be perverted in practice.

Perfectibility and Living—Who Are the "Living Dead"?

Perfectibility means that humans have the potential to improve themselves. Through examining those surviving the zombie apocalypse, *Dawn* explores ideas about healthy and unhealthy uses of this faculty of self-perfection. Specifically, the main plotline, following the story of the four comrades who escape to the mall, investigates this concept—and its pitfalls.

As already noted, according to Rousseau, humans can be physically alive while not actually living in the sense of fulfilling their human capacities and potential: "To live is not to breathe; it is to act; it is to make use of our organs, our senses, our faculties, of all the part of ourselves which give us the sentiment of our existence. The man who has lived the most is not he who has counted the most years but he who has most felt life. Men have been buried at one hundred who died at their birth."[45] The mere act of being alive does not mean we are truly living; we must make use of our bodies and faculties to interact with others and the material world. It is only when we experience our "sentiment of existence," then we are truly living.

The sentiment of existence is a complicated topic within Rousseau's psychology and moral theory. In short, it is one's awareness of one's consciousness.[46] It is the enjoyment of one's entire being.[47] When there is harmony between a man's faculties and desires, and he feels his sentiment of existence, he experiences happiness.[48] Happiness, however, requires a person to engage with his faculties fully, which results in satisfying all his desires. Thus, there are no remaining desires to be satisfied, and no faculties left unused.

One reason the sentiment of existence is complicated is that it is not a fixed phenomenon, occurring at a discrete point or moment.[49] This is due to the dynamism inherent in perfectibility itself. When a person uses her faculty of self-perfection, she develops new faculties (e.g., reason) and new desires (e.g., receiving love from others). Rousseau argues that to live healthily and completely, a man must expand his faculties and desires to his limit; this will allow him to experience as much of life as he possibly can.[50]

Expanding a person's faculties and desires, so they remain in harmony after this expansion, requires education. Most forms of education, however, do not facilitate this harmony. In particular, Rousseau takes aim at the education existing within liberal societies.[51] Indeed, this form of modern "society depraves and perverts men"[52] by teaching individuals that they are self-interested actors who form a political community primarily to protect themselves and their freedom "to choose and pursue their values for themselves." Rousseau argues that the result of this educational emphasis is a disharmony between our internal and external selves.

We can see this critique in both Rousseau's discussion of Locke's approach to education regarding economics,[53] and in important scenes in *Dawn* as Stephen, Peter, Roger, and Francine start to enjoy the relative security provided by the mall. Rousseau argues that Locke's ideal of a rational and industrious man is likely to be more concerned with the accumulation and consumption of property than experiencing life.[54] Those industrious and disciplined Lockeans who jealously guard life, liberty, and property are physically alive but not fully living in Rousseau's sense. As he puts it, "For the rich, boredom is their great plague. Amongst so many entertainments assembled at great expense, in the midst of so many people joining together to please them, boredom consumes them and kills them.... For them boredom is transformed into a horrible illness which sometimes deprives them of their reason and finally their lives."[55] Those able to enjoy the implied consumerism of Locke's liberal economics become bored. Able to satisfy their desires without having to use all their faculties, Rousseau thinks consumption deprives the rich of being alive. Instead of finding opportunities to exercise their faculties, they become complacent in enjoying comfortable self-preservation.

Rousseau thinks those not embracing this economic value and exchange system can live a more fulfilled life: such "people hardly ever get bored. Their life is active.... Many days of fatigue make them taste a few days of festival with delight"[56] By remaining active in order to survive, the poor enjoy their few "festival" days. They find harmony between their faculties and desires. Rousseau is not glorifying poverty nor turning a blind eye to its sufferings. But, while ordinary people can satisfy their desires to a lesser degree than the rich, they experience harmony and a form of active humanity that makes "good use" of life.[57] For those who fulfill Locke's supposed liberal ideal of acquisition and wealth, they can live a longer and more comfortable life, but they no longer experience life fully and are not fully conscious of their existence.

Romero's "Living Dead"

Dawn captures these ideas about self-perfection and the sentiment of existence by following four humans surviving the zombie apocalypse. Roger, Stephen, Peter, and Francine begin the film by experiencing life through awareness of their vulnerability (and the need for self-preservation). As Peter says to Roger: "We might not get out of any place alive. We almost didn't get out of here."[58] From the outset, what distinguishes these four humans from the many who expire around them, is that they use all their faculties to survive. Their bodies and minds are pushed to the limit. Their physical strength and endurance is tested through encounters with zombies, and even in the relatively protected confines of the helicopter, Stephen must overcome his body's lack of sleep to keep flying. Their capacity for reason is utilized in determining a safe spot to find fuel and shelter. Through these early scenes of flight and survival, *Dawn* shows humans using a range of abilities for self-preservation. It is not a comfortable life, but the group is active and alive in feeling (and defending) their existence from the living dead.

This starts to change when they become ensconced in the shopping mall. Upon entering the second floor, Peter and Roger find water, food, and shelter. The mall has suddenly provided them with everything they need for mere self-preservation. They no longer need to use their faculties in an active way to achieve this limited but essential end. Having the luxury to use their faculties for other objectives, they execute a "hit and run" within the mall to acquire a radio and other supplies. Initially, these scenes illustrate Rousseau's idea of the faculty of self-perfection. While, as discussed, animals would be satisfied with their self-preservation, Romero's humans, having achieved self-preservation, aspire to more. Thus, the four protagonist's desires expand (to include play and reading and sports) and they use their faculties to satisfy these new desires, which allows them to experience a greater sentiment of existence.

Eventually, however, this new emphasis leads to the mall residents being "corrupted" and experiencing "vices of the soul."[59] Over time, the four are able to turn the mall into their own miniature and self-sustained city. Having secured the entrances with trucks, locks, and alarms, they kill and clear out the zombies within their home. Freed from immediate bodily needs and mortal peril, they now use their perfectibility to do what they want. In short order, all four choose to consume—mostly without broader purpose. They take money from a bank, even though there is no economy, and it is worthless. Peter lackadaisically flips through books instead of using his freedom to read them with care. Francine rummages through cosmetics, even though she can determine the value of her own beauty. Roger engages in the same vanity as he tries on hats to look fashionable for a non-existent society. Stephen uses his time to play games, such as pinball. The mall allows them all to experience individual, fleeting pleasures that distracts them from feeling truly alive.

This consumerism continues to grow more elaborate—and emptier—over time. After a zombie bites Roger, he escapes reality by playing video games instead of living out his final days in a more robust and active fashion. Indeed, he and his friends are now like the zombies: their only focus is consuming. The zombies that surround *Dawn*'s humans are mindless: they have no choice. Instead, they are marked by machine-like programming and, absent human pity or perfectibility, the zombies consume without ever being satisfied. Their behavior and driving impulses never change over the course of *Dawn*. Humans, on the other hand, have a choice. But as what Loudermilk calls the "Mall Fantasia"[60] of *Dawn* takes over, Romero's four survivors choose no longer to be alive. Stephen, Francine, Peter, and Roger live without feeling their existence; their consumerism has transformed them into Rousseau's bored and dying rich and another version of Romero's "living dead."[61]

Only Francine is able to hold on to moments of living during this period of unchecked consumerism. She is active through compassionately feeding the animals in the pet store. When the group gives up on the goal of making it to Canada, she is the one who questions if their new home is truly good or if it is a prison. Francine rejects their new comfortable but passive life and asks: "What have we done to ourselves?"[62] She does not ask what or who has done this to them; she comprehends they are the culprits. It is at this point that Francine realizes there are better uses of her faculty of self-perfection than engaging in increasingly listless consumption. Remembering her goal of flying the helicopter, she has Stephen teach her how to use the machine. By actively extending her faculties to achieve her new, non-consumer desire (flight to what is perhaps a more realized life), Francine feels her existence again.

Tragically, this salvation is short-lived. The helicopter alerts motorcycle looters of the mall's existence. Facing this new threat, Francine again suggests the group abandon the mall; consumerism, after all, is not worth dying over. But not wanting to give up their "living dead" lifestyle, Peter and Stephen choose to endanger their own self-preservation by attempting to repel the looters, who eventually force themselves into the mall with a horde of zombies trailing behind. With the mall returned to a chaotic, uncivilized state, Francine prepares to leave. Peter, the only other remaining human from the original group, resigns to kill himself. Only when a group of zombies endangers his self-preservation does he become active instead of passive. Feeling his sentiment of existence again, he fights through the zombies to secure his desire for life by joining Francine on the helicopter.

This final scene, in which Peter comes close to killing himself, is important in prompting us to think about how *Dawn* brings to life Rousseau's criticism of how perfectibility is distorted in liberal societies. Rousseau argues that suicide is only endemic to humans in civil society: "Lucky to know only physical ills in his childhood—ills far less cruel, far less painful than are the other kinds of ills and which far more rarely make us renounce life than do the others! One does not kill oneself for the pains of gout. There are hardly any [pains] but those of the soul which produce despair.... Our greatest ills come to us from ourselves."[63] Suicide, according to Rousseau, requires the freedom to pursue perfection. Through our imagination, we can produce an ideal life that we desire. The problem, of course, is that many of us lack the faculties to achieve this desire. But this insufficiency only turns to despair in civil society, where our dependence on others and awareness of their social judgment awakens miserable feelings, such as jealousy, insecurity, and anxiety. Perhaps more troublesome, even those who achieve their ideal of perfectibility may well discover that it does not bring them happiness. These situations may put individuals into such despair that they want to kill themselves. For Rousseau, suicide is the failure of the "sentiment of existence"—instead of enjoying one's entire being and all its capacities, we experience disharmony between our faculties and desires, leading to misery.[64]

Peter's resignation to end his life shows that he sees no difference between the life he was living (e.g., wanton consumerism) and death. *Dawn*'s "consumer utopia"[65] seems to be an ideal of perfection that, upon actual achievement, turns out to be an unhealthy use of our faculties. Thus, it does not represent perfection because our faculties and desires are not in harmony. We do not feel our sentiment of existence through the ultimately passive nature of satisfying our bodily desires. Again, this only leads to boredom and the erasing of the difference between the mall's listless humans and the aimless walking dead. Ironically, in what he thinks are his final moments, Peter comes back to life. With his self-preservation endangered, he keenly experiences what Rousseau calls *amour de soi*, a form of self-love that is compatible with human happiness and fulfillment. Facing death, he feels pleasure in being alive; he feels his sentiment of existence, and he belatedly escapes with Francine.

Rousseau and Romero's Return to Nature

As seen in the previous section, Rousseau and Romero each present a case that the kinds of lives promoted by liberal societies are not healthy and complete for most, if not all, humans. So, what is the alternative? How can a human, therefore, live a good and rewarding life? Rousseau thinks we must "return" to nature. It is not clear that Romero's *Dawn* displays a similar longing, although I suggest a novel interpretation of Johnstown that may be consistent with Rousseau's thinking.

To be clear, we should not understand Rousseau's desired "return" to nature as an expressed hope that we can or should return to the state of nature, that is, to conditions that prevailed prior to formation of society and government. To attempt going backward, erasing our history, is a mistake.[66] Humans have developed abilities and knowledge beyond their initial situation. We now have desires that can only be satisfied by existing within society. A return to the state of nature is impossible, as we are no longer natural humans.

If not endorsing a reversion to the state of nature and undeveloped human existence, what does Rousseau mean when he says that we need to return to nature? As a modern political philosopher, he finds the truth of human nature not in a final purpose or *telos* but in how nature forms us. As described above, humans feel wholeness and harmony by nature: "…savage man, subject to few passions and self-sufficient, had only the feelings and the enlightenment suited to that state, that he felt only his true needs, looked at only what he believed it was in his interest to see, and that his intelligence made no more progress than his vanity."[67] "Savage" man experiences wholeness because his desires are not greater than his abilities and his abilities are not more developed than his desires. This natural harmony is his natural goodness. By returning to nature, Rousseau argues that we must restore this harmony to be morally and physically healthy.

Again, since today we have desires and faculties that did not exist in the state of nature (which occurred before society, before the development of culture, and before our growing dependence on others), we cannot return to this existence as a path to experiencing harmony. Indeed, as any fan of *Naked and Afraid* knows, we would be miserable living naked in the wilderness. Instead, we should *restore* the conditions and types of humans that existed in the state of nature, where we were naturally good and whole.[68] Through our faculty of perfectibility, Rousseau argues, we can identify the importance of restoring this natural goodness and wholeness. But we need to do so with our developed faculties such as reason, emotion, imagination, judgment, and morality. In whatever society we imagine, we need to have desires that can be satisfied by these faculties so we can restore the harmony we once felt by nature.

How to achieve the restoration of our natural goodness is a question that preoccupies Rousseau across his work. The noble savage of the *Second Discourse*, the citizen of the *Social Contract*, Emile, and the Solitary Walker are all possible options; the proper restorative path depends upon one's situation and natural abilities.[69] By returning to nature, Rousseau argues we can understand how to use *our* faculty of self-perfection in a manner to achieve *our* own well-being. What is clear, however, is that Rousseau rejects classical liberalism as a potential avenue to restore our natural goodness.

While *Dawn* also rejects classical liberalism, it is not clear if it offers a picture of a healthy society. Those in the city, at the outset of the film, are scared, chaotic, and desperate to escape. They cannot choose between their morality, which prevents them from killing their former family and friends who are now the zombies, and logic that informs them how to survive. Their desires and faculties are conflicted. Those who continue to cling to this dying society are constantly arguing about how they should respond to the zombie apocalypse, even as the threat draws nearer. They cannot provide for their most basic human desires: their own self-preservation is in jeopardy, and their capacity for pity is similarly stunted.

Romero's four survivors do experience a period of contentment in the mall. However, as we have examined, they are ultimately dissatisfied. Their full range of developed faculties remains unused, producing boredom and disharmony for each individual and the group as a whole. Fulfilling liberalism's view of "ourselves as freely choosing autonomous beings"[70] even within a tight-knit group yields vices and an unhealthy life.

Finally, the motorcycle raiders who attack the mall show joy in destruction, but they are not content. They display an insatiable and destructive appetite. This is another form of consumerism; one that devours everything in its path without finding limits to its desire. Their desire for destruction is what brings death upon their fellow survivors and themselves. Thus, Romero's presentation of the raiders suggests that they will never be satisfied.

Arguably, the only people that Romero shows as happy and content in the movie are those in the countryside outside of Johnstown. They are able to enjoy the simple pleasures in life. This does not mean that Romero meant this group of "rednecks" comprised an ideal community. But they may well be the closest approximation we can find in *Dawn* of Rousseau's project to restore our natures and experience harmony between our desires and our faculties. In these brief vignettes, we see national guardsmen, police, and civilian volunteers congregating with each other. They seem to be enjoying their efforts to defend their town from zombies. They share beer and coffee, play music, smoke cigarettes, pose for photographs, and laugh. They appear to have elements of a communal bond. But they are clearly outside confining degenerate human "anthills" (as Rousseau disparagingly calls cities), and instead seem "to be dispersed over the earth."[71]

Romero does not explore these itinerants enough for us to see if a true community exists, if the people are self-interested in hunting zombies, or if something else explains their behavior. If the citizens are going to achieve wholeness between their faculties and desires, however, they will have to embrace Rousseau's political solution. They will have to form a community that is similar to the political ideal that Rousseau sketches in the *Social Contract* and the beginning of *Emile*. This is a society directed by the general will, where each individual is working for the good of the society, instead of a society that is merely directed by aggregating different individuals' wills or wishes for themselves. As Rousseau elaborates, "Good social institutions are those that best know how to denature man, to take his absolute existence from him in order to give him a relative one and transport the *I* into the common unity, with the result that each individual believes himself no longer one but a part of the unity and no longer feels except within the whole."[72] A healthy society is one where the individual no longer thinks about him or herself but instead considers what is good for the whole. Liberal citizens can achieve pleasure through consumption or realizing whatever other good they seek, so long as they recognize the rights of others to do the same. But those operating pursuant to Rousseau's general will can only feel happiness through being good citizens, through putting the needs of the community above their own needs.

Does Romero's depiction of the community outside of Johnstown hint at his vision of a healthy and harmonious society? We do not see enough to answer this question, but there are some limitations to this interpretation. When flying over the area, Stephen says: "We're still pretty close to Johnstown. Those rednecks are probably enjoying the whole thing."[73] The use of "rednecks" is not a compliment.[74] Furthermore, in *Night of the Living Dead*, Romero brings forth issues of racism in a rural community near Johnstown, and the same or similar "rednecks" are involved in the murder of Ben.[75] In sum, there is not enough information to decide if this rural community is an example of a healthy society; the dark notes sounded in *Night* seem to give way to lighter motifs in *Dawn*, but the overall effect is ambiguous at best.

Setting this issue aside, we can still see *Dawn's* redneck group bringing together Rousseau's and Romero's specific criticisms of classical liberalism and modern society. As already indicated, Rousseau identifies the concentration of humans into cities as one of the greatest sources of our vice and misery. As he puts it unsparingly: "Cities are the abyss of the human species."[76] His image of "Men crammed together like sheep [who] would all perish in a very short time"[77] is later evoked in Romero's depictions of the entropy in Philadelphia and in the crowded mayhem of the mall in *Dawn's* final scenes.

Not surprisingly, part of Rousseau's recommended way out of this abyss is to retreat to more natural settings: "At the end of a few generations the races perish or degenerate. They must be renewed, and it is always the country which provides for this renewal."[78] Romero's depiction of Philadelphia compared to the countryside outside of Johnstown offers a similar gloss. Philadelphia, and every other city we hear of in the movie, has become the abyss of the human species. The dead are roaming freely and eating the living everywhere, but the problem is most intense in congested, dysfunctional urban areas. When trying to escape the apocalypse through the confines of a mall, and by restoring the comforts and security of city life, the group of cloistered survivors only succeed in transforming themselves into the "living dead." It is only by leaving this site (and its corrupting lifestyle) that Francine and Peter can exercise their faculty of perfectibility, in hope of restoring the wholeness which nature endowed them. It is altogether possible that the zombie apocalypse has freed them from classical liberalism's ideal of an acquisitive and restless consumerism. As Robin Wood explains, these two survivors "show themselves capable of autonomy and self-awareness."[79] While their prospects are uncertain,

> *Dawn* is perhaps the first horror film to suggest—albeit very tentatively—the possibility of moving beyond apocalypse. It brings its two surviving protagonists to the point where the work of creating the norms for a new social order, a new structure of relationships can begin…[80]

In this way, *Dawn* ends by embracing the longing to leave liberal, consumer-oriented society with the hope of creating "a new social order" that might restore our natural harmony and wholeness. While the outskirts of Johnstown may not represent this ideal, Francine's desire to create a healthy life in Canada engages our imagination.

This, perhaps, is a major component of the legacy of *Dawn* that continues to attract audiences to watch, reflect, and debate on the meaning of the film. Romero offers a convincing picture of the ills of liberalism and consumerism within the film. *Dawn*, however, does not provide a clear solution to this problem. The cities, the past centers of classical liberalism, are dying. The mall, a recreation of classical liberalism, transforms humans into the "living dead." The life of a raider is unsustainable. Francine's dream of relocating in Canada appears to be only a far-fetched, romantic longing. Even if the Johnstown group can survive the zombies, will the community put the town before their own individual desires, and how suspicious should we be of their motivations and prejudice? Like Rousseau, *Dawn* engages in important ideas, questions, and criticisms still roiling through the history of Western thought. While *Night of the Living Dead* brought Romero fame, *Dawn* ensures his legacy as a filmmaker that examines what it means to be a human.

Notes

1. Bishop, *American Zombie Gothic*, 129.
2. Hartz, *The Liberal Tradition*, 4.
3. Loudermilk, "Eating 'Dawn' in the Dark," 90–94; Riley, "The E-Dead: Zombies in the Digital Age," 195; Bishop, "The Idle Proletariat," 234–235; 237–238; Boluk and Lenz, "Infection, Media, and Capitalism," 135–136; Harper, "Zombies, Malls, and the Consumerism Debate."

168 Beyond the Living Dead

    4. Bishop, *American Zombie Gothic,* 15; Skal, *Monster Show,* 309.
    5. Orwin and Tarcov, "Introduction," xii–xiii.
    6. The chapter only investigates the 1978 version of the film. In a 2005 interview, Romero said the remake (in which he was not involved) lacks substance: "The first 15, 20 minutes were terrific, but it sort of lost its reason for being. It was more of a video game. I'm not terrified of things running at me; it's like Space Invaders. There was nothing going on underneath." Walters, "Simon Pegg Interview George A Romero."
    7. By *Day of the Dead* (1985) and *Land of the Dead* (2005) some of Romero's zombies display human faculties such as the capacity to plan and engage in irony. This essay, however, only examines zombies as they are presented in *Dawn*.
    8. Keetley, "Zombie Republic: Property and the Propertyless Multitude in Romero's Dead Films and Kirkman's *The Walking Dead*," 329–330.Shaviro, *The Cinematic Body,* 91.
    9. Bishop, "The Idle Proletariat," 236.
    10. Strauss, "What is Political Philosophy?," 39–40.
    11. Masters, *The Political Philosophy of Rousseau,* 197–204; Melzer, *The Natural Goodness of Man,* 108–113; Strauss, "On Classical Political Philosophy," 71–72.
    12. Strauss, "What is Political Philosophy?," 39.
    13. *Ibid.*, 39–48.
    14. Hudelson, "Liberals and Conservatives," 37; Forde, "Natural Law, Theology, and Morality in Locke," 396–397; Kautz, *Liberalism and Community,* 23; Tarcov, *Locke's Education for Liberty,* 1–8.
    15. Sorenson, "Rousseau's Liberalism," 443.
    16. My argument about the weaknesses of liberalism's view of human nature is not entirely original. Other scholars take up this claim and connect Romero's ideas to Karl Marx, George Hegel, Alexadre Kojève, and Francis Fukuyama. See, for example, Bishop, "The Idle Proletariat," 235; Harper, "Zombies, Malls, and the Consumerism Debate," Tait, "(Zombie) Revolution at the Gates," 63.
    17. Bloom, "Rousseau's Critique of Liberal Constitutionalism," 143–146; 166; Cullen, *Freedom in Rousseau's Political Philosophy,* 11–12; 19; Marks, *Perfection and Disharmony in the Thought of Jean-Jacques Rousseau,* 149–157; Masters and Kelly, "Introduction," xiii–xviii; Scott, "Introduction," XIII–XIV.
    18. Bloom, "Rousseau's Critique of Liberal Constitutionalism," 143–146; Masters, "Rousseau and the Rediscover of Human Nature," 110; Sorenson, "Rousseau's Liberalism," 443; 465–466.
    19. Cooper, "Between Eros and Will to Power," 106; 117; Cooper, *Rousseau & Nature,* xi; 39–40; Grace, "The restlessness of 'being,'" 137; Muchnik, "An essay on the principles of Rousseau's anthropology," 76; Scott, "The Theodicy of the *Second Discourse,* 709; Weiss, "Rousseau, Antifeminism, and Woman's Nature," 87; 90.
    20. Indeed, the historicism of Marx, Hegel, Kojève, and Fukuyama all find their origin from Rousseau's ideas of history. There is a teleological interpretation of Rousseau's work that can be found in Marks, *Perfection and Disharmony in the Thought of Jean-Jacques Rousseau,* 3; 38–39; 50–53; Smith, "Natural Happiness, Sensation, and Infancy in Rousseau's 'Emile,'" 93–94, 100–101. The literature on Rousseau has not fully addressed the teleological as compared to anti- teleological interpretations yet. I argue the anti-teleological is a stronger interpretation, as Rousseau does not argue there is one ideal that all humans should attempt to be.
    21. Drury, *The Political Ideas of Leo Strauss,* 157.
    22. *Ibid.*
    23. Rousseau, *Discourse on the Origin and the Foundations of Inequality Among Men.*
    24. Rousseau, *Emile,* 54.
    25. Forde, "The Charitable John Locke," 438–439; 450–458.
    26. Rousseau, *Discourse on the Origin and the Foundations of Inequality Among Men,* 54.
    27. Masters, *The Political Philosophy of Rousseau,* 136–146.
    28. Masters, "Rousseau and the Rediscovery of Nature," 114.
    29. Romero, *Dawn of the Dead,* DVD.
    30. *Ibid.*
    31. Amusingly, the scientist portrays himself as being devoid of emotion and pity—perhaps raising the question of whether he is fully human.
    32. Even in Romero's later films, such as *Land of the Dead,* the pity experienced by zombies like Big Daddy is directed at other zombies, suggesting that these "animals" recognize one another as a distinct species.
    33. Rousseau, *Discourse on the Origin and the Foundations of Inequality Among Men,* 71.
    34. *Ibid.*, 70.
    35. *Ibid.*, 71.
    36. Romero, *Dawn of the Dead,* DVD.
    37. Rousseau, *Discourse on the Origin and the Foundations of Inequality Among Men,* 72 (emphasis added).
    38. Romero, *Dawn of the Dead,* DVD (emphasis added).
    39. Rousseau, *Discourse on the Origin and the Foundations of Inequality Among Men,* 92.
    40. *Ibid.*, 137.
    41. Garrett, *Living with the Living Dead,* 9.
    42. Romero, *Dawn of the Dead,* DVD.
    43. *Ibid.*

44. Sandel, *Liberalism and the Limits of Justice*, xii.
45. Rousseau, *Emile*, 42.
46. Melzer, *The Natural Goodness of Man*, 35–46.
47. Grace, "The restlessness of 'being,'" 141.
48. Ibid., 140–143.
49. Ibid., 143–148.
50. Cooper, *Rousseau & Nature*, 20–21.
51. Ibid., 33; 89.
52. Ibid., 237.
53. Although not controversial to claim Rousseau criticizes Locke's ideas, there is a lack of literature on the subject. Marks, "Rousseau's Critique of Locke's Education for Liberty," 694–95.
54. Bloom, "Rousseau's Critique of Liberal Constitutionalism," 147; Kautz, "Privacy and Community," 254; Marks, *Perfection and Disharmony in the Thought of Jean-Jacques Rousseau*, 151–53.
55. Rousseau, *Emile*, 350.
56. Ibid., 350.
57. Ibid.
58. Romero, *Dawn of the Dead*, DVD.
59. Rousseau, *Emile*, 59.
60. Loudermilk, "Eating *Dawn* in the Dark," 93.
61. Bishop, *American Zombie Gothic*, 34–5.
62. Romero, *Dawn of the Dead*, DVD.
63. Rousseau, *Emile*, 48.
64. Ibid., 80–84. Wild animal deaths that might seem like instances of suicide, such as when whales beach themselves, or the mass deaths of lemmings are not in fact suicide. See: deCatanzaro, "Human suicide: a biological perspective," 265–272; Hamilton, "Do nonhuman animals commit suicide?" 278–279; Hogenboom, "Many animals seem to kill themselves, but it is not suicide"; Preti, "Animal suicide: Evolutionary continuity or anthropomorphism?" 1–3.
65. Bishop, "The Idle Proletariat," 242.
66. Rousseau, *Discourse on the Origin and the Foundations of Inequality Among Men*, 63.
67. Ibid., 88.
68. Cooper, *Rousseau & Nature*, 59–60; 117–118; 187–188; Melzer, *The Natural Goodness of Man*, 15–17; 49–51.
69. Cooper, *Rousseau & Nature*, 51–59; Melzer, *The Natural Goodness of Man* 89–108.
70. Sandel, *Liberalism and the Limits of Justice*, 9.
71. Rousseau, *Emile*, 59.
72. Ibid., 40.
73. Romero, *Dawn of the Dead*, DVD.
74. Rousseau's works, however, support the idea that those embracing classical liberalism's ideal of perfection look down at the simple souls of citizens in healthy republics. Thus, one wonders how thoughtful Stephen's comment is.
75. Romero, *Dawn of the Dead*, DVD.
76. Rousseau, *Emile*, 59.
77. Ibid.
78. Ibid.
79. Wood, *Hollywood From Vietnam to Reagan*, 107.
80. Ibid.

Conclusion

Do Not Go Gentle into That Bad *Night:* Humanism, Violence, and Plumbing the Romero Legacy

Bruce Peabody

Just over fifty years ago, George Romero's *Night of the Living Dead* (1968) premiered, and with it was born a growing national and world preoccupation with zombies as the subjects of mass and literary fiction, film, television, video games, and popular culture generally. This edited volume has contextualized, traced, and plumbed the meaning of the still-budding Romero legacy, drawing on a varied and cross-disciplinary group of thinkers and writers. The longevity, dynamism, and penetrating influence of Romero's creativity make the recently deceased filmmaker a worthy object of inquiry on his own. Moreover, his extensive body of work provides a prompt for taking stock of the shifting interest in zombies over the past half century, manifest in an array of popular and scholarly contexts. Studying Romero, and his creative and normative legacy, helps us better understand the current state of the zombie, especially their shifting depiction, forms, and capacities, and how the walking dead serve as markers of our evolving politics, artistic expressions, anxieties, and cultural tumult in the early decades of the twenty-first century.

Understanding the Rising Tide of the Dead

Since Romero's first zombie swayed amongst the headstones, popular and academic attraction to the dead has grown rapidly, "exploding into popular and cult movies," television, "blockbuster games" and comics.[1] As Greg Garrett argues, today, the zombie apocalypse inspired by Romero "represents one of the most important motifs in contemporary culture."[2] As just one measure of this claim, consider that from *Night's* release in 1968 to 2005, the relative frequency of references to "zombies" in American published books (as recorded by the Google Ngram Viewer tool) increased almost 900 percent (see Figure 1). This growth began in earnest in the 1970s and carried into the 1980s before leveling off at the end of the decade. A more recent surge transpired from just before the new millennium to 2005.

Overall, the twenty-first century "Zombie Renaissance" has been characterized by both an increasing volume in the production of popular, entertainment works depicting the undead and a diffusion of this material into diverse media: films, graphic novels,

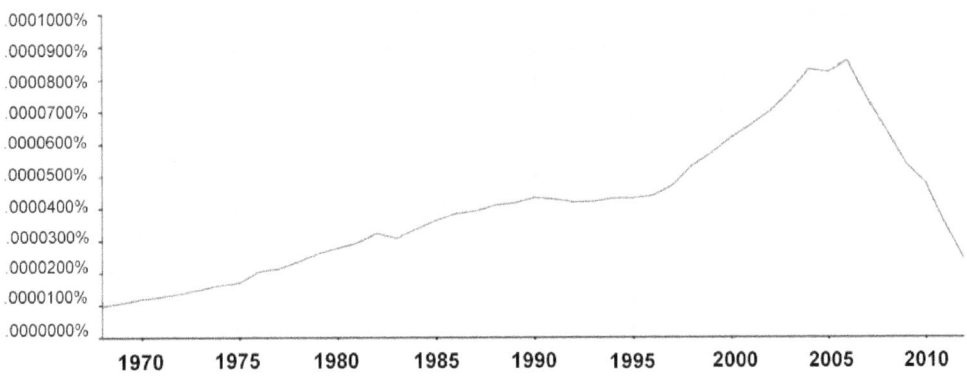

Relative incidence of the word "zombie" in American English books published from 1968 through 2012 (Source: Google Books Ngram).

books, video games, and, increasingly, mainstream press coverage.[3] One might add that the greater availability and variety of works about zombies has been accompanied by the rising profitability of this material: consider, in this regard, that the 2017 film *Get Out* (an admittedly non-traditional depiction of zombieism) grossed over $250 million and the movie version of *World War Z* grossed over half a billion dollars worldwide.

While academic interest in the living dead has arrived somewhat later to the scene, it has made up for this delay with imaginative commentary and scholarship, much of which has been referenced in the preceding essays. A significant portion of this published work has explored the historical and cultural evolution of zombies and interpreted our increased interest in the dead as a political, social, and cultural metaphor.[4] As dramatic and symbolic stand-ins, the undead help to spotlight, exaggerate, and focus on some crucial aspect of our society, especially by revealing our fears or by dramatizing inequities or ideologies embedded within our human relations. In the brutal contrast between zombie behaviors and ordinary human traits, desires, and *telos*—and in the related contrast between how we view ourselves and those trying to survive a zombie invasion—accounts of the walking dead encourage us to re-examine larger philosophical questions about the good life and living well.

This strategy of looking at zombies to look inside ourselves connects our absorption with zombie narratives with a wide range of social and political phenomena: from the nation's anxiety over the horrors of 9/11 and the threat of international and domestic terrorism to our collective response to the rise of social media (and the simultaneous glorification and erasing of online personality).[5] Other more recent academic projects in this vein trace a link between our attitudes towards the undead and responses to the Black Lives Matter movement (and its underlying cause of racial justice), immigration policy, and the rise of Donald Trump.[6] As Erin Cassese notes, "This is the utility of the zombie as a political metaphor—it's flexible; there is room enough for all our fears."[7]

More broadly, academicians have noted that the undead can teach us about "dangers facing the nation and globe,"[8] including a class of open-ended and relentless problems at hand in our new century: emerging and stubborn pandemics like COVID-19, climate change, the alienation of humans from work and social life, and the firehose of data sprayed at our collective brains. Scholars and other commentators have fastened upon the zombie figure to explain a wide range of intellectual puzzles, from the extended life of debunked ideas to exploring problems in the philosophy of mind.[9] Additionally, a growing literature on transhumanism (how we overcome "limitations for belonging to the human condition" by *intensifying* existing human traits) and posthumanism ("decentering" the human as a normative, historical, evolutionary, biological, and philosophical focus) often draws at least indirectly on zombie narratives.[10] As Erin Dolgoy and Kimberly Hale argue, understanding different depictions of zombies can help us explore alternatives to traditional notions of what it means to be human, and, more specifically, to consider the possibility that we might "change humanity to better fit the world, rather than changing the world to better suit humanity."[11] In these various ways, contemplating the zombie apocalypse is a set of thought experiments about what we value, and an invitation to tell the truth about where we are heading.

This essays in this volume contribute to many of these far-flung currents in zombie studies. For example, Cammie M. Sublette's essay discusses the legacy of slavery and the zombie genre's persistent interest in race. In Angela Tenga's essay, she explores the "Last Night story" as a "survivor narrative that is particularly suited to the conditions of the zombie apocalypse." Notwithstanding these and other broad contributions, the central purpose of this book has been to analyze the genealogy, meaning, and influence of Romero's six films about the living dead.

Romero as the Center of the Zombie Universe

But why this topic and why this focus—and why at this time? With, as noted, so much scholarship on the undead emerging over the past three decades, does the world really need another zombie book? The essays in this volume reflect an awareness that popular interest in zombies remains high, and that Romero and his six films about the undead are key to understanding how we got to our current zombie moment and where it goes next. Beyond just providing us with a set of (sometimes challenged) assumptions about how zombies look and act, the director is at the gravitational center of the zombie universe. Artists, authors, and scholars who produce stories about and analyses of the undead readily acknowledge Romero as the godfather of zombie films and the main engine for our culture's wider fascination with undead subjects. For example, over the years, numerous filmmakers and television producers working within the zombie genre, including such figures as Sam Raimi, Quentin Tarantino, Edgar Wright, Joss Whedon, and Jordan Peele have all expressed their appreciation for and awareness of Romero's legacy. Artists in various fields pay tribute to Romero in less explicit ways, mimicking the director's style, themes, and dramatic content. Indeed, even references to the zombie "renaissance" (or *re*-birth) point to an earlier etiology or birth where Romero stands as creator. After all, the director "invented almost single handedly" the modern representation of "cannibalistic, walking-dead ghouls" and inspired the mass public's outpouring of interest in these monsters.[12]

Besides his inspiring, precedential vision, another reason to put Romero at the center of a scholarly study of the dead is his longevity; the director's body of work is critical to studying the walking dead due to the length and productivity of his professional arc. The arc from *Night* to *Survival of the Dead* (2009), Romero's last zombie film, covers forty years, taking us from the Tet Offensive (and the beginning of the end of the Vietnam war) to the financial turmoil and capitalist cannibalism of the subprime mortgage crisis of 2007. In this way, Romero's career serves as a microcosm of a changing (and fractured) society. It is also a vehicle for tracking developments in how popular culture depicts zombies as well as the shifting contours of public interest in the undead. Put differently, in watching Romero's films (which serve as the longest and most enduring zombie franchise in history) we can learn about the foundations, growth, mainstreaming, transformation, and future of today's zombie narratives. Indeed, since Romero ushered in the modern zombie form, and, consequently, "didn't really have any rules" to follow in the genre, he was uniquely positioned to forge (and then rework and disrupt) expectations regarding what zombies did, and how a zombie film looked, worked, and unfolded.[13] In this way, Romero not only gave us an initial archetypal story about the rise, response to, and retreat from a viral zombie menace, but he was also creatively restless in showing us how to rework and play with that basic narrative. Throughout his career Romero was both iconic storyteller and cheerful iconoclast.

Admittedly, this volume is not the only one examining the artistic output and influence of the purported "Godfather of the Dead."[14] However, many books devoted to Romero represent variations of "fan books," offering some combination of hagiographic retrospectives, plot synopses, accounts of the production process of the various films, insider revelations and gossip about the personalities involved, and arguments about the relative merits of the director's respective works.[15] While still other books specifically centered on Romero are more scholarly,[16] the overall number is modest.

More to the point, this edited collection offers what are arguably three distinct features for helping us understand Romero's contribution to zombie studies. First, the essays gathered under this cover are the first collection published since the fiftieth anniversary of *Night of the Living Dead*. This feature of our book is not just opportunistic, but recognizes both the endurance of the *Dead* franchise and the greater distance we (the public, pundits, critics, scholars, and admirers and detractors of Romero's work) now have from *Night* and its successors, affording us enhanced critical and comparative perspective.

Second, and related, Romero's relatively recent death (in July 2017) provides an unfortunate boundary to his work that was previously missing. Until now, even sophisticated analyses of the artist's assorted roles (as director, author, screenwriter, editor, graphic novel contributor, mentor, interview subject, etc.) could not confidently discuss his legacy because the contours of his oeuvre were still expanding. The end of the director's career as a producer of entertainment helps to shift our focus fully from consumers to informed interpreters who are curious not just about Romero's existing influence on established thinkers, artists, and creative works, but also in anticipating and imagining his future impact, especially on emergent forms of the walking dead. In this light, Cammie Sublette's essay documents how Romero's *Night* lays down a grim sociological marker for charting the (lack of) progress we have made with respect to the experiences of black Americans and law enforcement, an analysis that is charged with additional meaning as the nation continues to reel from the implications of the 2020 killing of George Floyd and the resulting worldwide protests.

Third and finally, and as communicated in this book's descriptive subtitle, our authors are interested one way or another in the notion of legacy. The prior essays have measured the nature and span of Romero's creative and intellectual path, traced its idiosyncratic and often disruptive course, and assessed the value and meaning of the routes he and his armies of the dead have carved. Romero can be regarded as an independent, "maverick" (and harried) filmmaker,[17] a social and political satirist,[18] but he also draws on and contributes to the genre of the American western (as Gloria Pastorino in her essay makes clear), is an artistic and political "revolutionary" (as Emma Austin and Chera Kee discuss in their essays), and stands as an important figure in Italian cinema (as Fulvio Orsitto elaborates in his essay).

Understanding the Romero Legacy: Authority, Inheritance and the Span of the Dead

With each of these essays' different conclusions and interpretive glosses in mind, what broad observations can we make regarding how we should understand the Romero zombie legacy, now stretching into the twenty-first century? Etymologically, the notion of legacy points to two somewhat separate notions: the first derives from a *legatus*, an ambassador or other person with authority to conduct a mission, and the second refers to the more familiar notion of a gift by will or deeded inheritance.[19] The Romero legacy can be usefully considered in this dual light: serving as both authority figure and inherited resource.

With respect to the first understanding, we can appreciate that Romero's legacy has a retrospective and path-dependent character, representing a set of almost unavoidable historical and cultural reference points. One can make a strong case that no responsible scholar and no artist with even a modest degree of curiosity and cultural awareness can understand the contours of and contemporary interest in the undead without paying attention to the works of George A. Romero. His substantive ideas, directorial mien, and narrative inflections are now woven into our default portrait of what makes zombies move, moan, and absorb the attention of audiences and readers. To be sure, the vision first crafted in *Night* and stretching over four decades is both borrowed and new. Romero's undead ghouls are a "clever amalgam of images and tropes" from prior zombie narratives and other monstrous and dramatic films.[20] Indeed, many of the essays in this volume document the specific cultural and entertainment heritage that shaped Romero, including comic books, horror, sci-fi, and pulp fiction. The director freely conceded, and even celebrated, many of these influences.[21]

But while the zombie figure can be traced to centuries old folklore, and Pre-Code cinematic portrayals,[22] today, two decades into our new millennium, the zombie—both at home and on the world stage—remains Romero's creature. His stamp on the genre is both distinctive and decisive. As numerous scholars note, Romero has contributed to a set of canonical ideas about how zombies behave, what drives (and kills) them, and what it means to face a zombie horde. As Stephanie Zacharek puts it, Romero "didn't invent zombies.... But everything we think we know about zombies today began with him."[23] Romero's zombies (and the many walking dead that follow in his monsters' footsteps) move slowly, eat human flesh, must be destroyed with trauma to the head, reproduce through infection, and are self-propelled but largely unthinking. Along with films like *Zombie Flesh Eaters* (aka *Zombi 2*, 1979) and the *Evil Dead* series, Max Brooks's *Zombie Survival Guide* largely follows these conventions, noting, for example, that zombies "appear to be incapable of running. The fastest have been observed to move at a rate of barely one step per 1.5 seconds."[24]

Of course, much of what makes Romero's *Dead* series simultaneously durable and captivating is its relentless dynamism. Across and sometimes within Romero's films, the behavior, nature, and meaning of the living dead is varied and even evolving. The director's imitators have likewise freely borrowed from his model while deviating and sometimes transforming it. But even these updates are significant, in part, because they represent breaks from what is still a Romero baseline or venerable standard. Thus, while the *iZombie* television series gives us a group of intelligent, assimilated, emotional, and benevolent zombies, these figures are distinguished from a separate class of feral and "mindless" zombies known as "Romeros." Similarly, in the *Santa Clarita Diet*, protagonist Sheila Hammond continues to love and have sexual relations with her (living) husband even after she is "turned." Viewers are amused and disoriented by these developments, in part because they shatter the normal, well-understood rules of the zombie oeuvre—rules the television show otherwise honors (such as its adherence to the notion that zombies can only be "killed" with destruction of their brains).

Setting aside this notion of Romero as an authoritative reference point, we can also explore the director's legacy in its second (and intertwined) sense: Romero's work is a "gift by will" (with the "will" here being Romero's force of personality and clarity of vision), which offers a set of tools and perspectives which future scholars and artists can draw on, reinvent, or subvert. Romero's legacy in this sense is a resource for intellectual and creative projects today and into the future. Again, while other scholarship[25] and the essays in this book have pointed to many of these legacy-as-gift ideas, we bring this volume to a close by highlighting and explaining three particular aspects of the Romero heritage that have been especially influential: (1) his embrace of a discomforting ambiguity in presenting the threat and monstrousness of the zombie; (2) his emphasis on the inner struggles of his protagonists (and antagonists), rather than the raw, outward threat of the dead; and, finally, (3) his complex but unflagging embrace of humanism.

To begin with, as many scholars have noted, unlike other monsters and even creatures associated with the undead, the zombie is an especially disconcerting figure insofar as it "occupies a liminal or transitional and ambiguous space."[26] Zombies pass between the living and dead, civilization and chaos, and, perhaps most unsettling, they are jarringly poised between being monstrous and humane.[27] Unlike vampires, werewolves, ghosts (or more outsized beasts like dragons), zombies do not possess fantastic powers of shape-shifting or flight; indeed, their menacing traits (such as their physical decay, slowness of movement, greater effectiveness *en masse*, even their insatiable hunger) are recognizable problems or features of humanity. Kim Paffenroth elaborates that the zombie "is both still human, and yet no longer human: it cannot be treated just like a piece of trash, but also it should not be kept around."[28] Thus, the living dead must be destroyed in a way that somehow respects its humanity while recognizing its "impurity and contagion."[29] According to Greg Garrett, zombies "are popular villains because they have affinities to us yet seem alien."[30]

Romero's *Dead* series acknowledges the degree to which his living dead fill an "uncanny, interstitial space," and the director experiments with this awkward positioning to both engage and repulse his audience.[31] Through comic distortions (the dead as eager shoppers banging on the glass in *Dawn*), mimicked behavior (Bub learning how to use a phone and gun in *Day*), and explicit gestures to the uncanny border between humans and the dead (a recurring element in *Land*), Romero repeatedly exploits our uneasy recognition of our foe in a dizzying cycle that puts us on and off and on guard again. As Shaviro explains, Romero plays with the disruptive status of the zombie to transgress the "boundaries between humor and horror, between intense conviction and ludicrous exaggeration."[32]

Shaviro's comment points us to another signature contribution of Romero: his deployment of humor, especially to add to the disorientation of his viewers. It is not a new idea that "humor often provides horror-film viewers with a psychological escape from on-screen terrors."[33] But Romero invokes comedy and irony as part of his exploration of discomfort, incessantly punctuating and then resuming his climb through tension and horror. When Bub struggles to grasp and use a telephone, Dr. Logan encourages him to call his "Aunt Alicia," a banal and comical instruction that humanizes Bub and takes us away from the confines of the government base and the horrors of the world above—until we pause a beat and reflect on the fact that Aunt Alicia (assuming she ever existed) is now surely dead herself and certainly unavailable through a phone line. Zombies are a comedic foil for Romero because they teasingly suggest the prosaic absurdities in our own lives (consider the zombies struggling to maintain their balance on the crowded mall escalator in *Dawn*) and the ease with which we can lapse into monstrous behavior. These notions are certainly carried forward in films like *Shaun of the Dead* (2004), *Zombieland* (2009), *Zombieland Double Tap* (2019), and, even more poignantly and ironically in Jim Jarmusch's *The Dead Don't Die* (2019).

Ultimately, of course, Romero's humor gives way to a damning discomfort that finds its source at the unhappy road where the human and the monstrous meet. His audiences are horrified by the slaughter they encounter in all directions: we see ourselves destroyed by living corpses (and thereby experience our own mortality) as we simultaneously recognize that the protagonists' ruthless dispatch of the dead brings them (and us) closer to monstrous inhumanity. As Paffenroth concludes "it is not just horrible to watch zombies devouring humans, but it is more subtly and insidiously horrible to imagine the human characters in the movies slaughtering hundreds of zombies who look, and, to some extent, still act, exactly like human beings."[34] The effect of this is to leave the audience morally and ontologically de-centered. This legacy of discomfort has been widely imitated since Romero's *Night* debuted, both in other portrayals of zombies and more widely—perhaps most obviously in films that place the monstrous in children such as *The Omen, The Exorcist, Carrie*, and too many others to mention. Romero, like these many who followed him, blends our sympathies and fears into an impure alloy.

Related to this strategy of discomfort, some students of the dead contend that a major break from Romero took place with the rise of "fast" zombies found in *Nightmare City* (1980), *28 Days Later* (2002), the remake of *Dawn of the Dead* (2004), and *Zombieland* (2009).[35] But the fast vs. slow debate conceals a related but more important emphasis, and one where Romero's preferences have clearly won the day. As Simon Pegg observes, the "lolloping threat" of the walking dead is "a critical handicap which enabled survivors to take stock of their surroundings and regard their attackers with fascinated disgust as much as fear."[36]

In other words, the slowness of Romero's living dead creates a temporal space or break in which humans (both his characters and his audience) can express their character, reflect on their (mis)deeds, and fret. In emphasizing this interior struggle, Romero shifts our attention away from instant survival (as a problem of willpower and the physics of destruction) to psychological and social predicaments that may be our undoing. This move also trains our attention on the potential of humans to be self-destructive and even monstrous. As the director puts it succinctly, "In my work, usually the humans that are the worst…. I have a soft spot in my heart for zombies."[37] Indeed, because the dead have no "inner lives,"[38] zombie movies spotlight the psychological struggles and turmoil of the living. Romero's slow monsters serve as dramatic circuit breakers which facilitate the director's exploration of the best and worst in his humans. We can see this legacy of slowness and interiority in films like *Cemetery Man* (1994), *Shaun of the Dead* (2004), and the non-zombie movie *It Follows* (2014).

Romero's Humanism: We Are the Measure of the World

Perhaps the most consistent and sustained idea in Romero's *Dead* films, subsequently grappled with (and adopted) by countless filmmakers and writers, is his abiding humanism. Despite their bleakness, Romero's films are balanced or at least leavened by a persistent, life-affirming worldview that is both attractive to his audiences and artistically distinctive. Despite what some critics claim,[39] Romero does not celebrate nihilism or "the mere predations of the living dead"[40]

Humanism has a millennia-spanning history and represents a complex and not always intellectually uniform set of ideas. As Corliss Lamont recognizes there are "different kinds of humanists"[41] and varied humanisms. The broad intellectual tradition stretches from "Confucian China"[42] and the Socratic impulse "to call philosophy down from heaven" and direct it at "human things"[43] through the Renaissance shift from regarding a person as "a sinful and morally crippled creature" to "God's superior and talented collaborator charged with bringing to realization the potential inherent in His magnificent creation."[44] The humanist "ideals of human perfectibility, rationality, and agency"[45] found additional expression in the Enlightenment and in modern, secular forms which "are skeptical about the claim that there exists a god or gods"[46] and stress that the good life is achievable on earth, and ordinary human impulses and pleasures are "to be cultivated, not condemned."[47]

One notable aspect of this background is that it highlights how humanist principles often arose from periods of turmoil.[48] Mass violence, institutional and cultural dysfunction, and the inadequacy of the state to meet pressing needs ushered in new ideas directed away from established authority and towards the well-being and progression of regular people. The protracted havoc and misery delivered by the Black Death, for example, propelled an eventual transformation in how people understood their world, and destabilized the received authority of churches and monarchs. As the historian Barbara Tuchman summarizes

> If a disaster of such magnitude … was a mere act of God or perhaps not God's work at all, then the absolutes of a fixed order were loosed from their moorings. Minds that opened to admit these questions could never be shut. Once people envisioned the possibility of change in a fixed order, the end of an age of submission came into sight; the turn to individual conscience [and the foundation of Renaissance humanism] lay ahead.[49]

This context helps us further understand the relationship between Romero's humanism and the worlds of mayhem and disorder he creates. The waves of the living dead sweep away old orders and pin our attention to what we value in this life, in a manner that recalls medieval plagues, the religious wars that preceded the Enlightenment, and the horrors of the world wars that helped to birth modern humanism.

But what exactly is humanism—and how do we see it manifest in Romero's films? While the director's approach is always distinctly his own, his humanism roughly corresponds with Richard Cohen's description of a "worldview founded on the belief in the irreducible dignity of humans, a belief in the efficacy and worth of human freedom and hence also of human responsibility."[50] At the core of this perspective is the familiar concept that "man is the measure of all things"—that our moral aspirations and social arrangements should be based on standards of achievable human conduct, rather than rules set by God or inherited authorities.[51] As Dawn Keetley notes, this "generally humanist orientation" courses through zombie works generally since they consistently "position the human as the ideal from which we fell and to which we must return."[52] More specifically, we can highlight three features of the humanist paradigm that recur in Romero's films: (1) challenging and ultimately discrediting conventional institutions, especially those which are insufficient to protect us from new crises; (2) emphasizing the value of ordinary people; and (3) portraying and valuing a range of distinctly human attributes, some of which are essential for securing our autonomy.

First, as several essays in this book have noted, Romero's *Dead* series portrays a world in which previously dominant organizations and conventions are in eclipse or disarray. In addition to the unreliable role of government, the military, and news media, Romero's films are remarkably absent of religious figures and themes, despite the ubiquity of death. This is consistent with a longstanding humanist suspicion of organized religion and traditional claims to rule, and a reformist stress on approaching "moral and political issues rationally and fairly" rather than accepting answers from authority.[53] Gregory Waller goes so far as to suggest that *Night's* setting (a graveyard on a Sunday) "emphasizes the failure of religion in a secular age."[54] More broadly, Romero challenges the conventional family structure and prevailing racial and gender hierarchies, and he shows the payoff of this disruption in showcasing women and black men as the "chief protagonists" and the most effective, reasonable, and moral of his leaders.[55] Romero does not suggest that there is no role for, say, organized governance or society, but that the terms under which we design these entities must always focus on addressing human concerns and welfare.

A second humanist theme in Romero's work is his evinced respect for ordinary people and the inhabitants of what the director called "the real world."[56] Renaissance humanism famously expanded the subjects of art and literature from the powerful and well-born, providing us with accounts of the rest of society, using vernacular language and familiar scenes and settings. For his part, Romero does not judge grifters, hustlers, prostitutes, or rogues, especially if they show compassion, pluck, or some fealty to their fellow human beings. We each "count for one"[57] and our social status, wealth, and power—before or after the rise of the dead—is irrelevant to our moral worth. *Day's* prosaic and imperfect heroes include a female scientist, a "Jamaican helicopter pilot" and a "drunken Irish radio operator,"[58] and each of these figures communicates a range of "real world" human capacities and emotions, from fear to disgust to impatience and passion. Similarly, in *Night* there are no mad scientists, "no barons or knights," but instead "the characters are democratically ordinary."[59] Even Romero's choice to film in black and white, and his general reliance on amateur or unfamiliar actors reinforces this leveling and egalitarian impulse. The *Walking Dead's* Robert Kirkman extends this idea to zombie narratives generally, arguing that a "story about vampires or werewolves is a story about people going through that transformation.... But zombie stories are about human beings doing relatable things: protecting your family, finding food, building shelter."[60]

In the broadest recognition of these democratic values, Romero's humans demonstrate interest in and sympathy towards the living dead—at least when these monsters exhibit human traits.[61] After Cholo is bitten by a zombie in *Land*, Foxy offers to shoot him before he can reanimate. Cholo responds: "Nah, I've always wanted to see how the other half lives."[62] While a throwaway, comic line, it also gestures to the heart of Romero's reflexive and expansive humanism. As Waller explains, in Romero's films the living dead are also "recognizably ordinary" and "vulnerable."[63] They are young and old, often shown in their work or bed clothes, and they represent a wide swath of (former) humanity across demographic and social lines. As the director himself famously put it, "zombies are the blue-collar monster."[64] Riley's summation at the end of *Land*—the dead are "just looking for a place to go. Same as us"—simultaneously closes the gap between living and dead and underscores the simplicity and modesty of their desires.[65]

In *The Sky Is Falling: How Vampires, Zombies, Androids, and Superheroes Made America Great for Extremes*, Peter Biskind argues that an emergent extremism in popular culture is associated with the idea that some groups or individuals are so alien and threatening that they must be left out of the human race entirely. But George Romero's films have never embraced this perspective and have instead stood for an older proposition: that we might learn about our humanity through others, even (especially) through those that threaten our values and way of life.[66]

A third element of Romero's embrace of humanist values involves his depiction of a full range of distinctive and essential attributes, talents, and failings of humankind. His characters express (often extreme) emotion, empathy, humor, cooperation, pragmatism, loyalty, friendship, and, frankly, a range of less virtuous traits like selfishness, impulsivity, and willfulness. But these traits are identifiable as distinctively human, in part, because they are so antithetical to the mindless, emotionless, flesh eaters that constantly threaten to bring an end to humanity. Of course, Romero constantly plays with and blurs this division. The "zombies of *Day* wail in hunger and despair, are mainly bullied and abused by the living, and begin to exhibit individual personality traits."[67] In their capacity to express vociferous outrage, they may be more actively alive than the subdued human scientists and jaded soldiers. Indeed, the revolutionary consciousness, organization, and taste for "social justice" first exhibited (and then transmitted) by Big Daddy in *Land* suggest that Romero's dead assume what Lowenstein identifies as "increasingly 'human' traits."[68] Big Daddy expresses a compassion for his kind absent from many of the film's humans, and he ultimately becomes a figure of righteous indignation. Indeed, because Big Daddy is an effective and resourceful leader of the dead, he is able to do what the human Cholo cannot: destroy Fiddler's Green and deliver justice to Paul Kaufman.[69]

Besides furnishing us with portraits of different human types, emotions, and capacities, Romero's humanism also points to a rough path towards individual autonomy. In the world of the dead, surviving humans must use their full range of attributes—from tool-making, to conflict resolution, to empathy, to wider-scale social organization. In this way, Romero's films do "not simply or unequivocally valorize survival" but instead urge us to imagine more from the participating players, and, by extension, humanity as a whole.[70] Unlike what Greenberg describes as "cruel" horror that treats "characters and audience as dumb objects to be exploited toward enormous gain,"[71] Romero gives us countless figures who extend their lives, dignity, and agency through inventiveness and smart, proactive, and moral decision-making. The signature example of this figure is his first hero, the ordinary "working man,"[72] Ben, whose hands are as nimble as his mind. Unlike the other figures in the besieged farmhouse, he is "fully capable of active thought and rational action."[73] Pursuant to the humanist tradition, Ben's "heroic potential is shown in an ordinary context; he is just an intelligent and vital man caught in bad circumstances."[74]

Does the achievement and self-realization effected by *individuals* in Romero's films extend to humanity more widely? Do our efforts to learn about the world and our purpose in it through the struggles with the dead give rise to a broader humanist project of liberation for our species? As discussed in prior scholarship and elsewhere in this volume, both women and minorities in Romero's films show some capacity to become *more* self-actuating after the zombie apocalypse. But the more general prospects for social cooperation and human advancement in the *Dead* series seem pretty dim. While the director has affirmed that his dead "progress,"[75] it's not obvious we can extend this assumption to *homo sapiens* generally, particularly since our traditional notions of knowledge, development, and perfectibility depend upon an imaginable future that is incompatible with what Gwyneth Peaty calls "zombie time."[76]

So what does appreciating Romero's legacy of expressed humanism teach us about his work more generally? To begin with, it helps us better understand the terms of his normative critique of human behavior and social institutions. Romero does not tell his stories in the service of a grand meta-narrative, abstract ideology, or set of overarching political or religious precepts; instead his worldview, to the extent he discloses it, is centered on identifying and alleviating the conditions and suffering of humans as a whole. He skewers anyone who uses other people for their own ends, who acts cruelly, or otherwise consumes others literally or metaphorically. Thus, *Land of the Dead's* Kaufman is mostly odious because he allows the people of Uniontown to starve and denies them medicine—not because his autocratic rule degrades democratic principles or shoulders aside more meritorious leaders. The perversity of the clan battles between O'Flynn and Muldoon in *Survival* is that they sacrifice human lives for historic feuds and idiosyncratic beliefs about how best to handle the problem of the living dead, placing personal ego before society. Our conflicts over ideologies and history create what Sarge Crocket calls an "us-versus-them world" where we quickly forget the rationale for our discord and fight and kill pointlessly, propelled by inertia and atavism.[77]

Romero's humanist values also help us understand his critiques of consumer culture and purposeless living. The humanist tradition champions living under reason, self-rule, active and morally autonomous lives, and appreciating "what human beings are actually like, and of what will help them flourish in this world."[78] The mindless execution of Ben, the "Mall Fantasia"[79] of *Dawn,* and the insular and pointless exertions in *Day* are but three snapshots capturing Romero's concern that too many of us are, in the words of *Land's* Riley, merely "pretending to be alive."[80]

In sum, Romero's humanist values help to explain the characters he admires (those who try "to relate to each other" or who display "communitarian" values of "compassion and empathy"[81]), and those he dismisses or judges harshly (such as the various soldiers and militants he depicts as lacking the "will to sympathize"[82] with anyone outside their in-group). As Romero himself explained, the problem of the undead in his films is about ignoring "what we, the global community, should really be thinking about: something like … power to the people."[83]

In addition to revealing some prominent markings on Romero's moral compass, surfacing his humanist value system is also valuable in helping to explain the director's widespread appeal. As discussed, the version of humanism he embraces is neither ideological nor institutional; he does not advance any concrete set of political, religious, or moral beliefs and he does not obviously favor specific social structures (such as the family) or governing organizations. At the same time, Romero is no nihilist; his consistently human-centered emphasis spills out in his affection for his characters, his sympathy for their plights, and his big-hearted embrace of misfits, outcasts, nonconformists, and those who evince kindness towards others, even in the face of terror. Romero's principled but expansive point of view allows him to be both political and critical, to instruct without being didactic, to provoke without being too overt. His film's themes are broad enough and his endings sufficiently ambiguous that he neither condescends nor dictates, but gives his audience the freedom to consider multiple interpretations of his most important figures and events, while never losing sight of *homo sapiens* as his moral touchstone. And, of course, the humanist paradigm is sufficiently expansive and flexible that it allows Romero's concerns to evolve substantially from one film to the next.

Romero's valuation of the human species as a whole rather than privileging the worth or merit of particular individuals or archetypes has creative and artistic implications. His orientation is reflected in the mostly self-contained nature of his movies; he does not offer us an endless saga of connected plots and larger-than-life figures who stride from film to film. Instead, his loosely connected works track his democratic humanism: no one person is inherently more important than another. He takes all of his characters (and their stories), seriously without getting too invested in any one of them. Instead of giving us a virtuous, indefatigable, and seemingly indestructible hero like *The Walking Dead's* Rick Grimes, he offers dozens of grittier and more down to earth figures—any one of whom might die or face bleak prospects.

This stance makes Romero's characters more believable, grounded, and accessible, and gives the director greater authorial freedom and flexibility. He can assume his audience knows the basic backstory of his version of the zombie apocalypse, but is still at liberty to experiment with new aesthetics, styles, plots, and protagonists. Presumably, this creative latitude is part of his critique of *The Walking Dead* as a "soap opera";[84] Romero is not attracted to the AMC show's gradualism, prolonged character development, and interpersonal drama. Instead of the long-form zombie narrative, he prefers creative work with a shorter shelf life, as it facilitates greater originality and innovation. Romero can always rethink his themes, his zombies, his outlook, and his art; he owes nothing to inherited characters or storylines and does not seem to care too much about his prior audience's expectations.

Romero's humanism is not without its shortcomings. His basic concern with the plight of humanity, rather than his investment in particular humans can feel a little cold or harsh. Abrams has compared Romero and Max Brooks in asserting that they both adopt a journalistic, "pseudo-documentary" stance in their work.[85] As Abrams elaborates

> In "Night of the Living Dead," and "The Crazies," Romero mixed verité style and, in his words, "theatrical" story-telling. He quickly cross-cuts between events during action scenes, and uses naturalistically lit, sometimes out-of-focus takes to give viewers the impression that they're watching events happen in real-time.[86]

But in such a world, where all people (and stories) matter, and where each represents a piece of humanity's larger plight, any individual tale threatens to lose some of its significance and power, to become diluted in a dispassionate, somewhat distanced telling. In *Dawn*, Fran's narrative is salted with tragedy and personal loss and ends with a precarious future—which also describes Sarah's basic story arc in *Day*, and Sarge's account in *Survival*, and so on. Where "everybody [is] to count for one," the hazard is that everyone counts less.

Romero's situational and ahistoric approach, which eschews longer inter-film story arcs and reflects an encompassing interest in his fictional subjects, also poses challenges with respect to his audience's willingness to invest themselves in his protagonists. In *Land*, we feel compassion for Cholo and Slack, but the sentiment is somewhat abstract and blunted, since their future is untenable. Similarly, Romero's democratic, disjointed, and somewhat distancing aesthetic limits his characters' potential for personal and moral development. As Liebovitz points out, the zombie Bub's evolution is rapid and "heartfelt": over the course of a few days he goes from confused and shiftless to acquiring dawning appreciation of art, language, and memory, to being "grief-stricken" upon discovering the death of his "master," to becoming an agent of rage and vengeance.[87] But this progression is intense and almost frantic, and contrasts sharply with the fatalistic, jaded, and narrow emotional range of the humans that surround him.

Where We Stand at the End: Rebirth or Re-death?

In considering whether Romero's persistent humanism is one of his most important legacies, we can also take aim at the thesis more directly. In many ways, the rapid spread of the zombie apocalypse and the almost overnight collapse of our social order seems antithetical to celebrating and protecting humans as irreducible moral units. We might agree with Wood that zombie films are part of a general trend of horror: depicting "a spirit of negativity, an undifferentiated lust for destruction, that seems to be not far below the surface of the modern collective consciousness."[88] In films that portray the zombie pandemic, Renaissance and Enlightenment principles are in eclipse: "Reason and science are on the defensive, while behavior that was once beyond the pale—violence, lying, revenge—have become the new norm."[89] The dramatic tensions packed into *Night* are overcome by sacrificing "human dignity and human value," along with the sole figure who consistently upholds these values.[90] The humanist support of the "methods of science—skepticism, fallibilism, open debate, and empirical testing"[91] seems to come into question if not open repudiation in *Day*—and throughout the *Dead* series insofar as science provides no consistent or clear answers regarding how and why the dead rose from their graves.[92]

Even where Romero's survivors manage to find or create environments where they are not under imminent, existential peril, they often take actions that compromise human dignity and the worth of humanity as a whole rather than promoting it. Thus, when the mall survivors in *Dawn* achieve a measure of respite and freedom from the grind of mere survival, they isolate and become what Kyle Bishop describes as "feckless" consumers who surrender control over their own creativity and self-direction, and "ultimately lose that which makes them essentially 'human.'"[93] In *Day*, instead of facilitating cooperation and trust, the secure, enclosed scientific-military installation becomes a petri dish of hostility, humiliation, and degradation. *Diary of the Dead* (2007) expresses a similar concern that Romero's fictional subjects are diminishing rather than elevating the human condition. In Debra's final voiceover, she recounts how "Jason once said he thought he could help, maybe even save some lives."[94] But she ultimately concludes that he may have become disillusioned with humanity. After sharing his last video, which depicts "a couple of hometown Joes" who tie an undead woman to a tree and shoot her "just for kicks," she asks herself (and Romero's viewers): "Are we worth saving? You tell me."[95]

These, and countless other examples from Romero's *Dead* series might seem to cast the director's humanist inclinations in doubt. How sincerely can we hope to promote dignity and regard for others, when we constantly see these objects under attack in his films? Again, an obvious response to this challenge is simply to posit that these inhumane conditions will change once humans vanquish the dead. As Thomas Hobbes famously warned, an all-out war "wherein men live without other security than what their own strength and their own invention shall furnish them"[96] is inhospitable to human creativity, culture, and the exercise of the capacities and talents that make us a distinct species. War is possibly the most dehumanizing activity one can imagine; thus, if we can beat back the dead (or, more metaphorically, if we can stop our own penchant for conflict) we can go back to promoting our proper *telos*. In this interpretation, the promise of Romero's humanist vision is implicitly referenced at the outer boundaries of his work. Once the enemy is vanquished, we can be more fully human. Perhaps a new generation, not defined by an existential battle with the undead (or with hidebound divisions and ideologies), can help us realize our potential as a species.

But a serious problem with this response is that it seems to graft an agenda onto Romero's works that seems largely absent. The director does not appear especially interested in emphasizing the life to come, but is instead invested in the struggles of the moment. In *Land*, in what is arguably Romero's most hopeful ending—Dead Reckoning rumbles along a road with a cascade of fireworks overhead—the audience is under no illusions that "the North" will offer paradise.

Indeed, Romero gives us many indications that the way forward for his survivors will be treacherous if not impassable. The very last images that the director provided for us paint a dark picture of human prospects. At the very end of Romero's last film, *Survival of the Dead*, the reanimated O'Flynn and Muldoon engage in an endless, mindless, fruitless battle, pointing and discharging their (empty) guns at each other again and again. But what's notable about this *grand finale* is that the combatants' behavior deviates from what we have come to expect from the dead. Instead of wandering aimlessly, searching for humans to consume, or even haunting their old locales, O'Flynn and Muldoon exclusively hunt one another. Their bodies may be dead, but their inextinguishable drive comes from their lingering humanity; the twin patriarchs' hunger for revenge, and insatiable hatred, now override their undead taste for human flesh. When the living dead become more like the living, they still drive towards violence, albeit in a somewhat different form.

This idea, that destruction of others is core to our identity, is clearly at cross purposes with the humanist project. But it is a cultural impulse with a longstanding history, at least in the American context. As Richard Slotkin has argued, the idea of "regeneration through violence ... became the structuring metaphor of the American experience."[97] At the center of this cultural myth is the notion that "the redemption of American spirit or fortune [is] something to be achieved by playing through a scenario of separation [from society], temporary regression to a more primitive or 'natural' state" and, finally, rebirth and renewal through bloodshed and destruction.[98] While Slotkin chronicles this cycle of separation and violent rebirth primarily by recounting America's historical (and fictionalized) wars with Native Americans, it seems apposite to O'Flynn and Muldoon's endless struggles, and Romero's *Dead* series as a whole.

Understood in this light, our battles with zombies simply give vent to a destructive impulse to hunt "the other" that is core to our identity. In this interpretation, Romero does not give us his own preferred model of a post-apocalyptic society, or a clear path for ending the war with the dead, because these aspirations are somewhat beside the point. *Land of the Dead's* Fiddler's Green is corrupt, and *Survival's* "final answer" (teaching the dead to eat non-human flesh) is shrugged away by Sarge who abandons Plum Island and its wan promise of peace. We are left behind, with O'Flynn and Muldoon in endless conflict, and the implication that, as Tony Williams puts it, "the world they inhabit will also become extinct due to deadly behavioral mechanisms and institutional power politics that will eventually destroy everyone."[99] For Slotkin and Romero, our cultural assumptions and mythic backstory presume that we will continuously identify an enemy whom we will seek to destroy "root and branch" in a "savage war."[100] The director's forgiving, generous humanism is, therefore, balanced and perhaps undermined by his tough-minded, unforgiving, and even pessimistic view of how we see ourselves.

Bursting Through the Dam of the Dead

So who is George Romero and what is his legacy in this regard? Is he an irrepressible humanist, celebrating the potential of our species and our prospects for self-improvement, or an inveterate cynic? One suspects the obvious answer is the correct one: Romero is too interesting, too imaginative, and, presumably, too conflicted about the world around him to give us easy or consistent answers.

Clearly, he sees our existence (with and without the dead) as out of balance. But even in the throes of the zombie pandemic and even when presenting us with his protagonists' at the teetering edge of life, Romero consistently affirms his belief in the dignity of humans through two motifs. First, he treats his audience with sympathy and respect. Despite what Greenberg claims, Romero never fully embraces an amoral "cruel horror"—which entails a "cynical appraisal of the human condition," a "coolly harmful attitude toward the audience" and an eschewing of catharsis for a series exercises in "the viewer's capacity to endure psychic pain."[101] Instead, as several essays in this volume note, Romero punctuates his horror with winking and often campy humor and he provides caricatured violence that is more garish and comic than deliberately designed to target and punish viewers. Whenever the director comes close to breaking the third wall, it appears designed to acknowledge his audience's worth, to validate their experiences, and to bring us closer to thoughtful discomfort rather than cruelty. As he put it, "I'm kind of playing around a little bit to see if the violence can be that dominant a factor in the film and still enable the audience to get past it and experience the storyline and the allegory."[102] Violence is the test and not the payoff.

The second way in which we can see Romero's humanism bursting through the dam of the dead, is through his emphasis on moral choice. As discussed, an essential element of humanism is its view that "our individual responsibility for making moral judgements is unavoidable, an inevitable part of the human condition"[103] and not something we can leave for others. In Romero's films, the rising seas of the dead do not displace this responsibility, even if our long-term prospects are fraught. While bad things happen to good people in Romero's films, the fate of those who denigrate others and undermine the worth of their fellow humans is always worse—usually to an inflated and hyperbolic degree.

Furthermore, Romero values the struggle of his well-meaning protagonists, even when the payoff of these efforts are uncertain. As Stephen Law argues, the humanist admires the moral choices, good will, and ingenuity of people, and we judge that they have led "a meaningful life" even when their all too human efforts "end in the failure of [their] central project."[104] Romero puts the case bluntly: "We must make decisions for ourselves"[105] and not look to others for excuses or moral authority. In applying this idea to the terrors of the living dead, we can again borrow from a Renaissance idea, in noting that our battles with zombies are akin to the necessary but sometimes futile struggles against *fortuna*, "the blind vagaries of luck and fate."[106] Indeed, Waller has noted that Romero's zombies are "really no different from any other natural disaster"[107]—they are without apparent direction or obvious cause, and, at best, their destructive path can be ameliorated but not averted.

In summary, in facing the natural disaster of the dead, we can still express our humanity by exhibiting distinctive traits and by making hard but self- and species-affirming choices. As Mary Phipher puts it in a different context, "Facing death offers us an opportunity to work with everything we have within us and everything we know about the world. If we have been resilient most of our lives, most likely we will cope well with our own dying."[108] Or as Paffenroth explains, in the *Dead* series, even in the teeth of despair, "there is always some sense that choices still matter, that how we live our lives is important."[109] To the extent zombie stories raise the age old inquiry of "Why go on?,"[110] Romero's six films give us his insistent, humanist answer: because this is the only life we have, and in carrying on, especially in ways that strengthen our solidarity with others and exhibit our moral worth as a species, we give meaning to that fleeting, valuable existence.

Notes

1. Garrett, *Living with the Living Dead*, 6.
2. *Ibid.*
3. See Bishop, "Dead Man Still Walking"; Dendle, *The Zombie Movie Encyclopedia*; Hubner, Leaning, and Manning, *The Zombie Renaissance in Popular Culture*.
4. Biskind, *The Sky is Falling*, 77; Inguazano, *Zombies On Film*, 13; Skal, *The Monster Show*, 357.
5. Swanson, "The Only Metaphor Left," 379.
6. Gurr, *Race, Gender, and Sexuality in Post-Apocalyptic TV and Film*.
7. Cassese, "George Romero's Zombies." As Peter Biskind explains "zombies lend themselves to metaphoric interpretation; they are an all-purpose Them, with their significance in the eye of the beholder." Biskind, *The Sky is Falling*, 77.
8. Peabody, "Uncomfortable Fictions."
9. Krugman, *Arguing With Zombies*; Chalmers, "Consciousness and its Place in Nature"; Kirk, *Zombies and Consciousness*.
10. Sandu, "The Anthropology of Immortality," 3; Wolfe, *What is Posthumanism?*, xv.
11. Hale and Dolgoy, "Humanity in a Posthuman World," 345.
12. Bishop, *How Zombies Conquered Popular Culture*, 9.
13. Myers, "Interview with George A. Romero."
14. Flaherty, "Godfather of the Dead."
15. See, e.g., Wade, *Speak of the Dead*; Karr and Nicotero, *The Making of George A. Romero's Day of the Dead*.
16. Paffenroth, *Gospel of the Living Dead*; Seeßlen, *George A. Romero und Seine Filme*; Wetmore, *Back from the Dead*; Williams, *The Cinema of George A. Romero*.

17. Wade, *Speak of the Dead*, 69; Pegg, *Nerd Do Well*, 233.
18. As Romero himself explained, "I always used the zombie as a character for satire or a political criticism." MacKenzie, "George A Romero: 'The Walking Dead is a Soap Opera.'" See also, Newman, *Nightmare Movies*, 14; Schott, "Digital Dead"; Payne, "Laughing off a Zombie Apocalypse."
19. Stevenson, *Oxford Dictionary of English*, 1008.
20. Bishop, *How Zombies Conquered Popular Culture*, 9.
21. Williams, *George A. Romero: Interviews*, 10, 47, 50.
22. Bishop, *American Zombie Gothic*, 15; Vials, "The Origin of the Zombie in American Radio," 41; Garrett, *Living with the Living Dead*, 21.
23. Zacharek, "George A. Romero Made Movies About the Undead."
24. Brooks, *The Zombie Survival Guide*, 9.
25. See, e.g., Paffenroth, *Gospel of the Living Dead*, 8 (*Night's* "hopelessness struck a chord with people" and the unexpected bad ending became a future expectation in horror films).
26. Hubner, Leaning, and Manning, *The Zombie Renaissance in Popular Culture*.
27. Dargis, "Not Just Roaming, Zombies Rise Up"; Loudermilk, "Eating *Dawn* in the Dark," 85–6.
28. Paffenroth, *Gospel of the Living Dead*, 8.
29. Ibid.
30. Garrett, *Living with the Living Dead*, 9.
31. Shaviro, *The Cinematic Body*, 104.
32. Shaviro, *The Cinematic Body*, 101.
33. Worland, *The Horror Film: An Introduction*, 13.
34. Paffenroth, *Gospel of the Living Dead*, 9. See also Waller, *The Living and the Undead*, 302
35. Newbury, "Fast Zombie/Slow Zombie," 87; Levin, "Dead Run." The initial, graveyard zombie in *Night* actually moves fairly rapidly. It quickly closes in on Barbra and her car and then maneuvers from one side of the vehicle to the other. But this seems to be the exception in the Romero universe.
36. Pegg, *Nerd Do Well*, 198.
37. Quoted in Peters, "George Romero."
38. Biskind, *The Sky is Falling*, 77.
39. Garrett, *Living with the Living Dead*, 22.
40. Bishop, *American Zombie Gothic*, 3.
41. Lamont, *The Philosophy of Humanism*, 19.
42. Kurtz, *What is Secular Humanism*, 9
43. Strauss, *The City and Man*, 13.
44. Rossellini, *Know Thyself*, xx.
45. Wolfe, *What is Posthumanism?*, xiii.
46. Law, *Humanism*, 2.
47. Kurtz, *What is Secular Humanism*, 11–12.
48. Poole, *Wasteland*, 253–255.
49. Tuchman, *A Distant Mirror*, 123.
50. Cohen, "Introduction: Humanism and Anti-humanism—Levinas, Cassirer, and Heidegger," 9.
51. Kattsoff, "Man is the Measure of all Things," 452.
52. Keetley, "We're All Infected," 14.
53. Law, *Humanism*, 28.
54. Waller, *American Horrors*, 17.
55. Shaviro, *The Cinematic Body*, 87.
56. Williams, Tony, ed. *George A. Romero: Interviews*, 154.
57. Sabine, *A History of Political Theory*, 621.
58. Newman, *Nightmare Movies*, 285.
59. Waller, *American Horrors*, 19.
60. Peisner, "The Rise of 'The Walking Dead.'"
61. Lauro and Embry, "A Zombie Manifesto," 107 (*Land* gestures to a "humanist rather than a posthuman future").
62. George A. Romero, *Land of the Dead*, DVD.
63. Waller, *American Horrors*, 21.
64. Williams, *George A. Romero: Interviews*, 174.
65. Romero, *Land of the Dead*, DVD.
66. Montaigne, *The Complete Essays*, 228 ("On the Cannibals").
67. Newman, *Nightmare Movies*, 284.
68. Lowenstein, "Living Dead," 110.
69. Pegg, *Nerd Do Well*, 233 ("Bub, is perhaps the greatest mobile cadaver in the history of the genre, proving far more sympathetic and likeable than many of the human characters. We cheer him on at the end as he breaks free of his shackles and delivers ironic justice to his prime tormentor").
70. Shaviro, *The Cinematic Body*, 89.

71. Greenberg, *Screen Memories*, 168.
72. Waller, *American Horrors*, 19.
73. Ibid.
74. Ibid. As Shaviro elaborates, "The black man in *Night* is the sole character in the film who is both sympathetic and capable of reasoned action." Shaviro, *The Cinematic Body*, 88.
75. Williams, *George A. Romero: Interviews*, 153.
76. Peaty, "Zombie Time," 186.
77. Romero, *Diary of the Dead*, DVD.
78. Law, *Humanism*, 2.
79. Loudermilk, "Eating *Dawn* in the Dark," 93.
80. Romero, *Land of the Dead*, DVD.
81. Greene and Mohammad, *Zombies, Vampires, and Philosophy*, 338.
82. Abrams, "People Are Vectors."
83. Williams, *George A. Romero: Interviews*, 154–5.
84. MacKenzie, "George A Romero: 'The Walking Dead is a Soap Opera.'"
85. Abrams, "People Are Vectors."
86. Ibid.
87. Leibovitz, "Farewell George Romero."
88. Wood, *Hollywood From Vietnam to Reagan*, 84.
89. Biskind, *The Sky is Falling*, 14.
90. Waller, *American Horrors*, 27.
91. Pinker, *Enlightenment Now*, 10.
92. Paffenroth, "Apocalyptic Images," 147.
93. Bishop, "The Idle Proletariat, 235.
94. Romero, *Diary of the Dead*, DVD.
95. Ibid.
96. Hobbes, *Leviathan*, 77.
97. Slotkin, *Regeneration through Violence*, 5.
98. Slotkin, *Gunfighter Nation*, 12.
99. Williams, *The Cinema of George A. Romero*, 233.
100. Slotkin, *Gunfighter Nation*, 12.
101. Greenberg, *Screen Memories*, 149.
102. Swires, "Master of the Living Dead."
103. Law, *Humanism*, 110.
104. Law, *Humanism*, 121. Liel Leibovitz partly objects to this interpretation of Romero, arguing that while the director clearly rejects ideologies that reduce "all of humanity to a narrow scope of thought and feeling" he also repudiates humanism, which Liebovitz associates with an "obsession with personal happiness above all." Leibovitz, "Farewell George Romero." But this is a narrow reading of humanism that does not address Romero's conception which is not tethered to achieving or even aspiring to "personal happiness." After all, humans in the *Dead* films are rarely happy and have difficulty finding conditions or moments where they can even imagine sustained happiness.
105. Williams, *George A. Romero: Interviews*, 65.
106. Rossellini, *Know Thyself*, 387.
107. Waller, *American Horrors*, 21.
108. Pipher, "I'm Going to Die."
109. Paffenroth, "Apocalyptic Images," 148.
110. Garrett, *Living with the Living Dead*, 7–8.

Filmography

Absurd (see *Rosso sangue*)
Act of Violence (Fred Zinneman, 1949)
Africa addio (Gualtiero Jacopetti, and Franco Prosperi, 1966) aka *Africa: Blood and Guts*
Africa: Blood and Guts (see *Africa addio*)
The American Nightmare (Adam Simon, 2000)
Antropophagus (Aristide Massaccesi, aka Joe D'Amato, 1980) aka *The Grim Reaper* or *Zombie 7*
Antropophagus 2 (see *Rosso sangue*)
Apocalypse domani (Anthony M. Dawson aka Antonio Margheriti, 1980) aka *Cannibal Apocalypse* or *Invasion of the Flesh Hunters*
The Arabian Nights (see *Il fiore delle Mille e una notte*)
Armageddon (Michael Bay, 1998)
Army of Darkness (Sam Raimi, 1992)
Assault on Precinct 13 (John Carpenter, 1976)
El ataque de los muertos sin ojos (Armando De Ossorio, 1973) aka *The Return of the Evil Dead* or *Return of the Blind Dead*
The Beyond (see *...E tu vivrai nel terrore! L'aldilà*)
The Big Country (William Wyler, 1958)
Birth of the Living Dead (Rob Kuhns, 2012)
Black Lagoon (Rei Hiroe, 1954)
Black Orgasm (see *Orgasmo nero*)
Blacula (William Crain, 1972)
The Blair Witch Project (Daniel Myrick and Eduardo Sanchez, 1999)
The Blind Dead (see *La noche del terror ciego*)
The Blind Dead 3 (see *El buque maldito*)
The Blind Dead 4 (see *La noche de las gaviotas*)
The Blob (Irvin Yeaworth and Russell Doughten, 1958)
The Boys from Brazil (Franklin Schaffner, 1978)
Braindead (Peter Jackson, 1992)
Break to Freedom (Lewis Gilbert, 1953)
The Bridge over River Kwai (David Lean, 1957)
Il buono, il brutto e il cattivo (Sergio Leone, 1966), aka *The Good, the Bad, and the Ugly*
El buque maldito (Armando De Ossorio, 1974) aka *The Ghost Galleon* or *The Blind Dead 3*
Burial Ground: The Nights of Terror (see *Le notti del terrore*)
Candyman (Bernard Rose, 1992)
Cannibal Apocalypse (see *Apocalypse domani*)
Cannibal Ferox (Umberto Lenzi, 1981)
Cannibal Ferox 2 (see *Nudo e selvaggio*)
Cannibal Holocaust (see *Olocausto cannibale*)
Cannibal Holocaust 2: The Catherine Miles Story (see *Schiave bianche. Violenza in Amazzonia*)
Cannibal. The Last Survivor (see *Ultimo mondo cannibale*)
The Canterbury Tales (see *I racconti di Canterbury*)
Carrie (Brian De Palma, 1976)
Cemetery of the Living Dead (see *Cinque Tombe per un medium*)
Cemetery Man (Michele Soavi, 1994),
Children Shouldn't Play with Dead Things (Bob Clark, 1972)
Christina, princesse de l'érotisme (see *La nuit des étoiles filantes*)
Cinque Tombe per un medium (Massimo Pupillo, 1965) aka *Cemetery of the Living Dead* or *Terror-Creatures from the Grave*
City of The Living Dead (see *Paura nella città dei morti viventi*)
Cloverfield (Matt Reeves, 2008)
Cold Case (Meredith Stiehm, CBS, 2003–2010)
Contagion (Steven Soderberg, 2011)
The Country of Savage Sex (see *Il paese del sesso selvaggio*)
Creature from the Black Lagoon (Jack Arnold, 1954)
Creepshow (George A. Romero, 1982)
Criminal Minds (Jeff Davis, CBS, 2005–present) and spin-off: Beyond Borders
CSI (Anthony E. Zuiker, CBS, 2000–2015) and spin-offs: Miami, NY, and Cyber
Cut and Run (see *Inferno in diretta*)
The Dark Half (George A. Romero, 1993)
Dawn of the Dead (George A. Romero, 1978)
Dawn of the Dead (Zack Snyder, 2004)
Day of the Dead (George A. Romero, 1985)
The Dead Don't Die (Jim Jarmush, 2019)
Deadgirl (Marcel Sarmiento and Gadi Harel, 2009)
Death Smiles on the Murderer (see *La morte ha sorriso all'assassino*)
Deathdream (Bob Clark, 1974)
Il Decameron (Pier Paolo Pasolini, 1971) aka *The Decameron*
The Decameron (see *Il Decameron*)
Deep Impact (Mimi Leder, 1998)
Designated Survivor (David Guggenheim, ABC and Netflix, 2015–2019)
Diary of the Dead (George A. Romero, 2007)
A Dog's Life (see *Mondo cane*)
Don't Open the Window (see *No profanar el sueño de los muertos*)
...E tu vivrai nel terrore! L'aldilà (Lucio Fulci, 1981) aka *The Beyond* or *7 Doors of Death*

Eaten Alive! (see *Mangiati vivi!*)
El Dorado (Howard Hawks, 1967)
Emanuelle and the Last Cannibals (see *Emanuelle e gli ultimi cannibali*)
Emanuelle e gli ultimi cannibali (Aristide Massaccesi, aka Joe D'Amato, 1977) aka *Emanuelle and the Last Cannibals*
Erotic Nights of the Living Dead (see *Le notti erotiche dei morti viventi*)
Evil Dead (Sam Raimi, 1981)
Evil Dead II (Sam Raimi, 1987)
The Exorcist (William Friedkin, 1973)
Fear the Walking Dead, "Weak." (Colman Domingo, AMC, 2 Sept. 2018, written by Kalinda Vazquez).
A Few Dollars More (see *Per qualche dollaro in più*)
Fido (Andrew Currie, 2007)
Il fiore delle Mille e una notte (Pier Paolo Pasolini, 1974) aka *The Arabian Nights*
The First Purge (Gerard McMurray, 2018)
A Fistful of Dollars (see *Per un pugno di dollari*)
The Gates of Hell (see *Paura nella città dei morti viventi*)
Get Out! (Jordan Peele, 2017)
Geung see ga zuk (Ricky Lau, 1986) aka *Mr. Vampire II*
Geung see sin sang (Ricky Lau, 1985) aka *Mr. Vampire*
Geung see suk suk (Ricky Lau, 1988) aka *Mr. Vampire Saga*
The Ghost Galleon (see *El buque maldito*)
The Girl with All the Gifts (Colm McCarthy, 2016)
Go Home—A casa loro (Luna Gualano, 2018)
The Good, the Bad, and the Ugly (see *Il buono, il brutto e il cattivo*)
The Green Inferno (see *Natura contro*)
The Grim Reaper (see *Antropophagus*)
Gunfight at the OK Corral (John Sturges, 1957)
Halloween (John Carpenter, 1978)
Haunted Mansion (Rob Minkoff, 2003)
The Haunting (Jan de Bont, 1963)
Hell of the Living Dead (see *Virus—L'inferno dei morti viventi*)
High Noon (Fred Zinnemann, 1952)
Hondo (John Farrow, 1953)
Hostel: Part II (Eli Roth, 2007)
House by the Cemetery (see *Quella villa accanto al cimitero*)
I Eat Your Skin (Del Tenney, 1964)
I Walked with a Zombie (Jacques Tourneur, 1943)
In the Heat of the Night (Norman Jewison, 1967)
Incubo sulla città contaminata (Umberto Lenzi, 1980) aka *Nightmare City*
Inferno in diretta (Ruggero Deodato, 1985) aka *Cut and Run*
Invaders from Mars (Cameron Menzies, 1953)
Invasion of the Body Snatchers (Don Siegel, 1956)
Invasion of the Flesh Hunters (see *Apocalypse domani*)
Invisible Invaders (Edward Cahn, 1959)
It Follows (David Robert Mitchell, 2014)
iZombie television series (Diane Ruggiero-Wright, Rob Thomas, CW, 2015–2019)
Jungle Holocaust (see *Ultimo mondo cannibale*)
Killing Birds—Raptors (see *Uccelli assassini*)
King of the Zombies (Jean Yarbrough, 1941)

Land of the Dead (George A. Romero, 2005)
Last Cannibal World (see *Ultimo mondo cannibale*)
The Last Man on Earth (Ubaldo Ragona and Sidney Salkow, 1964)
Let Sleeping Corpses Lie (see *No profanar el sueño de los muertos*)
Life After Beth (Jeff Baena, 2014)
Ling huan xian sheng (Ricky Lau, 1987) aka *Mr. Vampire Part 3*
Little Big Man (Arthur Penn, 1970)
The Living Dead at Manchester Morgue (see *No profanar el sueño de los muertos*)
Ma (Tate Taylor, 2019)
The Magnificent Seven (John Sturges, 1960)
A Man Called Horse (Elliot Silverstein, 1970)
Man from Deep River (see *Il paese del sesso selvaggio*)
The Man Who Shot Liberty Valance (John Ford, 1962)
Mangiati vivi! (Umberto Lenzi, 1980) aka *Eaten Alive!*
Massacre in Dinosaur Valley (see *Nudo e selvaggio*)
Mr. Vampire (see *Geung see sin sang*)
Mr. Vampire II (see *Geung see ga zuk*)
Mr. Vampire Part 3 (see *Ling huan xian sheng*)
Mr. Vampire Saga (see *Geung see suk suk*)
Mr. Vampire 1992 (see *Xin jiang shi xian sheng*)
Mondo cane (Paolo Cavara, Gualtiero Jacopetti, and Franco Prosperi, 1962) aka *A Dog's Life*
Mondo cane n. 2 (Gualtiero Jacopetti and Franco Prosperi, 1963) aka *Mondo Insanity*
Mondo Insanity (see *Mondo cane n. 2*)
La montagna del dio cannibale (Sergio Martino, 1978) aka *Slave of the Cannibal God*
La morte ha sorriso all'assassino (Aristide Massaccesi, aka Joe D'Amato, 1973) aka *Death Smiles on the Murderer*
Natura contro (Antonio Climati, 1988) see *The Green Inferno*
NCIS (Donald P. Bellisario and Don McGill, CBS, 2003–present) and spin-offs: Los Angeles and New Orleans
New Guinea, Island of Cannibals (Akira Ide, 1974)
Night and Fog (see *Nuit et Bruillard*)
Night of the Comet (Thom Eberhardt, 1984)
Night of the Living Dead (George A. Romero, 1968)
Night of the Living Dead (Tom Savini, 1990)
Night of the Seagulls (see *La noche de las gaviotas*)
Nightmare City (see *Incubo sulla città contaminata*)
No profanar el sueño de los muertos (Jorge Grau, 1974) aka *Let Sleeping Corpses Lie* or *The Living Dead at Manchester Morgue* or *Don't Open the Window*
La noche de las gaviotas (Armando De Ossorio, 1975) aka *Night of the Seagulls* or *The Blind Dead 4*
La noche del terror ciego (Armando De Ossorio, 1972) aka *Tombs of the Blind Dead* or *The Blind Dead*
Le notti del terrore (Andrea Bianchi, 1981) aka *Burial Ground: The Nights of Terror* or *The Zombie Dead* or *Zombi Horror*
Le notti erotiche dei morti viventi (Aristide Massaccesi, aka Joe D'Amato, 1980) aka *Erotic Nights of the Living Dead*
Nudo e selvaggio (Michele Massimo Tarantini, 1985)

aka *Massacre in Dinosaur Valley* or *Cannibal Ferox 2*
La nuit des étoiles filantes (Jesús Franco, 1973) aka *Zombie 4: A Virgin Among the Living Dead* or *Christina, princesse de l'érotisme*
Nuit et Bruillard (Alain Resnais, 1955), also known as *Night and Fog*
Olocausto cannibale (Ruggero Deodato, 1980) aka *Cannibal Holocaust*
Oltre la morte (Claudio Fragasso, 1988) aka *Zombie 4: After Death*
The Omen (Richard Donner, 1976)
Orgasmo nero (Aristide Massaccesi, aka Joe D'Amato, 1980) aka *Black Orgasm* or *Voodoo Baby*
La orgía de los muertos (José Luis Merino, 1973) aka *Zombie 3: Return of the Zombies* or *The Hanging Woman*
Outbreak (Wolfgang Petersen, 1995)
Il paese del sesso selvaggio (Umberto Lenzi, 1972) aka *The Country of Savage Sex* or *Man from Deep River* or *Sacrifice!*
Papaya dei Caraibi (Aristide Massaccesi, aka Joe D'Amato, 1978) aka *Papaya, Love Goddess of the Cannibals*
Papaya, Love Goddess of the Cannibals (see *Papaya dei Caraibi*)
Paranormal Activity (Oren Peli, 2007)
Paura nella città dei morti viventi (Lucio Fulci, 1980) aka *City of The Living Dead* or *The Gates of Hell*
The People Under the Stairs (Wes Craven, 1991)
Per qualche dollaro in più (Sergio Leone, 1965), also known as *For a Few Dollars More*
Per un pugno di dollari (Sergio Leone, 1964), also known as *A Fistful of Dollars*
Pigsty (see *Porcile*)
Plague of the Zombies (John Gilling, 1966)
The Professionals (Richard Brooks, 1966)
Porcile (Pier Paolo Pasolini, 1969) aka *Pigsty*
Porno Holocaust (Aristide Massaccesi, aka Joe D'Amato, 1981)
Profondo rosso (Dario Argento, 1975), also known as *Deep Red*
Psycho (Alfred Hitchcock, 1960)
Quella villa accanto al cimitero (Lucio Fulci, 1981) aka *House by The Cemetery* or *Zombie Hell House*
I racconti di Canterbury (Pier Paolo Pasolini, 1971) aka *The Canterbury Tales*
Red River (Howard Hawks, 1948)
La regina dei Cannibali (Marino Girolami, 1980) aka *Zombie Holocaust* or *Zombi Holocaust*
The Return of the Evil Dead (see *El ataque de los muertos sin ojos*)
Return of the Blind Dead (see *El ataque de los muertos sin ojos*)
Revenge in the House of Usher (Jesús Franco, 1983) aka *Zombie 5: Revenge in the House of Usher*
Revenge of the Zombies (Steve Sekely, 1943)
Revolt of the Zombies (Victor Halperin, 1936),
Rio Bravo (Howard Hawks, 1959)
Roma contro Roma (Giuseppe Vari, 1964) aka *Rome Against Rome* or *War of the Zombies*
Rome Against Rome (see *Roma contro Roma*)
Rosso sangue (Aristide Massaccesi, aka Joe D'Amato, 1981) aka *Zombie 6: Monster Hunter* or *Absurd* or *Antropophagus 2*
Sacrifice! (see *Il paese del sesso selvaggio*)
Safe (Todd Haynes, 1995)
Salò (Pier Paolo Pasolini, 1975)
Santa Clarita Diet (Victor Fresco, Netflix, 2017–2019)
Schiave bianche. Violenza in Amazzonia (Mario Gariazzo and Franco Prosperi, 1984) aka *White Slave*, or *Cannibal Holocaust 2: The Catherine Miles Story*
The Searchers (John Ford, 1956)
7 Doors of Death (see *...E tu vivrai nel terrore! L'aldilà*)
The Seven Samurai (Akira Kurosawa, 1954)
Shane (George Stevens, 1953)
Shaun of the Dead (Edgar Wright, 2004)
The Shining (Stanley Kubrick, 1980)
Shock Waves (Ken Wiederhorn, 1977)
Slave of the Cannibal God (see *La montagna del dio cannibale*)
Snoop Dogg's Hood of Horror (Stacy Title, 2006)
Soldier Blue (Ralph Nelson, 1970)
Stagecoach (John Ford, 1939)
Stalag 17 (Billy Wilder, 1953)
Survival of the Dead (George A. Romero, 2009)
Tales from the Hood (Rusty Cundieff, 1995)
Teenage Zombies (Jerry Warren, 1959)
Terror-Creatures from the Grave (see *Cinque Tombe per un medium*)
Tombs of the Blind Dead (see *La noche del terror ciego*)
True Blood, "Never Let Me Go." (John Dahl, HBO, 19 July 2009, written by Alan Ball)
12 Monkeys (Terry Gilliam 1995)
24 (Joel Surnow and Robert Cochran, FOX, 2001–2010)
28 Days Later (Danny Boyle, 2002)
28 Weeks Later (Juan Carlos Fresnadillo, 2007)
The Twilight Zone (Rod Serling, 1959–1964)
Uccelli assassini (Claudio Lattanzi, 1987) aka *Zombie 5: Killing Birds* or *Killing Birds—Raptors*
Ultimo mondo cannibale (Ruggero Deodato, 1977) aka *Last Cannibal World* or *Cannibal. The Last Survivor* or *Jungle Holocaust*
Us (Jordan Peele, 2019)
Vampire in Brooklyn (Wes Craven, 1995)
Virus—L'inferno dei morti viventi (Bruno Mattei, 1981) aka *Hell of the Living Dead*
Voodoo Baby (see *Orgasmo nero*)
Voodoo Man (William Baudine, 1944)
The Walking Dead (Frank Darabont, 2010–present)
War of the Zombies (see *Roma contro Roma*)
Warm Bodies (Jonathan Levine, 2013)
White Slave (see *Schiave bianche. Violenza in Amazzonia*)
White Zombie (Victor Halperin, 1932)
The Wild Bunch (Sam Peckinpah, 1969)
World War Z (Marc Forster, 2013)
Xin jiang shi xian sheng (Ricky Lau, 1992) aka *Mr. Vampire 1992*
Zombi 2 (Lucio Fulci, 1979) aka *Zombie Flesh-Eaters*
Zombi 3 (Lucio Fulci and Claudio Fragasso, 1988) aka *Zombie 3*

Filmography

Zombi Holocaust (see *La regina dei Cannibali*)
Zombi Horror (see *Le notti del terrore*)
Zombie 3 (see *Zombi 3*)
Zombie 3: Return of the Zombies (see *La orgía de los muertos*)
Zombie 4: After Death (see *Oltre la morte*)
Zombie 4: A Virgin Among the Living Dead (see *La nuit des étoiles filantes*)
Zombie 5: Killing Birds (see *Uccelli assassini*)
Zombie 5: Revenge in the House of Usher (see *Revenge in the House of Usher*)
Zombie 6: Monster Hunter (see *Rosso sangue*)
Zombie 7 (see *Antropophagus*)
The Zombie Dead (see *Le notti del terrore*)
Zombie Flesh-Eaters (see *Zombi 2*)
Zombie Hell House (see *Quella villa accanto al cimitero*)
Zombie Holocaust (see *La regina dei Cannibali*)
Zombieland (Ruben Fleischer, 2009)
Zombieland Double Tap (Ruben Fleischer, 2019)

Bibliography

Abrams, Simon. "People Are Vectors: The Humanist Tradition in Zombie Narratives." *Balder and Dash,* June 20, 2013, https://www.rogerebert.com/balder-and-dash/people-are-vectors-the-humanist-tradition-in-zombie-narratives. Accessed October 20, 2019.
Adams, John Joseph (ed.). *The Living Dead.* San Francisco: Night Shade Books, 2008
Agamben, Giorgio. *Homo Sacer: Sovereign Power and Bare Life.* Stanford: Stanford University Press, 1998.
_____. *State of Exception.* Chicago and London: The University of Chicago Press, 2005.
Allan, Keith, and Kate Burridge. *Forbidden Words: Taboo and the Censoring of Language.* Cambridge: Cambridge University Press, 2006.
Alpert, Robert. "George Romero's *Night of the Living Dead* and *Diary of the Dead*: Recording History." *Cineaction* 95 (2015): 16–25.
Anderson, Benedict. *Imagined Communities.* London and New York: Verso, 1983.
Aristotle. *The Politics.* Translated and edited by Ernest Barker. New York: Oxford University Press, 1962.
Austin, Emma. "Zombie Culture: Dissent, Celebration, and the Carnivalesque in Social Spaces." In Hubner, Leaning, and Manning, *The Zombie Renaissance in Popular Culture,* 174–190.
Bacon, Thomas. "Are Marvel & DC Comics Really Close to Failing?" *Screen Rant.* March 4, 2019. https://screenrant.com/marvel-dc-comics-sales-failing. Accessed September 3, 2019.
Badley, Linda. "Zombie Splatter Comedy from Dawn to Shaun: Cannibal Carnivalesque." In McIntosh and Leverette, *Zombie Culture,* 35–53.
Baldwin, James. "A Report from Occupied Territory." *The Nation,* July 11, 1966. https://www.thenation.com/article/report-occupied-territory/. Accessed February 2, 2019.
Balfour, Brad. "George Romero Strives for 'Survival of the Dead.'" *Filmfestivaltraveler.com,* June 8, 2010, http://www.filmfestivaltraveler.com/film-arts/film-arts-interviews/765-george-a-romero-strives-for-survival-of-the-dead?showall=&limitstart. Accessed June 30, 2019.
Banes, Stephen. "A Word of Warning About Zombies." In Yoe and Banes, *The Chilling Archives of Horror Comics! Zombies,* 7-9.
Baschiera, Stefano, and Russ Hunter, eds. *Italian Horror Cinema.* Edinburgh: Edinburgh University Press, 2016.
Baudrillard, Jean. *America.* London and New York: Verso, 2010.
_____. *Symbolic Exchange and Death.* London, Thousand Oaks, New Delhi: Sage Publications, 1993.
Bauman, Zygmunt. *A Chronicle of Crisis.* London: Social Europe Edition, 2017.
_____. "Does the Richness of the Few Benefit Us All?" In Bauman, *A Chronicle of Crisis,* 101–112.
_____. *Liquid Times.* Cambridge: Polity Press, 2007.
Baumgartner, Robert. "'Main Objective: Don't Starve': Representations of Scarcity in Virtual Worlds." In Felcht and Ritson, "The Imagination of Limits: Exploring Scarcity and Abundance," 45–52.
Becker, Ernest. *Escape from Evil.* Washington: Free Press, 1975.
Bell, Alden (Joshua Gaylord). *The Reapers Are the Angels.* New York: Henry Holt and Company, 2010.
Bernard, Mark. "'The Only Monsters Here Are the Filmmakers': Animal Cruelty and Death in Italian Cannibal Films." In Baschiera and Hunter, *Italian Horror Cinema,* 191–206.
Bishop, Kyle William. *American Zombie Gothic. The Rise and Fall (and Rise) of the Walking Dead in Popular Culture.* Jefferson, NC: McFarland, 2010.
_____. "Battling Monsters and Becoming Monstrous: Human Devolution in *The Walking Dead.*" In Levina and Bui, *Monster Culture in the 21st Century: A Reader,* 73–85.
Biskind, Peter. *The Sky Is Falling: How Vampires, Zombies, Androids, and Superheroes Made America Great for Extremism.* New York: New Press, 2018.
_____. 'Dead Man Still Walking: Explaining the Zombie Renaissance.' *Journal of Popular Film and Television* 37.1 (2009): 16–25.
_____. *How Zombies Conquered Popular Culture: The Multifarious Walking Dead in the 21st Century.* Jefferson, NC: McFarland, 2015.

_____. "The Idle Proletariat: *Dawn of the Dead*, Consumer Ideology, and the Loss of Productive Labor." *The Journal of Popular Culture* 43.2 (2010): 234–248.

_____, and Angela Tenga, eds. *The Written Dead: Essays on the Literary Zombie*. Jefferson, NC: McFarland, 2017.

Bissette, Stephen R. "Introduction." In Howlett, *The Weird World of Eerie Publications: Comic Gore that Warped Millions of Young Minds!*, iv–xx.

Block, Alex Ben. "Filming *Night of the Living Dead*: An Interview with Director George Romero." In Williams, *George A. Romero. Interviews*, 8–17.

Bloom, Allan, "Rousseau's Critique of Liberal Constitutionalism." In Orwin and Tarcov, *The Legacy of Rousseau*, 143–167.

Boccaccio, Giovanni. *The Decameron* (David Wallace, ed.). Cambridge: Cambridge University Press, 1991.

Boluk, Stephanie, and Wylie Lenz, eds. *Generation Zombie. Essays on the Living Dead in Modern Culture*. Jefferson, NC: McFarland, 2011.

_____. "Infection, Media, and Capitalism: From Early Modern Plagues to Postmodern Zombies." *Journal for Early Modern Cultural Studies* 10.2 (2010): 126–147.

Booth, Robert A. "Organisms and Human Bodies as Contagions in the Post-Apocalyptic State." *Race, Gender, and Sexuality in Post-Apocalyptic TV and Film*. Ed. Barbara Gurr. New York: Palgrave Macmillan, 2015, 17–30.

Boudreau, Gary. "Code Name: Trixie." *Tales of the Zombie* 3. New York: Marvel, 1974, 72.

Bowring, Nicola. "Richard Matheson's *I Am Legend*: Colonization and Adaptation." *Adaptation*, vol. 8, no. 1, 2015, 130–44.

Brodesser-Akner, Taffy. "Max Brooks Is Not Kidding About the Zombie Apocalypse," *The New York Times*, 21 June 2013. https://www.nytimes.com/2013/06/23/magazine/max-brooks-is-not-kidding-about-the-zombie-apocalypse.html. Accessed May 20, 2020.

Brooks, Kinitra D. *Searching for Sycorax: Black Women's Hauntings of Contemporary Horror*. New Brunswick, NJ: Rutgers University Press, 2018.

Brooks, Max. *World War Z: An Oral History of the Zombie War*. New York: Broadway Books, 2007.

_____. *The Zombie Survival Guide*. New York: Broadway Books, 2003.

Brophy, Phillip. "Horrality: The Textuality of Contemporary Horror Films." *Screen*. January/February 1986. 27–1: 1–13.

Bruce, Barbara S. "Guess Who's Going to Be Dinner: Sidney Poitier, Black Militancy, and the Ambivalence of Race in Romero's *Night of the Living Dead*." In Moreman and Rushton, *Race, Oppression, and the Zombie: Essays on Cross-Cultural Appropriations of the Caribbean Tradition*, 60–73.

Brundage, W. Fitzhugh. *Lynching in the New South: Georgia and Virginia, 1880–1930*. Urbana: Illinois University Press, 1993.

Burgin, Xavier. *Horror Noire: A History of Black Horror*. 2019, Shudder Digital Streaming. Shudder Exclusive.

Butler, Bethonie. "Jordan Peele Made a Woke Horror Film." *The Washington Post*, February 23, 2017. https://www.washingtonpost.com/lifestyle/style/jordan-peele-made-a-woke-horror-film/2017/02/22/5162f21e-f549-11e6-a9b0-ecee7ce475fc_story.html?utm_term=.57d35cb716b0. Accessed July 1, 2018.

Canini, Mikko. *The Domination of Fear*. Amsterdam: Rodopi, 2010.

Cassese, Erin C. "George Romero's zombies will make Americans reflect on racial violence long after his death." *The Conversation*, July 26, 2017, https://theconversation.com/george-romeros-zombies-will-make-americans-reflect-on-racial-violence-long-after-his-death-81583. Accessed October 19, 2019.

Castro, Adam-Troy. "Dead Like Me." In Adams, *The Living Dead*, 369–376.

Chalmers, David. "Consciousness and Its Place in Nature." In Stich and Warfield, *The Blackwell Guide to the Philosophy of Mind*, 1–46.

Christie, Deborah, and Sarah Juliet Lauro, eds. *Better Off Dead: The Evolution of the Zombie as Post-Human*. New York: Fordham University Press, 2011.

_____. "A Dead New World: Richard Matheson and the Modern Zombie." In Christie, Deborah, and Sarah Juliet Lauro, eds. *Better Off Dead. The Evolution of the Zombie as Post-Human*. New York: Fordham University Press, 2011, 67–80.

Cianfarani, Carmine. "Society, Market and Industry." In *Italian Cinema of the Eighties*, 13:15. Rome: Ente Autonomo Gestione Cinema, 1984.

Claeys, Gregory, and Lyman T. Sargent, eds. *Utopia Reader*. New York: New York University Press, 2017.

Cochran, Russ. *Vault of Horror* No 1 (EC Classics 6) West Plains, MO: Ross Cochran Publishing, 1986.

_____. *Vault of Horror* No. 3. West Plains, MO: Ross Cochran Publishing, 1992.

Cohen, Richard A. "Introduction: Humanism and Anti-humanism—Levinas, Cassirer, and Heidegger." In Emmanuel Levinas, *Humanism and the Other*. Urbana: University of Illinois Press 2003, vii–xliv.

Colbert, Jade. "Colson Whitehead's Monsters—*Zone One* (Interview)." *The Varsity*, vol. 132, no. 17, 2012. https://thevarsity.ca/2012/01/30/colson-whiteheads-monsters-zone-one-interview/.

Combs, Richard. "Review of Zombies." *Monthly Film Bulletin*. February 1980. 47–553:33.

"Comic Book Code of 1954." *Wikisource*. https://en.wikisource.org/wiki/Comic_book_code_of_1954.

"Comics Code Revision of 1971." *Comic Book Legal Defense Fund*. http://cbldf.org/comics-code-revision-of-1971/.

Conterio, Martyn. *Interview with George A. Romero* [Originally published in *Starburst Magazine* (October 2013)]. https://medium.com/@mconterio/george-a-romero-interview-4c16169f56e0. Accessed November 12, 2018.

Conway, Gerry, and Steve Englehart (w), John Buscema (p), Joe Sinnott (i). "Nightmare in New Orleans!" *The Avengers* 1.152. New York: Marvel, 1976.

Cooper, Laurence D. "Between Eros and Will to Power: Rousseau and 'The Desire to Extend Our Being.'" *The American Political Science Review* 98.1 (2004): 105–119.

_____. *Rousseau & Nature: The Problem of the Good Life*. University Park: Pennsylvania State University Press, 1999.

Corkin, Stanley. *Cowboys as Cold Warriors. The Western and U.S. History*. Philadelphia: Temple University Press, 2004.

Craig, Johnny, Bill Gaines, and Al Feldstein. "Till Death" *The Vault of Horror* No. 28, 1952. Reprinted in Cochran, *Vault of Horror* No 1 (EC Classics 6) West Plains, MO: Ross Cochran Publishing, 1986.

Crump, Andy. "How *Get Out* Puts *Night of the Living Dead* in a New Light." *The Hollywood Reporter*, February 13, 2018. https://www.hollywoodreporter.com/heat-vision/get-flips-night-living-dead-head-1084105.

Cullen, Daniel E. *Freedom in Rousseau's Political Philosophy*. DeKalb: Northern Illinois University Press, 1993.

Curnette, Rick. 2006. "There's No Magic: A Conversation with George A. Romero." *The Film Journal*. Reprinted in https://thefilmjournalblog.wordpress.com/category/rick-curnutte/. Accessed November 23, 2018.

Curti, Roberto. *Italian Gothic Horror Films, 1957–1969*. Jefferson, NC: McFarland, 2015.

_____, and Tommaso La Selva. *Sex and Violence. Percorsi nel cinema estremo*. Turin: Lindau, 2003.

Dargis, Manohla. "Not Just Roaming, Zombies Rise Up," *The New York Times*, June 24, 2005. https://www.nytimes.com/2005/06/24/movies/not-just-roaming-zombies-rise-up.html. Accessed June 10, 2020.

Davis, Jack, Bill Gaines, and Al Feldstein. "The Chips are Down" *The Vault of Horror* No. 28, 1952. Reprinted in Cochran, *Vault of Horror* No 1 (EC Classics 6) West Plains, MO: Ross Cochran Publishing, 1986.

_____. "Foul Play!" *The Haunt of Fear* No. 19. May—June 1953. Reprinted in Grant Geissman. *Foul Play! The Art and Artists of the Notorious E.C. Comics*. Scranton, PA: HarperCollins Publishing, 2005, 83–89.

_____. "Graft in Concrete." *The Vault of Horror* No. 26, 1952. Reprinted in Cochran, *Vault of Horror* No. 3. West Plains, MO: Ross Cochran Publishing, 1992.

_____. "Reflection of Death!" *Tales from the Crypt* No. 23. April—May 1951. Reprinted in Grant Geissman. *Foul Play! The Art and Artists of the Notorious E.C. Comics* Scranton, PA: HarperCollins Publishing, 2005, 30–37.

De Andrade, Joaquim Pedro. "Cannibalism and Self-Cannibalism." In Johnson and Stam, *Brazilian Cinema*, 82–83.

deCatanzaro, Denys. "Human Suicide: A Biological Perspective." *Behavioral and Brain Sciences*. 3.2 (1980): 265–272.

Defoe, Daniel. *A Journal of the Plague Year* (George Rice Carpenter, ed.). New York: Longmans, Green, and Co., 1896.

Dendle, Peter. *The Zombie Movie Encyclopedia. 2000–2010*. Jefferson, NC: McFarland, 2012.

_____. *The Zombie Movie Encyclopedia*. Jefferson, NC: McFarland, 2001.

Derksen, Craig, and Darren Hudson Hick. "Your Zombie and You: Identity, Emotion, and the Undead." In Moreman and Rushton, *Zombies Are Us*, 14.

Desta, Yohana. "Get Out's $100 Million Success Destroys a Hollywood Myth." *Vanity Fair*, March 13, 2017. https://www.vanityfair.com/hollywood/2017/03/get-out-jordan-peele-box-office.

_____. "Jordan Peele's *Get Out* Almost Had an Impossibly Bleak Ending." *Vanity Fair*, March 3, 2017. https://www.vanityfair.com/hollywood/2017/03/jordan-peele-get-out-ending.

Diamond, Martin "Ethics and Politics: The American Way." In Horwitz, *The Moral Foundations of the American Republic*, 75–108.

Dolgoy, Erin A., Kimberly Hurd Hale, and Bruce Peabody, eds., *Short Stories and Political Philosophy: Power, Prose, and Persuasion*. Lanham, MD: Lexington Books.

Do Vale, Simone. "Trash Mob: Zombie Walks and the Positivity of Monsters in Western Popular Culture." In Canini, *The Domination of Fear*, 191–202.

Drezner, Daniel W. *Theories of International Politics and Zombies*. Princeton: Princeton University Press, 2014.

Drury, Shadia B. *The Political Ideas of Leo Strauss*. New York: Palgrave Macmillan, 2005.

Easton, David. *A Framework for Political Analysis*. Englewood Cliffs, NJ: Prentice-Hall, Inc., 1965.

Eckstein, Arthur M., and Peter Lehman, eds. *The Searchers. Essays and Reflections on John Ford's Classic Western*. Detroit: Wayne State University Press, 2004.

EFF, Electronic Frontier Foundation. "Patriot Act." https://www.eff.org/issues/patriot-act. Accessed October 6, 2019.

Eggertson, Chris. "BD Sits Down with Zombie Maestro George A. Romero!" *Bloody-Disgusting.com*, May 14, 2010, https://bloody-disgusting.com/news/20221/. Accessed July 2, 2019.

Engelhardt, Tom. *The End of Victory Culture. Cold War America and the Disillusioning of a Generation*. Amherst: University of Massachusetts Press, 1995 (revised 2007).

Esposito, Roberto. *Bíos. Biopolitics and Philosophy*. Minneapolis: University of Minnesota Press, 2008.

Felcht, Frederike, and Katie Ritson, eds. "The Imagination of Limits: Exploring Scarcity and Abundance," *RCC Perspectives* 2 (2015).
Feldstein, Al (w, p, i). "The Dead Will Return!" *The Vault of Horror* 13. New York: EC, 1950.
Fischer-Hornung, Dorothea, and Monika Mueller, eds. *Vampires and Zombies: Transcultural Migrations and Transnational Interpretations*. Jackson: University Press of Mississippi, 2016.
Flaherty, Joseph. "'Godfather of the Dead' George A. Romero Talks Zombies," Wired.com, June 15, 2010. https://www.wired.com/2010/06/george-a-romero-zombies/. Accessed June 12, 2020.
Forde, Steven. "The Charitable John Locke." *The Review of Politics* 71.2 (2009): 428–458.
Foundas, Scott. "Diary of the Dead: George Romero's Back." *Laweekly.com,* February 13, 2008, https://www.laweekly.com/diary-of-the-dead-george-romeros-back/. Accessed May 12, 2019.
Franklin, Daniel. *Politics and Film: The Political Culture of Film in the United States*. Lanham, MD: Rowman and Littlefield, 2006.
Gagne, Paul R. "Creepshow" in *Cinefantastique*. September-October 1982. 13–1: 17–35.
_____. "George Romero on Directing *Day of the Dead*." In Williams, *George A. Romero. Interviews*, 101–103.
_____. *The Zombies That Ate Pittsburgh: The Films of George A. Romero*. New York: Dodd Mead and Co., 1986.
Garrett, Greg. *Living with the Living Dead: The Wisdom of the Zombie Apocalypse*. New York: Oxford University Press, 2017.
_____. *A Long, Long Way: Hollywood's Unfinished Journey from Racism to Reconciliation*. New York: Oxford University Press, 2020.
Gaudiosi, John. "*Night of Living Dead* Helmer George A. Romero to Go Virtual in New 'Black Ops' Game." *Hollywood Reporter.* March 26, 2011. https://www.hollywoodreporter.com/news/night-living-dead-helmer-george-182294. Accessed March 14, 2020.
Geissman, Grant. *Foul Play! The Art and Artists of The Notorious E.C. Comics!* New York: Harper Design, 2005.
Gerber, Steve (w), and Pablo Marcos (a). "Voodoo Island." *Tales of the Zombie* 2. New York: Marvel, 1973.
Gillings, Joseph. "We're obsessed with zombies—which says a lot about today." *The Conversation*, February 23, 2015, https://theconversation.com/were-obsessed-with-zombies-which-says-a-lot-about-today-37552. Accessed June 8, 2019.
Giroux, Henry A. *Zombie Politics and Culture in the Age of Casino Capitalism*. New York: Peter Lang, 2011.
Giuliani, Gaia. *Zombie, alieni e mutanti. Le paure dall'11 settembre a oggi*. Firenze: Le Monnier Università, 2016.
Gottschall, Jonathan. *The Storytelling Animal: How Stories Make Us Human*. Boston: Houghton Mifflin Harcourt, 2012.
Grace, Eve. "The restlessness of 'being': Rousseau's protean sentiment of existence." *History of European Ideas*. 27.2 (2001): 133–151.
Gramlich, John. "Five Facts About Crime in the U.S." Pew Research Center website 17 October 2019, https://www.pewresearch.org/fact-tank/2019/10/17/facts-about-crime-in-the-u-s/. Accessed May 12, 2020.
_____. "Most Violent and Property Crimes in the U.S. Go Unsolved." Pew Research Center website 1 March 2017, https://www.pewresearch.org/fact-tank/2017/03/01/most-violent-and-property-crimes-in-the-u-s-go-unsolved/. Accessed May 12, 2020.
Grant, Barry Keith. "Taking Back the *Night of the Living Dead:* George Romero, Feminism, and the Horror Film." In Lauro, *Zombie Theory: A Reader*, 212–222.
Greenberg, Harvey R. *Screen Memories: Hollywood Cinema on the Psychoanalytic Couch*. Columbia, NY: Columbia University Press, 1993.
Greene, Richard, and K. Silem Mohammad (eds.). *Zombies, Vampires, and Philosophy: New Life for the Undead*. Chicago: Carus Publishing Company, 2010.
Guest, Kristen. *Eating Their Words: Cannibalism and the Boundaries of Cultural Identity*. Albany: State University of New York Press, 2001.
Gurr, Barbara, ed. *Race, Gender, and Sexuality in Post-Apocalyptic TV and Film*. New York: Palgrave Macmillan, 2015.
Gutmann, Amy. *Democratic Education*. Princeton, NJ: Princeton University Press, 1999.
Haidt, Jonathan. *The Righteous Mind: Why Good People Are Divided by Politics and Religion*. New York: Pantheon Books, 2012.
_____. "We Need a Little Fear." *The New York Times,* November 7, 2012, https://www.nytimes.com/2012/11/07/opinion/after-the-election-fear-is-our-only-chance-at-unity.html. Accessed June 6, 2019.
Hakola, Outi J. "Colliding Modalities and Receding Frontier in George Romero's *Land of the Dead*." In Miller and Bowdoin Van Riper, *Undead in the West: Vampires, Zombies, Mummies, and Ghosts on the Cinematic Frontier*, 133–149.
Hale, Kimberly Hurd, and Erin A. Dolgoy. "Humanity in a Posthuman World: M. R. Carey's The Girl with All the Gifts," *Utopian Studies* 29:3 (2018): 343–361.
Hall, Derek. 'Varieties of Zombieism: Approaching Comparative Political Economy through *28 Days Later* and *Wild Zero*.' *International Studies Perspectives* 12.1 (2011): 1–17.
Hamilton, Schott, and Conor Heffernan, eds. *Theorizing Zombiism*, Dublin: University College of Dublin Press, forthcoming.

Hamilton, William J. "Do Nonhuman Animals Commit Suicide?" *Behavioral and Brain Sciences.* 3.2 (1980): 278–279.
Hand, Richard J. "Disruptive Corpses: Tales of the Living Dead in Horror Comics of the 1950s and Beyond." In Fischer-Hornung and Mueller, *Vampires and Zombies: Transcultural Migrations and Transnational Interpretations,* 213–228.
_____. "Undead Radio: Zombies and the Living Dead on 1930s and 1940s Radio Drama." In Christie and Lauro, *Better Off Dead: The Evolution of the Zombie as Post-Human,* 39–49.
Harper, Stephen. "Zombies, Malls, and the Consumerism Debate: George Romero's *Dawn of the Dead,*" *Americana: The Journal of American Popular Culture* 1.2 (Fall 2002). http://www.americanpopularculture.com/journal/articles/fall_2002/harper.htm. Accessed July 29, 2019.
Harpold, Terry. "The End Begins: John Wyndham's Zombie Cozy." In Boluk and Lenz, *Generation Zombie: Essays on the Living Dead in Modern Culture,* 156–164.
Hartz, Louis. *The Liberal Tradition in America.* Orlando: Harcourt Brace, 1991.
Heer, Jeet, and Kent Worcester, eds. *Comics Studies Reader.* Jackson: University Press of Mississippi, 2009.
Heller-Nicholas, Alexandra. "Cannibals and Other Impossible Bodies: *Il Profumo Della Signora in Nero* and the *Giallo* Film." *Scope: An Online Journal of Film and Television Studies,* 22 (February 2012): 1–17. https://www.nottingham.ac.uk/scope/documents/2012/february-2012/heller-nicholas.pdf. Accessed July 29, 2019.
Henderson, Brian. "*The Searchers*: An American Dilemma." In Eckstein and Lehman, *The Searchers: Essays and Reflections on John Ford's Classic Western,* 47–74.
Hervey, Ben. *Night of the Living Dead* (BFI Film Classics). New York: Palgrave Macmillan, 2008.
Hetherington, Marc J., and Jonathan D. Weiler. *Authoritarianism and Polarization in American Politics.* Cambridge: Cambridge University Press, 2009.
_____, and Thomas J. Rudolph, *Why Washington Won't Work: Polarization, Political Trust, and the Governing Crisis.* Chicago: University of Chicago Press, 2015.
Higashi, Sumiko. "Night of the Living Dead: A Horror Film about the Horrors of the Vietnam Era." In Dittmar and Michaud, *From Hanoi to Hollywood: The Vietnam War in American Film,* 2000.
Hitz, Zena. "Degenerate Regimes in Plato's Republic." In McPherran, *Plato's Republic: A Critical Guide,* 103–131.
Hobbes, Thomas. *Leviathan.* Michael Oakeshott, ed. New York: Touchstone, 1997.
Hoberman, James, and Jonathan Rosenbaum. *Midnight Movies.* New York: Harper and Row, 1983.
Hogenboom, Melissa. "Many animals seem to kill themselves, but it is not suicide." *BBC* 6 July 2016. http://www.bbc.com/earth/story/20160705-many-animals-seem-to-kill-themselves-but-it-is-not-suicide. Accessed October 16, 2019.
Hogle, Jerrold. "Foreword." In Bishop, *American Zombie Gothic,* 3.
Horwitz, Robert H., ed. *The Moral Foundations of the American Republic.* Charlottesville: University of Virginia Press, 1986.
Howlett, Mike. *The Weird World of Eerie Publications: Comic Gore That Warped Millions of Young Minds!* Port Townsend, WA: Feral House, 2010.
Hubner, Laura, Marcus Leaning, and Paul Manning. *The Zombie Renaissance in Popular Culture.* New York and London: Palgrave Macmillan, 2015.
Hudelson, Richard. "Liberals and Conservatives." In Hudelson, *Modern Political Philosophy,* 30–43.
Hughes, Howard. *Cinema Italiano: The Complete Guide from Classics to Cult.* London: I. B. Tauris Books, 2011.
Ingels, Graham, Bill Gaines, and Al Feldstein. "Hook Line and Stinker" *The Vault of Horror* No. 26, 1952. Reprinted in Russ Cochran. *Vault of Horror No. 3.* West Plains, MO: Ross Cochran Publishing, 1992.
Inguanzo, Ozzy. *Zombies on Film: The Definitive Story of Undead Cinema.* Universe, 2014.
Isabella, Tony. "The Sensuous Zombie." *Tales of the Zombie* 1. New York: Marvel, 1973, 34–39.
Iyengar, Shanto, and Sean J. Westwood. "Fear and Loathing Across Party Lines: New Evidence on Group Polarization." *American Journal of Political Science,* 59:3 (2015): 690–707.
Jackson, Robert. "A Southern Sublimation: Lynching Film and the Reconstruction of American Memory," *The Southern Literary Journal,* Vol. 40, no. 2, 2008. www.jstor.org/stable/20077909.
Jancovich, Mark. *Rational Fears: American Horror in the 1950s.* Manchester: Manchester University Press, 1996.
Jim. "Exclusive Interview: Max Brooks on World War Z." *Eatmybrains,* 20 October 2006, https://www.eatmybrains.com/showfeature.php?id=55 Accessed May 10, 2020.
Johnson, Randal, and Robert Stam, eds. *Brazilian Cinema.* New York: Columbia University Press, 1995.
Jones, Andrew. "George Romero." *Starburst.* August 1982. 48: 40–43.
Kane, Joe. *Night of the Living Dead: Behind the Scenes of the Most Terrifying Zombie Movie Ever.* New York: Citadel, 2010.
Karr, Lee, and Greg Nicotero. *The Making of George A. Romero's Day of the Dead.* Medford, NJ: Plexus Publishing Ltd., 2014.
Kattsoff, Louis O. "Man Is the Measure of All Things." *Philosophy and Phenomenological Research,* 13:4, June 1953, 452–466.
Kaufman, Lloyd. "Cannibal Holocaust—Review by Lloyd Kaufman." In Slater, *Eaten Alive! Italian Cannibal and Zombie Movies,* 104–106.

Kautz, Steven. *Liberalism and Community*. Ithaca, NY: Cornell University Press, 1995.

_____. "Privacy and Community." In Orwin and Tarcov, *The Legacy of Rousseau*, 249–273.

Kay, Glenn. *Zombie Movies. The Ultimate Guide*. Chicago: Chicago Review Press, 2008.

Kearney, Richard. *On Stories*. Abingdon: Routledge, 2002.

Kee, Chera. "Beware the Zuvembies: Comics, Censorship, and the Ubiquity of *Not-Quite* Zombies." In Hamilton and Heffernan, *Theorizing Zombiism*, forthcoming.

_____. *Not Your Average Zombie: Rehumanizing the Undead from Voodoo to Zombie Walks*. Austin: University of Texas Press, 2017.

Keetley, Dawn,. "'Condemned to History by the Hate': David J. Moody's Hater and Postmillennial Rage." In Angela Tenga, Kyle William Bishop, and Dawn Keetley, *The Written Dead: Essays on the Literary Zombie*, 133–144. Jefferson, NC: McFarland, 2017.

_____. "Introduction: We're All Infected." In *"We're All Infected": Essays on AMC's the Walking Dead and the Fate of the Human*. Jefferson, NC: McFarland, 2014.

_____. *"We're All Infected": Essays on AMC's The Walking Dead and the Fate of the Human*. Jefferson, NC: McFarland, 2014.

_____. "Zombie Republic: Property and the Propertyless Multitude in the Post-Apocalyptic World," *Journal of the Fantastic in the Arts*, 25:2/3 (91) (2014): 295–313.

Keough, Peter. "Interview with George Romero." In Williams, *George A. Romero. Interviews*, 169–177.

Khan, Ali S. "Preparedness 101: Zombie Apocalypse," *CDC*, 16 May 2011, https://blogs.cdc.gov/publichealthmatters/2011/05/preparedness-101-zombie-apocalypse/. Accessed May 15, 2020.

Khazan, Olga. "In One Year, 57,375 Years of Life Were Lost to Police Violence: A New Study Find Police Killings Exact a Toll Greater Than Accidental Gun Deaths." *The Atlantic*, May 8, 2018. https://www.theatlantic.com/health/archive/2018/05/the-57375-years-of-life-lost-to-police-violence/559835/.

Kilgour, Maggie. *From Communion to Cannibalism: An Anatomy of Metaphors of Incorporation*. Princeton: Princeton University Press, 1990.

Kirk, Robert. *Zombies and Consciousness*. New York: Oxford University Press, 2005.

Kirkman, Robert, Charlie Adlard, and Cliff Rathburn, creator, writer, letterer. *The Walking Dead*. Issue 5. Tony Moore, penciler, inker, gray tones. Image Comics, Feb. 2004.

_____, Tony Moore, penciler, inker; Cliff Rathburn, gray tones. *The Walking Dead* Issue 6. Image Comics, Mar. 2004.

_____. *The Walking Dead. The Heart's Desire*. Issue 4, 30 November 2005.

Know, David. *Reel Terror. The Scary, Bloody, Gory, Hundred-Year History of Classic Horror Films*. New York, Thomas Dunne Books, 2012.

Kohn, Eric. "George Romero Says Nobody Will Finance His Next Zombie Movie and 'Night of the Living Dead' Wouldn't Get Made Today." Indiewire.com, October 27, 2016, https://www.indiewire.com/2016/10/george-romero-interview-night-of-the-living-dead-zombies-1201740739/. Accessed June 13, 2019.

Krugman, Paul. *Arguing with Zombies: Economics, Politics, and the Fight for a Better Future*. New York: W.W. Norton & Company, 2020.

Kuhns, Rob. *Birth of the Living Dead*. 2013. New York: Glass Eye Pix, 2018. Amazon Digital Services.

Kurtz, Paul. *What Is Secular Humanism?* Amherst, NY: Prometheus Books, 2007.

Kymlicka, W. *Politics in the Vernacular: Nationalism, Multiculturalism, and Citizenship*. Oxford: Oxford University Press, 2001.

Lacan, Jacques. *The Seminar of Jacques Lacan: Book 1, Freud's Papers on Technique, 1953–1954*. New York: W. W. Norton & Company, 1991.

Laist, Randy. "Soft Murders: Motion Pictures and Living Death in *Diary of the Dead*." In Boluk and Lenz, *Generation Zombie. Essays on the Living Dead in Modern Culture*, 101–112.

Lamont, Corliss. *The Philosophy of Humanism*. New York Continuum Publishing Company, 1990.

Lasswell, Harold D. *Politics: Who Gets What, When, How*. New York: Whittlesey House, 1936.

Lauro, Sarah Juliet. "Playing Dead: Zombies Invade Performance Art … and Your Neighborhood." In Christie and Lauro, *Better Off Dead*, 205–230.

_____, ed. *Zombie Theory*. Minneapolis: University of Minnesota Press, 2017.

_____, and Karen Embry. "A Zombie Manifesto: The Nonhuman Condition in the Era of Advanced Capitalism." *boundary 2. An International Journal of Literature and Culture*, 35:1, spring 2008, 85–108.

Law, Stephen. *Humanism: A Very Short Introduction*. New York: Oxford University Press, 2011.

Lee, Nathan. "Diary of the Dead." *Westword.com*, February 14, 2008, https://www.westword.com/film/diary-of-the-dead-5097552https://www.westword.com/film/diary-of-the-dead-5097552. Accessed June 28, 2019.

Leibovitz, Liel. "Farewell George Romero, the I.B. Singer of the Zombie Movie." *Tablet*, July 21, 2017, https://www.tabletmag.com/jewish-arts-and-culture/241274/farewell-george-romero. Accessed October 20, 2019.

Lenz, Wylie. "Toward a Genealogy of the American Zombie Novel: From Jack London to Colson Whitehead." In Bishop and Tenga, *The Written Dead: Essays on the Literary Zombie*, 98–119.

Levin, Josh. "Dead Run: How did movie zombies get so fast?" *Slate.com*, March 24, 2004, https://slate.com/culture/2004/03/how-did-movie-zombies-get-so-fast.html. Accessed June 9, 2020.

Levina, Marina, and Diem-My T. Bui (eds.). *Monster Culture in the 21st Century: A Reader*. London: Bloomsbury, 2014.
Levitsky, Steven, and Daniel Ziblatt. *How Democracies Die*. New York: Crown.
Lewis, Tyson E. "Ztopia: Lessons in Post-Vital Politics in George Romero's Zombie Films." In Boluk and Lenz, *Generation Zombie. Essays on the Living Dead in Modern Culture*, 90–100.
Lightning, Robert K. "Interracial Tensions in *Night of the Living Dead*," *CineAction* 53 (2000): 22–29.
Linnemann, Travis, Tyler Wall, and Edward Green. "The Walking Dead and Killing State: Zombification and the Normalization of Police Violence." In *Zombie Theory: A Reader*, 332–352.
Litwack, Leon. "Hellhounds," 8–37. In *Without Sanctuary: Lynching Photography in America*, Santa Fe: Twin Palms, 2003.
Lopes, Paul Douglas. *Demanding Respect: The Evolution of the American Comic Book*. Philadelphia: Temple University Press, 2009.
Loudermilk, A. "Eating *Dawn* in the Dark: Zombie desire and commodified identity in George A. Romero's *Dawn of the Dead*." *Journal of Consumer Culture* 3.1 (2003): 83–108.
Lowenstein, Adam. "Living Dead: Fearful Attractions of Film," *Representations* 110:1 (2010): 105–128.
_____. *Shocking Representation: Historical Trauma, National Cinema, and the Modern Horror Film*. New York: Columbia University Press, 2005.
Macek III, J.C. "The Zombification Family Tree: Legacy of Living Dead." *Pop Matters*, June 14, 2012. https://www.popmatters.com/159439-legacy-of-the-living-dead-2495844721.html?rebelltitem=1#rebelltitem1.
MacKenzie, Steven. "George A. Romero: 'The Walking Dead is a soap opera with occasional zombies.'" *The Big Issue*, Nov. 3, 2013, https://www.bigissue.com/interviews/george-romero-walking-dead-soap-opera-occasional-zombies/. Accessed October 20, 2019.
Maddrey, Joseph. *Nightmares in Red, White and Blue: The Evolution of the American Horror Film*. Jefferson, NC: McFarland, 2004.
Mahoney, Phillip. "Mass Psychology and the Analysis of the Zombie: From Suggestion to Contagion." In Boluk and Lenz, *Generation Zombie. Essays on the Living Dead in Modern Culture*, 113–129.
"Mails to the Zombie." *Tales of the Zombie* 3. New York: Marvel, 1974, 28–29.
Marcus, Millicent. *Filmmaking by the Book. Italian Cinema and Literary Adaptation*. Baltimore and London: Johns Hopkins University Press, 1993.
Marion, Isaac. *Warm Bodies*. New York: Atria Books, 2011.
Marks, Jonathan. *Perfection and Disharmony in the Thought of Jean-Jacques Rousseau*. New York: Cambridge University Press, 2005.
_____. "Rousseau's Critique of Locke's Education for Liberty." *The Journal of Politics* 74.3 (2012): 694–706.
Masters, Roger D., and Christopher Kelly. "Introduction." In *Discourse on the Sciences and Arts (First Discourse); and, Polemics*, xi-xxiii.
_____. *The Political Philosophy of Rousseau*. Princeton, NJ: Princeton University Press, 1968.
_____. "Rousseau and the Rediscovery of Human Nature." In Orwin and Tarcov, *The Legacy of Rousseau*, 110–140.
Matheson, Richard. *I Am Legend*. New York: Tom Doherty Associates Book, 1995.
McCloud, Scott. *Understanding Comics: The Invisible Art*. New York: Harper Perennial, 1993.
McElya, Micki. *Clinging to Mammy: The Faithful Slave in Twentieth-Century America*. Cambridge: Harvard University Press, 2007.
McGee, Mark Thomas. *Faster and Furiouser: The Story of American International Pictures*. Jefferson, NC: McFarland. 1995.
_____. *Invasion of the Body Snatchers: The Making of a Classic Paperback*. Albany, GA: BearManor Media. 2012.
McGregor, Don. "Night of the Living Dead Goes on, and on, and on, and on…" *Tales of the Zombie* 3. New York: Marvel, 1974, 50–55.
McIntosh, Shawn, and Marc Leverette (eds.). *Zombie Culture. Autopsies of the Living Dead*. Lanham, MD: Scarecrow Press, 2008.
McPherran, M.L. ed., *Plato's Republic: A Critical Guide*. Cambridge: Cambridge University Press, 2010.
Melzer, Arthur M. *The Natural Goodness of Man: On the System of Rousseau's Thought*. Chicago: University of Chicago Press, 1990.
Mendik, Xavier. "Body in a Bed, Body Growing Dead: Uncanny Women in Joe D'Amato's Italian Exploitation Cinema." In Weiner and Cline, *Cinema Inferno: Celluloid Explosions from the Cultural Margins*, 124–144.
Miccichè, Lino. "Introduction." In *Italian Cinema of the Eighties*, 9:11. Rome: Ente Autonomo Gestione Cinema, 1984.
Mill, J.S. *On Liberty*. Mineola, NY: Dover Thrift Editions, 2002.
Miller, Catriona. "Our endless appetite for zombies is because we're looking at ourselves." *The Conversation*, August 21, 2015, https://theconversation.com/our-endless-appetite-for-zombies-is-because-were-looking-at-ourselves-46425. Accessed May 11, 2018.
Miller, Cynthia J., and A. Bowdoin Van Riper (eds.). *Horror Comes Home: Essays on the Places Where Cinematic Terrors Dwell*. Jefferson, NC: McFarland, 2019.

_____. *Undead in the West: Vampires, Zombies, Mummies, and Ghosts on the Cinematic Frontier.* Lanham: Scarecrow Press, 2012.
Mitchell, Lee Clark. *Westerns: Making the Man in Fiction and Film.* Chicago: University of Chicago Press, 1996.
Montaigne, Michel de. *The Complete Essays.* New York: Penguin Classics, 1993.
Morehead, John. "Zombie Walks, Zombie Jesus, and the Eschatology of Postmodern Flesh." In Paffenroth and Morehead, *The Undead and Theology*, 101–123.
Moreman, Christopher M., and Cory Rushton (eds.). *Race, Oppression, and the Zombie: Essays on Cross-Cultural Appropriations of the Caribbean Tradition.* Jefferson, NC: McFarland, 2011.
_____. *Zombies Are Us. Essays on the Humanity of the Walking Dead.* Jefferson, NC: McFarland, 2011.
Muchnik, Pablo. "An Essay on the Principles of Rousseau's Anthropology." *Philosophy & Social Criticism* 26.2 (2000): 51–77.
Muir, John Kenneth. *Horror Films of the 1980s.* Jefferson, NC: McFarland, 2007.
Myers, Scott. "Interview with George A. Romero." *Go Into the Story*, July 18, 2017, https://gointothestory.blcklst.com/interview-written-george-a-romero-a67154d5ac20N/author, "The Last Man on Earth" *Monthly Film Bulletin*. 1 Feb 1967. 34:397: 27–28. Accessed October 19, 2019.
Netflix. Environmental Social Governance. 2019 Sustainability Accounting Standards Board (SASB) Report. https://s22.q4cdn.com/959853165/files/doc_downloads/2020/02/0220_Netflix_EnvironmentalSocialGovernanceReport_FINAL.pdf. Accessed April 15, 2020.
Newbury, Michael. "Fast Zombie/Slow Zombie: Food Writing, Horror Movies, and Agribusiness Apocalypse." *American Literary History* 24.1 (2012): 87–114.
Newby, Richard. "The Lingering Horror of *Night of the Living Dead*." *The Hollywood Reporter*, September 28, 2018. https://www.hollywoodreporter.com/heat-vision/why-night-living-dead-is-more-relevant-ever-1145708.
Newman, Kim. *Nightmare Movies: Horror on Screen Since the 1960s.* New York: Bloomsbury USA, 2011.
Nicotero, Sam. "Romero: An Interview with the Director of *Night of the Living Dead*." In Williams, *George A. Romero. Interviews*, 18–35.
Niles, Steven, and Chee. *George A. Romero's Dawn of the Dead.* San Diego: IDW Publishing, 2004.
Nyberg, Amy Kiste. "William Gains and the Battle over EC Comics." In Heer and Worcester, *Comics Studies Reader*, 58–68.
Olney, Ian. *Euro Horror. Classic European Horror Cinema in Contemporary American Culture.* Bloomington: Indiana University Press, 2013.
_____. *Zombie Cinema.* Quick Takes: Movies and Popular Culture Series. Series Editors: Gwendolyn Audrey Foster and Wheeler Winston Dixon. New Brunswick: Rutgers University Press, 2017.
Olson, Mancur. *The Logic of Collective Action: Public Goods and the Theory of Groups.* Cambridge, MA: Harvard University Press, 1971.
Onstad, Katrina. "Revolution cycle: Horror Auteur Is Unfinished With the Undead." *New York Times*, February 10, 2008, https://www.nytimes.com/2008/02/10/movies/10onst.html. Accessed June 30, 2019.
Ork, William Terry, and George Abbagnalo. "*Night of the Living Dead*—Interview with George A. Romero." In Williams, *George A. Romero. Interviews*, 3–7.
Orpana, Simon. "Spooks of Biopower: The Uncanny Carnivalesque of Zombie Walks." In Lauro, *Zombie Theory*, 294–315.
Orwin, Clifford, and Nathan Tarcov, "Introduction." In Orwin and Tarcov, *The Legacy of Rousseau*, xi-xiv.
_____. "Rousseau and the Discovery of Political Compassion." In Orwin and Tarcov, *The Legacy of Rousseau*, 296–320.
Paffenroth, Kim. *Gospel of the Living Dead.* Waco: Baylor University Press, 2006.
Paffenroth, Kim, and John W. Morehead,. "Apocalyptic Images and Prophetic Function in Zombie Films." In Paffenroth, *The Undead and Theology*, 145–164.
_____ and _____. *The Undead and Theology.* Eugene, OR: Wipf and Stock Publishers, 2012.
Pagano, David. "The Space of the Apocalypse in Zombie Cinema." McIntosh and Leverette, *Zombie Culture. Autopsies of the Living Dead*, 71–86.
Parry, Tyler. "Police Dogs and Anti-Black Violence." *Black Perspectives*, July 31, 2017. https://www.aaihs.org/police-dogs-and-anti-black-violence/.
Pasolini, Pier Paolo. *Scritti corsari.* Milan: Garzanti, 1975.
Patterson, Natasha. "Cannibalizing Gender and Genre: A Feminist Re-Vision of George Romero's Zombie Films." In McIntosh and Leverette, *Zombie Culture: Autopsies of the Living Dead*, 103–118. Lanham, MD: Scarecrow Press, 2008.
Paul, Louis. *Italian Horror Film Directors.* Jefferson, NC: McFarland, 2005.
Payne, Rodger A. "Laughing off a Zombie Apocalypse: The Value of Comedic and Satirical Narratives." *International Studies Perspectives* (2016): 1–14.
Peabody, Bruce. "Explaining the Paranoid Style in American Politics: System Disjuncture and Narratives of Fiction." In Sokolon, *Flattering the Demos*, 87–110.
_____. "Uncomfortable Fictions: Why 'Zombie Lit' should be on the President's Reading List—and Yours." *Americanpopularculture.com*, October 2011, http://www.americanpopularculture.com/archive/bestsellers/zombie.htm. Accessed November 11, 2011.

_____. "What Thomas Hobbes Can Tell Us About Donald Trump and Conflicts of Interest." *Washingtonpost.com*, December 4, 2016, https://www.washingtonpost.com/news/monkey-cage/wp/2016/12/04/what-thomas-hobbes-can-tell-us-about-donald-trump-and-conflicts-of-interest/. Accessed December 5, 2016.

Pearson, Kit, and Marv Wolfman (w) and Pablo Marcos (a). "The Thing from the Bog!" *Tales of the Zombie* 1. New York, Marvel, 1974.

Peaty, Gwyneth. "Zombie Time: Temporality and Living Death." In Keetley, *"We're All Infected': Essays on AMC's The Walking Dead and the Fate of the Human*, 186–200.

Peele, Jordan. "Jordan Peele Crashed a *Get Out* College Course." *The Late Show with Stephen Colbert*. YouTube. November 6, 2017. https://www.youtube.com/watch?v=vKbyfdJXoDg. Accessed July 24, 2018.

_____. "Jordan Peele *Get Out* Keynote." *2017 Film Independent Forum*. YouTube. October 23, 2017. https://www.youtube.com/watch?v=YnpDiuE8HJU. Accessed July 1, 2018.

Pegg, Simon. *Nerd Do Well: A Small Boy's Journey to Becoming a Big Kid*. New York: Gotham Books, 2011.

Peisner, David. "The Rise of 'The Walking Dead.' The tortured history of TV's goriest show." *Rollingstone.com*, October 31, 2013, https://www.rollingstone.com/tv/tv-news/the-rise-of-the-walking-dead-183738/. Accessed June 6, 2020.

Peters, Maquita. "George Romero, 'Night of the Living Dead' Director, Dies at 77." *NPR.org*, July 16, 2017, https://www.npr.org/sections/thetwo-way/2017/07/16/537589005/george-romero-night-of-the-living-dead-director-dies-at-77. Accessed June 10, 2020.

Phillips, Tom. "Games industry pays tribute to George A. Romero." *Eurogamer*. https://www.eurogamer.net/articles/2017-07-17-games-industry-pays-tribute-to-george-a-romero. Accessed Mach 14, 2020.

Pifer, Lynn. "Slacker Bites Back: Shaun of the Dead Finds New Life for Deadbeats." In Christie and Lauro, *Better Off Dead: The Evolution of the Zombie as Post-Human*, 163–174.

Pinker, Steven. *Enlightenment Now: The Case for Reason, Science, Humanism, and Progress*. New York: Random House, 2018.

Pipher, Mary. "I'm Going to Die. I May as Well Be Cheerful About It." *New York Times*, March 6, 2020, https://www.nytimes.com/2020/03/06/opinion/mortality-death.html. Accessed May 28, 2020.

Poole, Scott W. *Monsters in America: Our Historical Obsession with the Hideous and the Haunting*. Waco: Baylor University Press, 2011.

Porton, Richard. "Blue Collar Monsters" *Filmhäftet*. 2002. 119: 2.

_____. *Wasteland: The Great War and the Origins of Modern Horror*. Berkley: Counterpoint, 2018.

Preti, Antonio. "Animal suicide: Evolutionary continuity or anthropomorphism?" *Animal Sentience*. 2.20 (2018): 1–3.

Proffitt, Jennifer M., and Rich Templin, "'Fight the Dead, Fear the Living': Zombie Apocalypse, Libertarian Paradise?" In *Thinking Dead: What the Zombie Apocalypse Means*.

Randell, Karen. "Lost Bodies/Lost Souls: *Night of the Living Dead* and *Deathdream* as Vietnam Narrative." In Boluk and Lenz, *Generation Zombie. Essays on the Living Dead in Modern Culture*, 67–76.

Ransome, Noel. "How George Romero's Progressive Politics Gave Way to 'The Walking Dead's' Nihilism." *Vice.com*, July 18, 2017, https://www.vice.com/en_ca/article/j5qk48/how-george-romeros-progressive-politics-gave-way-to-the-walking-deads-nihilism. Accessed July 1, 2019.

Reed, Scott. "Rhetoric Goes Boom(er): Agency, Networks, and Zombies at Play." In Boluk and Lenz, *Generation Zombie. Essays on the Living Dead in Modern Culture*, 219–47.

Reeves Sanday, Peggy. *Divine Hunger: Cannibalism as a Cultural System*. Cambridge: Cambridge University Press, 1986.

Riley, Brendan. "The E-Dead: Zombies in the Digital Age." In Boluk and Lenz, *Generation Zombie*, 194–205.

Roberson, Chris, and Michael Allred. *iZombie*. Burbank: Vertigo/DC Comics, 2010–2012.

Rocha, Glauber. "The Tricontinental Filmmaker: That Is Called the Dawn." In Johnson and Stam, *Brazilian Cinema*, 76–82.

Romero, George. A, Tommy Castillo, and others., Alex Maleev, Dalibor Talajic and Andrea Mutti. *Empire of the Dead* # 1–15 US: Marvel Comics, 2014–2015.

_____. "Preface." In Russo, *The Complete Night of the Living Dead Filmbook*, 6–7.

_____. "10 Questions for George Romero." *Time.com*, June 7, 2010, http://content.time.com/time/magazine/article/0,9171,1992390,00.html. Accessed June 6, 2019.

_____. *Toe Tags: The Death of Death* #1–6 US: DC Comics, 2004–2005.

Rossellini, Ingrid. *Know Thyself: Western Identity from Classical Greece to the Renaissance*. New York: Doubleday, 2018.

Rousseau, Jean-Jacques. *Discourse on the Origin and the Foundations of Inequality Among Men*. In *The Major Political Writings of Jean-Jacques Rousseau: The Two Discourses & The Social Contract*, edited and translated by John T. Scott, 38–151. Chicago: University of Chicago Press, 2012.

_____. *Emile: or On Education*. Translated by Allan Bloom. New York: Basic Books, 1979.

Rubinstein, Richard, quoted in N/Author. "Romero Rubinstein 'Knights' for UA-overseas; producers Detail other Deals." *Variety*. 27/6/1979: 6.

Russo, John. *The Complete Night of the Living Dead Filmbook*. Pittsburgh: Imagine Inc, 1985.

_____. *Night of the Living Dead*. Glasgow: Collins, 1981.

Rustblade. "Dawn of the Dead—Double Cd + Comic Book + Poster." 2018. http://www.rustblade.com/product/dawn-of-the-dead-double-cd-comic-book-poster/. Accessed January 3, 2019.

Ryan, Michael, and Douglas Kellner. *Camera Politica: The Politics and Ideology of Contemporary Hollywood Film*. Bloomington: Indiana University Press, 1988.

Sabin, Roger. *Comics, Comix and & Graphic Novels: A History of Comic Art*. London: Phaidon Press Ltd., 2001.

Sabine, George. *A History of Political Theory*. Hinsdale, IL: The Dryden Press, 1973.

Salazar, Juan Francisco, and Stephen Healy. "We're all The Walking Dead—we just don't know it yet." *The Conversation*, March 30, 2015, https://theconversation.com/were-all-the-walking-dead-we-just-dont-know-it-yet-39489. Accessed June 3, 2016.

Sandel, Michael. *Liberalism and the Limits of Justice*. New York: Cambridge University Press, 1998.

Sandu, Antonio. "The anthropology of immortality and the crisis of posthuman conscience." *Journal for the Study of Religions and Ideologies*, 14:40 (2015): 3–26.

Schmeink, Lars. *Biopunk Dystopias: Genetic Engineering, Society, and Science Fiction*. Liverpool: Liverpool University Press, 2017.

Schott, Gareth. "Digital Dead: Translating the Visceral and Satirical Elements of George A. Romero's *Dawn of the Dead* to Videogames." In Moreman and Rushton, *Zombies Are Us*, 141–150.

Schweitzer, Dahlia. *Going Viral. Zombies, Viruses, and the End of the World*. New Brunswick: Rutgers University Press, 2018.

Scott, John T. "Introduction." In *The Major Political Writings of Jean-Jacques Rousseau: The Two Discourses & The Social Contract*, XIII-XLIV.

_____. "The Theodicy of the *Second Discourse*: The 'Pure State of Nature' and Rousseau's Political Thought." *The American Political Science Review* 86.3 (1992): 696–711.

Seabrook, William. *The Magic Island*. New York: Harcourt, Brace, 1929.

Seeßlen, Georg T. *George A. Romero und seine Filme*. Bellheim: kuk, 2010.

Seligson, Tom. "George A. Romero: Revealing the Monster within Us." In Williams, *George A. Romero: Interviews*, 74–87.

Sennitt, Stephen. *Ghastly Terror! The Horrible Story of the Horror Comics*. Manchester: HeadPress, 1999.

Shakespeare, William. *Macbeth* (Barbara A. Mowat and Paul Werstine, eds.). New York: Simon & Schuster, 2013.

Shaviro, Steven. *The Cinematic Body*. Minneapolis: University of Minnesota Press, 1993.

Shermeyer, Kelli. "'Systems Die Hard': Resistance and Reanimation in Colson Whitehead's *Zone One*." In Bishop and Tenga, *The Written Dead: Essays on the Literary Zombie*, 120–132.

Shipka, Danny. *Perverse Titillation: The Exploitation Cinema of Italy, Spain and France, 1960–1980*. Jefferson, NC: McFarland, 2011.

Simpson, Philip L. "The Zombie Apocalypse Is Upon Us! Homeland Insecurity." In Dawn Keetley, "*We're All Infected*," 29.

Skal, David J. *The Monster Show: A Cultural History of Horror*. New York: Farrar, Straus and Giroux, 2001.

Skulan, Tom, and Carlos Kastro, Eric Mehéu, and Eric Stanway. *Night of the Living Dead No. 1*. Albany: FantaCo Enterprises Inc., 1991.

_____. *Night of the Living Dead Nos. 2-4*. Albany: FantaCo Enterprises Inc., 1992.

_____. *Night of the Living Dead: Prelude*. Albany: FantaCo Enterprises Inc., 1991.

Slater, Jay, ed. *Eaten Alive! Italian Cannibal and Zombie Movies*. London: Plexus Publishing Limited, 2006.

Slotkin, Richard. *Gunfighter Nation. The Myth of the Frontier in Twentieth-Century America*. Norman: University of Oklahoma Press, 1998.

_____. *Regeneration Through Violence: The Mythology of the American Frontier, 1600–1860*. Norman: University of Oklahoma Press, 2000.

Smith, Jeffrey A. "Natural Happiness, Sensation, and Infancy in Rousseau's *Emile*." *Polity* 35.1 (2002): 93–120.

Smith, Justine. "Dawn of the Dead had an alternate ending that's even bleaker than the original." *Lwlies.com*, September 1, 2018, https://lwlies.com/articles/dawn-of-the-dead-alternate-ending/. Accessed June 5, 2019.

Soderberg, Branden. "Civil Rights-Era Horror Classic *Night of the Living Dead* Still Resonates." *City Paper*, March 6, 2019. https://www.citypaper.com/film/bcp-060816-night-of-the-living-dead-20160607-story.html.

Sokolon, Marlene, ed. *Flattering the Demos*. Lanham, Maryland: Lexington Books, 2018.

Sondrol, Paul C. "Totalitarian and Authoritarian Dictators: A Comparison of Fidel Castro and Alfredo Stroessner." *Journal of Latin American Studies*, 23: 3 (1991): 599–620.

Sontag, Susan. "The Imagination of Disaster." *Commentary*, 40.4 (1965): 42–48.

Sorenson, L. R. "Rousseau's Liberalism." *History of Political Thought* 11.3 (1990): 443–466.

Sorlin, Pierre. *Italian National Cinema. 1896–1996*. Bristol: Routledge, 2001.

Stein, Elliot. "The Night of the Living Dead." *Sight and Sound*. Spring 1970. 39:2: 105.

Stevens, Dana. "Diary of the Dead George Romero's bleakest zombie movie yet." *Slate.com*, February 15, 2008, https://slate.com/culture/2008/02/george-romero-s-diary-of-the-dead-reviewed.html. Accessed June 6, 2019.

Stevenson, Angus, ed. *Oxford Dictionary of English*. Oxford: Oxford University Press, 2010.

Stoker, Bram. *Dracula*. Edited by Eleanor Bourg Nicholson, San Francisco: Ignatius Press, 2012.
Strauss, Leo. *The City and Man*. Chicago: University of Chicago Press, 1978.
_____. "On Classical Political Philosophy." In Gildin, *An Introduction to Political Philosophy: Ten Essays by Leo Strauss*, 59–79.
_____. "What Is Political Philosophy?" In Gildin, *An Introduction to Political Philosophy: Ten Essays by Leo Strauss*, 2–57.
Sublette, Cammie M. "The House That White Privilege Built: Jordan Peele's *Get Out* and the Haunting Legacy of Plantation Slavery." In Miller and Bowdoin Van Riper, *Horror Comes Home: Essays on the Places Where Cinematic Terrors Dwell*, 83–94.
Surmacz, Gary. A. "Anatomy of a Horror Film" *Cinefantastique*. September 1970. 14:1: 15–26.
Sutler-Cohen, Sara. "Plans Are Pointless; Staying Alive Is as Good as It Gets. Zombie Sociology and the Politics of Survival." In Moreman and Rushton, *Zombies Are Us. Essays on the Humanity of the Walking Dead*, 183–193.
Swanson, Carl Joseph. "'The Only Metaphor Left': Colson Whitehead's *Zone One* and Zombie Narrative Form." *Genre* 47.3 (2014): 379–405.
Swires, Steve. "Master of the Living Dead." *Starlog Magazine*, No. 21, April 1979, 44–47.
Tait, R. Colin. "(Zombie) Revolution at the Gates: The Dead, The 'Multitude' and George A. Romero," *Cinephile* 3:1 (2007): 61–70.
Tarcov, Nathan. *Locke's Education for Liberty*. Lanham, MD: Lexington Books, 1999.
Thoreau, Henry David. *Civil Disobedience and Other Essays*. Overland Park, Kansas: Digireads.com Publishing, 2017.
Thoret, Jean-Baptiste, ed. *Politiques des zombies: L'Amérique selon George A. Romero*. Paris: Ellipses Édition, 2015.
Thrower, Stephen. *Beyond Terror: The Films of Lucio Fulci*. Godalming: FAB Press, 2017.
Tosca, Susana. "Reading Resident Evil: Code Veronica X." *Proceedings of DAC03*. 2003: 206–216. https://static.aminer.org/pdf/PDF/000/256/173/hypertext_and_comics_towards_an_aesthetics_of_hypertext.pdf. Accessed March 14, 2020.
Totaro, Donato. "Porcile." In Slater, *Eaten Alive! Italian Cannibal and Zombie Movies*, 39–41.
Towlson, Jon. "Rehabilitating Daddy. Or How Disaster Movies Say It's Ok to Trust Authority" in *Paracinema* #16, June 2012, pp. 10–12.
Townsend, Allie. "Colson Whitehead's Pop Culture Zombies." *Time*, 15 Oct. 2011, http://entertainment.time.com/2011/10/15/origins-colson-whitehead-on-pop-culture-zombies/.
Trombetta, Jim. *The Horror! The Horror! Comic Books the Government Didn't Want You to Read!* New York: Abrams ComicArts, 2010.
Tuchman, Barbara. *A Distant Mirror: The Calamitous 14th Century*. New York: Random House, 2011.
Vallan, Giulia D'Agnolo. "A Pinewood Dialogue with George A. Romero." *Museum of the Moving Image*. January 11, 2003, http://www.movingimagesource.us/files/dialogues/2/49247_programs_transcript_pdf_244.pdf. Accessed October 20, 2019.
Vervaeke, John Christopher Mastropietro, and Filip Miscevic. *Zombies in Western Culture: A Twenty-First Century Crisis*. Cambridge: Open Book Publishers, 2017.
Vials, Chris. "The Origin of the Zombie in American Radio and Film: B-Horror, U.S. Empire, and the Politics of Disavowal." In Boluk and Lenz, *Generation Zombie. Essays on the Living Dead in Modern Culture*, 41–53.
Viano, Maurizio. *A Certain Realism: Making Use of Pasolini's Film Theory and Practice*. Berkeley: University of California Press, 1993.
Wade, Chris. *George A. Romero on Screen*. Lulu.com, 2019.
_____. *Speak of the Dead: George A. Romero's Original Dead Trilogy*. Lulu.com, 2016.
Wallace-Sanders, Kimberly. *Mammy: A Century of Race, Gender, and Southern Memory*. Ann Arbor: University of Michigan Press, 2011.
Waller, Gregory A. *American Horrors: Essays on the Modern American Horror Film*. Urbana: University of Illinois Press, 1987.
_____. *The Living and the Undead: From Stoker's Dracula to Romero's Dawn of the Dead*. Urbana: University of Illinois Press, 1986.
Walters, Ben. "Simon Pegg interviews George A. Romero." *Time Out London* 8 September 2005. https://web.archive.org/web/20070217113705/http://www.timeout.com/film/new/631.html. Accessed March 1, 2020.
Weber, Max. *From Max Weber: Essays in Sociology*. H. H. Gerth and C. Wright Mills, eds. New York: Oxford University Press, 1958.
Wein, Len (w), Gene Colan (p), Frank Giacoia (i). "March of the Dead!" *Strange Tales* 171. New York: Marvel, 1973.
Weiner, Robert G., and John Cline, eds. *Cinema Inferno: Celluloid Explosions from the Cultural Margins*. Toronto: Scarecrow Press, 2010.
Weiss, Penny A. "Rousseau, Antifeminism, and Woman's Nature." *Political Theory* 15.1 (1987): 81–98.
Wells, Paul. *The Horror Genre from Beelzebub to Blair Witch*. London: Wallflower Press, 2000.
Wertham, Fredric. *Seduction of the Innocent*. New York: Rinehart & Company, 1954.

Wetmore, Kevin J., Jr. *Back from the Dead: Remakes of the Romero Zombie Films as Markers of Their Times.* Jefferson, NC: McFarland, 2011.
Whitehead, Colson. *Zone One.* New York: Anchor Books, 2012.
Wile, Rob. "Jordan Peele's *Get Out* Is the Most Profitable Film of 2017," *Money,* August 8, 2017. http://money.com/money/4891175/get-out-jordan-peele-most-profitable-movie-2017.
_____. *Post-9/11 Horror in American Cinema.* New York and London: The Continuum International Publishing Group, 2012.
Wilkinson, Alissa. "George Romero Didn't Mean to Tackle Race in *Night of the Living Dead,* but He Did Anyway." *Vox,* July 22, 2017. https://www.vox.com/culture/2017/7/22/15985492/night-of-living-dead-movie-week-george-romero-zombies-get-out-jordan-peele.
Williams, Tony, ed. *The Cinema of George A. Romero: Knight of the Living Dead.* London and New York: Wallflower Press, 2003 (2nd ed. 2015).
_____. *George A. Romero: Interviews.* Jackson: The University Press of Mississippi, 2011.
_____. "George A. Romero on *Survival of the Dead.*" In Williams, *George A. Romero: Interviews,* 178–184.
Winkler, Martin M. "Homer's *Iliad* and John Ford's *The Searchers.*" In Eckstein and Lehman, *The Searchers. Essays and Reflections on John Ford's Classic Western,* 145–170.
Without Sanctuary: Lynching Photography in America. Allen/Littlefield Collection, Special Collections, Robert W. Woodruff Library, Emory University. Santa Fe: Twin Palms, 2003.
Wolfe, Cary. *What Is Posthumanism?* Minneapolis: University of Minnesota Press, 2010.
Wood, Amy Louise. *Lynching and Spectacle: Witnessing Racial Violence in America, 1890–1940.* Chapel Hill: University of North Carolina Press, 2009.
Wood, Mary. *Italian Cinema.* New York: Berg, 2005.
Wood, Robin. *Hollywood from Vietnam to Reagan … and Beyond.* New York: Columbia University Press, 2003.
_____. "An Introduction to the American Horror Film." In B. Nichols, ed., *Movies and Methods (Vol II),* 195–219.
_____. "Neglected Nightmares" *Film Comment.* March/April 1980. 16:2: 30–32.
Wood, Wally (p & i). "The Thing from the Sea." *Eerie* #16. New York: Avon, 1954.
Worland, Rick. *The Horror Film: An Introduction.* Hoboken, NJ: Wiley-Blackwell, 2006.
Wright, Bradford W. *Comic Book Nation: The Transformation of Youth Culture in America.* Baltimore: Johns Hopkins University Press, 2001.
Xavier, Marlon. *Subjectivity, the Unconscious and Consumerism.* London: Palgrave Macmillan, 2018.
Yoe, Craig, and Steve Banes, eds. *The Chilling Archives of Horror Comics! Zombies.* San Diego: IDW Publishing, 2012.
Young, Iris Marion. *Responsibility for Justice.* Oxford: Oxford University Press, 2011.
Young, P. Ivan. "Walking Tall or Walking Dead? The American Cowboy in the Zombie Apocalypse." In Keetley, *We're All Infected: Essays on AMC's The Walking Dead and the Fate of the Human,* 56–67.
Zacharek, Stephanie. "George A. Romero Made Movies About the Undead Full of Messages for the Living." *Time.com,* July 17, 2017. https://time.com/4861329/george-a-romero/. Accessed October 19, 2019.
Zani, Steven, and Kevin Meaux. "Lucio Fulci and the Decaying Definition of Zombie Narratives." In Christie and Lauro, *Better Off Dead: The Evolution of the Zombie as Post-Human,* 98–115.
Zealand, Christopher. "The National Strategy for Zombie Containment: Myth Meets Activism in Post-9/11 America." In Boluk and Lenz, *Generation Zombie: Essays on the Living Dead in Modern Culture,* 231–247.
Zinoman, Jason. "Jordan Peele on a Truly Terrifying Monster: Racism." *The New York Times,* February 16, 2017. https://www.nytimes.com/2017/02/16/movies/jordan-peele-interview-get-out.html.
Žižek, Slavoj. *How to Read Lacan.* New York and London: W.W. Norton & Company, 2006.
_____. *The Metastases of Enjoyment.* On Women and Causality. London and New York: Verso, 1994.
_____. *Violence.* New York: Picador, 2008.

About the Contributors

Emma **Austin** is a senior lecturer at the University of Portsmouth. Her academic research focuses on interrogating zombies and horror texts in popular culture. Besides running an undergraduate unit on researching horror for the last five years and offering additions to A-Level teaching packages on horror, she has appeared on undead-related speaking panels such as the Barbicans *Battle of Ideas* in 2017 and Portsmouth Comic Con in 2018.

Benjamin Isaak **Gross** is an assistant professor in the Department of Sociology and Political Science at Jacksonville State University. His research focuses on political philosophy. He is especially interested in examining how engaging with nature through the modern scientific project affects our understanding of human nature, politics, and society.

Chera **Kee** is an associate professor of English at Wayne State University. Her research interests include film and media studies, pop culture, fandom, horror, race and gender, and she has published extensively on zombies, including her book *Not Your Average Zombie: Rehumanizing the Undead from Voodoo to Zombie Walks* (2017).

Fulvio **Orsitto** is the administrative director of the Georgetown University Florence Campus, Villa le Balze, and formerly an associate professor at California State University at Chico. His book publications include several articles and the edited volumes, including *TOTalitarian ARts: The Visual Arts, Fascism(s), and Mass-Society* (2017), and *Boom ... e dintorni. Il miracolo economico italiano tra cinema, televisione e letteratura* (2017).

Gloria **Pastorino** is a professor of Italian and French at Fairleigh Dickinson University, where she also teaches English and world literature, drama, and film. Her publications include *Othello. As Interpreted by Luigi Lo Cascio* (Bordighera 2020), several articles on Italian theatre, film, cinema and migration, mafia and masculinity, and translations for American productions of plays by Dario Fo, Luigi Pirandello, Mariangela Gualtieri, Romeo Castellucci, Lella Costa and Juan Mayorga.

Bruce **Peabody** is a professor of government and politics at Fairleigh Dickinson University. He is the author of *Short Stories and Political Philosophy: Power, Prose, and Persuasion* (2019), *Where Have All the Heroes Gone? The Changing Nature of American Valor* (2017) and *The Politics of Judicial Independence* (2011).

Cammie M. **Sublette** is the Head of the Department of English at the University of Arkansas–Fort Smith. Her research specializes in African American literature, food studies, horror and zombie films. She is the coeditor of an interdisciplinary book on food studies, titled *Devouring Cultures: Perspectives on Food, Power, and Identity from the Zombie Apocalypse to* Downton Abbey (2015).

Angela **Tenga** is an associate professor of English at Florida Institute of Technology. Her research interests include fictional representations of the monstrous, the fictional construction of criminality, and early English literature. She has coedited *The Written Dead: Essays on the Literary Zombie* (2017) and *Plant Horror: Approaches to the Monstrous Vegetal in Fiction and Film* (2016). Her work has also appeared in scholarly journals including *The Journal of Popular Culture, Gothic Studies,* and edited collections.

Index

Numbers in ***bold italics*** indicate pages with illustrations,
f following a number indicates a figure

Aaron (fictional character, *The Searchers*) 57
Abrams, Simon 181–182
absence, of religious figures in Romero 178
accuracy, of media reporting 73–74, 79*n*83
Agamben, Giorgio 63, 65
Al (fictional character, *Fear the Walking Dead*) 92
AIP *see* American International Pictures
alienation, in *I Am Legend* 87
Allan, Keith 112*n*15
allegory for discrimination, zombies as 9, 14*n*52, 16
allegory for modern inequality, *Land of the Dead* as 101, 124–125, 130, 131
American Horrors (Waller) 9, 15, 120, 178, 180, 185
American International Pictures (AIP) Edgar Allan Poe horror film series 20
American Zombie Gothic (Bishop) 14*n*46, 30*n*14, 57, 85, 89–90; on colonization zombies and 152; on *Dawn of the Dead* 11, 126, 138*n*16, 163; on humanism of Romero 177; on the state in zombie media 119, 126, 138*n*16
Amy (fictional character, *The Walking Dead*) 88, **88**
Anderson, Benedict 7–8
Andrea (fictional character, *The Walking Dead*) 88, **88**
animal trait, instinct as 158–159
animals, zombies as 158
Anthropocene 81
anthropophagism 100, 102–103
"Anubis" (Romero) 17–18
apocalyptic plague narrative 82
approach to filmmaking, auteuristic 98, 111*n*3
Argento, Dario 27, 72
Aristotle 129, 134
Arthur Katz (fictional character, *Diary of the Dead*) 134–135
Austin, Emma 15–31
auteuristic approach, to filmmaking 98, 111*n*3
authoritarianism 123, 131
Avenging a Crime (film) 149
awareness, of consciousness 161–162

Baldwin, James 151
Banes, Stephen 35
Barbara (fictional character, *Night of the Living Dead*) (Savini) 13*n*13, 43
Barbra (fictional character, *Night of the Living Dead*) (Romero) 13*n*13, 21, 62, 85–86; Ben and 144–145; as feminist character 152*n*9; Rose compared with 145–146
Baron Samedi (fictional character, *Strange Tales*) 48

Bauman, Zygmunt 7
Becker, Ernest 91
Beecher, Henry Ward 111
Bell, Alden 95–96
Ben (fictional character, *Night of the Living Dead*) 18, 43–44, 52*n*53, 55–57, 61–62, 64f; Bishop on 85; as black character 66–67, 74f, 144–146, 148–150; brother of 90; Last Night Story of 89, 93–94; as lone hero 70, 85–86, 180
Ben (fictional character, *28 Days Later*) 128f
Ben Cortman (fictional character, *I Am Legend*) 57
Bernard, Mark 103
The Beyond (*E tu vivrai nel terrore!*) (film) 109
Beyond Terror (Thrower) 99, 106–107, 109, 112*n*8
Bianchi, Andrea 108
The Big Country (film) 56, 58f, 60, 69
Big Daddy (fictional character, *Land of the Dead*) 73, 105, 118, 129–131, 134, 168*n*32, 179–180
biopolitics, zombie films and 8
Biopunk Dystopias (Schmeink) 5, 6, 8
Bishop, Kyle William 4, 14*n*46, 30*n*14, 39, 57; on Ben (*Night of the Living Dead*) 85; on colonization zombies and 152; on *Dawn of the Dead* 119, 126, 138*n*16, 156, 163; on humanism of Romero 177; on popularity of zombies in popular culture 172, 174; on the state in zombie media 119, 126, 138*n*16; on *The Walking Dead* 89–90
Biskind, Peter 179, 182, 185*n*4
Bissette, Stephen R. 39
black character, Ben (*Night of the Living Dead*) as 66–67, 74f, 144–146, 148–150
black men, killed by police 151–152, 173
black protagonists, in horror films 143–144
blood, in films of Romero 74, 75f
Boccaccio, Giovanni 82–83
Bowring, Nicola 87, 93
Boy (fictional character, *Survival of the Dead*) 128, 137
brain, role of in zombie films 59, 66, 80, 92
Breckinridge Scott (fictional character, *World War Z*) 94
broken states, in Romero 120–122
Brooks, Max 82, 93–94, 118, 119, 135, 139*n*49; on *Dawn on the Dead* (Snyder) 152*n*7; on zombie conventions of Romero 174
Brophy, Phillip 15, 19, 27, 30*n*5, 32
brother, of Ben (fictional character, "Dead Like Me") 90
Brother Voodoo (fictional character, *Strange Tales*) 48
Bruce, Barbara 145

207

Index

Bub (fictional character, *Day of the Dead*) 78n52, 105, 123, 129, 160, 175–176, 182, 186n69
Burial Ground (*Le notti del terrore*) (film) 108
Burridge, Kate 112n15
Bush, George W. 6
Butler, Bethonie 153n23

camera angles, of *Night of the Living Dead* 39–40, 52n42–43
Camera Politica (Ryan & Kellner) 117, 120, 130
Canada 13n11, 126, 128, 139n49, 140n92, 163, 167
Cannibal Holocaust (*Olocausto cannibale*) (film) 104, 114n41
"The Cannibal/The Zombie" (Slater) 103, 105
cannibal zombies 32–33, 50, 50n5, 105–106
cannibalism 11, 32, 66, 99–100, 111–112n5; in Italian cinema 112n15, 113n28; metaphorical 101–102; Slater on 103
"Cannibals and Other Impossible Bodies" (Heller-Nicholas) 112n5
Captain Henry Rhodes (fictional character, *Day of the Dead*) 25, 43, 121, 123f; authoritarian rule of 122–123, 139n46
Cassese, Erin 171
catastrophe films 2
Catholicism 9, 14n47, 100, 109, 112n15
cause, of zombification 42
Cemetery of the Living Dead (*Cinque Tombe per un medium*) (film) 114–115n46
A Certain Realism (Viano) 98, 111n2
characters in EC comics, as trapped 24
"The Chips Are Down" (Davis, Gaines & Feldstein) 22
Cholo (fictional character, *Land of the Dead*) 124–125, 179
Chris (fictional character, *Get Out*) 144–147, 150
Christie, Deborah 56–57
Cianfarani, Carmine 112n6
cinema, Italian 99, 112n6, 140n90
The Cinema of George A. Romero (Williams) 35, 40, 184
The Cinematic Body (Shaviro) 66, 72–73, 77n22, 130, 140n90; on *Dawn of the Dead* 133; on resourcefulness of humans in Romero 179–180
cities, Rousseau on 167
City of the Living Dead (*Paura nella città dei morti viventi*) (film) 108–109
"Civil Disobedience" (Thoreau) 129
"Civil Rights- Era Horror Classic *Night of the Living Dead* Still Resonates" (Soderberg, B.) 153n27
Claeys, Gregory 126
classical: liberalism 156–157, 167; political philosophy 156
Clinging to Mammy (McElya) 146–147
Cohen, Richard 178
Cold War 10, 35
color in EC comics, use of 21–22, 25–26
Comanche Indians 58
comic adaptations, of Romero 28
Comic Book Nation (Wright) 38
comic books 10, 19–29, 34; gore in 38, 45
Comics Code Authority 33–34, 38, 44, 52n57
Comics, Comix and & Graphic Novels (Sabin) 26
The Complete Night of the Living Dead Filmbook (Romero) 39
"Condemned to history by the Hate" (Keetley) 142n168
consciousness, awareness of 161–162
consumerism 3, 11; in *Dawn of the Dead* 100–101, 125–126, 162–163

Contagion (film) 2, 108
Corkin, Stanley 70
The Country of Savage Sex (*Il paese del sesso selvaggio*) (flim) 103–104
COVID-19 2, 4, 5, 171
Cowboys as Cold Warriors (Corkin) 70
Craig, Johnny 20–21
Creed, Jason 24
Creepshow (film) 19, 27–28, **28**
"Creepshow" (Gagne) 24
Creepy (magazine) 38
crime, perceived increase in 1–2, 12n4
Crocket (fictional character, *Survival of the Dead*) 127, 137
Crump, Andy 151

Dale (fictional character, *The Walking Dead*) 88, **88**
D'Amato, Joe 103, 108–109, 114n44
Davis, Jack 22, 23, 26
Dawn of the Dead (Romero) (film) 3, 11, 13n13–15, 19, 25; consumerism in 3, 100–101, 125–126, 162–167, 180; healthy society in 165; release of 106–107; Rousseau and 155–160; use of color in 26; Western elements in 60, 67–68, 74n25
Dawn of the Dead (Snyder) (film) 144, 152n7
"*Dawn of the Dead* had an alternate ending that's even bleaker than the original" (Smith) 126–127
Day of the Dead (film) 3, 13n16, 22, 26, 30n34; government in 121, 135, 138n33; morality in 43, 73, 101–102, 182
"Dead Like Me" (Troy-Castro) 81–82, 90
"A Dead New World" (Christie) 56–57
"The Dead Will Return" (Feldstein) 42
Dean Armitage (fictional character, *Get Out*) 146–147
Death Smiles on the Murderer (*La morte ha sorriso all'assassino*) (film) 106–107
Debbie (fictional character, *The Searchers*) 60
Debra (fictional character, *Diary of the Dead*) 68, 122, 124, 134–135, 183
The Decameron (Boccaccio) 82–83
Defoe, Daniel 82–83
Demanding Respect (Lopes) 44
democracy 6, 70, 129, 136
Dendle, Peter 1, 4, 108
Deodato, Ruggero 104
destructiveness 72, 73, 75–76
Diary of the Dead (film) 4, 13n17, 24, 73–74, 101–102; humanity in 182–183; presence of government in 121, 134–135; *Stagecoach* compared with 63
discomfort, with humanity of zombies 176
Discourse on the Origin and the Foundations of Inequality Among Men (Rousseau) 158–160, 165
"Disruptive Corpses" (Hand) 43
A Distant Mirror (Tuchman) 177
distinction, between human and zombie state 84, 97n18, 157–158, 171, 175–176
distribution, of resources 135–136
Divine Hunger (Reeves Sanday) 99–100
Dr. Logan (fictional character, *Day of the Dead*) 25, 105, 122–123, 176
Dr. Penny Jones (fictional character, *Empire of the Dead*) 50
Dolgoy, Erin 172
Dracula (Stoker) 83
dream states, in Romero 127–128, 140n82

Eaten Alive! (*Mangiati vivi!*) (film) 103
Eaten Alive! (Slater) 104, 114n41, 114n43

EC *see* Entertaining Comics
economy, in films of Romero 139*n*49
Eddie Murry (fictional character, "The Thing from the Sea") 36
education, Rousseau on 161–162, 169*n*53
Eerie (magazine) 37
Emile (Rousseau) 157, 161, 162, 164, 165–167
Empire of the Dead (Romero) 50
"The End Begins" (Harpold) 124
The End of Victory Culture (Engelhardt) 10, 55, 60, 69, 78*n*58
end titles, of *Night of the Living Dead* 74f
enemies, as sub-human 63, 65–67
Engelhardt, Tom 10, 55, 60, 69, 78*n*58
Entertaining Comics (EC) 15–16, 19–20, 50*n*13; characters morality of 24, 43–44; freedom of artists of 26; moral justice in 25, 36; treatment of human body in 26, 36, 51*n*23
Eric Northman (fictional character, *True Blood*) 83
Escape from Evil (Becker) 91
Ethan (fictional character, *The Searchers*) 57–59, 60–61
Everett, Bill 44

faithful slave narrative 146–147
false states, in Romero 124–127
Famous Monsters of Filmland (magazine) 38
"Farewell George Romero" (Liebovitz) 182, 187*n*104
fast-running zombies 107–108, 176–177
Fear the Walking Dead (TV Series) 82, 92
Feldstein, Al 21, 22, 23, 42
fiction, horror 34
Fiddler's Green 124
Fido (film) 43, 50
films: catastrophe 2; post-9/11 3; of Romero humor in 176; in theaters for spectacle 99, 112*n*7
A Fistful of Dollars (film) 56, 70, 71
Floyd, George 173
Forbidden Words (Allan & Burridge) 112*n*15
Ford, John 56
formula, for zombie films 80
Forster, Marc 12*n*5
found-footage subgenre 104
Francine (fictional character *Dawn of the Dead*) 26, 68, 73, 126, 128; on life in the mall 163–164
Frankenstein 68, 78*n*52
free will, of humans in Romero 185
freedom, of EC artists 26
Freudstein (fictional character, *House by the Cemetery*) 109–110
From Communion to Cannibalism (Kilgour) 100
From Max Weber (Weber) 120, 135
Fulci, Lucio 99, 107, 108–110

Gagne, Paul 24, 39
Gaines, William 10, 21, 42–43
Garrett, Greg 160, 170, 175–176
"George A. Romero Made Movies About the Undead" (Zacharek) 174
"George Romero's Zombies" (Cassese) 171
Get Out! (film) 11, 144–150, 153*n*23; influence of *Night of the Living Dead* on 143, 147–148
ghouls, zombies contrasted with 54, 76*n*4, 87, 105
giallo subgenre 109
Girolami, Marino 104–105
Glenn (fictional character, *The Walking Dead*) 89
Go Home (*A casa loro*) (film) 110–111
Going Viral (Schweitzer) 5, 13*n*35
Golem (mythological character) 105

gore: in comics 38, 45; horror films and 18, 19, 27, 40, 72
Gospel of the Living Dead (Paffenroth) 80, 86, 92, 126, 175; on similarities between humans and zombies 176
government, in zombie films 118, 119–120, 132–136, 138*n*20, 178
government, social coordination in 136
"Graft in Concrete" (Davis, Gaines & Feldstein) **23**
Greenberg, Harvey 184
Greta (fictional character, *Death Smiles on the Murderer*) 106
Gross, Benjamin Isaak 155–177
Gualano, Luna 110–111
"Guess Who's Going to Be Dinner" (Bruce) 145
Gunfighter Nation (Slotkin) 183–184

Haidt, Jonathan 137
Haiti 32, 152
Hale, Kimberly 172
Hand, Richard 35, 43
Harper, Stephen 100–101
Harpold, Terry 124, 139*n*50
Harry Cooper (fictional character, *Night of the Living Dead*) 62, 67, 86, 145
Hays Code 71
Heller-Nicholas, Alexandra 112*n*15
"Hellhounds" (Litwack) 150
Henderson, Brian 69
heroes 2–3, 10, 18, 46, 83, 126, 144, 178
Hervey, Ben 49–50
Hetherington, Marc 122
High Noon (film) 69–70
HIV/AIDS 9–10
Hobbes, Thomas 119–120, 183
Hoberman, James 19–20
Hollywood from Vietnam to Reagan (Wood, R.) 127, 129, 167, 182
The Hollywood Reporter (website & magazine) 151
"Homer's *Iliad* and John Ford's *The Searchers*" (Winkler) 61
"Hook, Line and Stinker" (Ingels, Gaines & Feldstein) 23
horrality 10, 15, 19, 27
"Horrality" (Brophy) 15, 19, 27, 30*n*5, 32
The Horror! (Trombetta) 34
horror comics, as society critique 35, 42–43
Horror Films of the 1980s (Muir) 109
horror media, race relations in 90, 130–131, 141*n*114
House by the Cemetery (*Quella villa accanto al cimitero*) (film) 109–110
House Un-American Committee (HUAC) 69
How Democracies Die (Levitsky & Ziblatt) 136
"How 'Get Out' Puts 'Night of the Living Dead' in a New Light" (Crump) 151
How Zombies Conquered Popular Culture (Bishop) 172, 174
Howard, Robert 46
Howlett, Mike 46
HUAC *see* House Un-American Committee
human and zombie state, distinction between 84, 97*n*18, 157–158, 171, 175–176
human characteristics: perfectibility as 159–160, 161–162; pity as 158
humanism 177–182
Humanism (Law) 185
"Humanity in a Posthuman World" (Hale & Dolgoy) 172
humanity of zombies, discomfort with 176

humans in Romero, free will of 185
humans, in zombie films of Romero 23, 42–43, 52n54, 54–55, 76n5; cooperation of 129–131, 135, 137, 175, 178, 180; Romero on 75, 178; self-destructiveness of 72, 73, 75–76, 119–120, 182–183
humor, in films of Romero 176

I Am Legend (Matheson) 16, 24, 56, 81; alienation in 87
"The Idle Proletariat" (Bishop) 156, 168n16
"I'm Going to Die" (Phipher) 185
"The Imagination of Disaster" (Sontag) 2–3, 12n7
Imagined Communities (Anderson) 7–8
In the Heat of the Night (film) 67
Indians, portrayal of 55–57, 63, 69–70
inequality, racial 11, 123, 147–148, 173
influence, on Italian cinema of VHS 99
influence on video games, of Romero 29
Ingels, Graham 23, 25–26
instinct, as animal trait 158–159
"Interracial Tensions in *Night of the Living Dead*" (Lightning) 138n4, 145
"Introduction" (Bissette) 39
"Introduction: Humanism and Anti-humanism" (Cohen) 178
"An Introduction to the American Horror Film" (Wood, R.) 132, 141n129
Invasion of the Body Snatchers (film) 17, 54
Invisible Invaders (film) 17
Isabella, Tony 45
Italian cinema 112n6, 114n37; influence of VHS on 99; violence in 102–103
Italian Cinema (Wood, M.) 112n6
Italian Horror Film Directors (Paul) 104, 106, 108, 114n38–39, 114n44
iZombie (TV Series) 9, 49, 53n68, 97n53, 175

Jackson, Robert 149
jiangshi (Chinese mythological character) 115n46
Jim (fictional character, *The Walking Dead*) 89
John (fictional character, *Day of the Dead*) 121, 128, 137
Johnstown 166, 169n74
Jones, Duane 144–145
"Jordan Peele Made a Woke Horror Film" (Butler) 153n23
"Jordan Peele on a Truly Terrifying Monster: Racism" (Zinoman) 144–145, 151
A Journal of the Plague Year (Defoe) 82–83
Judy (fictional character, *Night of the Living Dead*) 40, 149
Julie (fictional character, *Warm Bodies*) 92–93
June (fictional character, *Fear the Walking Dead*) 92

Kaufman (fictional character, *Land of the Dead*) 24, 43, 73, 78–79n82, 101, 124–125, 127, 130, 134–136, 138n20, 140n82, 179–180
Kay, Glenn 108, 115n53
Kearney, Richard 83–84
Kee, Chera 32–51
Keetley, Dawn 7, 130, 131, 142n168, 178
Kellner, Douglas 117, 120, 130
Keough, Peter 12n1
Kilgour, Maggie 100
King, Martin Luther 14n56, 66, 148, 153n27
King, Stephen 19, 24, 27
Kirkman, Robert 81, 87–88, 178–179

Lacan, Jacques 71–72
Laist, Randy 74

Lamont, Corliss 177
Land of the Dead (film) 43, 65f, 68, 73, 77–78n51; as allegory of modern inequality 101, 124–125, 130, 131; hopeful ending of 101, 124–125, 131
Lasswell, Harold 135
Last Cannibal World (Ultimo mondo cannibale) (film) 104
The Last Man on Earth (film) 17–18, 114n46
Last Night story (Whitehead) 80–88
Last Night story, of Ben 89, 93–94
Law, Stephen 185
legacy, of Romero 174
Leibovitz, Liel 182, 187n104
Lenz, Wylie 82
Lenzi, Umberto 103–104, 107–108
Leone, Sergio 70–71
Leviathan (Hobbes) 119–120, 183
Levitsky, Steven 136
Lewis, Tyson E. 65
liberalism 129–130, 155–157, 167
Liberalism and the Limits of Justice (Sandel) 160
Lightning, Robert K. 138n4, 145
"The Lingering Horror of Night of the Living Dead" (Newby) 145
Liquid Times (Bauman) 7
Litwack, Leon 150
Living with the Living Dead (Garrett) 160, 170, 175–176
Locke, John 161, 162, 169n53
lone fighter, Western hero as 69–70
lone hero, Ben as 70, 85–86, 180
Lopes, Paul Douglas 44
"Lost Bodies/Lost Souls" (Randell) 66, 67
Lowenstein, Adam 5–6, 67
lynching 67, 74, 148–150, 153–154n38
Lynching and Spectacle (Wood, A.) 149

Macbeth (Shakespeare) 96
Machiavelli, Niccolò 156
The Magic Island (Seabrook) 32, 105
The Magnificent Seven (film) 70
"Mails to the Zombie" 46
Malcolm (fictional character, *The Reapers Are the Angels*) 95–96
Malcolm X 66, 153n27
The Man Who Shot Liberty Valance (film) 61
Mapache (fictional character, *The Wild Bunch*) 71
Marion, Isaac 80, 92
Mark Spitz (fictional character, *Zone One*) 84
Marks, Jonathan 169n53
Martin (fictional character, *The Searchers*) 60–61
Martino, Sergio 114n44
Massaccesi, Aristide 106; *see also* D'Amato, Joe
Massacre in Dinosaur Valley (Nudo e selvaggio) (film) 114n44
Matheson, Richard 16, 24, 56, 81, 87
McCarthy, Joseph 69–70
McElya, Micki 146–147
media reporting, accuracy of 73–74, 79n83
metaphorical cannibalism 101–102
Miccichè, Lino 112n6
Midnight Movies (Hoberman & Rosenbaum) 19–20
military service, EC artists and 35
mind, philosophy of 171
Mitchell, Lee Clark 70–72
modern political philosophy 156
mondo subgenre 11, 98, 103–104, 114n41
The Monster Show (Skal) 138
moral justice, in EC comics 25, 36

morality, of EC comics characters 24–25, 43–44
Motion Pictures Production Code 26–27
Muir, John Kenneth 109
Muldoon (fictional character, *Survival of the Dead*) 127, 137, 183
Muselmann (Agamben) 63, 65

narrative: apocalyptic plague 82; faithful slave 146–147; survival 81
National Guard 123–124
nationalism, *The Walking Dead* and 8
necessitas legem non habet (necessity knows no laws) 6
"Neglected Nightmares" (Wood, R.) 133
Nerd Do Well (Pegg) 139*n*45, 176–177
Newby, Richard 145
Newman, Kim 118, 126, 133
"The Night of the Living Dead" (Elliot) 18
Night of the Living Dead (Hervey) 49
Night of the Living Dead (Romero) (film) 1, 3, 8, 10–11, 13*n*12, **41**; as allegory for Vietnam War 150, 153*n*40; camera angles of 39–40, 52*n*42–43; cannibal zombies and 32; end titles of 74f; fiftieth anniversary of 173; influences on 16–19, 22–26, 34; *Invasion of the Body Snatchers* compared with 17, 54; as Last Night story 86–87; presence of government in 121; Romero on 25, 54, 76*n*2; success of 16, 143
Night of the Living Dead (Savini) (film) 13*n*13, 43
Nightmare City (Incubo sulla città contaminata) (film) 107–108
Nightmare Movies (Newman) 118, 126, 133
No Name (fictional character, *A Fistful of Dollars*) 70–71

Official Night of the Living Dead (Skulan) 28, 30*n*40
O'Flynn (fictional character, *Survival of the Dead*) 137, 142*n*170, 183
Olney, Ian 152
On Stories (Kearney) 84
"The Only Monsters Here Are the Filmmakers" (Bernard) 103
Orsitto, Fulvio 11, 98–116
"other," zombies as 106, 110–111, 170, 171, 184, 185*n*4

Paffenroth, Kim 80, 86, 92, 117–118, 126; on success of zombie as villain 175, 176
Pagano, David 9
pages, "splash" 20
panels, splat 15, 22, 26
paranoia 134, 145, 147–148
parodies 2, 12*n*6
Parry, Tyler 148, 153*n*30
Pasolini, Pier Paolo 11, 98, 102–103, 111*n*1, 111–112*n*4–5, 112*n*21–22; later films of 102, 113*n*27; Romero and 113*n*26
Pastorino, Gloria 1–14, 55–74, 98–116
Paul, Louis 104, 106, 108, 114*n*44
Paul Kaufman (fictional character, *Land of the Dead*) 24, 43, 73, 78–79*n*82, 101; Fiddler's Green and 124–125, 125f; humanism and 180
Paul Redeker (fictional character, *World War Z*) 94–95
Peabody, Bruce 11, 117–142, 170–187
Peckinpah, Sam 70–72
Peele, Jordan 11, 143–144
Pegg, Simon 139*n*45, 176–177
Peisner, David 178–179
"People Are Vectors" (Abrams) 181–182
perceived increase, in crime 1–2, 12*n*4
perfectibility, as human characteristic 159–160, 161–162

Perry (fictional character, *Warm Bodies*) 92–93
Perverse Titillation (Shipka) 103
Peter (fictional character, *Dawn of the Dead*) 101, 126, 131, 160, 162; self-preservation and 163–164
The Philosophy of Humanism (Corliss) 177
philosophy of mind 171
Phipher, Mary 185
physically untouched zombies 36
"Pigeons from Hell" (Howard) 46
Pigsty (Porcile) (film) 98, 102, 111*n*1, 111–112*n*5, 112*n*21; *The Walking Dead* and 113*n*25
Pittsburgh 66, 68, 78*n*51, 78*n*82, 90, 98
pity, as human characteristic 158
Plum Island 127
police, black men killed by 151–152, 173
"Police Dogs and Anti-Black Violence" (Parry) 148, 153*n*30
political critique, zombie films as 2, 4, 69, 117, 121–122; *Dawn of the Dead* 133
political philosophy: modern classic contrasted with 156
Politics (Aristotle) 129, 134
Politics: Who Gets What, When, How (Lasswell) 135–136
portrayal, of Indians 55–57, 63, 69–70
portrayal, of violence in films of Romero 26–27, 131–132
post-9/11 films 3
presence of government, in *Diary of the Dead* 121
preservation of humanity, storytelling as 84, 94, 95
Production Code Administration 39
pulp magazines 35–36
Pupillo, Massimo 114*n*46

R (fictional character, *Warm Bodies*) 92–93, 97*n*53
race relations, in horror media 90, 130–131, 141*n*114, 145
racial inequality 11, 123, 147–148, 173
radio dramas 35, 51*n*18
Ramón (fictional character, *A Fistful of Dollars*) 71
Randell, Karen 66, 67
"Reading Resident Evil" Tosca 29
The Reapers Are the Angels (Bell) 95–96
Reeves Sanday, Peggy 99–100
references, to zombie in books 170–171, 171f
refuge: in Westerns and in zombie films, contrasted with 57, 60; in zombie films 57, 124–128
"Rehabilitating Daddy" (Towlson) 3
religion, zombification and 9, 112*n*15
"A Report from Occupied Territory" (Baldwin) 151
resources, distribution of 135–136
Responsibility for Justice (Young) 118–119
Return of the Living Dead (film) 2
return to nature, in Rousseau 164–165
revenge, zombies and 33
"Richard Matheson's *I Am Legend*" (Bowring) 87, 93
Rick Grimes (fictional character, *The Walking Dead*) 7, 87–88, 181
Riley (fictional character, *Land of the Dead*) 130, 134, 179, 180
Ringo Kid (fictional character, *Stagecoach*) 65
"The Rise of 'The Walking Dead.'" (Peisner) 178–179
Robert Neville (fictional character, *I Am Legend*) 56–57, 61, 87
Roger (fictional character, *Dawn of the Dead*) 68, 125–126, 163
Rome Against Rome (Roma contro Roma) (film) 114*n*46
Romero, George A. 1, 3–4, 6–7, 9–10, 15, 172; absence

of religious figures in 178; on classic horror 17; comic adaptations of 28; *Dead* series 19, 24, 92, 128, 131–133, 135, 138, 174–175, 178, 180, 184–185; humanism of 177–182; on humans in his films 75, 119, 138, 138n21, 177, 180–181; influence on video games of 29; influences on 174; legacy of 173–175; on *Night of the Living Dead* 25, 66, 67, 77n45, 99, 141n126; politics of 133–135; on social commentary 119, 122, 132, 174, 185; on *Survival of the Dead* 136–137; on *The Walking Dead* 181; as zombie comics writer 29, 39; on zombie walks 12n1; on his zombies 22, 54, 78n60, 177, 179
Rose Armitage (fictional character, *Get Out*) 145–147, 150
Rosenbaum, Jonathan 19–20
Rousseau, Jean-Jacques 155–166, 168n20; on cities 167; on education 161–162, 169n53
"Rousseau's Critique of Locke's Education for Liberty" (Marks) 169n53
"Rousseau's Liberalism" (Sorenson) 156–157
Rowlandson, Mary 55
Ruth (fictional character, *I Am Legend*) 56, 87
Ryan, Michael 117, 120, 130

Sabin, Roger 26
Sandel, Michael 160
The Santa Clarita Diet (TV Series) 175
Sarah (fictional character, *Day of the Dead*) 26, 78n52, 122–123, 127–128, 139n33; on cooperation 130, 136
Savini, Tom 13n13, 25, 27–28, 31n40
Scar (fictional character, *The Searchers*) 58, 60, 69
Schmeink, Lars 5, 6, 8
Schweitzer, Dahlia 5, 13n35
Screen Memories (Greenberg) 184
Scritti corsari (Pasolini) 111–112n5
Seabrook, William 32, 105
The Searchers (film) 56, 57–60, 69
"*The Searchers*" (Henderson) 69
Second Discourse (Rousseau) 157–158
Seduction of the Innocent (Wertham) 38
semi-states, of Romero 122–124
The Seminar of Jacques Lacan (Lacan) 71–72
Sennitt, Stephen 19–20
"The Sensuous Zombie" (Isabella) 45
sexploitation 108
Shakespeare, William 96
Shaviro, Steven 66, 72–73, 77n22, 130, 140n90; on *Dawn on the Dead* 133; on resourcefulness of humans in Romero 179–180; on similarities between humans and zombies 176
Sheila Hammond (fictional character, *The Santa Clarita Diet*) 175
Sheriff McClelland (fictional character, *Night of the Living Dead*) 148, 149
Shermeyer, Kelli 84–85
Shipka, Danny 103
Shocking Representation (Lowenstein) 67
Siegel, Don 17
similarities between humans and zombies 176, 179
Simon Garth (fictional character, *Tales of the Zombie*) 44–46, **47**, 49
Simpson, Phillip 4
Skal, David J. 138
Skulan, Tom 28
The Sky Is Falling (Biskind) 179, 182, 185n4
Slater, Jay 103, 109–110
Slave of the Cannibal God (*La montagna del dio cannibale*) (film) 114n44
slave-style zombies 32–33, 50, 105, 114n46

Slotkin, Richard 183–184
Smith, Justine 126–127
social coordination, of government 136
"society critique, horror comics as 35, 42–43
Society, Market and Industry" (Cianfarani) 112n6
Soderberg, Branden 153n27
Soderberg, Steven 2, 108
"Soft Murders" (Laist) 74
Sondrol, Paul C. 139n45
Sontag, Susan 2–3
Sorenson, L.R. 156–157
"A Southern Sublimation" (Jackson) 149
special effects 25, 38, 72, 99, 103, 108
spectacle, films in theaters for 99, 112n7
"splash" pages 20, 21
splat panels 15, 22, 26
Stagecoach (film) 62, 64f, 65f; *Diary of the Dead* compared with 63
Stanley (fictional character, "Hook, Line and Stinker") 23
status quo, in Romero 129
Stein, Elliot 18
Stephen (fictional character, *Dawn of the Dead*) 68, 73, 126, 128, 160; on Johnstown 166; life in mall and 163–164
Stine, R.L. 34
Stoker, Bram 83
stories, vampire 83, 96n12
storytelling: as preservation of humanity 84, 94, 95; value of 83–84, 91
stragglers, in *Zone One* 91–92
Strange Tales (Marvel) 46, 49
subgenre: found-footage 104; mondo 103–104
sub-human, view of enemy as 63, 65–67
Subjectivity, the Unconscious and Consumerism (Xavier) 100–101
Sublette, Cammie M. 143–154, 172
survival narrative 81
survival of characters, in horror films 148, 153n28
Survival of the Dead (film) 8, 22, 58f, 59f, 60; government in 121, 127; metaphorical cannibalism in 101–102; Romero on 136–137; self-destructive humans in 74–75, 137–138, 183
swarm, zombies as 5–6
sympathetic, zombies as 29, 36
Synder, Zack 144
"Systems Die Hard" (Shermeyer) 84–85

Tait, R. Colin 117, 140n82
Tales of the Zombie (Marvel) 33, 44–45, 52n59
Tarantini, Michele Massimo 114n44
Temple (fictional character, *The Reapers Are the Angels*) 95–96
Tenga, Angela 11, 80–98, 172
terrorism: attacks of 2001 1, 134; zombies as metaphor for 6–7
thanatopolitics 65, 77n39
"The Thing from the Bog!" (Pearson, Wolfman & Marcos) 45
"The Thing from the Sea" (Wood, W.) 36, **37**
Thoreau, Henry David 129
Thrower, Stephen 99, 106–107, 109, 112n8
"Till Death" (Craig, Gaines & Feldstein) **21**, 22
Tom (fictional character, *Night of the Living Dead*) 62, 68, 149
Tosca, Susana Pajares 29
"Totalitarian and Authoritarian Dictators" (Sondrol) 139n45

"Toward a Genealogy of the American Zombie Novel" (Lenz) 82
Towlson, Jon 3
trapped, EC comics characters as 24
traumatic change, in zombie media 80–81, 82–83
treatment of human body, in EC comics 26, 36, 51n23
Trombetta, Jim 34
Troy-Castro, Adam 81–82, 90
True Blood (TV Series) 83
Trump, Donald 1–2, 73, 171
trust in authorities, zombie films and 4, 6, 93, 117
Tuchman, Barbara 177
28 Days Later (film) 5, 119, 128f
2001 terrorist attacks 1, 134

"Uncomfortable Fictions" (Peabody) 120, 139n26
The Undead and Theology (Paffenroth) 117–118
"Undead Radio" (Hand) 35
USA Patriot Act 6
utopia 3, 124
Utopia Reader (Claeys & Sargent) 126

value, of storytelling 83–84, 91, 94
vampire stories 83, 96n12
Vari, Giuseppe 114n46
Vault of Horror (EC comics) 20–21
VHS *see* video home system
Viano, Maurizio 98, 111n2
video home system (VHS) 99
Vietnam War 39, 62, 65–66, 77n44, 134; *Night of the Living Dead* as allegory for 150, 153n40
violence: in Italian cinema 102–103, 113n28; in Westerns 71–72, 78n77
Violence (Žižek) 69
virtue and virtuous traits 90, 179, 181
voodoo, zombies and 9, 14n46, 32–33, 152

The Walking Dead (Kirkman) 81, 87–90, **88**
The Walking Dead (TV series) 6–8, 14n41, 49, 50, 59f; reference to *Porcile* in 113n25; Rick Grimes in 181
Wallace-Sanders, Kimberly 147
Waller, Gregory 9, 15, 120, 178, 180, 185
Warm Bodies (film) 50
Warm Bodies (Marion) 80, 92–93
Warren, James 38–39
"We Need a Little Fear" (Haidt) 137
Weber, Max 120, 135
Weiler, Jonathan D. 122
The Weird World of Eerie Publications (Howlett) 46
We're All Infected (Keetly) 7, 178
Wertham, Fredric 38
Western hero, as lone fighter 69–70
Westerns 55, 63; violence in 71
Westerns (Mitchell) 70–72
White Zombie (film) 98, 105
Whitehead, Colson 80–82, 84, 91
Why Washington Won't Work (Hetherington & Weiler) 122, 13940
The Wild Bunch (film) 71–72, 74f, 75f, 78n76

Williams, Tony 35, 40, 184
Winkler, Martin 61
Without Sanctuary (Emory University) 149
Wood, Amy Louise 149
Wood, Mary 112n6
Wood, Robin 127, 129, 131, 133, 167, 182
Wood, Wally 36
"A Word of Warning" (Banes) 35
World War Z (Brooks) 82, 93–94, 118, 142n158
World War Z (film) 2, 12n5, 171
worth of humanity, in films of Romero 68–69
Wright, Bradford 38

Xavier, Marlon 100–101
Xolelwa Azania *see* Redeker, Paul

Young, Iris Marion 118–119

Zacharek, Stephanie 174
Ziblatt, Daniel 136
Zinoman, Jason 144–145, 151
Žižek, Slavoj 69
Zombi 2 (film) 107
"The Zombie Apocalypse Is Upon Us!" (Simpson & Bishop) 4
Zombie Cinema (Olney) 152
zombie comic writer, Romero as 29, 39
zombie films: biopolitics and 8; formula for 80; government in 118, 119–120, 138n20, 178; as political critique 2, 4, 69, 117, 121–122, 133; refuge in 57, 124–128; role of brain in 59, 66, 80, 92; traumatic change in 80–81; trust in authorities and 4, 6, 93, 117; ; *see also specific films*
Zombie Holocaust (*La regina dei Cannibali*) (film) 104–105
The Zombie Movie Encyclopedia (Dendle) 1, 4, 108
Zombie Movies (Kay) 108, 115n53
zombie Renaissance 11–12, 33, 173
"Zombie Republic" (Keetley) 130, 131
"Zombie Revolution at the Gates" (Tait) 117
The Zombie Survival Guide (Brooks) 119, 135, 139n49, 174
"Zombie Terror" (EC Comics) 35, 51n16
zombie walks, Romero on 12n1
zombies: as allegory for discrimination 9, 14n52, 16; as animals 158; cannibal 32–33, 50, 50n5, 105–106; fast-running 107–108, 176–177; frequency of references to 170, 171f; ghouls contrasted with 54, 76n4, 87, 105; as metaphor for terrorism 6–7; as "other" 106, 110–111, 170, 171, 184, 185n4; physically untouched 36; revenge and 33; slave-style 32–33, 50, 105, 114n46; as sympathetic 29, 36, 50; voodoo and 9, 14n46, 152
"Zombies, Malls, and the Consumerism Debate" (Harper) 100–101
Zombification: cause of 42; religion and 9
Zone One (Whitehead) 80–82, 84; stragglers in 91–92
"Ztopia" (Lewis) 65
zuvembies 33, 46, 48, **48**

www.ingramcontent.com/pod-product-compliance
Ingram Content Group UK Ltd.
Pitfield, Milton Keynes, MK11 3LW, UK
UKHW050527150426
5217IPUK00026B/1838